Refugees Now

Refugees Now

Rethinking Borders, Hospitality, and Citizenship

Edited by Kelly Oliver,
Lisa M. Madura, and
Sabeen Ahmed

ROWMAN &
LITTLEFIELD
INTERNATIONAL
London • New York

Published by Rowman & Littlefield International Ltd.
6 Tinworth Street, London, SE11 4AB, U.K.
www.rowmaninternational.com

Rowman & Littlefield International Ltd.is an affiliate of Rowman & Littlefield
4501 Forbes Boulevard, Suite 200, Lanham, Maryland 20706, USA
With additional offices in Boulder, New York, Toronto (Canada), and Plymouth (UK)
www.rowman.com

British Library Cataloguing in Publication Data
A catalogue record for this book is available from the British Library

ISBN: HB 978-1-7866-1162-8
PB 978-1-7866-1163-5

Library of Congress Cataloging-in-Publication Data

Names: Oliver, Kelly, 1958- editor. | Madura, Lisa M., editor. | Ahmed, Sabeen. 1991- editor.
Title: Refugees now : rethinking borders, hospitality and citizenship / edited by Kelly Oliver, Lisa M. Madura and Sabeen Ahmed.
Description: London ; New York: Rowman & Littlefield International, 2019. | Includes bibliographical references and index.
Identifiers: LCCN 2018056628 (print) | LCCN 2019014123 (ebook) | ISBN 9781786611642 (Electronic) | ISBN 9781786611628 (cloth) | ISBN 9781786611635 (pbk.)
Subjects: LCSH: Refugees—Civil rights. | Refugees—Government policy. | Refugees—Legal status, laws, etc.
Classification: LCC HV640 (ebook) | LCC HV640 .R41834 2019 (print) | DDC 362.87/561—dc23
LC record available at https://lccn.loc.gov/2018056628

Contents

Acknowledgments

The editors would like to thank everyone involved in the *Refugees Today* workshop in Vienna, Austria, in August 2016, which was supported by grants from Vanderbilt University and the University of Vienna.

We acknowledge earlier versions of two chapters that have been previously published as journal articles: Serena Parekh, “Beyond the Ethics of Admission: Stateless People, Refugee Camps, and Moral Obligations,”*Philosophy and Social Criticism* (August 2013), and Jade Schiff, “Welcoming Refugees: Mindful Citizenship and the Political Responsibility of Hospitality,” *Signs* (February 2018).

Introduction

Sabeen Ahmed and Lisa Madura

"In a way, the refugee crisis is a misnomer," journalist Patrick Kingsley writes in his 2017 book *The New Odyssey*. "There is a crisis, but it's one caused largely by our response to the refugees, rather than by the refugees themselves."[1] The *Guardian*'s first-ever migration correspondent, Kingsley recounts months of travel across the Middle East and North Africa, chronicling relationships with smugglers on the coasts of Egypt and refugees waiting weeks for aid, painting a picture of their plight rarely portrayed in Western media. His book is at once a devastating portrait of today's refugee crisis and a searing critique of the West's political impotence, affective indifference, and ethical irresponsibility in the face of the largest wave of mass migration since World War II. Kingsley is not the first to try to articulate the crisis on its own terms, however; many scholars now write of the theoretical groundings of the figure of the "refugee"—scholarship that is increasingly characterized as "critical refugee studies"—aiming to propose and analyze solutions that are sensitive to the full scope of statelessness as an existential, phenomenological, ethical, and, ultimately, *human* experience.[2]

Writing as an exile in America after her departure from Europe in 1941, Hannah Arendt observed that the denationalized migrants of the era of the world wars were viewed by the European states "not as individuals but as compact ethnic groups" and were "attacked and persecuted not as individuals but as members of a people or a splinter group of people lacking the protection of a state."[3] Arendt was one of the first modern thinkers to problematize the refugee not merely in terms of her juridical ontologization but as a crucial—if not necessary—corollary of contemporary nation-statehood. It is unsurprising that her work has had such a far-reaching influence in so many strands of critical political philosophy, taken up both in the context of statelessness and well beyond it. Her characterization of the problem of modernity as the crisis of the "right to have rights" is echoed in Judith Butler's writings on dispossession, Seyla Benhabib's work on human rights and migration, and, most recently, Giorgio Agamben's theoretical revival of the figure of *homo sacer*. The subject of modernity, these writings together suggest, is the subject stripped of her *political* status—whether in the context of second-class citizenship, incarceration, or forced migration, among many other iterations—and who, by making visible the farce of human rights, illustrates that membership in the political community is the very ground of membership in the community of human beings. In the words of Athena Athanasiou, "dispossession"—of one's home, of one's state, of one's citizenship—"works by rendering certain subjects, communities, or populations unintelligible by eviscerating for them the conditions of possibility for life and the 'human' itself."[4]

The problem of political subjecthood is perhaps more acute today than it has been ever before. We inhabit a world riddled with environmental catastrophes, armed conflicts both domestic and foreign, chasms of economic disparity between the rich and poor, large-scale human rights violations, and an ever-rising tide of populist and extremist nationalism driving social, political, and cultural divides from east to west. A common theme across these conflicts, as Kingsley and other journalists record almost daily—and which makes writings by such theorists as Arendt perennially relevant—is the unprecedented and increasing number of displaced persons and populations. As of 2017, the United Nations reports that there are 65.6 million persons forcibly displaced worldwide "as a result of persecution, conflict, violence, or human rights violations."[5] Of these, 22.5 million are registered refugees—with more than half of them being children—and 10.3 million were newly displaced during 2016 alone. Yet only 189,300 refugees were resettled across thirty-seven countries, "including those resettled with UNHCR's assistance,"[6] while nine of the top ten refugee-hosting countries were and have historically been located in the Global South (the exception—and the country hosting the largest number of refugees today—is Turkey).[7] By the time this book is in print, the numbers will have changed and, given the ever-polarizing and increasingly radicalizing hostility fueling our current political climate, likely for the worse.

In recent years—years in which the so-called European migrant crisis has come to dominate public and political discourse in the Anglo-American and European worlds—a number of excellent academic texts and anthologies have been published, with contributions from Ayten Gündoğdu,[8] Sarah Fine and Lea Ypi,[9] and Reece Jones,[10] adding to earlier writings by Matthew Gibney,[11] Emma Haddad,[12] and many others. As these writings tell us, the refugee is no longer ignored, not out of any sense of ethical progress but simply because she *cannot* be ignored. Her presence permeates land and sea, constantly exposing the West's supposed solutions—political agreements, border security, humanitarian refuge—as mechanisms of elimination and security, whether biopolitical or within the theoretical contours of classical sovereignty—spatial containment, physical exclusion, incarceration.

In line with these timely writings, the refugee serves as the central focus of this volume as well. However, we would like to clarify that the term "refugee" as it appears in this volume is often used as an umbrella term for migrants, stateless persons, and internally displaced persons as a general ontological referent rather than in strict adherence with the legal definition of "refugee." As articulated in Article 1A(2) of the 1951 UN Convention Relating to the Status of Refugees, the "refugee" is a person who,

> owing to well-founded fear of being persecuted for reasons of race, religion, nationality, membership of a particular social group or political opinion, is outside the country of his nationality and is unable or, owing to such fear, is unwilling to avail himself of the protection of that country; or who, not having a nationality and being outside the country of his former habitual residence as a result of such events, is unable or, owing to such fear, is unwilling to return to it.[13]

For the purposes of international law, in other words, the registered "refugee" is a legal categorization that must be *recognized as such*, without which the guarantee of non-refoulement is absent. The "refugee," then, should not be confused with the "migrant": the migrant, so named mainly in economic contexts, is one who has left her country, seeks to settle elsewhere, and, as Richard Falk notes, "has no status in international law and has no special claim to protection."[14] These distinctions are crucial when considering contemporary stateless persons, such as Syrians fleeing civil war, economic migrants seeking material security, the environmentally displaced, or those living in what the United Nations calls "protracted" situations—one in which 25,000 or more refugees "from the same nationality have been in exile for five or more years in a given asylum country"[15]—all which trouble our ability to offer determinative and widely applicable legal and policy-oriented solutions.

The decision to utilize the term "refugee" as a generalized marker for statelessness and displacement, made by many of the authors in this book and by others beyond it, is not to ignore or undermine the particularities of the "legal" figure, whether from the UN Refugee Convention or elsewhere. We do, however, recognize that the contingent, historical context in which the UN Refugee Convention was drafted has generated normative understandings of refugeehood that can be problematic for the inclusivity of similarly politically vulnerable persons.[16] In this sense, we utilize the term "refugee" in order to include those whose political and, above all, *existential* experiences of displacement render them similarly deprived of resources for "bare life."

This volume gathers together chapters concerned with the ontopolitical precarity of statelessness and displacement and the power plays undergirding the deeply insufficient, so-called solutions to the "refugee problem," masking what Hannah Arendt once recognized as "the trend of international negotiations simply to *ignore* the existence of refugees."[17] The chapters in this volume are committed to a common goal of understanding the refugee, offering various ways to conceptualize, engage with, and "do right" by forcibly displaced or otherwise stateless persons, with many contributors arguing for specific ways to overhaul worldwide norms and legal and political apparatuses that are doing further harm to already vulnerable populations. These harms are expansive in scope, with dimensions both legal (insofar as they involve a deprivation of political status) and ontological (in that they deprive individuals of certain fundamental human rights). As do so many writings on the topic, these chapters often engage, perhaps inevitably, with the works of Hannah Arendt, Jacques Derrida, Giorgio Agamben, and others who have laid the theoretical groundwork for theories of statelessness. Beyond merely utilizing these existing theories, however, the authors in this volume also critique and expand on them as a way to develop novel and as-yet-unexplored approaches to our unique, contemporary context. Divided into five thematized parts that explore the various dimensions of the phenomenon of statelessness, these chapters together provide a critical commentary on material responses to contemporary refugee crises as a means of opening pathways to more pointed assessments of both the political and the ideological underpinnings of statelessness.

Part one provides some of the conceptual machinery for understanding the politics of contemporary global human migration. In "Refugees and the Politics of Indignity," David Owen expresses the need for political rather than simply moral intervention for displaced persons. Owen develops a two-pronged theory of dignity—one of dignity *of* one's person and the other of dignity *in* one's person—to illustrate how the current humanitarian framing of displacement generates a hierarchical dignitary regime that ascribes a supererogatory status to refugee intervention. Nöelle McAfee's "Refugees and the Right to Politics" argues that, by the light of the self-understanding of democratic nation-states, all those in their midst should be seen as having political rights. She further argues that even in the absence of this recognition, those not recognized as having rights can and do in fact harness political power. In response to the flow of migrants and refugees the world over, the international community should, for both normative and political reasons, find a way to recognize noncitizens' rights, even if this means rethinking the limits of state sovereignty. Furthering a theme introduced by Owen, Mladjo Ivanovic's chapter interrogates the inadequacies of humanitarian efforts that pose as engaged compassion while in reality serving to regulate and manage populations. Taking up the writings of Theodor Adorno in particular, Ivanovic explores the question of moral agency and the hypocrisy of a humanitarian imaginary that romanticizes suffering but that is itself produced out of a culture that thrives on exclusion and persistent inequality.

Part two foregrounds the philosophical notion of hospitality and its normative implications. The chapters in this part draw critical attention to the way our social imaginings of who (or what) the foreigner is provide an alibi for ethical irresponsibility and lead to indifference about or violence toward those in need of sanctuary. Lisa Madura initiates this discussion by addressing the political and ethical complexities that come with thinking and acting hospitably in the context of global human migration. Drawing on the work of Emmanuel Levinas and Jacques Derrida, Madura takes up issues of sovereignty, security, and risk as she interrogate states' use of propaganda and manipulation of fear, arguing for a reorientation of our ethical and political priorities with respect to refugees and immigrants. In her chapter, Jade Schiff talks about the anxieties generated by the arrival of the refugee and recommends "mindful citizenship" as a way to allay these anxieties while simultaneously fostering hospitable practices of welcoming. She argues that by adopting mindful citizenship, we position ourselves to take responsible action when confronted by the arrival of the refugee in need. In the final chapter of part two, Peg Birmingham provides a segue from discussions of hospitality to discussions of political status and rights. She takes the universal "right to politics"—or the "right to have rights" as expressed by Hannah Arendt—alongside Etienne Balibar's observation that a political world organized by sovereign, territorially discrete nation-states is inadequate to deal with such a universal right. Birmingham suggests that the figure of the refugee is not just a problem *for* "the political" conceived in terms of sovereign national borders but, rather, that it is a figure on which we must found a new conception *of* the political.

Part three addresses issues of political status and public representation, detention and deportation, and the Eurocentric frameworks of analysis that perpetuate exclusionary practices. In the first chapter, Kelly Oliver attends to the inhumane practices of refugee camps and detention centers and argues for their abolition. To this end, she calls for a rethinking of the category of "refugee," citing the many problems of distinguishing between citizen, noncitizen, and refugee and recommending that we replace current political approaches to refugees with a theory of "earth ethics" centered on the relational responsibility engendered by our sharing a common planet. In an evaluative assessment of the ethics of admission, Serena Parekh then argues for the need to clarify our moral obligations toward stateless persons and calls for a broadening of the scope of consideration beyond mere de jure refugees to include those who exist outside of established and codified political communities. By drawing attention to the ontological harm of statelessness, Parekh sees an opportunity to expand the philosophical understanding of obligation in a way that reaches those who, for a number of reasons, may never be resettled politically. Finally, Sabeen Ahmed adds a critical dimension to refugee scholarship by interrogating Giorgio Agamben's oft-explored notion of *homo sacer* and this figure's inability to account for contemporary refugee crises. Ahmed shows how Agamben's refugee—and texts that take up this figure similarly—is paradigmatic of a particular sociohistorical moment, the Jewish Holocaust, and therefore is ontologically incapable of capturing the situation of the non-European refugee of today.

In part four, we turn to the politics of human migration as it relates to place. These chapters address the practical challenges faced by refugees as well as the global community tasked with providing resettlement. Chong Un Choe-Smith, in her aptly titled "Political Refugees and Economic Migrants: A Distinction without a Difference?," challenges this titular distinction. By exploring the consequences of physical and economic insecurities, Choe-Smith suggests that the categorical division between these two groups does not constitute a morally significant difference such that international and domestic laws and policies should prioritize one over the other. Eduardo Mendieta then takes us into a discussion of the rights of immigrants and the duties of nation-states. Although there exists a complex tension between human rights and citizen rights, Mendieta situates the right of mobility within a discourse of the human right to life, illustrating that there emerges a concomitant right to emigrate built into our very understanding of human rights. He concludes by interrogating the consequences of this right to emigrate on the part of receiving nations and their duties to provide asylum. Gertrude Postl's chapter explores the concept of *Heimat* and the question of what it means "to be at home" in the face of loss and exile, interrogating the meaning of both "home" and "hospitality" when it comes to welcoming the foreigner. Postl focuses on the social alienation involved in losing not only one's home but also one's culture and language and suggests that it is only through reclaiming language that one can codify the possession of *Heimat* as well as critique it. Julia Kristeva ends part four by asking us to identify the "foreigner within ourselves" as a means of guiding how we think about and act toward the foreign Other. Kristeva utilizes psychoanalytic theory to diagnose a condition of identity confusion that exists for both foreigners and their hosts. By "domesticating foreignness," Kristeva wonders if we can't open up "a universal conciliation presiding over the universality *of the "human race,"* envisioning a "paradoxical community" that is developing on the contemporary world stage where we do not recoil at foreignness but share in it.

Finally, part five brings us to the topic of narrative and testimony. In "I Am Not Your Canvas: Narratives, Nostalgia, and the (Re)claiming of Refugee Voices," Anna Gotlib addresses the issue of "narrative erasure," or the way refugees' own stories, desires, demands, and intentions have been silenced and excluded from "master public narratives." As Gotlib shows, the stories of refugees are stifled or replaced by master narratives constructed to reflect the needs and interests of host societies, thus compromising the moral agency and life prospects of those who are presented within these narratives. What is needed, then, is for the Global North to stand down from its role in defining identities and circumscribing prospects so that the refugees may reclaim their voices and gain agency over their own narratives and futures.

Gotlib's discussion of narrative erasure is followed by two provocative pieces that shift the point of view from thinking *about* the refugee to thinking *with*, or giving witness to, the refugee. The previous chapters in this volume are concerned principally with the refugee as an abstract figure appearing on the contemporary social and political landscape against the irreducibility of this figure's lived experience. Esther Hutfless and Elisabeth Schäfer provide an unconventional and thoughtfully written adaptation of a film they directed in a format that breaks away from the previous chapters to great effect.[18] Although invoking abstractions is necessary in theoretical scholarship, their "How to Be a Refug(e)e for a Stranger" reminds us that the ethical emerges only from the intercorporeal confrontation *with* the Other as a living, breathing, historically situated agent of experience in her own right. In an effort to return to the singular individual behind the figure, Hutfless and Schäfer bring us face-to-face, so to speak, with the personality at the center of the many discourses explored in this volume: the refugee herself. Finally, in response to and echoing the work of Hutfless and Schäfer, Eva-Maria Aigner brings the volume to a close with a treatment of how to develop hospitable space in *writing*. She suggests that philosophical writing, especially those with human lives as their subjects, must take responsibility for itself by admitting to the impossibility of perfect translation and absolute representation. Aigner's contribution to this volume is both revealing and performative, taking on itself the sort of literary risks required to preserve an ambiguity in language that is necessary when speaking about the Other for whom no concept is ever adequate.

At their core, these chapters examine the theoretical, material, and political dimensions of the largest humanitarian disasters of our time, centered not simply on the volume of externally displaced persons but also on the internally displaced, victims of war and climate change, and, above all, the future ramifications of today's inaction. The feature unifying this diverse collection, however, is the need to expose the unacknowledged realities responsible for both the magnitude of these crises and the concomitant need to supplement theoretical approaches from more philosophically diverse perspectives. It is in the service of this end that *Refugees Now* aims to contribute to rich scholarship in the growing field of critical refugee studies while preserving and recognizing the limits of scholars to ever fully capture the experiences of Otherness that time and time again exceed theory's linguistic and technical boundaries. We hope this collection makes good on that promise both to other interested scholars and to those invested in more deeply understanding the complexities of statelessness today.

NOTES

1. Patrick Kingsley, *The New Odyssey: The Story of the Twenty-First-Century Refugee Crisis* (New York: Liveright Publishing Corporation, 2017), 6.

2. See, for example, Dan Bulley, *Migration, Ethics & Power: Spaces of Hospitality in International Politics* (London, UK: SAGE Publications Ltd., 2017); Étienne Balibar, *Citizenship*, trans. Thomas Scott-Railton (Cambridge, UK: Polity Press, 2015); Giorgio Agamben, *Homo Sacer: Sovereign Power and Bare Life*, trans. Daniel Heller-Roazen (Stanford, CA: Stanford University Press, 1998); Peter Gatrell, *The Making of the Modern Refugee* (Oxford, UK: Oxford University Press, 2013); Sam Okoth Opondo and Michael J. Shapiro, *The New Violent Cartography: Geo-Analysis after the Aesthetic Turn* (Abingdon, OX: Routledge, 2012); Thomas Nail, *The Figure of the Migrant* (Stanford, CA: Stanford University Press, 2015); and Zygmunt Bauman, *Strangers at our Door* (Cambridge, UK: Polity Press, 2016).

3. Hannah Arendt, "The Disenfranchised and the Disgraced," in *The Jewish Writings*, ed. Jeromy Kohn and Ron H. Feldman (New York: Schocken Books, 2007), 233.

4. Judith Butler and Athena Athanasiou, *Dispossession: The Performative in the Political* (Cambridge: Polity Press, 2013), 20.

5. UN High Commissioner for Refugees (UNHCR), "Global Trends: Forced Displacement in 2016," June 2017, http://www.unhcr.org/5943e8a34.pdf, 2.

6. UNHCR, "Global Trends," 3.

7. UNHCR, "Global Trends," 14.

8. Ayten Gündoğdu, *Rightlessness in an Age of Rights: Hannah Arendt and the Contemporary Struggle of Migrants* (Oxford: Oxford University Press, 2015).

9. Sarah Fine and Lea Ypi, eds., *Migration in Political Theory: The Ethics of Movement and Membership* (Oxford: Oxford University Press, 2016).

10. Reece Jones, *Violent Borders: Refugees and the Right to Move* (New York: Verso, 2016).

11. Matthew J. Gibney, *The Ethics and Politics of Asylum: Liberal Democracy and the Response to Refugees* (Cambridge: Cambridge University Press, 2004).

12. Emma Haddad, *The Refugee in International Society: Between Sovereigns* (Cambridge: Cambridge University Press, 2008).

13. James C. Hathaway and Michelle Foster, *The Law of Refugee Status*, 2nd ed. (Cambridge: Cambridge University Press, 2014), 2.

14. Richard Falk, "Refugees, Migrants and World Order," in *The Refugee Crisis and Religion: Secularism, Security and Hospitality in Question*, ed. Luca Mavelli and Erin K. Wilson (Lanham, MD: Rowman & Littlefield, 2017), 26.

15. U.S. Department of State, "Protracted Refugee Situations," https://www.state.gov/j/prm/policyissues/issues/protracted (accessed July 8, 2018).

16. As noted by Erin K. Wilson and Luca Mavelli's introduction to *The Refugee Crisis and Religion*, "The provisions of the Refugee Convention, with their emphasis on the violation and abuse of human rights, are a reflection of the post–Second World War political climate, when understandings of displacement were informed by the ideological conflict of the Cold War" (Wilson and Mavelli, 11). Wilson and Mavelli are here drawing from Alexander Betts, *Survival Migration: Failed Governance and the Crisis of Displacement* (Ithaca, NY: Cornell University Press, 2013).

17. Arendt, "The Disenfranchised and the Disgraced," 234, emphasis added.

18. This film was made for a collaborative workshop on refugees between Vanderbilt University and the University of Vienna funded by both universities. Some of the chapters in this volume came out of work done at that workshop.

Part I

HUMANITARIANISM AND HUMAN RIGHTS

Chapter One

Refugees and the Politics of Indignity

David Owen

Even as the status of refugee formally denotes a commitment to the dignity of persons, the position of asylum seekers and refugees is increasingly one in which that commitment is notional rather actual, especially in the so-called developed world. Kelly Oliver has recently drawn attention to this point by analyzing the character of the global refugee regime as one of "carceral humanitarianism," which picks out the sense in which it increasingly combines logics of humanitarianism and of detention or encampment.[1] My focus in this chapter is more limited than Oliver's analysis of the global regime (though supportive of it) in that its aim is to try to understand the normative dynamics of the phenomenon that Didier Fassin highlights when he comments that "whereas many European states once regarded asylum as a right, they now increasingly treat it as a favor"; my primary focus is on the corollary also advanced by Fassin that this development required that "the image of refugees had to be transformed from victims of persecution entitled to international protection to undesirable persons suspected of taking advantage of a liberal system."[2]

The chapter begins by sketching out a picture of refugeehood which is conceptually connected to the political legitimacy of the international state system and, specifically, to a cosmopolitan conception of the dignity of persons. In the second section, it turns to showing how this picture was made vulnerable by a failure of international cooperation and has been undermined in public political culture through a transformation of both the general orientation to refugeehood (from one of dignity to one of suffering) and the image of the refugee, where these transformations have enabled a politics of indignity. I conclude the chapter by drawing attention to the relationship between humanitarianism and dignitary hierarchy that this politics has established.

REFUGEES, LEGITIMACY, AND DIGNITY

The current legal specification of the figure of the refugee is provided by international refugee law, which, strictly speaking, consists of "international and regional conventions, General Assembly resolutions and resolutions of various ad hoc groups with regional competence (e.g., the EEC Ad Hoc Group on Immigration), customary law and domestic legislation."[3] However, the primary instruments of contemporary international refugee law are the 1951 Geneva Convention Relating to the Status of Refugees and the 1967 New York Protocol to the Convention Relating to the Status of Refugees, and, taken together, these instruments provide the basic definition of the refugee:

> One who owing to a well-founded fear of being persecuted for reasons of race, religion, nationality [as belonging to a "people"], membership of a social group or political opinion is outside the country of his nationality [as membership of a state] and is unable or, owing to such fear, is unwilling to avail himself of the protection of that country; or who, not having a nationality and being outside the country of his habitual residence . . . is unable, or, owing to such fear, is unwilling to return to it.[4]

This specification of the criteria of refugeehood has been much discussed,[5] and there are regional instruments that adopt more expansive criteria—for example, in Africa, the Organization of African Unity's 1969 Convention Governing the Specific Aspects of Refugee Problems in Africa, and, in Latin America, the 1984 Cartagena Declaration on Refugees.

The first way of thinking about the modern legal figure of the refugee is as a political subject whose exceptional status serves to reproduce the imagined reconciliation of an international order of nominally equal sovereign states with a cosmopolitan commitment to the dignity of human persons. To grasp this way of picturing the institution of refugeehood, we can note that the primary norm through which the reconciliation of the international order of states and a cosmopolitan commitment to the equal dignity of human beings is expressed and, ideally, secured is the human right to a nationality. It is this commitment that grounds the acknowledgment that de jure statelessness is a fundamental normative problem for a legitimate international order of states. This norm fairly naturally gives rise to a picture of refugeehood as a form of de facto statelessness that similarly poses a legitimacy problem for the international order of states and where the international refugee regime acts as a legitimacy-repair mechanism that, ideally, reasserts the reconciliation of an international order of (nominally equal) states with a cosmopolitan commitment to the dignity of human persons.[6] Reflecting on and defending the current refugee regime, Matthew Price notes that

> citizens of burdened societies lack protection of their basic rights, but they retain their standing as members. The appropriate stance of outsiders to burden societies is to lend assistance, not to condemn their failings. Asylum is an inappropriate tool for addressing the needs of those fleeing burdened societies.[7]

By contrast, Price contends, asylum as a mode of "surrogate membership" in another state is the appropriate response for dealing with those of its citizens targeted by outlaw states as states that flout "the requirements of international legitimacy by violating basic human rights—such as the peremptory human rights norms recognized by customary international law"—since it provides these persecuted citizens whose very standing as members is being denied with protection "in a manner that also expresses the condemnation that is deserved."[8] Although, as I have argued elsewhere,[9] Price's argument is not without limitations, it nicely exemplifies the connection between refugeehood, asylum, and membership that structures the dignity-based picture of refugees.

We can flesh out this picture further by reflecting further on dignity as a complex phenomenon that encompasses a normative status, a practical relation to oneself, and a mode of conduct and comportment. Although historically dignity has been seen as legitimately differentiated in hierarchical terms (the dignity of the monarch being distinct from the dignity of her subjects, for example, who were also distinguished by rank), moral dignity is now identified as a single status of basic equality ascribed to all human beings and given clear legal expression as universal human rights.[10] More colloquially, as Jeremy Waldron puts it nicely,

> A person's dignity is not just some Kantian aura. It is their social standing, the fundamentals of basic reputation that entitle them to be treated as equals in the ordinary operation of society. Their dignity is something they can rely on—in the best case implicitly and without fuss, as they live their lives, go about their business, and raise their families.[11]

That at least is the ideal—and this sense of dignity as a normative status protected by law and respected by one's fellow human beings is central to our contemporary use of the concept and grounds my opening claim that the refugee is a figure whose exceptional status serves to reproduce the imagined reconciliation of an international order of nominally equal sovereign states with a cosmopolitan commitment to the dignity of human persons. It does so because the refugee is defined in terms of the denial of their dignity as members of political society by their home state.

To develop the analysis I want to offer, it will be helpful to distinguish two different ways in which one's dignity can be denied. The first is the breaching of one's rights. The person who assaults me or burglarizes my home thereby denies, in a very practical sense, my dignity. Yet although such actions deny one's dignity, they do not thereby *target* one's dignity; that is, they are not qua breaches of rights expressively focused on rejecting one's claim to dignity in the way that actions such as degradation, contempt, insult do. These actions are called "dignitary harms" precisely because they are focused on rejecting one's entitlement to dignity as an equal status. We might say that the former denies the dignity *of* one's person as a bearer of equal status expressed in human or civic rights, while the latter rejects the dignity *in* one's person that grounds one's entitlement to equal status. It is both true and important that a breach of the rights to which I am entitled as part of my dignity as an equal may be expressed in a way that also constitutes a dignitary harm (e.g., torture). The same act may comprise both injury and insult. It is also true that some dignitary harms may also be breaches of rights; think, for example, of libel and slander. In these cases, insult is injury. While these exceptions reinforce the point that breaches of human (or civic) rights and dignitary harms are generally distinct categories of wrong even though both may be manifest in the same action, they have a particular importance with respect to refugeehood since persecution by the state "for reasons of race, religion, nationality [as belonging to a "people"], membership of a social group or political opinion" necessarily takes the form of *either* a breaching of one's basic rights that targets one's standing as a member of political society (e.g., imprisonment or torture based on religious or political beliefs) *or* a denial of one's standing as a member of political society that is itself injurious (e.g., state defamation of ethnic or social groups). We can come at the same general point concerning dignity in a slightly different way by distinguishing what Michael Rosen calls "respect as observance" and "respect as respectfulness." The former denotes observing (and not undermining) your human or civic rights: I recognize the dignity *of* your person by not breaching these rights or undermining your ability to exercise them. The second refers to an attitude with which I interact with you: I acknowledge the dignity *in* your person by engaging respectfully with you. State persecution involves the denial of the dignity of your person as a member of political society and/or the denial of the dignity in your person as a member of political society.

The Refugee Convention thus expresses a cosmopolitan commitment to the dignity of human beings both in its substantive specification of the figure of the refugee (persecutions based on race, religion, and so on are attacks on the dignity of persons) and in the structuring of the current regime in terms of the *grundnorm* of non-refoulement, that is, a binding obligation on any state to which a claim to asylum is made not to return persons who, on the basis of an impartial process of adjudication, are found to satisfy the criteria of refugeehood to the state from which they have fled or to another state in which they would lack protection of their human rights. More formally, the legal duty of non-refoulement

> encompasses any measure attributable to the State which could have the effect of returning an asylum seeker or refugee to the frontiers of territories where his or her life or freedom would be threatened, or where he or she is at risk of persecution, including interception, rejection at the frontier, or indirect *refoulement*.[12]

Notice that this legal duty of non-refoulement is not only an expression of the moral duty to protect asylum seekers or refugees from these serious threats to their dignity but also, at the same time, a way of communicating to all states (including the state to which application is made) the standing of asylum seekers and refugees as individuals entitled to equal dignity.

Understanding refugeehood within this dignity-based framework helps us to distinguish the specificity of refugees and their exceptional status as those who are entitled to claim the protection of a state that is not their own; however, it can also offer guidance for the treatment of refugees precisely because it is a matter of not only respecting their rights, that is, the dignity of their person, but also engaging respectfully with them in acknowledging the dignity in their person. However, as the remarks by Fassin cited in the introduction indicate, this normative picture of refugeehood has largely been displaced in the public political culture of the "developed" world in ways that have supported the rise of a politics of indignity with respect to refugees—and it is to this development that we now turn.

HUMANITARIANISM, SUFFERING, AND SUSPICION

We can introduce the transformations with which this section is concerned by returning to the current regime and binding duty of non-refoulement, where an important implication of this principle is that the current regime places no restrictions on the numbers of refugees to whom a state owes a duty of non-refoulement. This does *not* entail that refugees have a right to asylum in the state to which they make application (a possibility advocated, discussed, and rejected in the drafting of both Article 14 of the Universal Declaration of Human Rights and the 1951 Convention on Refugees). On the contrary, as long as the duty of non-refoulement is not breached, states can come to bilateral, multilateral, or omnilateral arrangements with one another concerning the distributions of the presence of refugees and responsibilities for the costs of refugee protection. This point is important—even if, in practice, the state of application is still typically the state of asylum—because it points to the fact that responsibility for the protection of refugees is specified by the current regime in a way that is maximally consistent with respect for the autonomy of states. Under this current legal structure, it is up to states, jointly or collectively, to work out terms of reasonable cooperation for the fair distribution of refugees; if (or to the extent that) they fail to do so, the duty of non-refoulement entails that the default condition is that the state to which application is made bears the responsibility of ensuring the provision of asylum.

This normative structure of the contemporary refugee regime involves an important normative claim and constructs a practical dilemma. The normative claim is that discharging the duty to refugee protection takes priority over fairness of distribution of the responsibility for refugee protection. The practical dilemma is that, to the extent that refugees are perceived as burdens on the states that protect them and the costs of protecting refugees become significant, the current regime gives rise to a situation in which states, collectively, have an interest in effective and fair refugee protection but individually see themselves as having an interest in minimizing their individual burden. What lies behind this collective action problem with respect to refugeehood as a global public good is a particular picture and self-understanding of the state. Matthew Gibney describes this self-understanding thus:

> Above all else . . . the state is fundamentally an answer to the question of who is responsible to whom in the modern world: states are responsible to their own citizens. The survival of the state as an entity over time rests, moreover, on its ability to portray itself convincingly as an answer to such a question. As a consequence, the claims of outsiders are assessed by states, including liberal democratic ones, through a logic that deprecates the interests and needs of outsiders—a logic that is exceedingly sensitive to the potential damage to its own authority involved in forcing its citizens to incur costs for the sake of strangers.[13]

The failure of the international community to develop robust institutional mechanisms of state cooperation in the face of significant refugee flows enables (or at least fails to qualify or displace) the particular self-understanding of the state that Gibney identifies, and, as James Hathaway and R. Alexander Neve noted in motivating the last serious proposal for reform of the international refugee regime, the lack of fair apportionment of refugee protection was a key contributor to the reluctance of states to admit refugees for whom, in virtue of the principle of non-refoulement, they thereby bear sole responsibility for what often amounts to indefinite protection.[14] The primary expression of this political logic is what we may call an "ideology of humanitarianism," according to which obligations to refugees are pictured in terms of humanitarian aid as moral obligations that we should fulfill, as long as the costs of doing so are low, rather than as obligations of justice. Rather than acknowledging the figure of the refugee as a condition of legitimacy of the international order of states, this logic recasts the refugee as a supplicant whose suffering should move us as a matter of moral solidarity but to whom our relationship is one of beneficence rather than justice. Humanitarianism as an attitude addresses (unchosen) suffering in the figure of a victim requiring aid and does not distinguish between the sources or causes of suffering—thus, a person subject to injustice (persecution) and a person subject to misfortune (natural disaster) are taken as equivalent from a humanitarian standpoint. It finds expression as a "politics of rescue" rather than a "politics of dignity." As the numbers seeking asylum in the "developed world" have grown over the past thirty years (alongside the entrenchment of human rights in the domestic law of these "advanced states"), so this political logic has asserted itself in two general ways.

The first way in which it appears is as the undermining of the distinctive character of the figure of refugees and hence their exceptional status. The key move here is to note, first, that there are a variety of others, apart from those who are persecuted by states, whose basic needs are not met by their own states—most obviously, people suffering from famine or environmental disasters or lack of economic opportunity—and, second, that there are many internally displaced persons who are unable or unwilling to cross the border into another state to claim protection. This puts pressure on the existing legal specification of the refugee by identifying this figure as simply one among a plurality of those with whom we should stand in relations of moral solidarity according to need—and by de-differentiating the figure of the refugee from such others enables the political undermining of the exceptional status of the refugee.

The second manifestation of this political logic comes with humanitarianism's introduction of the issue of costs for the agent who aids—or can aid—the victim and, hence, its distinction between what is morally obligatory and what is morally supererogatory. This dimension of humanitarian framing enables the issue of costs to be construed ambivalently and indeterminately across two dimensions—the cost to the state considered in isolation and the cost to the state in comparative perspective—while allowing states to determine what count as "low costs." The issue of costs finds expression in three main rhetorical forms:

1. We cannot afford . . . (primary duty to our own citizens, already under strain)
2. We are being taken advantage of . . . (by other states that are not contributing or by refugees who could have settled elsewhere)
3. It would be cheaper to protect . . . (somewhere else, over there)

Each of these modes of argument avails itself of the humanitarian calculus of costs in ways that would justify a humanitarian choice not to offer aid and support the representation of the admission of any refugees as a supererogatory act of charity (i.e., despite the fact we cannot afford or are being taken advantage of or it would cheaper elsewhere, we still admit some refugees). It may, of course, be the case that these arguments typically involve misrepresentations of the facts that enable the self-serving disavowal of responsibility. My point is simply that they conform to the structure of argument that a humanitarian framing requires.

All of these rhetorical appeals to costs can be seen in the political transformation of the treatment of those claiming refuge in "developed" states, which can be summarized in terms of four main features: (1) declining rates of recognition over the past forty years, (2) increasing use of detention practices, (3) the proliferation of nonarrival measures, and (4) the restriction of the rights of asylum seekers. These measures have been enabled by a transformation of the image of the refugee from a person entitled to protection into an object of suspicion—the switch to a default presumption of the "bogus asylum seeker" who seeks to use the asylum route for economic immigration and to a picture of those whose refugee claims cannot easily be disallowed as motivated by economic reasons for seeking entry to "developed" states rather than elsewhere, say, to the camps in neighboring states to their state of origin, and hence as acting in ways that are—in some indeterminate sense—taken to be unfairly burdensome toward the citizens of these "developed" states. Whereas the former picture is of someone who is not entitled to refugee status seeking to abuse the migration system of a state for personal advantage, the latter is of someone who is entitled to refugee status abusing the refugee system for personal advantage by seeking refuge *here*. Each of these pictures performs two acts: first, it identifies the asylum seeker as an objection of suspicion, and, second, it situates the citizens of developed states as the potential victims or dupes of unscrupulous asylum seekers, whether or not they have legitimate claims to refugee status.

To analyze the political work performed by these distorted pictures of asylum seekers and refugees, it will be helpful to return to the language of dignity and the distinction drawn earlier between "respect as observance" and "respect as respectfulness." Consider the general point that although breaches of your human rights may be more serious than dignitary harms (being murdered is typically worse than being humiliated), it can also be the case that the latter may be more fundamental than the former in the specific sense that dignitary harms act to undermine the target's claim to dignity as equal status. Recognizing this point helps account for an important phenomenon. As Rosen puts it,

> One of the features that have characterised many of the most violent and destructive acts of the twentieth century has been the humiliation and symbolic degradation of their victims. . . . It seems to be a fact about human nature that human beings are able more easily to engage in the most violent behaviour towards one another if at the same time they expressively deny the humanity of their victims.[15]

Dignitary harms work by introducing hierarchy into a category that marked equality, by differentiating the dignity due to different types of person. Such harms work to cultivate attitudes of "soul-blindness" (in Stanley Cavell's apposite phrase), in which "they" are seen as lacking the entitlement to the standing that "we" rightly possess. It may be helpful here to introduce briefly an example explored by Raymond Gaita concerning James Isdell, Protector of Aborigines in Western Australia in the 1930s, who administered a program in which children of mixed blood were (typically forcibly) removed from the Aboriginal mothers "and placed in circumstances in which (it was hoped) most of them would have children with lower class whites":

> Responding to the question, how did he feel taking children from their mothers, Isdell answered that he "would not hesitate from a moment to separate any half-caste from its Aboriginal mother, no matter how frantic her momentary grief might be at the time." They "soon forget their offspring," he explained.[16]

As Gaita remarks, these words, coming from Isdell, "marked his sense of the kind of gulf that existed between 'them' and 'us.' 'Our' children are irreplaceable; 'theirs' are not.'"[17] Isdell was not ignorant of the facts concerning the victims of his actions; rather, "he suffered a kind of blindness to the meaning of what they did and suffered":

> Although the grief of the women who had lost their children was visible and audible to him, he did not see in the women's faces or hear in their voices grief that could lacerate their souls and mark them for the rest of their days. It was literally unintelligible to . . . Isdell that sexuality, death and the fact that at any moment we may lose all that gives sense to our lives could mean to "them" what it does to "us."[18]

Isdell could not see that "their" loves, griefs, joys, and desires go deep in "them" and have depth in the same way that they do for "us." "They" lack the kind of individuality that shows itself in "our revulsion in being numbered rather than called by name and that gives human beings the power to haunt those who have wronged them, in remorse."[19] We might think of the response to the photograph of the drowned Syrian child Alan Kurdi as an all-too-brief instance of soul-dawning against this general background of soul-blindness.

Since the mid-1980s, the cultivation of soul-blindness with respect to refugees as well as immigrants more generally has been something like a project for significant sectors of news media and politics—"indignity advocates" as we might call agents such as the U.K. newspaper the *Daily Mail*—perhaps as a reaction to the spread of human rights and human rights organization in the 1970s. Thus, for example, following the relative closure of routes of legal labor migration in the post-OPEC United Kingdom, antimigration discourses in the United Kingdom mobilized around the rhetorical figure of the "bogus" asylum seeker. The absence of significant evidence for the widespread existence of this phenomenon did not in any way affect its political salience in generating public anxiety and cultivating an attitude of epistemic injustice toward refugees that took the form of hermeneutic indignity.[20] Hermeneutic indignity refers to "the lived experience of being unfairly disadvantaged in rendering one's social experience intelligible, to others and possibly even to oneself." A group is subject to hermeneutic indignity, for example, if they lack the resources to get their stories heard or if their accounts of their social position are resisted by the cultivation of "willful not knowing" on the part of socially privileged actors. In support of this claim, we can note that the study published as *Bad News for Refugees*, reviewing media coverage of refugee issues in 2006 and 2011, found the following:

1. The existence of "persistent and overwhelmingly hostile coverage of refugees and asylum in much of the national media"
2. The blurring in news accounts of the distinction "between refugees, asylum seekers and other migrants"
3. The "relative absence of the voices of refugees or those who represent them, as any form of balance to the inaccurate and partial reporting"[21]

This position of hermeneutic indignity, as the authors document, had negative consequences both for "the stability of existing communities" in the United Kingdom and for refugees themselves in terms of social isolation and stigmatization.[22] It is hard to resist the conclusion that this epistemic dignitary harm has a wide presence in our public political culture and plays a significant role in enabling testimonial indignity as the rhetorical refiguring of the asylum seeker as either presumptively bogus or as otherwise taking advantage of the "generous" and "tolerant" character of the United Kingdom. This testimonial indignity displayed itself in and enabled a more skeptical and inquisitorial evaluation of refugee claimants in which the focus on the notion of "a reasonable fear of persecution" was displaced by a focus on, for example, visible bodily signs of proof of torture or abuse.[23]

These epistemic dignitary harms in turn shaped public acceptance of political policies, such as nonarrival measures as well as policies that engaged in more general dignitary harms through the quasi criminalization of asylum seekers and the introduction of detention practices, loss of right to work, and draconian restrictions on welfare provision as well as increasingly limited access to adequate legal representation and rights of appeal—justified largely in terms of reducing incentives for abuse. At the same time, this regime of indignity—this insertion of hierarchy into the order of equal dignity—plays a further significant political role in that it asserts to citizens of the state, under conditions of increasingly high levels of inequality within the state, that the state privileges them over strangers—that their dignity is of a higher rank. In other words, dignitary harms directed at targeting the claim to dignity of refugees and asylum seekers enable the construction of hierarchical dignitary regimes that breach the dignity of refugees and asylum seekers but do so in ways that support the capacity of the state to draw legitimation from citizens.

What is most salient about the political use of the humanitarian framing of refugeehood is that it maintains the rhetorical form of a commitment to the moral equality of persons as vulnerable to suffering while allowing cost-based arguments effectively to support the proliferation of dignitary hierarchies between citizens and refugees and between "deserving" or "worthy" recipients of aid (perhaps most notably orphaned children who are visibly of a young age) and those who are undeserving or unworthy of our support. Thus, in the past year in the United Kingdom, we have seen a limited coalition built around admitting child refugees and, on their admission, a demand by the *Daily Mail* that they be subject to dental checks to determine that they were indeed children.[24] Indeed, one might think that from the standpoint of contemporary opponents of equal dignity, one of the great merits of the rhetorical functioning of the humanitarian standpoint in public political culture is precisely that it facilitates the appearance of a formal commitment to moral equality with substantive attitudes and policies that deny it.

GRATITUDE, INDIGNITY, AND HUMANITARIANISM

This chapter began with Fassin's remark that "whereas many European states once regarded asylum as a right, they now increasingly treat it as a favor," where this development required that "the image of refugees had to be transformed from victims of persecution entitled to international protection to undesirable persons suspected of taking advantage of a liberal system."[25] In the preceding section, I offered an account—with evidence drawn from the

U.K. example that I know best—of the conceptual and epistemic dynamics of this transformation of the normative status of asylum seekers and refugees in terms of a politics of indignity. In concluding, I want to reinforce this picture by drawing attention to one of its outcomes in public political culture by considering the relationship between dignitary hierarchy and humanitarianism from another direction.

If we reflect back on a world in which dignitary hierarchy was the accepted form of social order, we can note that the default demand of superiors to inferiors with respect to decent treatment was that the inferiors exhibit gratitude. To fail to exhibit gratitude was both shameful and an indicator of being "uppity," that is, indicating an attitude by which the inferior claimed a status or rights to which they were not taken to be entitled. Gratitude was expected, and exhibiting gratitude was a performance of knowing your place (even if the performance was not genuine). From the presumed contemporary perspective of the moral equality of human beings, this demand for gratitude was a demand for and an affirmation of indignity.

At least in public political culture, it seems to me that current forms of humanitarianism support a similar demand for gratitude on the part of refugees. Let me be clear here. Refugees might well feel gratitude toward a state that admitted them, for example, on the grounds that this state acknowledged their right to protection when others did not conform to this requirement, but they wrong no one if they neither feel nor exhibit such gratitude. The demand for gratitude—the presumption that a failure to exhibit gratitude is a shameful failing—is something else. In general, we not only do not take it that observing a person's rights is grounds for them to feel gratitude toward us, but we also would regard the thought that they should exhibit such gratitude as a failure to acknowledge their dignity. To the extent that the humanitarian outlook manifests itself in public political culture as a demand for gratitude on the part of the rescued to the rescuer, it supports dignitary hierarchy.

Addressing the entrenchment of the humanitarian picture of refugees in our public political culture, however, requires recognizing that transforming the political imagination of refugeehood toward a politics of dignity requires taking seriously the point that such a politics is a matter of not simply "respect as observance" but also "respect as respectfulness." Consider that while law is well suited to regulating "respect as observance," it is a more limited instrument in relation to regulating "respect as respectfulness." Rather, the burdens of such regulation—of cultivating human and civic relations of respect as respectfulness—fall on state representatives and officials as well as the citizens and residents of states in their attitudes toward and interactions with asylum seekers and refugees. This does not mean that state governments lack political measures that can support (or undermine) practices of respectfulness, but it does entail that refugee justice cannot be divorced from the everyday attitudes and practices of state representatives and officials as well as the citizens and residents of a state and that cultivating a politics of dignity for refugees must be a mutually reinforcing legal, political, and cultural project if it is to be at all robust. This is also, fundamentally, a process in which refugee voices must be heard.

NOTES

1. See Kelly Oliver, *Carceral Humanitarianism: Logics of Refugee Detention* (Minneapolis: University of Minnesota Press, 2017).

2. Didier Fassin, "From Right to Favour," *The Nation*, April 5, 2016, https://www.thenation.com/article/from-right-to-favor.

3. Patricia Tuitt, *False Images: The Law's Construction of the Refugee* (London: Pluto Press, 1996), 9. See also Guy S. Goodwin-Gill and Jane McAdam, *The Refugees in International Law* (Oxford: Oxford University Press, 2007).

4. 1951 Convention Relating to the Status of Refugees, Article 1 A (2), and 1967 New York Protocol to the Convention Relating to the Status of Refugees, Article 1 (2).

5. See Andrew E. Shacknove, "Who Is a Refugee?," *Ethics* 95, no. 2 (1985): 274–84; Matthew Gibney, *The Ethics and Politics of Asylum: Liberal Democracy and the Response to Refugees* (Cambridge: Cambridge University Press, 2004); Matthew E. Price, *Rethinking Asylum: History, Purpose, Limits* (Cambridge: Cambridge University Press, 2009); Matthew Lister, "Who Are Refugees?," *Law and Philosophy* 32 (2013): 645–71; David Owen, "In Loco Civitatis: On the Normative Structure of the International Refugee Regime," in *Migration in Political Theory*, ed. Sarah Fine and Lea Ypi, 269–90 (Oxford: Oxford University Press, 2016); and David Miller, *Strangers in Our Midst: The Political Philosophy of Immigration* (Cambridge, MA: Harvard University Press, 2016).

6. See Owen, "In Loco Civitatis."

7. Price, *Rethinking Asylum*, 73.

8. Price, *Rethinking Asylum*, 73.

9. See Owen, "In Loco Civitatis."

10. This is not to say that human and civic rights exhaust the notion of moral dignity, only that they are a clear expression of it.

11. Jeremy Waldron, *The Harm in Hate Speech* (Cambridge, MA: Harvard University Press, 2012), 5.

12. Erika Feller, Volker Türk, and Frances Nicholson, eds., *Refugee Protection in International Law: UNHCR's Global Consultations on International Protection* (Cambridge: Cambridge University Press, 2003), 178–79. See also Goodwin-Gill and McAdam, *The Refugees in International Law*, 201.

13. Gibney, *The Ethics and Politics of Asylum*, 211.

14. James C. Hathaway and R. Alexander Neve, "Making International Refugee Law Relevant Again," *Harvard Human Rights Journal*, no. 10 (1997) 115–211.

15. Michael Rosen, *Dignity* (Cambridge, MA: Harvard University Press, 2012), 97.

16. Raymond Gaita, *Good and Evil* (Basingstoke: Palgrave Macmillan, 1991), 332.

17. Gaita, *Good and Evil*, 333.

18. Gaita, *Good and Evil*, 333–34.

19. Gaita, *Good and Evil*, 156.

20. The concepts of "hermeneutical indignity" and "testimonial indignity" in this section are adapted from Miranda Fricker, *Epistemic Injustice* (Oxford: Oxford University Press, 2007).

21. Gregg Philo et al., *Bad News for Refugees* (London: Pluto Press, 2013), 165.

22. Philo et al., *Bad News for Refugees*.

23. Didier Fassin, *Humanitarian Reason: A Moral History of the Present* (Berkeley: University of California Press, 2012).

24. Sam Tonkin, "Another All-Male Coachload of 'Child' Migrants Arrives in Britain—but Officials WON'T Say How Many There Are and WON'T Do Dental Checks to Prove They're Really Children," *Daily Mail*, October 19, 2016, http://www.dailymail.co.uk/news/article-3850840/Third-batch-child-migrants-begin-journey-Calais-Jungle-UK-Home-Office-admit-two-thirds-past-children-lied-age-officials.html.

25. Fassin, "From Right to Favour."

Chapter Two

Refugees and the Right to Politics

Nöelle McAfee

A central tenet of political sovereignty is that all people have a right to collective self-governance and that their prerogative to rule themselves should be free from undue encroachment by others. This tenet works fine when people stay in "their own" place, but what comes of it when 3.3 percent of the world's population is on the move?[1] With such a significant number of people migrating from one sovereign state to another, whose sovereignty takes precedence: individuals' or collectives'? In no small way, today's flow of migrants and refugees presents a challenge to the global order of nation-state sovereignty. Contrary to those who claim that stateless persons lack fundamental human rights—that any right depends on state membership—migrants and refugees enact in their claims to dignity and their political aspirations a nonsovereign politics. Their right to politics manifests itself in every moment of collective deliberation, of self-government, of performative calling for something new to come into being.

In the first part of this chapter, I describe the current human rights regime and how it fails to meet the fundamental rights of those it was originally designed to protect. Namely, it denies refugees political rights of self-governance. The second part draws on theorists who think about "the political" in broader terms, bringing to light other ways we might internationally organize ourselves. With their help, I argue that in an era of mass migration, any nation-state founded on ideals of democratic self-governance, that is, the notion that all affected by public matters be able to help direct those matters, needs to grant political rights to all affected. This includes not only those resettled into host countries but also refugees in camps. Otherwise, these states have violated the principles of the Universal Declaration of Human Rights, which calls for rights for all, not only citizens.

HUMAN RIGHTS AND THE LIMIT CONDITION OF THE REFUGEE

This right to politics, as I describe it here, exceeds the usual conceptualization of human rights. International human rights regimes have for more than half a century recognized two fundamental sorts of rights: (1) civil and political rights and (2) welfare rights, such as economic, social, and cultural rights. The first empowers; the second protects. In more recent years, minority rights and environmental rights have also emerged so that now rights fall into four general categories:

- First, *political and civil rights*, for example, the right to participate in governance, as stated in Article 21 of the UN Universal Declaration of Human Rights
- Second, *social or welfare rights*, which can include basic goods such as education, food, and employment
- Third, *rights of women, minorities, and groups* to protect vulnerable populations from discrimination and denial of basic human rights
- Fourth, a bit less obvious and still controversial, *environmental rights* because of the impact that environmental degradation has on basic human welfare and livelihood

All four of these kinds of rights are laid out in an array of international documents and agreements, especially the first two, starting with the 1948 Universal Declaration of Human Rights. They are internationally recognized to the extent that sovereign nations have signed on to the various conventions. Created within and by an international system of state sovereignty, they aim to provide safeguards for members of nation-states. But while they claim to be universal, the hard truth is that these rights are always tethered to particular political attachments.

That tether breaks when people have to flee their state and seek refuge elsewhere. Their first immediate need is shelter. Given the deplorable living conditions of many refugees worldwide, warehoused in camps and bereft of basics needed for sustaining life, much attention has understandably gone to guaranteeing refugees the class of rights known as "welfare rights": decent housing, sustenance, and medical care. While civil and political rights are usually taken to be the most vital for human dignity, throughout the refugee crisis of recent years, political and civil rights for refugees (both in camps and resettled in host countries) have largely been ignored, seen as either untenable for stateless persons, utopian, or even dangerous for state sovereignty.

Civil and political rights meet their limit in the figure of the refugee, the limit condition of sovereignty and human rights. Why do civil and political rights elude the refugee? Those most in need of rights—refugees—seem excluded from the first kind for the following reasons:

- Political rights seem to exist only within the province of a state and only for those who are members of that state.
- A certain reading of Arendt agrees that stateless peoples are bereft of rights.
- The immediate need seems to be for non-refoulement and welfare rights, that is, primarily support and protection, not empowerment.

As enumerated in the 1948 Universal Declaration of Human Rights, civil and political rights include these: the right to life, liberty, and security of person (Article 3); the right to recognition everywhere as a person before the law (Article 6); equal protection of the law (Article 7); due process in court (Articles 8 to 11); freedom from arbitrary interference with one's privacy, family, home, or correspondence (Article 12); freedom of movement and residence within the borders of each state (Article 13); the right to leave any country, including one's own, and to return to one's country (Article 13); the right to seek and to enjoy in other countries asylum from persecution (Article 14); the right to a nationality (Article 15); the right to freedom of opinion and expression (Article 19); the right to freedom of peaceful assembly and association (Article 20); the right to take part in the government of one's country, directly or through freely chosen representatives (Article 21); and a social and international order in which the rights and freedoms set forth in the declaration can be fully realized (Article 28).

Most of these rights are negative, in Isaiah Berlin's sense, providing protection from interference, from harm, from restrictions. Berlin's notion is that there is an "area within which the subject . . . is or should be left to do or be what he is able to do or be, without interference by other persons."[2] The underlying assumption is that sovereign subjectivity is prior to and should be immune from the vagaries of the group. Freedom from incursion presupposes a self that is ontologically prior to any collectivity, and so its rights would also be prior and independent of any collective affirmation. As negative liberties, the civil and political rights in the declaration position political agency as a matter of freedom from infringement, not freedom to shape a common world.

Only Articles 19 to 21 safeguard positive liberty, that is, "freedom to develop and act" rather than merely "freedom from incursion." These include freedom of association, speech, and self-government. Contrary to Berlin's mistaken view that any collective aspirations could endanger the sovereign individual, the civic republican tradition, beginning with Aristotle, holds that being part of deciding with others what ought to be done is central to a life that is human. From a Kantian kingdom of ends to Arendt's space of appearance to Jürgen Habermas's public sphere, being human requires being treated with dignity, as someone who helps choose collective ends, not someone merely subject to others' decisions. So that there are a few articles of positive freedom in the declaration is a good thing. But of these enumerated freedoms—association, speech, and self-government—the latter is denied to the refugee. Self-government is restricted to political freedom in one's own country. There is no such political right outside one's "own" sovereign sphere.

State sovereignty, in fact, explicitly excludes the involvement of those who are not members of the polity. As a report for the UN High Commissioner for Refugees (UNHCR) states,

> Refugees, like other aliens, are entitled to the same freedom of expression, association and assembly as citizens. However, the granting of political rights is often seen as a threat to the national cohesion of the country of asylum or to its relations with the country of origin.[3]

Even the primary international convention on refugees, the 1951 Refugee Convention, lacks any mention of political rights for refugees.[4] Subsequent conventions on refugees mention only freedom of movement. While no state is required to grant political rights to aliens, they do retain the discretion to do so, at least under the 1992 European Convention on Participation of Foreigners in Public Life at Local Level, which makes it possible for foreigners who have lawfully been resident in their territory for five years to vote in local elections. So too, Article 8b of the Treaty on the European Community entitles EU citizens to take part in municipal elections outside their own country as long as they are residents there.[5] On the whole, though, other than a few accommodations for legal residents, the refugee lacks any formal right to political participation in the host country.

This, of course, is exactly the irony of the situation. Created in the aftermath of World War II, in which tens of millions of people had to flee their countries and homes, the 1948 Declaration of Human Rights does not protect refugees' civic and political rights. From a civic republican point of view, such rights are paramount for one's humanity. One of those refugees, Hannah Arendt, pointed out this massive contradiction. Without mentioning the declaration by name, she writes,

> No paradox of contemporary politics is filled with a more poignant irony than the discrepancy between the efforts of well-meaning idealists who stubbornly

> insist on regarding as "inalienable" those human rights, which are enjoyed only by citizens of the most prosperous and civilized countries and the situation of the rightless themselves.[6]

But are refugees really rightless? As Diana Meyers writes, "Human rights covenants are strong on moral fanfare and weak on legal enforcement."[7] Meyers notes that the one population that actually has any recourse to seeking legal enforcement of these basic human rights is the refugee population. Defined as someone "outside his or her country of nationality or habitual residence who is unable or unwilling to return due to a well-founded fear of persecution based on his or her race, religion, nationality, political opinion, or membership in a particular social group," the refugee is able, under the 1951 Geneva Convention on refugees, to "apply for asylum in the hope of gaining a safe haven," Meyers writes. "The right to asylum numbers among the very few remedies available to victims of human rights abuse, and it is recognized by three-quarters of the world's states." The refugee is both the "most destitute" and "the most protected by international law."[8] Hence, failures to ensure the rights of refugees point to a more catastrophic failure of the international community to protect the rights of all.[9]

So the figure of the refugee, the most protected class of human beings protected by the international human rights agreements, is bereft of the most human of rights. In a world order regime of nation-states, the stateless refugee is at the mercy of her host country. As Yasemin Sari writes,

> The equal status one enjoys while in their country of origin is put on hold once the individual is outside their territory. The human right to asylum is in place in order to remedy this fundamental inequality in which the refugee finds herself once they are outside of their country of origin—without the protection of civil and political rights. In turn, the refugee's equality (recognized by the UDHR) as a rights-bearer becomes dependent on a host state's willingness to acknowledge such equality.[10]

Based on the horrific experience during World War II where countries failed to provide asylum to those fleeing Nazi Germany, the 1951 Convention Relating to the Status of Refugees prohibits expelling or returning refugees who might, because of race, religion, nationality, politics, or social group identity, be endangered if returned to the country from which they are fleeing. For the refugee, much is put on hold. While protected by the bedrock principle of non-refoulement, for many, the way it has been met is in the refugee camp.[11] The refugee in exile can have her life on hold for decades.

According to the U.S. State Department, 10.3 million people live in a protracted refugee situation, defined as a situation in which 25,000 or more refugees from the same country have been seeking asylum in another country for five or more years. As the UNHCR puts it, these "refugees find themselves in a long-lasting and intractable state of limbo. Their lives may not be at risk, but their basic rights and essential economic, social, and psychological needs remain unfulfilled after years in exile":

> Protracted refugee situations are some of the most compelling humanitarian challenges confronting governments around the world. People in protracted refugee situations are often deprived of freedom of movement, access to land, and legal employment. UNHCR estimates that the average length of major protracted refugee situations has increased from 9 years in 1993 to 17 years at the end of 2003.[12]

As the International Justice Resource Center puts it, "Countries with limited national resources and/or limited legal frameworks for protecting refugees who nonetheless host large refugee populations" often hinder refugees' freedom of movement. Warehousing refugees in camps limits their access to work and education. Some countries, such as Kenya and Ethiopia, specify by law that refugees' movements may be restricted, limited to living in designated areas, such as refugee camps. Moreover, refugee warehousing provides only a way station to membership in a political community. Someone may reside within a nation's borders, but in a camp, one does not have membership there. Hence, they are denied their right to the first of the four categories of rights I laid out above, the right to politics, thereby effectively denying them their humanity. And since our own humanity depends on how we treat others, denying others the right to politics denies our own humanity as well. This is a central evil of the refugee camp.

There are only three decent outcomes for the refugee: voluntary temporary asylum, voluntary repatriation, or full membership in a new community. Some Syrians may be waiting out the war in a neighboring country, waiting for the time that it is safe to go home, not wanting to exchange their old citizenship for a new one. Others, such as those welcomed by Canadians since the death of Alan Kurdi, have found a new home and a path to citizenship in a new country. The worst outcomes are interminable warehousing in refugee camps, illegal entry bereft of basic rights in another country, or forced repatriation. The rule of law, domestic or international, that designates who may enter and join a political community usually rests on democratic notions of self-governance of all involved. Since Kant, countries that understand themselves to be democratic abide by the notion that the people should be governed by laws that they did or would authorize. But the refugee without political rights is denied participation in developing the rule of law. She is subject to laws that she has no hand in making.

REFUGEES AND THE RIGHT TO POLITICS

Now I turn to how we might think more capaciously and justly about the political rights of refugees. Here I draw on political theorists who think more expansively about the political, including Agamben, Arendt, Cornelius Castoriodis, and Jacques Rancière. With their aid, I argue that all those affected by public matters—wherever they are—should be able to help govern those matters. One need not have a transcendent notion of human dignity to ground this all-affected principle, for it is immanent in the practices and principles of existing nation-states.

What would actually be involved in taking this class of civil and political rights seriously for the 65 million refugees in the world today, both all those resettled and the nearly 12 million people currently living in protracted situations? The latter, warehoused in perpetuity, live in political limbo, rooted in place but without any rights of self-governance. Even the former, those who have been resettled, lack any fundamental right to self-governance. How do the limits of state sovereignty function to negate the civil and political rights of stateless persons? And what would come of the very concept of borders and state sovereignty if refugees were granted these most fundamental rights? Just asking these questions points to what is really at stake in the debate over refugee rights (as well as all immigrants' rights): the sovereignty of a nation-state to limit participation to only those who are already members and, in turn, the sovereignty of those members to deny political rights to those whose very presence calls into question state sovereignty.

While those large questions loom in the background, I will not approach them directly. Rather, I aim to consider why refugees should be seen as having any claim to political rights at all, especially in an order of nation-state sovereignty where a notion of political rights for refugees can hardly be comprehended. But, of course, the more I press this matter, the more I will push up against those looming questions.

The refugees is usually seen as the figure of need and want, not political agency. As Giorgio Agamben puts it,

> The separation between humanitarianism and politics that we are experiencing today is the extreme phase of the separation of the rights of man from the rights of citizen. In the final analysis, however, humanitarian organizations—which today are more and more supported by international commissions—can only grasp human life in the figure of bare or sacred life, and therefore, despite themselves, maintain a secret solidarity with the very powers they ought to fight.[13]

Drawing on Hannah Arendt's poignant depiction of the refugee, a new kind of human being—"the kind that are put in concentration camps by their foes and internment camps by their friends"[14]—Agamben seems to be conceding that there are only universal human rights for those who belong to a particular political state. If that is the case, then what good are universal human rights if there is an absence of particular state membership or when one is fleeing the deprivations that a particular state is imposing? Where an international doctrine of international human rights ought to provide security to everyone precisely to help those most in need, refugees are the most vulnerable and bereft. Today, as millions are seeking refuge from violence and terror at home, to think that losing one's state means losing one's political rights is devastating.

But on another reading of Hannah Arendt, this is not quite the case. As Katherine Howard reads Arendt, even stateless persons have the most fundamental political right, what Arendt enigmatically referred to as the right to have rights.[15] Through this right, they can enact a nonsovereign stateless politics, a politics of belonging in the face of exclusion. Specifically, Howard takes on Jacques Rancière's claim that Arendt's conceptualization of the political forecloses stateless people from appearing in the political realm or undertaking political action of their own. Howard argues that Arendt's discussion of stateless persons should be read in conjunction with her theory of politics as speech and action. To be expelled from a state and its rights does not mean being excluded from the world and the power that comes from "political action which is stubbornly human in the face of dehumanizing systems."[16] The refugee has power beyond the nation-state, the power to speak, act, and enact. The right to politics, as Howard sees it, is "one enacted insofar as we are community-building creatures."[17] Wherever people gather, with or without the papers of citizenship, they have a nonsovereign power that can "transcend and challenge given structures, including those devoted to oppression and dehumanization."[18]

I agree with Howard's reading of Arendt's project and the right to have rights. To it, I add that this right is always already operating, even as formulated in *Origins*, where, Arendt writes, "We become aware of the existence of a right to have rights (and that means to live in a framework where one is judged by one's actions and opinions) and a right to belong to some kind of organized community, only when millions of people emerged who had lost and could not regain these rights because of the new global political system."[19] The paradox in the way Arendt puts it is that the right *exists* but is not acknowledged in a world regime of sovereignty and the Rights of Man. Arendt is contrasting what rights look like from the vantage point of the sovereign nation-state, where rights are the properties of individuals, to what they look like from the vantage point of human plurality.[20]

Efforts to delimit refugees' political rights ignore a crucial reality: the political exceeds mechanisms of elections and governments. It also exceeds the deliberative will-formation of those recognized as citizens of a nation-state. For example, it was the *political* struggles of women, laborers, black folk, and other disenfranchised people that led to political rights for women, laborers, black folk, and other now enfranchised people. While the human rights regime seems unaware of this, theorists have been thinking this through for decades. Starting in the 1980s, liberalism, which had long focused on the state and the limits of its power, came under scrutiny by communitarians for its lack of attention to civic life and by feminists who criticized its patriarchal, universalist assumptions.[21] More recently, theorists such as Wendy Brown, Judith Butler, Jacques Rancière, and others, largely following Arendt, have been calling for a more radically democratic politics. What emerged from these disparate phenomena was a new imaginary of politics that is not centered on the state or the usual apparati of power. This alternative imaginary notices the ways in which problems are named, framed, and deliberated throughout many regions of society, including those arenas seen as outside the political. It also attends to the kind of power that is created horizontally among people in association. It sees the world in a way in which politics is not only what governments do but also what all involved and affected engage in.

Pace Arendt and Habermas, the political arises whenever two or more people come together to address matters of public concern and whenever something needs to be addressed in the midst of disagreement. Politics takes place in the camp and between the camp and the country, whenever people move about, whenever they appear in public with others. For example, in seven of nine camps in Thailand along its border with Myanmar, refugees democratically elect their own committees to run the day-to-day affairs of the camp and oversee matters of education, health, and justice.[22] For another example, for more than a decade in camps in Benin, Togolese refugees engaged in various forms of representation and political participation. Describing these, Clara Lacadet writes,

> The emergence of 'refugee politics' is considered not as an epiphenomenon, but as an aspiration that is found in numerous camp contexts, and which is indicative of the tensions brought about by the confrontation between refugees and humanitarian organizations. It is in fact a hybrid form of politics, at the crossroads between traditional political representation (electing a president, nominating representatives) and the categorization advocated by humanitarian organizations in an attempt to give an increased voice to vulnerable groups.[23]

The conception of the political that I have in mind includes two rather distinct, sometimes oppositional sources for thinking about the political. The first I borrow from Benjamin Barber: politics is the practice of deciding what to do when participants have no basis for agreement yet nonetheless have to decide. "A political question thus takes the form," as Benjamin Barber put it in 1984, "What shall we do when something has to be done that affects us all, we wish to be reasonable, yet we disagree on means and ends and are without independent grounds for making the choice?"[24] Barber points out that at the heart of politics is the process of deciding what action to take "under the worst possible circumstances, when the grounds of choice are not given a priori or by fiat or by pure knowledge."[25] That is, politics is the practice of deciding what to do when there is no objective truth of the matter.[26]

Whoever has the authority to decide is a citizen, Barber further argues, and in a monarchy, there is only one citizen, the king. In a democracy, supposedly all affected are able to decide. To this, some might say, perhaps the citizens of a nation-state might well decide to close their borders or deny refugees any political rights. But in an era of mass migration—in fact, as of this writing, 3.3 percent of the world's population are migrants[27]—using the norms underlying democracy to grant some the power to deny democratic power to others is both hypocritical and incoherent. Democracy's fundamental principle is that all who are affected by matters of common concern should be able to shape those matters. No one should be subject to a law that he or she had no hand in making. Democracy's normative legitimacy rests on all affected having political agency. This is why political agency itself is often the object of political struggle; that is, *the struggle for political agency itself is a political matter*.

Today, who "counts" as a political agent, that is, as someone able to participate fully and equally in the process of charting one's own life and community? Today, in the United States alone, not the undocumented, not people under age eighteen, not resident aliens, not most felons, not many homeless, and not refugees. And throughout the world, as entire nations are drowned by rising seas, as encroaching deserts cause mass migrations, as civil wars force people from their home, the questions of "who counts" and "who decides" will come knocking more frequently.

Politics, then, is not only the process of *deciding* but also the process of *contesting the narrow hold* that some have over the levers of power. Along these lines, politics is also the ceaseless contestation between groups over who gets what, where, and when; conflicting visions over what principles ought to guide public policymaking; struggles over identity and inclusion in the public world; and conflicts between the pull of tradition and demands for change. In the starkest terms, Jacques Rancière reminds us, beginning with the ancients, "the whole basis of politics" has been "the struggle between the poor and the rich," especially insofar as the poor have been excluded from the political order. In refugee politics, the struggle is between those deemed the wretched of the earth and those deemed to be proper citizens. For Rancière, politics begins when those who have had no part demand to have a part.[28] So, contrary to his claims about the stateless, his own political theory opens up a way of thinking about refugee politics. This demand "is the actual institution of politics itself."[29] Otherwise, there is a "natural order of domination," much as Aristotle explained in terms of why it makes perfectly good sense for men to rule their wives and their slaves, for these others lack the capacity to rule themselves. When those deemed lacking insist on their capacity and equal right of self-rule, domination's hold begins to erode, and politics begins.

By thinking of politics this way, much more broadly than formal systems of sovereign politics, it is obvious that "rightless" people take part in politics all the time, just as the young Dreamers do in the United States. Threatened with deportation, bereft of formal political rights, they speak and act together, visibly and loudly, demanding to take part. In the process of their demands, they are being political. While they might not be recognized as citizens, they are clearly political agents. And they are very directly challenging the limits and borders of the sovereign state.

"Politics exists because no social order is based on nature, no divine law regulates human society," writes Castoriadis. And, I would add, no sovereign order can limit political agency. There is no natural *arkhé* or foundation that will settle matters. Plato infamously tried to fabricate a natural order that would preempt any need for political adjudication to settle matters, thus keeping people (or, rather, the poor masses) in their supposedly proper place. His myth of the metals, a lie he fabricated to dupe most of the people into accepting rule by others, held that those with bronze in their blood should be ruled by those with gold and silver in theirs.[30]

For Plato's attempt to keep the people in their proper place, as Rancière notes, it was already too late, for democracy had "already passed that way."[31] Thanks to Cleisthenes, the Greek politician who in 500 BCE changed Athenian governance from rule by elite to rule by the demes (however limited), any supposed natural order lost its authority. Instead of the authority of nature, there was now the authority of all citizens regardless of family lineage or wealth. The democratic dictum was essentially the Protagorean one: the measure of what is right or true was human, not natural or divine, intelligence. There was no external standard for adjudicating measures or deciding what ought to be done in the midst of disagreement. The introduction of democracy brought with it the fact of disagreement, uncertainty, and the peril of having to judge in such circumstances.

In our time, the Universal Declaration of Human Rights tries to keep politics in its proper place: in the domain of one's "own" state. But the 65 million refugees in the world today—as well as the rest of the 3.3 percent of the world's population in migration—are bound to upset this order. Democracy has already passed this way. The figure of the "alien" is also the figure of a human being, the supposed bearer of civil and political rights. Since democracy has already passed this way, attempts to keep some from ever participating in those matters to which they are subjected will stand as performative contractions of the very order that attempts to keep order. "The refugee must be considered for what he is," Agamben writes, "nothing less than a limit concept that radically calls into question the fundamental categories of the nation-state, from the birth-nation to the man-citizen link, and that thereby makes it possible to clear the way for a long-overdue renewal of categories."[32] Agamben continues this thought in a negative direction: toward a politics in which "bare life is no longer separated and excepted"; that is, Agamben seems resigned to the wretched wrenching away of human dignity. But I think that the refugee poses a limit in the other direction, as a figure who faces the citizen, a reminder that the citizen can lose everything too if dignity is not also granted to the person washed ashore. The visage of the refugee is both a remainder and a reminder of what sovereign states try to excise: the fact of the "alien's" political power.

To begin to bring this chapter to a close, note the two claims I am making: one is that, by the light of the self-understanding of democratic nation-states, all those in their midst should be seen as having political rights. The other is that even in the absence of this recognition, those not recognized as having rights can and do in fact harness political power. In effect, then, the longer the international community fails to find a way to recognize noncitizens' rights, the more political turmoil it might face. Any encounter with an "alien's" political power is an encounter with the reality of the artifice and fragility of human rights. In a postmetaphysical age, most people recognize at some level or another that human rights conventions are human creations, not abstract, timeless truths. And so are sovereign states. Just as our conventions are made, they can be undone or remade. "The bringing about of a history in which society not only knows itself, but *makes itself* as explicitly self-instituting," Castoriadis writes, "implies a radical destruction of the known institution of society, in its most unsuspected nooks and crannies, which can exist only as positing/creating not only new institutions but a new *mode* of instituting and a new relation of society and of individuals to the institution." The international community with all its nation-state "parts" can and should reimagine its human rights conventions.

The only thing that stands in the way of such an understanding, again to borrow from Castoriadis, is "the fictive and finally incoherent non-place of identitary logic-ontology," to think that the way things are is the way they must be. "The self-transformation of society concerns social doing—and so also politics, in the profound sense of the term—the doing of men and women in society, and nothing else."[33] Rights are not only made—they are performatively constituted and lived. As I have written elsewhere, "Behaving humanely toward another is a way of acknowledging the dignity of the object of our attentions; but more so it speaks volumes about our own humanity."

What is the case now can be superseded, as Castoriadis suggests, by radical questioning and the creation of new political imaginaries. "Each society also brings into being its own mode of self-alteration."[34] No society, no criteria, no norms exist naturally, meaning that none come into being without the artifice of some creatures. If politics is an art itself, it is an art of self-making and world-making, of deciding together under the worst possible circumstances what merits being and what does not.

In her essay "We Refugees," Arendt closes with the figure of the "conscious pariah," the Jew who insists "upon telling the truth, even to the point of 'indecency, [and gets] in exchange for their unpopularity one priceless advantage: history is no longer a closed book to them and politics is no longer the privilege of Gentiles."[35] These conscious pariahs know that "the outlawing of the Jewish people in Europe has been followed closely the outlawing of most European nations." Moreover, as "refugees driven from country to country," they represent "the vanguard of their peoples—if they keep their identity." In other words, the refugee can be a political actor: the refugee, by her actions and words, can fell sovereign states, can change history.

Hence, in response to the flow of migrants and refugees the world over, the international community should, for both normative and political reasons, find a way to recognize noncitizens' rights, even if this means rethinking the limits of state sovereignty. At a minimum, all refugees should have the right to self-governance of their own immediate living situation. There should also be experiments in alternative forms of political representation, which may be limited at first but provide a clear path toward full political participation. In an era of mass migration, doing anything less would undermine the very legitimacy of state sovereignty, the right for all subject to the laws to also be authors of the laws.

NOTES

1. World Migration Report 2018, https://publications.iom.int/system/files/pdf/wmr_2018_en.pdf, 13.

2. Isaiah Berlin, *Four Essays on Liberty* (London: Oxford University Press, 1969), 121–22.

3. Ruma Mandal, "Political Rights of Refugees," UN High Commissioner for Refugees, November 2003, http://www.refworld.org/pdfid/3fe820794.pdf, iv.

4. 1951 Convention Relating to the Status of Refugees, http://www.unhcr.org/en-us/1951-refugee-convention.html.

5. Mandal, "Political Rights of Refugees."

6. Hannah Arendt, *The Origins of Totalitarianism* (New York: Harcourt, 1948), 279.

7. Diana Meyers, *Victims' Stories and the Advancement of Human Rights* (New York: Oxford University Press, 2016), 29.

8. Meyers, *Victims' Stories and the Advancement of Human Rights*, 30–31.

9. The 1951 Convention's definition of the refugee excludes the vast number of people internationally who have been internally displaced or have been forced to flee their countries for other reasons. Hence, according to the International Justice Resource Center, "Countries in the Americas and Africa experiencing large-scale displacement as the result of armed conflicts found that the 1951 Convention definition did not go far enough in addressing the protection needs of their populations. Consequently, both Article 3 of the Cartagena Declaration and Article 1(2) of the 1969 OAU Convention extend refugee status to an individual who 'owing to external aggression, occupation, foreign domination or events seriously disturbing public order in either part or the whole of his country of origin or nationality, is compelled to leave his place of habitual residence in order to seek refuge in another place outside his country of origin or nationality.' OAU Convention Governing the Specific Aspects of the Refugee Problem in Africa, art. 1(2); *accord* Cartagena Declaration on Refugees, Colloquium on the International Protection of Refugees in Central America, Mexico & Panama, art. 3. The African Union is unique in having a convention that specifically addresses the protection needs of IDPs. African Union Convention for the Protection and Assistance of Internally Displaced Persons in Africa. Finally, the United Nations High Commissioner for Refugees (UNHCR) provides protection to IDPs and stateless individuals in addition to 1951 Convention refugees."

10. Yasemin Sari, "Resettlement and a Right to Place: Resettlement as a Condition for the Sense of Self," Agenda for International Development, July 7, 2017, http://www.a-id.org/en/news/refugees-and-a-right-to-place-resettlement-as-a-condition-for-the-sense-of-self.

11. https://www.odi.org/sites/odi.org.uk/files/odi-assets/publications-opinion-files/9851.pdf.

12. http://www.state.gov/j/prm/policyissues/issues/protracted.

13. Giorgio Agamben, *Homo Sacer: Sovereign Power and Bare Life* (Stanford, CA: Stanford University Press, 1998), 133.

14. Hannah Arendt, "We Refugees," in *Altogether Elsewhere: Writers on Exile*, ed. Marc Robinson (Boston: Faber and Faber, 1994), 111.

15. Katherine Howard, "The 'Right to Have Rights' 65 Years Later: Justice beyond Humanitarianism, Politics beyond Sovereignty," *Global Justice: Theory, Practice, Rhetoric* 10, no. 1 (2017): 79–98.

16. Howard, "The 'Right to Have Rights' 65 Years Later," 87.

17. Howard, "The 'Right to Have Rights' 65 Years Later," 92.

18. Howard, "The 'Right to Have Rights' 65 Years Later," 93.

19. Arendt, *The Origins of Totalitarianism*, 296–97.

20. Arendt, *The Origins of Totalitarianism*, 297–98.

21. See Alison Jaggar, *Feminist Politics and Human Nature* (Lanham, MD: Rowman & Littlefield, 1983) and Michael Walzer, *Spheres of Justice: A Defense of Pluralism and Equality* (New York: Basic Books, 1983).

22. Elisabeth Olivius, "Sites of Repression and Resistance: Political Space in Refugee Camps in Thailand," *Critical Asian Studies* 49, no. 3 (2017): 289–307, doi: 10.1080/14672715.2017.1333268.

23. *Journal of Refugee Studies* 29, no. 2 (June 1, 2016): 187–207, https://doi.org/10.1093/jrs/fev021, 187.

24. Benjamin Barber, *Strong Democracy: Participatory Politics for a New Age* (Berkeley: University of California Press, 1984), 120–21.

25. Barber, *Strong Democracy*, 120–21.

26. I am not arguing against truth per se. There may are certainly many empirical and logical truths. But the absence of truth is the very sine qua non of politics. This is in two senses. First, the question "what should we do?" on matters that are not simply prudential do not admit of truth. For example, when it is a question of how to use scarce resources, toward what end, the answer will be tethered to what participants value. There is no set of facts that can answer the question. Second, politics arises because of disagreement over what should be done. If there were agreement on a matter, then it would not be the subject of political inquiry or contestation.

27. World Migration Report 2018, https://publications.iom.int/system/files/pdf/wmr_2018_en.pdf, 13.

28. Jacques Rancière, *Dis-agreement* (Minneapolis : University of Minnesota Press, 1999), 11.

29. Rancière, *Dis-agreement*, 11.

30. Plato, *Republic*, 414c–417b.

31. Rancière, *Dis-agreement*, 16.

32. Agamben, *Homo Sacer*, 134.

33. Cornelius Castoriadis, *The Imaginary Institution of Society* (Cambridge, MA: MIT Press, 1987), 373.

34. Castoriadis, *The Imaginary Institution of Society*, 372.

35. Arendt, "We Refugees," 119.

Chapter Three

Humanitarian Melancholia

Humanitarianism and the Need for Morality of Thinking

Mladjo Ivanovic

Gruesome scenes of unbearable human suffering and institutional callousness not seen in Europe since World War II have today become daily routine. Images of boats and life jackets littering the beaches, bodies of children drowned at sea, overcrowded camps set up by the UN High Commissioner for Refugees, and families stranded at a border standing in the cold next to a barbed-wire fence are just some of the scenes of catastrophic conditions that define the present humanitarian crisis. Sadly, these images represent the experiences of only a small portion of those attempting to escape horrific conditions in their home countries. Millions of refugees from the Middle East, for example, remain interned in massive refugee camps in Turkey, Jordan, and Lebanon, yet their hardships rarely reach the front pages of Western media.[1] Since the beginning of the "migration crisis" in 2012, European leaders and the general public have ignored the real causes of why people are seeking refuge in Europe and instead focus on idle justifications of inhumane policies that have condemned thousands of people to death in the Mediterranean. What is being cast as a "migrant problem" is in fact a collision of European state interests, outdated international law, and impotent humanism—one that drowns in the iconography of human misery yet fails to mobilize solidarity toward those who are escaping appalling conditions. This is not an accident; these faults are both moral and political. They point to a multifaceted dimension of reasoning about humanitarian tragedy as well as the formation or sustenance of individual and collective identities of Western spectators and humanitarian victims.

In following the mutations of these identities as historical and political processes that shape our moral impulse toward distant others, this chapter offers an analysis of how representations and knowledge about their suffering invites us to contemplate the conditions of those who flee to affluent

European societies. Every attempt to mediate knowledge about their horrifying experiences also articulates a relationship that shifts our awareness into an acknowledgment of how suffering of those afflicted is inseparable from our own position in the world and the conditions that we enjoy (regardless of whether or not we acknowledge the obligations that this relationship entails). Although this seems to be an epistemic shift, it is nonetheless propelled by the underlying ontological negotiations and material practices of a society that take place in the formation of our experiences in regard to ourselves, the world we inhabit, and other human beings.

At the heart of these processes lies the acknowledgment of a fundamental change in the ways that the suffering of refugees as *distant others* is represented and articulated in contemporary political culture. We have been witnessing a degeneration of the liberal humanitarian principles of solidarity. We instead find a docile, narcissistic kind of self-reflection, devoid of significant political engagement with the "evils of the world."[2] While there are still institutional and individual efforts to mobilize a political force from this moral encounter between Western spectators and vulnerable strangers, it seems that the liberal premise of the success of moral education that habituates social agents into adopting the moral dispositions to act on behalf of those who are in dire need reveals the limits of an outdated ideology. Rather than improving ties of solidarity and fostering the awareness to acknowledge and respect differences among people and the sociocultural ethos they may share, today's target of humanitarian practices and discourses seems to be part of an ontological lottery that involves the reduction of humanity to social and cultural divisions. Hence, any radical alternative to the current humanitarian situation of millions of forcefully displaced people needs to take into account the tumultuous dynamics between history and our present reality. There is a sense of the world beyond the West, but it is a different world—a world that confronts us with uncomfortable but vital questions of power, responsibility, and justice and that, in doing so, calls us to reflect on historical choices that have ultimately designed our present unjust global political, social, and economic conditions.

This chapter is divided into two main parts. The first identifies some of the weaknesses of humanitarian discourse and practices, and it has an analytical dimension in that it attempts to tease out the political forces, cultural habits, forms of knowledge, skills, and expertise that were folded into the organization and form of subjectivity that is at the center of humanitarian attention. A growing problem of our political culture is an increased difficulty in mobilizing solidarity with people who are culturally and geographically distant from us. In witnessing the dire circumstances of millions of forcefully displaced people today, this is a problem that cannot continue to be ignored. Although there is an increasing amount of literature on humanitarianism, most of these (often brilliant) analyses stop at one of two institutional levels:[3] they focus on either the deficiencies of institutional management or the political shortcomings of current policies that result from an inability (and unwillingness) of governments or nonprofit officials and workers to struggle for a more just world. Although identifying these shortcomings is welcome (and necessary), I leave them aside and focus on showing the inherent inconsistencies and ideological tendencies of humanitarian principles and practices that are the hallmark of today's humanism.

The second part focuses on offering an alternative way of thinking about responsibility and solidarity. Following the work of critical social theorists, I argue that our way of apprehending the world is in itself a historical and critical process. Accordingly, I propose a transformationalist interpretation of Theodor Adorno's critique of cognitive and material dispositions that results in reductive habits of cognition and atrophied moral agency. While my reading of Adorno finds his work partially open to the possibility of ethics beyond the common liberal understanding, what I find ultimately helpful in addressing today's issues of humanitarianism is the guiding thread of his work that shows how epistemology ought to be ethical and that ethics should in turn be political. Adorno's insistence on the primacy of the object of our knowledge invites us to think morally and see the priority of the Other as a crucial feature of any ethical relationship. Ultimately, by drawing attention to the ways in which the explication of the realms of human vulnerability depend on our capacity to leave our own epistemic and ontological position to reflect on the values and norms that often manifest themselves as subordinating and exploitative, this chapter charts a way to understand how the transformation of humanitarian agency can take place.

HUMANITARIANISM AND ITS DISCONTENTS

When we reflect on urgent social challenges tied to the current failures of humanitarian "management" and inclusion of forcefully displaced people in Western societies, the questions of solidarity with those who seek refuge within our borders cannot be examined separately from the organizational structure that dominates our present moral discourse. *Humanitarianism* articulates a site wherein different dimensions of the moral, economic, and political intersect with and determine one another in various ways that come to define what humanism and solidarity are. What I understand as humanitarianism in the contemporary conventional context is a definite set of ideas and practices that can be located materially in their institutional and discursive forms. In other words, as Didier Fassin has insightfully put the point, humanitarianism ultimately stands for a system of governance that designates "the deployment of moral sentiments in contemporary politics."[4] The political economy of moral sentiments is evident in the ways in which it nourishes political discourses and legitimizes political practices, particularly where these discourses and practices are focused on the disadvantaged and the dominated, whether at home (e.g., the poor, the immigrants, or the homeless) or farther away (e.g., refugees, migrants, or the victims of famine, epidemics, or war). Such a humanitarian assemblage includes but also exceeds the intervention of the state, local administrations, international bodies, political institutions more generally, spatial organizations, technical standards, procedures, and systems of monitoring.

In the contemporary political culture, the discourse of affects and humanitarian values offer a high political return. Yet this ongoing attempt to treat humanitarianism as a symbol of what is good about the world—as an echo of the possibility of a more humane world—has the tendency to conceal inequalities on which humanitarianism draws its purpose and validity. One reason that humanitarian language has steadily increased over the past few decades is that after a century of ideologies and bloodshed, it still offers a seductive simplification of our reality without real commitment to action. Sympathy can allow an entire generation to imagine the discovery and expression of solidarity, an empty solidarity, not through ideas of responsibility, reparations, and social criticism but instead in the management of expedient moral sentiments and caretaking. What is worse, many seem to believe that good intentions are enough. The humanitarian discourse has always focused the impact of its practices and knowledge on the attitudes of the public and the messages that such knowledge aims to convey. As such, it denotes a certain way of looking at the world. As humanitarian organizations increasingly ally themselves with governments and corporate donors—and by doing so compromise in ways that ultimately corrode their core organizational values—it seems to me that the issue is not how to justify political undertones of a shifting humanitarian ideology but, rather, whether and how humanitarianism can sustain its ethics.

The problem, as I see it, must be approached from two specific critical lines. The first is primarily political and concerns earlier descriptions of humanitarianism as reminiscent of the neoliberal political and economic logic. Recent humanitarian interventions show how spatial organizations, procedures, and systems of monitoring have become the means for exercising violence and for governing those who are unwanted in the West. The collusion of these technologies of humanitarianism, human rights advocacy, and international law, including the attendant military and political powers, constitute what Eyal Weizman has described as our *humanitarian present*.[5] The driving force of humanitarianism is accordingly no longer a sense of naive but engaged compassion but instead a highly specialized and concerted international effort to manage populations that are seen as posing risks. Within this present condition, all political opposition, social activism, and institutional reforms are replaced by the elasticity of measures, degrees, negotiations, proportions, and administration. Thus, as humanitarianism aligns with forces that it ultimately aims to challenge, the humanitarian spectator and the victim become a site wherein political, aesthetic, and ethical transformations and negotiations take place.

This brings us to a second problem closely related with the increasing commodification of private emotions and philanthropic obligations, namely, the production of administrative knowledge as an intrinsic aspect of today's humanitarian practice. This epistemological dimension of humanitarianism and the ethics of solidarity turns on questions of representation and the articulation of knowledge that are the modus operandi of increasingly institutionalized neoliberal logic of measures, standards, microeconomic explanations, and strategic depictions of afflicted individuals, often at the cost of actual insight into systemic causes of environmental degradation, global poverty, and violence. Such a reduction of humanitarian methodology into a form of depoliticized managerialism further suggests that the instrumentalization of humanitarian practice and humanitarian discursive regimes has a direct impact on epistemic and affective dispositions of subjects who are vessels of humanitarian agency. Because suffering is also characteristic language of the contemporary world and that compassion has become a significant political force, the Western humanitarian subject is exposed to the constant risk of renouncing objectification in her description and ultimately of reinforcing the social construction to which she unwittingly contributes. Being a product of social processes that differentiate our "self" from others and condition our capacity for affective attachment and reflexive engagement with the political conditions of human vulnerability, we are confronted with the uncomfortable but vital question of our cultural situatedness, privilege, and ontologically unstable alterity and, finally, with justice in its national and international contexts.

The political and epistemic problems of the current state of humanitarianism reflected in the ongoing apathy of European societies for the hardships of refugees warehoused in refugee camps on the Greek islands and in Turkey, Lebanon, and Jordan are closely related. The best way to think through the challenges of humanitarianism and the contemporary humanitarian agency of European spectators is not only to conceive humanitarianism as something that is confronted with the subject who has inadequate motivation or inadequate goals in regard to solidarity with others. Both aspects, which are actually true, are a reflection of deeper processes of subject formation and the associated development of moral and political dispositions within contemporary Western moral and political agency. Taking into account that humanitarianism seems to be a self-repairing mechanism of a system that engenders inequalities and human deprivation, the fact that these inequalities and injustices ultimately help humanitarianism validate its own existence point to ideological tendencies of a discourse that is unavoidably bound up with a history of colonialism, racism, sexism, and human exploitation.

This paradox at the heart of the humanitarian field requires us to examine not only the structural issues tied with humanitarianism in its institutional form but also the moral and political implications that such a structure has on the individual agency. In other words, if we reflect on the pitfalls of public engagement with the hardships of refugees, one has to be clear about what kind of impact humanitarianism has on both the material conditions of people affected by humanitarian crises and the constitution of the moral dispositions of Western spectators on whose donations and engagement humanitarianism ultimately depends. Today, most of the moral and political appeal of humanitarianism is informed by an emphasis on urgency and vulnerable iconography of poverty and violence. Yet we should reflect on what has been ultimately gained through such public depictions and what has been lost. What really happens when we use images of suffering? Do we speak of inequality? Do we invoke human trauma in order to recognize the underlying systematic nature of violence? And, more generally, what are the consequences when we mobilize compassion rather than challenge underlying injustices? Are scales of humanitarianism different than scales of justice?

These kinds of questions are closely related to each other. They help us understand how shortcomings of humanitarianism are mere symptoms of deeper social and political problems inextricably linked to the moral and political dispositions of the twenty-first-century individual. Reflecting on the intersection of epistemological issues and the articulation of knowledge about human suffering plays a crucial if often unacknowledged role in grounding the humanitarian ontology of the precarity of others. To deal with these processes properly, we must consider the standards by which we measure and evaluate others and the social conditions that surround them. These standards often overlook and/or obscure the extent to which the very material and epistemological preconditions for moral agency and recognition of moral and political obligations are themselves space wherein ontological negotiations about the understanding and identity of others take place. As a product of negotiation (and representation), the refugee is turned into an object without voice, without meaning other than that given to her by the political and moral discursive apparatus of the West.

Finally, not only do these epistemological and ontological negotiations take place within a power-saturated reality, but they also circumscribe and define who we are, our sense of self, the way we are perceived by others, what we are able to see, and who the Other is. Additionally, they impose a condition of "reproducibility," a prerequisite that allows for the perpetuation of social conditions whose history (and longevity) often mistakenly influences us to believe they are "natural" in some way rather than a product of historical choices that have been made at the cost of conquered, enslaved, and oppressed people. Yet in light of shifting social and cultural contexts, the reproducibility of power relations also entails a possibility to break out of previous oppressive contexts. Only when we detach from reductive accounts of "knowing" and "seeing," when we reconfigure the direction from which power flows, do these hegemonic imaginaries fall apart. Hence, by whatever approach we choose to distance ourselves from these imaginaries, it is obvious that radical social transformation depends on our capacity to purge ourselves from epistemic, ontological, social, moral, and political privilege. Only by installing different configurations of power and by making the emergence of different patterns and ways of thinking, seeing, and caring is such a change possible. Despite a difficult social and political reality, there seems to exist hope for a more inclusive and perhaps all-encompassing relation with others that transcends the narrow and exclusionary logic of humanity to which our political culture abides.

THEODOR ADORNO AND "MORALITY OF THINKING"

A glimpse at the current state of humanitarianism and the refugee crisis sufficiently indicates the general tendency of the Western public to differentiate from and select which people are worthy of assistance. Although this is an important feature of how our social structures guide our perception and knowledge of instances of human suffering, such an account does not fully articulate the complexity of the current humanitarian situation. We have seen that questions about the ways in which vulnerable others are represented in our media-saturated culture and whether such a spectacle of suffering has the power to move us to action point to broader social contexts and invoke issues tied with social forces under which our subjectivity is formed. Thus, the problem of Western humanitarian agency cannot be addressed properly by pointing only at the imperative to act on vulnerable others. Previous pages show how such a view must be complemented with an analysis of the epistemic and ontological dimensions of the Western humanitarian agency.

In the remainder of this chapter, I turn to the question of what reforms are necessary to make humanitarian appeals an effective means to encourage a better acknowledgment of the individual and collective responsibilities amid a reality of exploitation and injustice.

When we look back on the work of early Frankfurt School, we can see that moral agency is situated and arises out of the very nature of social conditions and cognitive capacities that are mournfully defined by their instrumental nature. Taking into account such an ontological and epistemological entrapment of agents, critical theorists caution that individuals seem to be unable to acknowledge others and engage with them as objects of moral concern. Underneath the cognitive and material dispositions of a damaged social world lies a form of subjectivity that is unable to awake to an immanent call for solidarity toward others who endure inhumane conditions.

Social Pathologies and Pathologies of Thinking

The question of the relationship between reductive tendencies of Eurocentric thinking is central to Adorno's account of rationality—specifically, to whether his insights about the ideological, oppressive nature of our cognitive dispositions can explain the ethical deficit of the contemporary moral/humanitarian agent. His analysis suggests that something takes place with the way we appropriate the world around us and that this elementary process of appropriation in itself unlaces scores of avenues for violent social relations and public coldness and indifference.[6] This occurs because the encounter with other human beings (and the subject's articulation of them) rests on the knower's values, previous knowledge, cultural norms, biases, social conditions, media portrayals, and so on, which determine the success (or failure) of the encounter with the precarity of the other. Adorno himself conceives of thinking as an operation of identification. This process involves bringing something specific and particular (the manifold given to us through the senses) under something general (concepts). While all thinking intrinsically has this structure, only the dominant instrumental form of rationality holds that the synthesis performed by conceptual subjugation of the sensible world actually captures reality's all-essential properties.

In arguing about the limits of such rationality, Adorno complains about something more fundamental. It is the thought that any form of being subsumed under concepts, even the most apt one, misses something about its target—and if this inconsistency is not reflected on, then thought unavoidably does injustice to objects of cognition. Instead of saying what something is, identity thinking says what it falls under—what it is an example or representative of, what it consequently is not, or what social powers want it to be. If we take into account that our perceptions of other human beings follow the same dynamics, Adorno's doubts about the cognitive adequacy of our experience leads to general suspicion about our capacity to act morally regarding injustices done to others. If we translate this into our position as humanitarian spectators of instances of suffering, it seems that we unavoidably apply reductive standards to such conditions because in our perceptions, we follow our own standpoint in evaluating circumstances that victims of humanitarian crises as objects of our knowledge experience. These standards go to the heart of the problems that I addressed earlier, namely, that we experience others in a way that is predetermined and, as such, subsume complex social circumstances to an articulation that is in itself devoid of acknowledging the weight and standpoint of people who are the target of our cognitive and affective ascriptions.

Such a stance, however, highlights once again the interrelation between the workings of social ontology of human beings and the limits of our cognitive apparatus. The fact that our social world tends to produce consciousness in a way that is exclusionary and discriminatory makes the process of witnessing a peculiar endeavor. The jigsaw of failures of our current humanitarianism, then, is in our inability to see the world and our place in it for what they are. This is not conducive to having the capacity for moral agency because if our moral capacity depends on our epistemic dispositions to recognize others and award them with specific ontological status by applying norms determined by social circumstances, then this process not only results in our perpetuating the conditions we should criticize but also places under question the nature and possibility of humanitarianism in general.

An attempt to understanding distorted cognitive capacities as the outcome of processes of social development in modernity positions the modern subject at odds with the professed needs and challenges of an ethically fragile world. The way in which Adorno attempts to respond to this kind of challenge is by discerning objects of thought that are decentered, historically conscious, attuned to the fact of pluralism, and recognized in their specific particularity despite all forms of reduction. When used to analyze relations of cognitive accounts of oppression and domination, this way of conceptualizing thinking implies that our cognitive dispositions do not sufficiently attend to the fact that identifying always involves disregarding what is "nonidentical" and incommensurable in the particular object of our thinking. It thereby violates a commitment inherent in its understanding of concepts themselves: concepts are directed toward capturing what they are not. Consequently, since such a cognitive model of thinking does not consider what is left out as essential about the object or, rather, it is not conceived or recognized as essential, we are left with an ideological understanding of the world and its entities. This not only leaves our knowledge of others fragmented or false but also creates a background wherein ontological formation and recognition of other people takes properties of sociopolitical manipulation that serves the political and economic interests of those in power. Such processes of objection assume a certain image that simultaneously determines what is essential about objects and about the ways they are accessible to us. This not only often conceals marginalization and oppression of those whom we conceive alien and unwanted but also keeps us in a state of lethargy because our own reflective capacities obscure (rather than illuminate) relations of power that cause and sustain unjust conditions.

Nonidentity and Constellations

The critique of such constitutive aspects of our cognitive dispositions depends on an effort to reconstruct intuitive, premediated knowledge of subjects whose agency is deemed constitutive of the hierarchies that are consequently proved to be the most effective and long-standing instrument of social domination. Insofar as the subject's cognitive dispositions articulate and sustain social identities that are inherently a product of social relations, the first step in overcoming this mutually reinforcing relation between social conditions and cognitive dispositions is to disentangle one from the other. Adorno connects this process to an inherent potential of thinking to reconcile with its immediate object. As he puts it, "While doing violence to the object of its synthesis, our thinking heads a potential that waits in the object, and it unconsciously obeys the idea of making amends to the piece for what it has done."[7] Such making of amends would require a reflection on thinking itself and the problematic nature of its orientation toward identity, what Adorno calls the *second reflection*. It would require a positioning of thinking away from fitting the world into conceptual schemes and others in already predetermined values within an evaluative frame constituted toward giving the object priority.[8] Indeed, in *Minima Moralia*, Adorno even speaks of adhering to a "morality of thinking," wherein such morality is manifested in epistemic sensitivity toward the limits and objectifying veneer of a thinking subject:

> Even when sophistication is understood in the theoretically acceptable sense of that which widens horizons, passes beyond the isolated phenomenon, considers the whole, there is still a cloud in the sky. It is just this passing-on and being unable to linger, this tacit assent to the primacy of the general over the particular, which constitutes not only the deception of idealism in hypostazing concepts,

> but also its inhumanity, that has no sooner grasped the particular than it reduces it to a through-station, and finally comes all too quickly to terms with suffering and death for sake of a reconciliation occurring merely in reflection—in the last analysis, the bourgeois coldness that is only too willing to underwrite the inevitable.[9]

In other words, although Adorno correctly objects to a form of thinking as an immanent reduction and equation of truth with immutability, a wider, tragic aspect of identity thinking should form the basis of a critique of distinctively pathological tendencies of modernity that still plague our militaristic, exploitative, humanitarian present. If thinking is to avoid collapsing into ideology, it must draw its normative motivation from within the existing social world, not from an abstract metaphysical account as such. One can capture this stance well if one reflects on Adorno's understanding of nonrational cognitive experiences that are rooted in somatic awareness of the finitude and contingencies of human vulnerability. Such experiences (e.g., the suffering of living beings) may provide impulses for thinking that may result in heightened reflexivity and increased individual and collective decentralization from historically known forms of control and discursive cognitive models from which they draw their validity and justification.

Adorno's way to achieve this pivots on two fulcrums: it both addresses the epistemological (and ethical) primacy of the object and at the same time offers a conceptual strategy for allowing that primacy. First, in conjunction with his critique of identity thinking, Adorno insists that the priority of object is not in itself the denial of the necessity of the subject's contribution to knowledge acquisition. Rather, it is a way to correct the tendency of a distorted cognitive model to ignore its reductive processes and ideological contribution. Whatever is contained in the others-objects themselves requires human subjectivity to be illuminated through either acknowledging their own needs or creating adequate space for them to be encountered. In this way, the vulnerability of others is unlocked by the subjects acknowledging the historical dynamics and relational character of the objects and conditions they cognize.[10] This cannot happen by stubbornly applying our own categories, values, or norms to them. Objects require our understanding to remain open to more fluid forms of gathering concepts into relational clusters, and this in turn requires the subject to move beyond her own epistemic situatedness in order to avoid reinforcing fixed categorizations of her own norms and cultural standards.

One way to realize this, Adorno believes, is to employ a multitude of concepts, at the same time acknowledging the diversity of historical contexts that they are embedded in, and reflexively bring them into what he, following Walter Benjamin, calls *constellations*. The reference to Benjamin's notion of constellations helps Adorno reconstruct modern thought forms by taking this epistemological metaphor and bringing into focus the temporal and historical tensions between concepts and the objects they are referring to. He describes the mediating function of constellations in terms of discontinuous dialectical critical mediation and emphasizes their abrupt irruptive appearance as a dialectical image that disrupts the homogenized continuum of history. As he puts it,

> The constellation illuminates the specific side of the object, the side which to a classifying procedure is either a matter of indifference or a burden. . . . It lends objectivity to them by the relation into which it puts the concepts, centered about a thing. Language thus serves the intention of the concept to express completely what it means. By themselves, constellations represent from without what the concept has cut away within: the "more" which the concept is equally desirous and incapable of being. By gathering around the object of cognition, the concepts potentially determine the object's interior. They attain, in thinking, what was necessarily excised from thinking.[11]

Hence, the significance of this conceptual strategy lies in its connecting or mediating power—that is, in its potential to bring together material objects with overarching discursive narratives, without reducing one to the other.

The intertwining of material and epistemic aspects of our knowledge puts forward the reflexive disclosing effect of decoupling objects from their sedimentary meanings and ideological representations. Such a process enables the subject to comprehend a broader conception of social conditions and other people and at the same time prevent the singular specificity of the historical phenomenon from being dominated, eclipsed, or incorporated in reductive accounts of articulation. Drawing on social genesis and the dynamics of cultural and geopolitical change, Adorno explains the significance of this strategy as follows:

> The history locked in the object can only be delivered by a knowledge mindful of the historic positional value of the object in its relation to other objects—by the actualization and concentration of something which is already known and is transformed by that knowledge. Cognition of the object in its constellation is cognition of the process stored in the object. As a constellation, theoretical thought circles the concept it would like to unseal, hoping that it may fly open like the lock of a well-guarded safe-deposit box: in response, not to a single key or a single number, but to a combination of numbers.[12]

The ideal toward which this reconfiguration of thinking aims is a disclosure of ways in which discursive framing is related to historical objects, and exactly through their configuration and discursive interrelationship, they receive meaning and recognition and invoke responsibilities to those who reflect on them.

In this sense, at least as far as Adorno's understanding of constellations goes, if our grasp of events that result in human suffering aims to detach from reductive accounts of evaluative frameworks and ontological differentiation that separate humanity from the privileged and those marginalized, it should be located at the intersection of tensions and relations between different historical processes. Thus, to understand the conditions that some human beings endure, we need to understand how these people are situated in an epistemic and ontological vortex that positions the articulation of their lives against the backdrop of broader historical and political phenomena. Whether one agrees with the details of this strategy, Adorno's insights help us to think differently about objects of our knowledge. This helps us understand not only all the pitfalls of the moral agency of the "Western" humanitarian subject but also that as much as objects of our knowledge, we are also the product of the same relations of power and social, gendered, and racial classifications that pervade different dimensions of our existence. Although our ontological and epistemological genesis stems from the same set of ideological processes that position different individuals within the same modality of global power, one must be clear regarding the intricate differences in these positions and the obligations that such differences entail. Social emancipation and transformation of an unjust world are processes that explore the relationship between different objects in their historical complexity, and as such, they receive actualization in constant tension between our cognitive, ethical, and political agency and social conditions that are directly or indirectly the result of relations of power that we must be able to contest.

In the end, our active efforts to overcome the limitations of epistemic and ontological norms that guide our recognition of other people can help us direct our articulation of others in a way that will help them reveal themselves as inevitable objects of our moral concern. The success of such moral solicitation depends on the success of creating space wherein the other can present herself independent of any thematization. Cultural conditioning too often drowns out the call of distant others so that their voices go unheard. As I understand the lesson drawn from Adorno's philosophy, if we do not first approach ways in which we comprehend others, we will not be able to recognize them on their own terms, and the Western subject will remain locked in a self-identifying imaginary. Only if we detach from reductive forms of thinking will we be able to approach others ethically and be aware of the responsibilities that our position in the world demands from us. While ascription cannot be completely suspended, as all our perceptions are culturally conditioned, comprehending the Other through multiple angles and possible interpretations can help us encounter them in their humanity and historical locatedness. We need to invite the Other into a reciprocal relationship, and in this relationship, the other can teach us something about ourselves too.

TOWARD A NEW HUMANISM

Throughout this chapter, I have argued that by invoking human vulnerability and suffering as the moral cornerstones of solidarity, humanitarianism collapses important political questions of responsibility and justice with moralizing discourses around which the Western public is called to organize a charitable action toward the misfortune of refugees and non-Western others. Ironically enough, compassion and the representation of human suffering—the two structural aspects of the humanitarianism—fail to mobilize and sustain moral dispositions to act on the vulnerability of others. One of the lessons taken from the current humanitarian crisis and management of refugees by European countries is that compassion cultivates a flawed disposition of solidarity that often ignores the historical injustices and contemporary inequalities sustained by a dehumanizing logic of the global market and neoliberalism. In the case of media representations that expose Western subjects to human vulnerability and gruesome atrocities, the extent to which such portrayals make available the normative discourses that subtly regulate moral and political threshold of the Western spectator, such practices are ultimately instruments of power.

By analyzing the entanglement of moral impulses with the economy and the ways in which such entanglement is manifested through diverse mechanisms that form what we understand as our humanitarian present, I sought to demonstrate how humanitarianism has capitalism as its necessary condition of possibility. In other words, humanitarianism manifests all communicative, representational, and institutionalized paradoxes and ideological tendencies of neoliberalism, which ultimately thrives on inequality, suffering, militarism, and moral selectivism. Thus, rather than directing my analysis at limits of current international law and international institutions, avoiding a naive denunciation of humanitarian management has helped me focus on the inner mechanisms of the production of "humanity" under the inhumane conditions of an unjust global order. This is why reflecting on calls for cultivating compassionate dispositions toward distant others discloses the underlying logic of economic domination of all spheres of social life, wherein solidarity not only is rendered a matter of consumerist choice but also has prioritized the pursuit of the self-assertion and pleasures of the Western identity over the morality of otherness and justice.

By hinting at very complex accounts of how such hierarchies form and sustain our agency in a way that prevents us from looking at others without the reductive lens of Eurocentrism, I have tried to go beyond a figure of the humanitarian victim and problematize the subjectivity of the spectator. Instead of despairing for the inhumanity of perpetrators and social conditions that their agency brings into existence, my intention was to call into question the historically invariable role of bystanders. Similarly entangled in ontological formation and defined by often-unexamined certainties of "objective" knowledge that aims to vindicate the history of the West (and the present choices that the West makes), the bystander often becomes arbitrarily collectivized in the hegemonic figure of the Western actor. This is an actor who, for the most part, remains blind and ignorant about her own role in perpetuating historical inequalities and injustices done to others whose agency is commonly ignored or rendered insignificant. This is why I have strongly defended a return toward an ethics and epistemology of otherness portrayed through work of Theodor Adorno. My interpretation of his theory has shown that regardless of how much the subjectivity remains a product of historically layered inequalities and injustices, our cognitive dispositions remain a vehicle of emancipatory social processes. By incorporating a critique of epistemic elements and placing somatic impulses in regard to evidence of human vulnerability at the forefront of political agency, Adorno envisions a moral force that helps us redefine the sense of responsibility, individual engagement, and solidarity among people. This is the reason that he insisted that answering the calls of human misery is possible only if we cultivate our capacities in a way to make that feeling sensitive to determinations and limitations that remain an inherent aspect of our political culture. Any attempt to ground ethics in universal principles will be too abstract and too weak to guide our actions amidst different geopolitical contexts. Furthermore, it will separate morality from the nondiscursive, materialistic motive, which Adorno thinks is necessary for a successful moral response. For Adorno, the role of judgment remains important, but this judgment would not be about the application of a principle but rather a recognition of which core features of deplorable crimes against humanity are present in specific situations. In this way, moral agency receives the kind of foothold in human beings that the universalism of Enlightenment culture and Kantian ethics evidently lack.

Going back to the relation between the evidence of human suffering and our moral obligations, what lessons for the solidarity with others can we draw from this analysis of our epistemic dispositions and how they guide our moral and political faculties? Adorno's insistence on the moral-political imperative of sheer human vulnerability and the somatic reactions that exposure to instances of human suffering entails seems to serve a twofold purpose here. First, somatic reactions escape rationalization and as such avoid pitfalls of an atrophied reason—simultaneously pushing us to reflect on causes that result in such conditions. Second, such impact on our faculties and subsequent reflection on the meaninglessness of human suffering at the same time illuminates pathologies and limits of our agency, thus enabling us to transcend them. When we consider this in light of critiques of liberal notions of humanitarianism that I have introduced in this chapter, such a reading of Adorno could itself be seen as a call to or gesture of solidarity with the suffering of the marginalized subjects who have suffered so much due to historical and present injustices perpetuated in the name of progress and the lethal ideals of monological Eurocentrism. Taking into account that solidarity and moral engagement with others depend on the humanity that we recognize in the appeals that their inhumane conditions make on us, the first step toward a new form of solidarity is the disenchanting enchantment of the humanitarian imaginary and values that are created by an environment that thrives on exclusion and historical inequalities. Hence, as Adorno reminds us, one cannot distinguish the analysis of morality from questions of the proper form of politics. The problem with solidarity today is that human suffering and human vulnerability are mediated by processes that, rather than closing gaps, create and sustain distance between different cultural, moral, and political perspectives. In order to approach the Other ethically, such a process for Adorno requires recognizing not only the vulnerability of the gaze that stares at us (or the violently subjugated particularity of the nonidentical) but also the mask that conceals the environment that mercilessly negotiates her ontological (and subsequently moral) value and an account of reason that ultimately dehumanizes the other into an object of our perception. Thus, such a critical notion of solidarity suggests that the blind faith of our political culture in compassion alone is an insufficient condition for grounding an ethics of solidarity insofar as, without critical judgment and self-critique, our affective dispositions tend to collapse either into self-absorption or voyeurism—both narcissistic engagements with distant others that fuel injustices rather than overcoming them.

By indicating different layers of epistemic and ontological determinations that reduce the European capacity to include non-Europeans in their sociopolitical environment, I wanted to show how questions of humanitarianism and solidarity cannot be properly addressed without raising questions of justice and responsibility. If we want to discuss the reach and limits of the existing humanism, it is necessary to interrogate the implications of our situatedness, wherein every normative negotiation takes place within a normative frame that enables epistemic and ontological negotiation of different social groups and different cultural contexts. Analyzing historical, social, and global injustices without addressing specifically epistemic forms of violence and oppression would fail to address and overcome the complexity of such processes of domination. As we have seen from critical accounts of Adorno and other social theorists, such epistemic forms of violence ultimately limit the capacity of agents to escape the marginalization that occurs as an effect of the epistemic biases and epistemic domination that each sustain and reinforce for each other. Referring to the intertwining of cognitive deficiencies, material conditions, and lack of public interest to address social maladies, we have seen that these forms of oppression are inevitable parts of the social structure of our globalized capitalist world and as such should be a primary target of an analysis of present humanitarianism and humanitarian agency.

In the end, one can easily conclude that there is no such thing as an epistemic innocence because we always operate within grids of intelligibility that determine what can be intelligible and what is rendered invisible. Retrospectively, looking at the exclusionary logic of Eurocentrism, the legacy of colonialism, and the forms of agency that echo and sustain them, I have referred to ways how the colonial "hangover" and present requirements of the global market force humanitarianism to remain discursively confined within a dehumanizing and violent past—one plagued by domination, exploitation, and annihilation. At the very source of our current difficulties regarding the inclusion of "subaltern" others in western European and North American societies, one can ultimately find failures in both basic human self-understanding and the understanding of others. Such failures account for false ontological formations regarding others, and they show how our ethical and political agency often falls prey to cultural biases, the incommensurability of experiences, and the reductive, violent nature of mediation and ascription of knowledge toward epistemically disadvantaged agents, such as refugees, immigrants, asylum seekers, and so on. If our aim is to envision and create new forms of social relations between "West" and Global South, we must stop relying on discursive and normative commitments to what is essentially an ethnocentric solidarity that imagines otherness and historicity from the position of a subject—that is ignorant of and indifferent to her own complicity and privilege. By doing this, we are making a first step toward living a wrong life right.

NOTES

1. For more on this theme, see Kelly Oliver, *Carceral Humanitarianism: Logics of Refugee Detention* (Minneapolis: University of Minnesota Press, 2017), 20–28.

2. See Lillie Chouliaraki, *The Ironic Spectator* (Cambridge: Polity Press, 2013), and Kelly Oliver, *Carceral Humanitarianism: Logics of Refugee Detention* (Minneapolis: University of Minnesota Press, 2017).

3. For example, see Michael Barnett, *Empire of Humanity: A History of Humanitarianism* (Ithaca, NY: Cornell University Press, 2011); Deen K. Chatterjee, ed., *The Ethics of Assistance: Morality and the Distant Needy* (Cambridge: Cambridge University Press, 2004); Simon Chesterman, Michael Ignatieff, and Ramesh Thakur, eds.,

Making States Work: State Failure and the Crisis of Governance (New York: United Nations University Press, 2005); B. S. Chimni, "Globalization, Humanitarianism, and the Erosion of Refugee Protection," Refugee Studies Centre Working Paper (Oxford: Oxford University Press, 2000); Didier Fassin, *Humanitarian Reason: A Moral History of the Present* (Berkeley: University of California Press, 2012); Didier Fassin and Mariella Pandolfi, eds., *Contemporary States of Emergency: The Politics of Military and Humanitarian Intervention* (New York: Zone Books, 2010); and Martha Nussbaum, *Creating Capabilities: The Human Development Approach* (Cambridge, MA: Belknap Press, 2011).

4. Fassin, *Humanitarian Reason*, 2.
5. Eyal Weizman, *The Least of All Possible Evils* (New York: Verso, 2011), 4.
6. Theodor Adorno, *Negative Dialectics*, trans. E. B. Ashton (New York: Verso, 2005), 11.
7. Adorno, *Negative Dialectics*, 30.
8. Adorno, *Negative Dialectics*, 183–88.
9. Theodor Adorno, *Minima Moralia*, trans. E. F. N. Jephcott (New York: Verso, 2006), 74.
10. Adorno, *Negative Dialectics*, 52.
11. Adorno, *Negative Dialectics*, 162.
12. Adorno, *Negative Dialectics*, 163.

Part II

HOSPITALITY, CARE, AND RESPONSIBILITY

Chapter Four

Hospitality and the Political Economy of Care

Lisa M. Madura

As the foregoing chapters have made evident, the contemporary global climate is largely one of hostility toward immigrants. The displaced in need of protection and opportunity are met with resistance and are forced into a liminal existence. Refugees fleeing war-torn countries are living in tent cities outside of metropolitan Europe with only the minimal resources afforded them by humanitarian organizations. Undocumented immigrants in the United States are treated as criminals, being held in unsanitary and overcrowded detention facilities while they await deportation hearings, in some cases for years. Residents of the United States, both documented and undocumented, are targets of racial discrimination perpetuated by a deepening fear of the foreign other, who is believed to threaten the "at home" of American life. Crises of forced migration raise important ethical questions about the economy of care. As members of a global community, what do we owe one another? What are the political and moral dimensions of the host–guest relationship? When is the host justified in turning the guest away? The works of Emmanuel Levinas and Jacques Derrida provide valuable resources for thinking through these questions, each philosopher contributing to the development of an ethical conception of hospitality rooted in human alterity. I take their conception of hospitality to serve as a framework within which we can understand and deal with two conflicting impulses—the ethical impulse to unconditionally welcome the other in need and the political impulse of self-preservation, which forecloses hospitality and leads to discrimination and exclusion.[1]

In this chapter, I provide a sketch of the Levinasian–Derridian theory of hospitality, which redraws the boundaries of ethics and politics to reveal a persistent and, in some ways, tragic tension between them. With this tension in view, I diagnose an imbalance in the popular attitudes and practices of the Western world with respect to immigration and forced migration. Looking primarily at immigration and refugee politics in the United States, I tap into the rhetoric of relevant discourses and examine the ways that propagandistic appeals to sovereignty and fear motivate an unjust prioritizing of political concerns over ethical responsibilities. More specifically, I argue that assumptions about sovereignty authorize the state to police membership to an unjustified extreme and that propagandistic tropes that dehumanize the foreign other reinforce the apparent justice of this extreme policing. I propose that a shift in ethical orientation is needed to correct the overvaluing of political concerns that drive us to consider the migrant other primarily in terms of risk management. By diagnosing the lack of hospitality toward immigrants and refugees, I hope to move the conversation about the economy of care as it concerns migrant others in the direction of establishing more hospitable practices. This chapter is an invitation to think otherwise about the immigrant and the refugee, to think along with Levinas and Derrida about what is unthinkable about the other, and therefore to think otherwise than categorically, otherwise than economically, otherwise than reflexively.

LEVINAS AND ETHICS AS HOSPITALITY

Emmanuel Levinas locates the root of discrimination and violence in the ontological distinction we make between "same" and "other." This distinction ordinarily arises from perceived (or assumed) characteristics that set people apart from one another. The term "otherising" is an expression often used in theories of oppression to pick out special instances of marginalization, where difference is marketed as a justification for exclusion and violence. By contrast, Levinas uses the term "other" to capture what is distinctive about human beings that gives them value beyond metrics of difference. He takes otherness—radical alterity or singularity—to be what commands hospitality. Put in these terms, my moral responsibility is for the other qua other. Alterity grounds my responsibility for other people rather than justifying my indifference. In constructing his notion of ethics, Levinas develops a theory of relating to another person that does not do violence by categorizing her but instead recognizes her as essentially exterior to any conceptual framework. He wants us to see that the categories through which we ordinarily group and understand our experience do not capture the other's singularity. At the heart of alterity ethics and thus of hospitality is the requirement that we take the other not as an object—a thing that can be described and summed up by a finite list of characteristics—but as irreducibly singular and valuable *as such.* Ethics, for Levinas, is a metaphysical relationship that respects alterity and responds to rather than sums up the singular other.

Taking the other as singular has radical consequences for the economy of care. We ordinarily consider ourselves responsible to our friends and family because we stand in a definitive relation to them. By virtue of having a socially sanctioned connection to my sister, my parent, or my child, I am ethically bound to them. And by acquiring friendships or entering into communities of association, I sign myself up for the responsibility of caring for and about certain others. These associations are believed to generate a sort of moral authority whereby people can make normatively binding demands on one another. Levinas offers an alternative conception of ethics, arguing that relations of ethical obligation do not obtain only for those people with whom I share some definitive social connection. On his view, ethical consideration is owed to every single person. We are beholden to the stranger just as much as we are to our family. The form that such ethical consideration takes is, on Levinas's view, best understood as unconditional receptivity or a "welcome," hence Derrida's characterization of Levinasian ethics as "an immense treatise *of Hospitality*."[2] In a slogan, hospitality involves being unconditionally receptive to the needs of others and unconditionally inclusive of others in need.

Levinas makes the case for the absolute and unconditional nature of hospitality by drawing on two facts about human life. The first has been mentioned—human beings are singular in a way that cannot be captured by the panoramic of ontology, meaning that any attempt to categorize or thematize, when directed toward a person, is an act of violence. The second fact about human life is that it is socially grounded, meaning that the very existence of an autonomous self depends on some prior social embeddedness. The idea that we are entitled to pick and choose who to welcome, who is deserving of our welcome, is the function of a mistaken assumption about self-sovereignty. But, Levinas argues, the social condition that founds all human life and reason destroys the notion of the wholly sovereign ego. My existence is grounded in social connectedness, not separation and freedom. Levinas writes, "The 'at home' [*Le 'chez soi'*] is not a container but a site where *I can,* where, dependent on a reality that is other, I am, despite this dependence or thanks to it, free."[3] The "at home" that appears to be at stake in welcoming the migrant others is imagined to be an entitlement, something that is wholly mine and that I am justified in preserving at any cost. This notion of entitlement is what I want to resist. The illusion of self-sovereignty can be broken open by the realization of our fundamental sociality.

It is not what I have in common with another person that makes me responsible for her. Instead, Levinas argues that the ethical relationship is established before commonality or difference.[4] I am equipped with the ontological instruments to identify difference only because I am part of a community prior to or beyond difference. Levinas thus redefines otherness as denoting every human person's ability to resist categorization. On this view, ethics amounts to a respect for the other's *otherness* and is described as "the welcoming of the other by the same" and "the calling into question of the same by the other."[5] Both of these descriptions invite us to understand ethics not as a system but as an orientation and an attitude. An attitude of hospitality emphasizes the ethical imperative to welcome the other *unconditionally*, which prioritizes the singular individual over the particularities of their existence.[6] To be hospitable is to welcome the other beyond categories.

The ethics of hospitality is not a system, as this would require and entail definite terms and normative reasons, and that is the work of politics. Ethics is the orientation that gives rise to the system. Cruelty and injustice occur when one ignores the other, and it is, in part, the misunderstanding of my self as sovereign that leads me to justify inhospitality.[7] Linking ethical responsibility to singularity and fundamental sociality comes with a profound consequence; I am responsible for the other before I can even have reflective awareness of this responsibility. Levinas concludes that because the social relation precedes ontology, it also precedes any conditions I may set for ethical commitment. I am committed to the other before I am free to commit or free to refuse commitment. This makes hospitality absolute and unconditional.

DERRIDA AND THE PARADOX OF HOSPITALITY

In his deconstruction of Levinasian ethics, Derrida grapples with the conflict between the law of absolute hospitality and the paradox that arises from its implementation. Derrida appropriates ideas from Levinas's *Totality and Infinity* and engages in an examination that exposes the tensions that arise when a theory of hospitality is translated into practice.[8]

To be hospitable is to offer something to the other—food, shelter, comfort, safety, opportunity, or rights. And it means doing so with no regard for the particularities of the other—beyond the contingencies of *existents*. In Derrida's words, the declaration of absolute hospitality states, "Let us say yes *to who or what turns up*, before any determination, before any anticipation, before any *identification*, whether or not it has to do with a foreigner, an immigrant, an invited guest, or an unexpected visitor, whether or not the new arrival is the citizen of another country, a human, animal, or divine creature, a living or dead thing, male or female."[9] Derrida picks up where Levinas leaves off, adding that unconditional and absolute responsibility, that is, ethics as hospitality, cannot translate itself into concrete, empirical laws without paradox. This is because there is an insoluble antinomy between the law of hospitality—the law that demands unconditional welcome of the new arrival—and the laws that make hospitality practicable—those rights and duties that are always conditioned and conditional.[10] This antinomy characterizes the conflict between, on the one hand, one's ethical impulse that is guided by the law of hospitality and, on the other, the totalizing tendencies of one's political orientation that are necessary for the construction of positive laws. The insolubility comes from the interdependence between the two. Ethics requires positive laws in order to be made effective, but positive laws can come about only through a violation of the ethical principle of nonreduction. This is the tragedy of the tension.

Giving anything, whether it be food, shelter, or citizen rights, requires totalizing, limiting, and condemning certain individuals while including others. Not only does an offer of hospitality to one person entail the withholding of hospitality from innumerable others, but hospitality always involves making an offering, whether material or symbolic. However, I cannot invite a stranger into my home without first having a home, and maintaining a home requires that I protect it and preserve it, which involves occasionally closing it off to others. This shows that the possibility of hospitality requires one to be, from time to time and in a certain measure, inhospitable.[11] So how do we *act* hospitably? Ethics, for Levinas, is a matter of bracketing similarities and differences and welcoming the other unconditionally. If ethics and politics are essentially in conflict with one another, as this theory suggests, then we are faced with the question, can there be a sociopolitical manifestation of ethics as hospitality? If so, what does it look like?

The political, as Levinas conceives it, is needed to regulate the economy of care. It determines who receives hospitality and how much so as to preserve the "at home" and ensure the possibility of ethics and of future hospitality. Derrida comments that "[unconditional hospitality] wouldn't be effectively unconditional if it didn't have to become effective," that is, concrete and determinate.[12] Without implementation, hospitality remains abstract and illusory. The problem we face is that the norms and conditions, duties and rights—the laws that are necessarily imposed on the host as well as the guest—facilitate as well as corrupt and pervert the law of absolute hospitality. The paradox of hospitality shows that every attempt to satisfy one's ethical responsibility invariably betrays the principle itself. As Derrida puts it, "Absolute hospitality must not be offered out of duty, but must be graciously offered beyond debt and economy."[13] When negotiating between the ethical responsibility to help others and the political limitations necessary for any functioning society, where do we draw the line between the self and the other? My social circles are, for the most part, chosen by me, so any support I may provide for them or any welcome that I extend to them is not an ethical gesture but a political one.

To summarize, hospitality occurs when I welcome the other beyond categories, common interests, shared history, and ideology. The responsibility we feel for those close to us—our friends, family, or fellow citizens—is our ethical impulse constrained by personal (i.e., political) interests. It involves conceptualization, discrimination, and therefore a categorial violation of even the other to whom I extend a welcome. Not only am I behaving inhospitably toward those whom I shut out, but I am also acting inhospitably toward my selected beneficiaries because the welcome I extend is conditional; it is based on how I understand the other in relation to me. We find ourselves in a constant state of tension between our ethical responsibility to help the stranger and the political requirements for practical sustenance of oneself and one's personally chosen allies. Complicating this tension is the fact that politics at once makes hospitality possible and denatures hospitality. To be sure, I am not just straddling two mutually exclusive yet equally imposing responsibilities. Rather, ethics and politics are mutually exclusive *and* mutually dependent.[14] Ethics cannot be realized without politics, and politics does not exist without ethics.[15] Derrida positions himself on the side of Levinasian ethics while at the same time calling attention to the aporia of such an ethic. I submit that the paradoxical nature of hospitality is not grounds to reject it. Rather, we ought to preserve it as the goal of our intersubjective relationships while maintaining awareness of the ways that every engagement in hospitality involves a violation of hospitality.

What Derrida's conclusions tell us is that our social and political lives cannot be conducted free of moral loss. This conclusion further implies that we must decide where the moral losses are to be taken. Correcting injustice in one place creates injustice somewhere else. I mean to do more than present this conception of hospitality and burden my readers with the myriad ways in which the global community is failing to effect hospitality. I am rather recommending that we take this conception seriously, which means allowing it to motivate our actions and to shift our attitudes in a way that comes with risk. I am claiming that, when we live in a world where no decisions come without moral loss, we must choose where to take the hit. If I am advocating anything or prescribing a way forward, it is that in matters of human migration and the refugee crisis, the world, especially the parts of the world with relevant resources, ought to take the risk.

THE MYTH OF SOVEREIGNTY AND THE TRANSITIVITY OF HOST AND GUEST

Hospitality is often typified by a host–guest relationship. If we think of the host as the one in the position to give, the one extending the welcome, and the guest as the one in the position to receive, the one being welcomed, we think too simply. This way of understanding hospitality overlooks that the host—the supposedly sovereign individual in the position of power—is as dependent on the guest as the guest is on the host. Taking ethics as hospitality helps us break out of the liberal social paradigm of aggregated, autonomous individuals whose moral responsibility is simply a matter of mutual noninterference. Restructuring our moral attitudes requires not only seeing that our fundamental condition is social but also seeing the ways in which the same who welcomes the other is also beholden to the other. In other words, the host is not only a host but always also a guest. Hospitality entails realizing that my very sovereignty is precarious. Being hospitable to the other—playing the role of the host—involves confronting my own limitations with respect to the other and my own dependence with respect to all others.

One may object that if my ethical responsibility for the other comes from my dependence on the other, then ethics doesn't enjoy the metaphysical priority that Levinas would have us believe. It would seem that hospitality is nothing more than giving back what is owed, which is precisely paying a debt within a circumscribed economy. This objection rests on a misapprehension of the nature of dependence in this context. The relationship between the host and guest, the same and other, is one of indebtedness prior to the possibility of reciprocity and therefore without regard for reciprocity. It is not because I may need the other in the future that I extend hospitality to the other but rather because I am always already dependent on the other. The purpose of pointing out this dependence is that even within the rational structures by which we explain and justify turning away, the host appears not to be sovereign but to need the guest. Not only does the notion of sovereignty make sense only in relation to another from which I distinguish myself, but my apparent sovereignty is sustained by the other that I resist.

This interdependence between the host and guest means that one cannot be wholly sovereign any more than one can be wholly for-the-other. Because it is not possible for one to be purely ethical or purely political, one's protectionist tendencies must be checked by an attitude of hospitality while one's ethical impulse is at the same time supplemented by political measures of self-preservation. The task is always to bear in mind that ethics and politics are, in fact, inextricably linked and to avoid letting self-preservation overshadow hospitality. This task involves clearing away the misunderstanding that sovereignty automatically derives from autonomy and is an absolute right that can be pursued without regard for the other. It further involves contending with the fact that hospitality is risky; welcoming the other always involves the possibility that the other will threaten or destroy my own well-being and create conditions for the impossibility of future hospitality.

In order to identify whether a guest is a potential threat, we are forced to apply categories. What this means is that inhospitality is not only justified but also necessary. The guest is always potentially a parasite, so to ensure the security of one's home for future hospitality, one must scrutinize the newcomer. The recognition of this fact, coupled with a growing ideology that takes anything alien or foreign to be a threat, has produced a trope where immigrant is metonymic for parasite. According to this ideology, in order to ensure the protection *of* a certain chosen group of people, there must be protection *against* certain others. If I pick and choose whom I extend hospitality to based on what I know about them and what sort of assurances I can deduce from this information, I am not being hospitable. But if I am not assured of my own safety and of the security of those resources that allow for hospitality, then my very ability to be hospitable is at stake. Furthermore, by welcoming the other who is a stranger, I place others for whom I am also responsible at risk. My own safety and the safety of those around me is never guaranteed. This leads me to focus my attention on self-preservation. I am disposed to see the other *as* a parasite or a threat and to take myself as sovereign. The inescapable possibility that the guest will do me harm explains my tendency toward reductive exclusion. However, that we must vet our guests contributes to the mistaken belief that there is a greater responsibility to the self than to the other. This belief operates on my political reasoning such that, by reducing the other to a potential threat, I feel justified in turning them away.

In the sociopolitical arena, current immigration policies are concerned primarily with the interests of the host nation. Campaigning on the platform of hospitality, the host becomes a despot as it targets a group and justifies their exclusion by promoting the dehumanizing trope of the foreigner as a parasite and a threat. This propaganda eclipses pertinent empirical and theoretical facts. It takes state sovereignty for granted, ignoring the deep dependence that states have on one another and on immigrants. It strategically overestimates the risk of harm that comes with welcoming the foreigner, further justifying the state's authority to manage its borders and doing so at the expense of lives that are not measurable in terms of risk management. This eclipsing is maintained by rhetoric that reinforces reductive exclusion and creates a false sense of justice. The most pervasive examples of propagandizing tropes circulating at present are the labeling of Latin American immigrants as "illegals" and the Islamophobia stemming from the September 11, 2001, terrorist attacks. The host is thus a despot insofar as he occupies a position of power vis-à-vis the guest and uses the very ideal of hospitality in a way that undermines hospitality. The host says it is precisely because he is hospitable—because he has the interests of the other at heart—that he must let one person in but not another. Herein lies the danger. The aporia of hospitality forges a territory wherein racism and classism can be cloaked in the disguise of justice and civil protection. As the remainder of this chapter will demonstrate, U.S. immigration policy and contemporary discourses concerning the refugee crisis reveal how the interdependence of politics and ethics has given way to a prioritization of politics over ethics.

THE POLITICS OF IMMIGRATION

Since the early twentieth century, illegal immigration has been the central problem of U.S. immigration policy. The "illegal" immigrant came into existence in the 1920s and is a concept that has since been reified and stigmatized in public discourse. Broadly speaking, persons are considered illegal if they reside in the United States without a current visa and do not meet the going qualifications for citizenship and naturalization. Introducing the concept of citizen illegality came with significant consequences. With the aim of maintaining the racial and cultural purity of American national identity, "illegality" is an invented category foisted on the migrant, marking a person as illicit and using that mark as grounds for exclusion and expulsion. The United States systematically excludes undesirables from membership through both symbolic and material measures. Such measures include public attitudes that cast the foreigner as illegitimate and parasitic, institutions and laws that deprive undocumented immigrants of health care benefits and exclude them from other federal programs, and the violent policing of borders to physically bar people from entry as well as the active policing of communities to incarcerate and expel undocumented individuals.

Immigration policy and the associated conditions for citizenship reflect the categories valued in the forming of a national identity. Immigration policy is taken to be indispensable to a functioning society while at the same time being an instrument of discrimination used to reinforce values on the lines of race, ethnicity, religion, sexuality, and, most prominently in the twenty-first century, class. In the early twentieth century, the identity of the United States was determined largely by policies that regulated the racial demographics of the United States by implementing a quota system to determine which individuals were eligible for citizenship.[16] In her work, Mae M. Ngai looks at the history of immigration in the United States and reveals patterns of exclusion that have reoccurred over the decades. At present, it is the socioeconomic value of an individual that is emphasized by conditions for citizenship. Ngai writes, "The controversies over immigration policy taking place at the beginning of the twenty-first century center on whether immigrants contribute positively or deleteriously to the nation's economy and culture." She goes on to observe that while the conditions for citizenship may shift, "there is virtually no political support for open or numerically unrestricted immigration."[17] There is no support for unrestricted immigration because it would mean certain death for the "sovereign" nation-state. For practical purposes—those laid out in Derrida's deconstruction—some degree of regulation is necessary.

As I have mentioned, qualifications for citizenship in the United States began on mainly racial grounds and have since been redefined in terms of national economic interests rather than overt racial bias. To include some and not others on the basis of economic interests may not seem morally problematic; however, the structural violence that grounds economic motivations is of the same nature as that which grounded the racial motivations that would now be considered (at least publicly) morally unacceptable. The United States has reformulated the "immigration problem" as a threat to resources and national security rather than a threat to the racial and cultural purity of the nation-state, as it was presented in the early versions of immigration policy.[18] It is evident that such explicit racism has not been eradicated but has been replaced by a more subtle form of racial bias and justification for exclusion in the form of national security defense and economic interest. Current immigration controls appear to be the newest iteration of a history of American exceptionalism that discriminates against the foreign "other" and attempts to preserve the familiar "at home" of the Anglo-American nation-state.

As I have expressed already, welcoming the foreigner is never completely hospitable because it is not unconditional. Even instances that seem welcoming, in fact, commit categorial violence through reductive *inclusion*. Take, for example, Barack Obama's 2015 immigration reform, which states that certain undocumented children and parents may obtain temporary legal status as long as they meet specific conditions.[19] All those who do not meet the conditions face deportation. The seemingly hospitable act of including some entails two corresponding moments of inhospitality: the inhospitable act of reductive inclusion of those deemed fit on the basis of ascribed categories and the inhospitable act of reductive exclusion of all others. And because the host is the one with the power to decide membership, the host is always also a despot. The despotism of the host is further demonstrated by the fact that the United States has contributed to the destitution of the many immigrants against whom it secures its borders. Ngai makes this point in saying that "Americans want to believe that immigration to the United States proves the universality of the nation's liberal democratic principles; we resist examining the role that American world power has played in the global structures of migration. We like to believe that our immigration policy is generous, but we also resent the demands made upon us by others and we think we owe outsiders nothing."[20]

Taking Ngai's point, we can figure that this double standard is sustained by the abiding belief in self-sovereignty, which deems hospitality as something supererogatory. Learning to view the other in their singularity and moreover recognizing that our sense of sovereignty is derivative points to the reality that no amount of generosity will absolve us of our responsibility for one another and that we are not being truly hospitable even when we grant citizenship or some provisional version thereof. In other words, we will recognize that we are never doing enough. An ethic of hospitality forces us to question the supposedly natural and fixed categories currently informing attitudes toward immigrants. By highlighting our culturally influenced and fear-based image of the foreigner, I hope to make evident the need for the global community to develop a more hospitable system for receiving the migrant other.

PROPAGANDISTIC TROPES: THE IMMIGRANT AS PARASITE

The present sociopolitical situation in the United States is such that self-preservation is being used to legitimize unnecessarily violent and inhumane treatment of anyone who presents as a foreigner. Such mistreatment is buttressed by the belief that immigrants are parasitic on the host society as well as by the belief that the host nation is fundamentally sovereign and so is beholden only to itself. To think of the immigrant other as a parasite not only makes it seem as if the immigrant is out to take what is rightfully "ours" but also imbues them with a sense of contamination, as if to say that the immigrant is infecting the nation and making it sickly when in fact the opposite is often the case. The trope of immigrant as parasite permeates the mainstream attitude toward the foreigner and leads to the mistreatment of anyone perceived to be a foreigner, whether that person is a natural-born citizen, a refugee seeking asylum, or a documented or undocumented immigrant.

It is worth repeating at this stage that hospitality requires one to make an offer beyond debt and economy. Ethics is a nonreciprocal relationship with the other because it is prior to the instruments that allow us to define reciprocity. In being treated as a parasite, the immigrant is divested of her status as a singular other who *counts as such*. The seemingly commonsensical way of talking about immigrants in terms of benefit for the nation-state reinforces inhospitable practices by drawing an image of the foreigner as an other to whom nothing is owed but of whom much can be demanded. As this logic goes, if the other is a potential liability, then before we take them in, we need assurance that we will be benefited in some way. It has to be worth the risk.

Current immigration policy follows this logic, implying that someone can become a citizen as long as they benefit but do not hinder the country to which they are being naturalized. This measure, though perhaps justified to a degree, is taken to extremes at the expense of hospitality for all parties. It casts the foreigner as a potential liability but also implies that those who do "belong" belong only because they meet the conditions of membership, that is, are individuals *of a certain kind*. To this point, Derrida states, "From the point of view of the law, the guest, even when he is well received, is first of all a foreigner, he must remain a foreigner. Hospitality is due to the foreigner, certainly, but remains, like the law, conditional, and thus conditioned in its dependence on the unconditionality that is the basis of the law."[21] Taking others as individuals of a certain kind is an inevitable part of understanding each other and of establishing rights and laws. However, the point that Derrida is at pains to express is that a welcome extended under these circumstances does not qualify as a gesture of pure hospitality.

Insofar as sovereignty is the basis on which the host nation justifies its monopoly on setting the terms of engagement, the host has an investment in maintaining the appearance of sovereignty. Immigration policy that is highly conditional expresses two conflicting thoughts: it says that the host nation both does and does not need the immigrant. To preserve the appearance of sovereignty, the host nation does not want to admit that it benefits from the immigrant, but the very conditions for immigration state that the other is welcome only if they have something to offer in return. This perversion of logic is maintained so as to keep the motivating scales tipped toward self-preservation.

PROPAGANDISTIC TROPES: THE REFUGEE AS THREAT

The other case of global inhospitality that I would like to address is the recent "refugee crisis." The largely inhospitable response to asylum seekers and specifically those migrating from Middle Eastern countries can be explained by looking at how the terrorist attacks of September 11 have shaped Western attitudes toward the Middle Eastern other. Hours after the September 11 attacks, David Horowitz published an article in which he blamed the United States for being weak and overconcerned with cashing in on "peace dividends." In the article, he demands that the United States throw all resources into national defense, and he promotes racial and ethnic profiling: "It's time to tighten our security systems, beginning with airport checks. It's time to let the profiling of potential terrorists—and that does mean Islamic and Palestinian terrorists—outweigh the objections of the ACLU and other leftists groups."[22] In the same address, Horowitz makes the alarmist claim that the political left has "alliances with anti-American radicals at home and abroad," and he calls to "step up the monitoring of all groups who have declared war on the United States." This is just one example of the broad-strokes rhetoric that is often employed by public figures and that paints Muslims as the other about whom the United States should be centrally concerned. Anti-Muslim sentiments are often packaged in pro-American and pro-freedom terms and sold to the public as a concern for the interests of the nation. The fear inspired by the September 11 attacks has been leveraged into widespread Islamophobia through political rhetoric demonizing Muslims worldwide. This is not to say that all fear-based responses are irrational or unjustified. However, the answer to the threat of terrorism seems to be not less hospitality, as Horowitz and others suggest, but, in certain respects, more hospitality. I return to this thought at the end of this section, but before I do so, I would like to register some examples of categorial violence at work.

Among the institutions inculcating discriminatory attitudes and practices is the Federal Bureau of Investigation (FBI), which issued a report in 2006 outlining the radicalization process said to give rise to "homegrown terrorists."[23] The report opens with the key judgment that "the radicalization cycle is generally composed of four steps: pre-radicalization, identification, indoctrination, and action." Aside from the metaphysically problematic way this report implicates individuals as future threats by calling the initial stage "pre-radical," the report further offers identifying markers of a potential threat, including "wearing traditional Muslim attire," "growing facial hair," and "frequent attendance at a mosque or prayer group." To be sure, protecting against a threat requires identifying what the threat is and where it is likely to manifest, which further involves isolating identifying features of those who may pose a threat. It follows that self-preservation comes at the expense of hospitality. However, not all inhospitality is created equal. In Levinasian terms, justice is the ontological attempt at realizing ethics. The aim, then, should be to limit reductive practices that do violence to the other. All intentionality involves violence simply by reducing the other to a category, but reducing the other to an externally imposed category about which they have no say takes categorial violence to the level of injustice. This same preemptive discrimination employed in the FBI report was promoted by Donald Trump, who, at his campaign rallies, would read the Al Wilson song "The Snake." The song tells the story of a trusting woman (an American) who saves a snake (a refugee) from freezing by inviting him into her home. As the woman comforts the snake, he bites her. She asks the snake why he would do such a thing after she was so kind to him. Trump quotes the venomous snake's reply: "'Oh shut up, silly woman' said the reptile with a grin, 'you knew damn well I was a snake before you took me in.'"

The injustice of categorial violence is happening not only in the United States. Following the November 2015 Paris attacks and the subsequent 2016 attacks in Brussels, a worldwide attitude of inhospitality gained greater traction. France began shutting down mosques and policing Muslim communities.[24] The United Kingdom implemented a formal deradicalization scheme that involved profiling members of the community and subjecting anyone judged to be in a "pre-radical" stage to a deradicalization process. Echoing Horowitz's call to action a decade and a half earlier, politicians and leaders are pointing to terrorist attacks executed by resident citizens of Middle Eastern descent as justification for denying asylum to refugees. Furthering this agenda, Donald Trump persistently attempted to implement by way of executive order what has come to be known as the "Muslim ban," which would temporarily suspend the United States Refugee Admissions Program and deny entry into the United States for anyone coming from a list of seven countries, all of which are mainly Muslim. Islamophobia expresses a conflation of religion with extremist ideology and a reduction of anyone of Middle Eastern descent to the category of Islamic extremist, resulting in hostility toward the most vulnerable and the most in need of hospitality—those fleeing the same enemy against whom the United States and other European powers are trying to defend themselves. Conflict in the Middle East has forced the migration of millions of people now seeking asylum in neighboring European countries. The influx of refugees hit crisis levels in 2015 as a result of the deteriorating situation in their countries of origin, where violence is generated by ideological wars, race and gender discrimination, and religious persecution.

Returning for a moment to the transitivity of "host" and "guest," Derrida points out that the host–guest relationship always involves a transgression of the Same by the other. The host is always also a guest in the sense that welcoming the other requires a certain vulnerability on the part of the one that welcomes. To draw on a different example, in June 2015, Dylann Roof opened fire in a church in Charleston, North Carolina, killing nine people, all of whom were African American. Roof later confessed that his intention was to incite a race war. This event illustrates the highest degree of vulnerability that a host exposes herself to in granting hospitality. Roof entered the church but did not immediately launch into an assault. He was welcomed into the Bible study, he sat down, he participated in prayer, and he made himself at home before shooting. Offering hospitality means figuratively and literally laying oneself bare before the other. The risk that hospitality brings is often a risk of losing one's life. When the cost of hospitality is life, how can we justify *not* closing ourselves off? The law of absolute hospitality does not permit the host to consider such risks, but the *laws* of hospitality—the concrete duties and responsibilities that stake a claim on justice—have come to consider such risks above all else. We must not forget that the practical consequences of inhospitality are equally critical. Domestic terrorist attacks committed by citizens who have been recruited and radicalized by terrorist organizations can often be traced to political and social marginalization and exclusion, to inhospitality.

TOWARD HOSPITABLE PRACTICES

Conditions for citizenship are the effective strategy for maintaining the sovereignty of a nation and preserving a desired national identity. In Levinasian terms, placing conditions on membership ensures the "at home" of the Same. We cannot have a nonjuridical concept of membership because the very notion of inclusion implies exclusion, and determining who to include and exclude must be done on the basis of positive law dictated by categorial values. It follows that insofar as assigning membership entails conditions for membership, it can never be hospitable in the absolute sense. Ngai writes, "Indeed, nationalism's ultimate defense is sovereignty—the nation's self-proclaimed, absolute right to determine its own membership, a right believed to inhere in the nation-state's very existence, in its 'right of self-preservation.'"[25] The presumptive right to sovereignty overlooks the fact that sovereignty is not fundamental, nor does it exist in the absence of the other.

What makes reductive exclusion especially pernicious is that certain forms of categorial violence are a necessary part of ordering our social world. The mechanisms of conscious experience involve a cognitive disposition to categorize. On a social scale, the cognitive disposition to categorize manifests itself through the necessarily reductive parameters of social organization. To be more concrete, society operates in part through a distribution of resources as well as of benefits and burdens, and this distribution always involves some criteria set up in advance to determine who gets what and how much. As a consequence, particularly vulnerable categories of people become targets for exclusion and expulsion. What makes an individual or a group of people vulnerable to categorial violence and reductive exclusion is, as previously mentioned, the ontological distinction we make between "same" and "other."[26] The more "other" I take a person or group to be, the greater ontological distance I place between me/us and them. When we narrowly understand moral responsibility as owed only to those closest to us—our friends, family, and other personally chosen allies—the ontological distance felt between anyone who does not belong to my social circle results in a feeling of justified indifference toward them. The ontological distance is made greater by the dehumanizing tropes that have permeated public thinking, such as illegal alien, parasite, and threat.

A final diagnostic thought: underwriting the propaganda of fear is the more pervasive but lesser acknowledged fear of the loss of control when the comfort of one's "at home" in disrupted by difference. When we encounter something unfamiliar, incomprehensible, and "foreign," we experience a loss of control and ownership over our world—a loss of "sovereignty." We are made uncomfortable by the presence of that which we cannot assimilate into an already formed body of knowledge and which we cannot make sense of on our own terms. The propaganda of fear capitalizes on this fact of human psychology. The tropes serve to mitigate this fear in two ways: they give us some way to make sense of the foreign other, which reestablishes some control, but they also give us justification for excluding the foreign other from our spaces so that we do not have to contend with the discomfort of sharing a world with what is other-than-myself. If a fear for our lives was the only fear motivating reductive exclusion, then it would not be simply "foreign" offenders who were marked as "terrorists," but that term would be extended to the perpetrators of violence against people of color who are often white and often Christian and who often claim to be acting for the sake of preserving American culture. The fact that the term "terrorist" is not extended to this latter group reveals what is actually at stake for the promoters of inhospitality. What is at stake is the feeling of familiarity and control that comes with being surrounded by people who look, behave, talk, and pray like "we" do.

As much as Levinas and Derrida emphasize the demand for hospitality, they also show that we have a material reason to separate. As a community, we welcome those who benefit us and place physical and symbolic barriers before those who do not. A theory of hospitality makes evident the demand for a limiting jurisdiction with regard to inclusion. However, this demand is exploited in the social and political arena to legitimize unjust discrimination. Dehumanizing tropes are publicly circulated in the interest of protecting ideological biases. As "our" interests shift, so too do our conditions for membership and thus our conception of what makes someone "other." These divisive categories are the weapons of reductive exclusion. Looking forward, destabilizing the historically sedimented cultural attitude that maintains the immigrant as hostile and parasitic and that encourages despotism on the part of the host will require establishing a criterion for recognizing corruption in our cognitive bias and replacing invidious knowledges with those informed by a conception of ethics as hospitality.

NOTES

1. It was brought to my attention by an anonymous reviewer that framing ethics and politics according to Levinas's schema, as I do, appears in conflict with the largely Arendtian approach to politics taken by many of the other authors in this volume. To clarify, I do not take what I am doing to be inconsistent with an Arendtian approach. Politics, for Arendt, is productive. It is where human progress is made. Politics, as Arendt understands it, is a matter of disclosing one's particularity by occupying the public sphere and expressing oneself through word and deed. Instead of seeing an inconsistency between their views, one might consider the Arendtian public sphere to be the enabler of Levinasian ethics. Ethics, for Levinas, is a matter of *response*-ability. The ethical moment par excellence occurs when one is present for and responds to the singular Other who appears in their particularity. What Arendt calls "politics" is just what Levinas identifies as the precarious moment of balance between politics and ethics. As will be made evident in this chapter, politics (as Levinas uses the term) is both an obstacle to—and a condition for the possibility of—ethics. Levinas and Arendt are using the word "politics" in different ways, but their philosophies are not necessarily irreconcilable.

2. Jacques Derrida, *Adieu to Emmanuel Levinas*, trans. Pascale-Anne Brault and Michael Naas (Stanford, CA: Stanford University Press, 1999), 21.

3. Emmanuel Levinas, *Totality and Infinity: An Essay on Exteriority*, trans. Alphonso Lingis (Pittsburgh, PA: Duquesne University Press, 1969), 37.

4. Levinas, *Totality and Infinity*, 305. "Same" is a term Levinas uses to refer to the Self or the Ego. He often talks about the tendency of the Western intellectual world (and Western philosophy in particular) to engage in a "reduction of the other to the Same," which means setting the other up as something graspable by my understanding. In doing this, I metaphorically incorporate the other into my Self. The objective of Levinasian ethics is to respect the other as something that I cannot grasp, something utterly exterior.

5. Levinas, *Totality and Infinity*, 43.

6. Levinas, *Totality and Infinity*, 44–46.

7. Levinas, *Totality and Infinity*, 52.

8. Derrida's primary treatment of hospitality is found in his work *Of Hospitality: Anne Dufourmantelle Invites Jacques Derrida to Respond*, trans. Rachel Bowlby (Stanford, CA: Stanford University Press, 2000); in his works appearing in *The Gift of Death*, trans. David Wills (Chicago: University of Chicago Press, 2008); and in "Hostipitality," in *Acts of Religion*, ed. Gil Anidjar, 356–420 (New York: Routledge, 2002).

9. Derrida, *Of Hospitality*, 77.

10. Derrida, *Of Hospitality*, 76.

11. Derrida, *Of Hospitality*, 55.

12. Derrida, *Of Hospitality*, 79.

13. Derrida, *Of Hospitality*, 83.

14. Levinas, *Totality and Infinity*, 300.

15. For a more extensive explanation of how this interdependence works and specifically the controversial claim that politics cannot exist without ethics, see Lisa M. Madura, "Global Migration and the Ethics of Hospitality" (master's thesis, University of Nevada, Reno, 2016), available at ProQuest Dissertations & Theses.

16. See Chapter 1, Sec. 201, of the Immigration Act of 1924, May 26, 1924.

17. Mae M. Ngai. *Impossible Subjects: Illegal Aliens and the Making of Modern America* (Princeton, NJ: Princeton University Press, 2004), 5.

18. This is not to say that racism is no longer an explicit motivation for reductive exclusion. The rise of the alt-right is evidence that people do still consider racial purity to be a compelling justification for excluding select groups from membership in a community or citizenship in a nation.

19. *American Immigration Counsel*, "The Dream Act, DACA, and Other Policies Designed to Protect Dreamers," September 6, 2017, https://www.americanimmigrationcouncil.org/research/dream-act-daca-and-other-policies-designed-protect-dreamers.

20. Ngai, *Impossible Subjects*, 11.

21. Derrida, *Of Hospitality*, 71, 73.

22. David Horowitz, "Horowitz's Notepad Special: This Is War," *FrontPage Mag*, September 11, 2001, http://archive.frontpagemag.com/readArticle.aspx?ARTID=21215.

23. "The Radicalization Process: From Conversion to Jihad," *U/FOUO Federal Bureau of Investigation Intelligence Assessment*, Counterterrorism Division, May 2006.

24. Rowen Scarborough, "France Cracks Down on Islamic Radicalism after Paris Attacks, Shutters Mosques," *Washington Times*, January 28, 2016, http://www.washingtontimes.com/news/2016/jan/28/france-cracks-down-on-islamic-radicalism-after-par/?page=all.

25. Ngai, *Impossible Subjects*, 11.

26. "Other" is in quotes to indicate that I am using it in the non-Levinasian way described at the beginning of this chapter.

Chapter Five

Welcoming Refugees

*Mindful Citizenship and the Political Responsibility of Hospitality**

Jade Larissa Schiff

The urgency of responding to the Syrian refugee crisis may occlude important questions about political responsibility. First, who bears responsibility for refugees' suffering and why? Questions of responsibility are often framed as questions of liability: those who cause or contribute directly to harm are responsible for its consequences. However, this answer obscures how a diverse collection of actors is implicated in harm because they contribute to and benefit from social, political, and economic structures and processes that produce and exacerbate it. This generates structural injustice, which imposes a political responsibility that Iris Young analyzes according to a "social connection model." Refugees suffer structural injustice in an international order that privileges sovereign boundaries over movement and citizenship over noncitizenship, an international society that privileges conformity over nonconformity, and a global economy in which the stateless are deemed superfluous. Because implication in structural injustice comes about through everyday practices, it often passes unnoticed. Crises such as the one in Syria expose such injustice and may facilitate the assumption of political responsibility. Relatively privileged states (and their citizens and residents) that benefit from the structural injustice refugees suffer bear a political responsibility of hospitality toward them.

Second, why do we sometimes struggle to acknowledge and assume this responsibility? Arguments against admitting refugees are often driven by concerns about scarcity and by xenophobia. I reinterpret these as symptoms of anxiety and resentment. Refugees embody the uprootedness of a global-

*I want to thank Emily Beausoleil, Amy Eckert, Ayten Gündoğdu, Matthew Moore, Serena Parekh, Bernard Schiff, and two anonymous reviewers for helpful comments on previous drafts of this chapter.

ized world that the privileged share with them, though we occupy different positions in it. Their arrival generates anxieties about the contingency and vulnerability of home from which we are normally insulated. Refugees become targets of resentment, and this inhibits us from assuming our political responsibility of hospitality.

In the third and fourth sections of this chapter, I argue that the cultivation of "mindful citizenship" might mitigate these anxieties and resentments and help us assume our political responsibility. Mindful citizenship entails nurturing mindfulness in each other and letting go of individual *and* collective anxieties and resentments. Although Young warns that focusing on the self can distract us from assuming political responsibility and combating structural injustice, assuming political responsibility *requires* some work on the self that we can undertake with and alongside others.

The purpose of this chapter is to raise these questions, not to settle them, to stimulate and provoke new thoughts about our political responsibilities toward refugees. What I undertake here is thus intended to be an experiment in thinking that gestures toward new ways of responding to these perilous times. The election of Donald Trump and the resurgence of white nationalism and xenophobia have plunged the United States and the world into an unprecedented crisis. In the face of that crisis, we must act. Some of that action must be immediate, but the urgency of immediate action must be accompanied by care and attention lest we react in ways that exacerbate the crisis rather than ameliorate it.

REFUGEES, STRUCTURAL INJUSTICE, AND THE POLITICAL RESPONSIBILITY OF HOSPITALITY

What constitutes a refugee crisis? Under the 1951 UN Convention and 1967 Protocol, a refugee is someone who, "owing to a well-founded fear of being persecuted for reasons of race, religion, nationality, membership of a particular social group or political opinion, is outside the country of his nationality, and is unable to, or owing to such fear, is unwilling to avail himself of the protection of that country." According to the United Nations, as of 2014 there were approximately 60 million refugees, and their numbers have since increased.

This constitutes a crisis in two senses. First, the failures of states to admit refugees in sufficient numbers and of governments and international organizations to offer adequate aid exacerbate their suffering. Massive displacements challenge a global order defined by principles of sovereignty. This challenge demands fundamental transformations in our approach to refugee crises. However, for those of us who live in relative privilege, the existence of even huge numbers of refugees does not challenge our sense of having a secure home in the world. We do not *experience* it as a crisis. From this perspective, a refugee crisis is a sudden, massive influx of refugees that poses such a challenge and provokes both public declarations of hospitality and aggressive opposition. I emphasize this second sense of a crisis because it casts the problem of political responsibility in starkest relief.

A number of actors—states, the United Nations, and relief organizations—have a mandate to care for refugees during crises and not. But who bears responsibility for *generating* these crises and why? The usual answer is those whose actions displace masses of people. This response is based on a "liability model of responsibility." We assign responsibility to agents whose faulty actions are causally connected to a harm as long as their actions were voluntary "and performed with adequate knowledge of the situation."[1] Bashar al-Assad and his regime are most directly responsible for the Syrian crisis. Assad's regime has driven millions out of Syria through state violence, including the indiscriminate use of barrel bombs and chlorine gas, which constitutes war crimes. The ensuing civil war between the government (supported by militias and Shiite groups) and Sunni rebels, which has drawn in American, French, Russian, and other forces, has exacerbated the crisis. These actors share responsibility to varying degrees, though Assad and his allies bear the largest share.

Assigning liability is vital but insufficient. It obscures the responsibility shared by a broader network of actors who contribute to the structures and processes against the background of which the crisis erupted and to which it draws our attention. To address this responsibility, we must examine more closely the harm that refugees suffer. They are thrust into structural positions of disadvantage in an international state system that privileges sovereign boundaries over movement and citizenship over noncitizenship, an international society that privileges conformity over nonconformity, and a global economy that finds the stateless superfluous. Along with Serena Parekh, I call these cases of "structural injustice" that generate a distinctly political form of responsibility. While Parekh focuses on the "refugee regime" itself, I examine the conditions that thrust refugees into positions of structural disadvantage in the first place.

Structures consist of rules and resources deployed against the background of an unequally shared world. People occupy different social positions, and structure "consists in the connections among these positions and their relationships, and the way the attributes of positions internally constitute one another through those relationships."[2] Structures do not merely enable and constrain action. Rather, "a social structure *exists* only in the action and interaction of persons; it exists not as a state, but as a process."[3] These actions "often have future effects beyond the immediate purposes and intentions of the actors."[4] Structural injustice "exists when social processes put large categories of persons under a systematic threat of domination or deprivation of the means to develop and exercise their capacities, at the same time as these processes enable others to dominate or have a wide range of opportunities for developing and exercising their capacities."[5] Structural injustice does not arise from wrongful individual or collective actions. It "occurs as a consequence of many individuals and institutions" pursuing their interests "within given institutional rules and accepted norms."[6]

The international states system, international society, and the global political economy are structures. In these, refugees suffer structural injustice because their homelessness prevents them from exercising fundamental political capacities, while these structures enable others to do so. Hannah Arendt recognized this implicitly when she argued that stateless peoples lost not only civic rights, which can be denied to members of political communities, but also the right to *have* rights. They suffered "the deprivation of a place in the world which makes opinions significant and actions effective."[7] While contemporary protests against conditions in refugee camps show that refugees *can* create fleeting public spaces,[8] during crises this may be impossible. This leaves them even more vulnerable to structural injustice.

In the international system, states occupy different positions and have different relationships to each other. These relationships are dynamic: states can be longtime allies (the United States and Great Britain) or allies of convenience (Russia and Syria), or they can be implacable enemies (the United States and North Korea) or circumstantial ones (Russia and France). Some states are more powerful than others, but they normally interact on terms of formal equality. The foundation of that equality is legal sovereignty: externally, states regulate their own borders. While this principle is challenged by international human rights law, it remains a source of tension concerning refugees. Internally, sovereignty entails a legitimate monopoly on violence[9] and on domestic policymaking, which have also been challenged by international human rights law. Hence, refugees present a political challenge domestically where resources are at stake.

In the international states system, refugees suffer structural injustice. Despite increasingly porous borders, the system privileges boundaries over movement[10] and citizenship and residency over noncitizenship and refugee status. Citizens and residents are in principle guaranteed the security of external sovereignty and the protection and welfare afforded by internal sovereignty, though both are unequally distributed by gender, race, class, ability, and so on. Because refugees are either in constant motion or housed in the sometimes permanent temporariness of camps, they either lack these protections entirely or enjoy them at the pleasure of unaccountable host states. This arbitrary control is a form of domination[11] that penalizes refugees *because* they are refugees. Because the international system allows citizens and others to develop and exercise their capacities through relatively regular (if unequal) access to state resources while frequently leaving refugees at the state's mercy, the latter suffer structural injustice.

Refugees also suffer structural injustice in international society, which exists when "a group of states, conscious of certain common interests and common values, form a society in the sense that they conceive themselves to be bound by a common set of rules" that are "established by dialogue and common consent"[12] and "share in the workings of common institutions."[13] The rules of international society are the norms to which actors agree to conform, including rules of diplomacy, the terms by which actors are deemed legitimate and illegitimate, and shared views of appropriate and inappropriate conduct. These rules are constituted and legitimated by conformity to their requirements. Nonconforming actors—such as terrorist groups and "rogue states"—are excluded from the community. The position of refugees is more dire: they cannot choose to conform or not because they are practically invisible and thus are excluded from the normative community.

Structural injustice is one consequence of this exile. The norms that define legitimate actors and appropriate behaviors and thus that authorize international actors to develop and exercise their capacities constrict the abilities of refugees to develop and exercise theirs. For example, sovereignty is not only a legal principle but also a social norm. Notwithstanding international humanitarian law, relationships among states are governed by a norm of noninterference. If refugees have been mistreated in their home or host state, they have no assurance that their pleas will be heard or answered. States and relief organizations may respond, but refugees are at the mercy of their goodwill.

Finally, refugees suffer structural injustice in the global political economy. Economic interactions between state and nonstate actors are governed by market forces and by the rules of international trade set by organizations such as the International Monetary Fund. They are also shaped by the relative power of actors. The rules and dynamics of the global economy enable and constrain states and other actors through trade pacts, the imposition of tariffs and sanctions, and other tools. Refugees suffer structural injustice because their capacities to participate in and benefit from the global economy are constricted, while those of citizens and legal residents are enhanced through states' economic activities. While microeconomies may develop in refugee camps, this labor is invisible in the global economy, to which it is effectively useless and refugees are "superfluous humanity."[14] Many refugees have no enforceable right to the prosperity of host states except insofar as those states may deign to increase aid. Thus, refugees' opportunities are limited, while citizens and other residents enjoy the fruits of the state's participation in the global economy.

Who is responsible for structural injustice? When structural processes produce injustice, direct and even indirect causal connections are difficult to trace and the demands of "adequate knowledge" often too strenuous, so a liability model is inadequate.[15] Instead, Young proposes a "social connection model of responsibility." In it, "individuals bear responsibility for structural injustice because they contribute by their actions to the processes that produce unjust outcomes." Responsibility comes "from belonging together with others in a system of interdependent processes of cooperation and competition through which we seek benefits and aim to realize projects."[16] For Young, "all the persons who participate . . . in the ongoing schemes of cooperation that constitute these structures are responsible for them in the sense that they are part of the process that causes them."[17] This is political responsibility.

But as I have asked elsewhere, how can we acknowledge and experience our implication in structural injustice and assume political responsibility for it when it is generated by activities so quotidian as to pass unnoticed?[18] Ordinarily, the contingent social structures, processes, and practices that shape our lives appear natural, even necessary. Pierre Bourdieu calls this "misrecognition," a disposition that conceals the contingent character of social life and the domination it sustains. Our lives are shaped by unreflective habits, or a *habitus* that makes the world seem familiar and predictable. *Habitus* operates unconsciously, and the unconscious is "the forgetting of history" that makes *habitus* like a "second nature."[19] Thus, *habitus* is "history *turned into* nature, i.e. denied as such."[20] Historical amnesia is underwritten by misrecognition, which naturalizes social and political orders so that we take them for granted rather than question them. "Every established order tends to produce (to very different degrees and with very different means)" the naturalization of its arbitrariness by reproducing systems of classification. These systems "[reproduce] . . . the power relations of which they are the product, by securing the misrecognition . . . of the arbitrariness upon which they are based."[21] Misrecognition naturalizes relationships of domination of subordination between those who benefit from the global order and refugees whose lives are constricted by it. The felt naturalness of this order conceals our implication in their suffering. This makes it difficult to assume responsibility for transforming what is simply how things *are*.[22]

Misrecognition can break down in the face of crises such as the current refugee crisis. Crises disrupt our *habitus* by disrupting the practical context it helps us navigate.[23] They destabilize everyday life and call into question the self-evidence of our world. "When the social world loses its character as a natural phenomenon . . . the question of the natural or conventional character . . . of social facts can be raised."[24] Acknowledging the contingency of the existing global order can facilitate the acknowledgment of our everyday implication in the suffering of refugees and enable us to assume our responsibility for it.

Crises expose how political responsibility for the suffering of refugees extends beyond those most directly responsible for it. Political responsibility extends to the citizens and residents of relatively privileged countries who benefit from existing global orders. It is grounded in the concrete structures and practices that condition our and others' lives. It is forward looking and also has powerful implications for the present. Our responsibility to refugees is political because it is shared by virtue of participation in "schemes of cooperation" that generate and sustain structural injustice. That injustice is a consequence of our common pursuit of aims such as security, prosperity, and participation in international society. In the long term, beneficiaries of globalization have a political responsibility to promote changes that distribute its benefits more equitably. In democracies, this may include joining organizations that pressure governments to admit more refugees and ease the path to citizenship. Globally, it could mean encouraging governments that house refugees temporarily to increase aid and improve camp conditions. Citizens and residents could also coordinate to pressure refugee organizations to be more proactive in securing refugees' welfare.

These measures point toward a political responsibility of hospitality. This is a responsibility of relatively privileged states and their relatively privileged citizens and residents toward the stateless. It is political because it involves coordinated action to pursue the project of hospitality. While states are ultimately the gatekeepers for refugees, citizens and residents of democracies can generate political pressures for hospitality from within. This responsibility is shared by all states and their citizens and residents in principle, but *how* it is shared must be decided through political coordination among unequal parties. Countries that can afford to accept more refugees ought to shoulder larger burdens of this political responsibility.

Some countries have done so admirably. While many regarded Canada's plan to admit 25,000 Syrian refugees as inadequate, Canadian hospitality was displayed in other ways. Prime Minister Justin Trudeau met a plane carrying refugees at the airport to tell them "you are home" and to distribute parkas to protect against the Canadian winter. They were granted permanent residency, and some citizens opened their homes to provide material and emotional support.[25] France took in slightly more refugees and pledged to admit 24,000 more even after the Paris attacks. These numbers were eclipsed by Germany, which pledged to admit a million refugees. These responses demonstrate the assumption of a political responsibility of hospitality not only by states but by citizens as well.

HOMELESSNESS AND RESENTMENT

Powerful forces can inhibit our capacity and willingness to assume our political responsibility of hospitality. Several countries have been very *inhospitable to* Syrian refugees. Denmark admitted 17,000 but then adopted a law allowing authorities to confiscate their valuables to help cover the costs of admitting them, a practice reminiscent of Nazi confiscations of Jewish property.[26] Denmark also tightened its borders to prevent entry from Germany. Sweden required that everyone entering from Denmark present an ID, a practice that had been discontinued in the 1950s.[27] Hungary closed its border with Croatia entirely and diverted refugees to Slovenia.[28] Slovenia erected razor wire along its Croatian border ostensibly to "direct" the flow of refugees.[29] The initially tepid welcome of the United States turned hostile when President Trump ordered an immigration ban preventing Syrian and other nationals.

I interpret these reactions as symptoms of anxiety and resentment. A number of commentators have noted the resentment toward Syrian refugees in Turkey, Jordan, and Lebanon, which has led to discrimination in housing and medical care, economic exploitation, and violence.[30] This resentment stems from concerns that refugees are taking citizens' jobs and straining resources, such as schools and hospitals. In the United States, the alt-right and President Trump himself make similar claims. Without denying these sources, I think the resentment has much deeper roots. While refugee crises may facilitate the assumption of responsibility, they are also profoundly disorienting because they expose "the conventional character of socially established identities, implicit standards and explicit norms."[31] A sudden influx of refugees raises acute questions of national identity and implicit standards of belonging that are ordinarily taken for granted, and they introduce different, sometimes conflicting norms into a political community. More fundamentally, they disturb the secure sense of home that people in positions of relative privilege enjoy. These disturbances can produce profound anxiety and resentment toward those we perceive as its cause.[32] There is some evidence of a psychic dimension to our responses to refugees. King Abdullah II of Jordan has said that the influx of refugees has brought "'the psyche of the Jordanian people' to the boiling point."[33] This points to a symptomatic reading (in the Freudian sense of a behavioral manifestation of anxiety) of the resentments with which refugees are met. We resent the presence of those who remind us of the contingency of our enjoyment of home, of our implication in their suffering, and of our responsibility to combat the structural injustice that engenders it. How we respond to this disturbance shapes our capacities to assume a political responsibility of hospitality.

Some scholars have suggested that the homelessness of refugees is emblematic of a modern condition that Friedrich Nietzsche first diagnosed as a consequence of the death of God. The end of belief in transcendence erased a signpost that helped human beings orient themselves in the world.[34] Nietzsche asked,

> We children of the future, how could we be at home in this today? We feel disfavour for all the ideals that might lead one to feel at home even in this fragile, broken time of transition. The ice that still supports people today has become very thin; the wind that brings the thaw is blowing; we ourselves who are homeless constitute a force that breaks open ice and other all too thin "realities."[35]

Nietzsche's "children of the future" famously sought a home founded on new ideals—a transvaluation of modern values. The ambiguity of his "we"—are the children of the future an elite few who alone can transcend the barrenness of modernity and must carry others with them, or are we all children of the future?—suggests that homelessness might be constitutive of the human condition.[36] A number of scholars have associated Nietzschean homelessness with the concrete homelessness of refugees. Daniel Warner has asserted that "we are all refugees."[37] Nicholas Xenos identifies their displacement with "the general phenomenon of modernity that Simone Weil called 'uprootedness.'"[38] Finally, Michael Dillon identifies the refugee "as a figure of the political abjection that is integral to the political subjectification of political modernity."[39]

The homelessness of the modern subject and its representation by the refugee are made manifest by globalization. Since 1648, states have become political, territorial, and even spiritual and cultural homes. Increasingly intensive and extensive globalization challenges the sanctity of these homes. However, the effects of this challenge are unequally distributed, and the identification of the refugee with the modern subject obscures this fact. For example, I am a legal permanent resident of the United States and a professor in a small town with a reasonable cost of living. I live comfortably here and am largely insulated from the vicissitudes of globalization. But what if I am confronted with an influx of people who remind me that the home I take for granted is potentially fragile? I hope that my response would be gracious and welcoming, but I am not immune to the anxieties and resentments that make some respond to refugees with hostility.

MINDFULNESS AS A WAY OF LIFE

How can we mitigate these anxieties and resentments and be more responsive to the plight of refugees? I think mindfulness can help facilitate our assumption of responsibility and maintain a disposition to undertake it in an ongoing way. Rooted in Buddhism and Hinduism,[40] mindfulness has become increasingly secularized and widespread in popular culture and is receiving growing scholarly attention. Here I treat it as a way of life.

Mindfulness starts from the belief that unhappiness arises from attachments and aversions that are rooted in the past and projected into the future and so keep us from being fully present to ourselves and in the world. It resists the historical sickness that Nietzsche diagnosed: "He who cannot sink down on the threshold of the moment and forget all the past . . . will never know what happiness is."[41] It also resists dwelling in a future where, as Arendt put it, "Progress and Doom are two sides of the same medal."[42] Mindfulness may enable us to let go of our attachment to the false sense of invulnerability that the arrival of refugees disturbs and help us avoid being overwhelmed by our aversion to the anxieties and resentments that their arrival provokes. Some studies have linked mindfulness meditation to increased compassion, and perhaps cultivating mindfulness might engender greater hospitality as well.[43]

Jon Kabat-Zinn offers seven principles of mindful living. They are not definitive or exhaustive, but they are accessible and transposable into politics: nonjudging, patience, beginner's mind, trust, nonstriving, acceptance, and letting go. The first principle, nonjudging, means assuming "the stance of an impartial witness to [our] own experience[s]" and examining our reactions to them.[44] We frequently categorize our experiences automatically as good, bad, or neutral. These judgments keep our minds in constant motion instead of allowing us the stillness to examine our experiences.[45] If we can observe neutrally the anxieties and resentments that refugees stir up, we may be able to let go of them, to address the suffering we see, and to assume our political responsibility of hospitality.

The second principle, patience, entails accepting that "sometimes things must unfold in their own time." Rather than embracing or fleeing negative emotional reactions, we give ourselves room to have them. We accept our minds' wanderings into the past and future, and this enables us to bring ourselves back to the present.[46] In the face of a refugee crisis, patience can help us acknowledge and accept our anxieties and resentments rather than pushing them away or judging ourselves for them. Patience can prevent us from being consumed by our aversive reactions.

The third principle, beginner's mind, entails viewing the familiar as unfamiliar, seeing ourselves and the world with fresh eyes, and approaching them with wonderment rather than taking them for granted.[47] Beginner's mind can help us discover or reconsider our anxieties and resentments about refugees. When undertaken from a neutral, patient, nonjudging perspective, we can let go of them in order to better assume our responsibility of hospitality. Beginner's mind might also help us examine and transform the unconscious habits that sustain structural injustice and develop new, conscious ones that support a struggle for global justice.

The fourth principle, trust in oneself, means relying on our own intuition and authority in becoming more fully ourselves rather than relying on others' esteem or authority.[48] We need not appeal to some "authentic" self, which has become less plausible as we have come to understand ourselves (through Karl Marx, Hannah Arendt, and others) as contingent, ongoing projects of self-fashioning. Becoming more fully ourselves can mean coming to terms with our vulnerability and the privilege that normally insulates us from them and with the contingency of our experience of home and the anxieties and resentments that it generates. If we trust our own intuition and authority in attending to these reactions, we are more likely to be able to let go of them.

The fifth and sixth principles are nonstriving and acceptance. They are often interpreted as encouraging passivity, but this is mistaken. Striving keeps us from being present centered because it entails evaluation and self-judgment. *Non*striving does not preclude having goals but rather facilitates their achievement by freeing us from the self-punishment and paralysis that may accompany self-judgment if we do not realize them.[49] Acceptance "means seeing things as they actually are" rather than wishing that they were otherwise, which consumes energies that could be used to *change* how things are in order to move toward our goals. Acceptance entails neither passivity nor resignation. Instead, it allows us to notice injustice and our reactions to it so that we can address both. It thus enables rather than discourages assuming our political responsibility of hospitality.

The final principle is letting go. It means not clinging to the world as we think it is or want it to be and allowing ourselves to experience it as it is. Letting go is the ultimate goal and the benefit of mindfulness. Through it, we can immerse ourselves in the present, unimpeded by the judgments, expectations, preconceptions, defenses, attachments, aversions, and distrust that ordinarily filter our experiences and condition our reactions to them. We tend to hold on to pleasing thoughts and feelings (such as the sense of being at home in the world that privilege helps to secure), to reimagine pleasurable situations, and to rid ourselves of or flee from unpleasant ones. Elevating some aspects of experience over others in this way prevents us from being in the present and accepting things as they are—things such as the arrival of refugees, the displacements of globalization, and the anxieties and resentments that attend our confrontations with them.[50] Letting go of these feelings can help us make more conscious choices in the face of what is and take responsibility for those choices. It can also help us *together* in assuming our political responsibility of hospitality toward refugees: it can provide a foundation for practices of mindful citizenship.

POLITICAL PRINCIPLES AND PRACTICES OF MINDFUL CITIZENSHIP

Several political theorists have explored the political possibilities and limits of mindfulness.[51] Mindful politics entails embedding individual mindfulness practices in the shared projects of political life.[52] While its Buddhist and Hindu roots may connote asceticism, mindfulness practices are always anchored in and responsive to our practical contexts and lived experiences. Some scholars worry that mindfulness might be coopted by regressive political projects, such as neoliberalism[53] and patriarchy.[54] In the context of our political responsibility of hospitality, the risk is that mindfulness can produce a quietism that leaves unchallenged both structural injustice and the exclusionary impulses that undermine hospitality. Young warned that focusing on the self in the way that mindfulness requires can distract us from bringing about structural change.[55] However, coming to terms with our implication in structural injustice and cultivating the dispositions necessary to combat it demands some work on the self.[56] Mindful politics involves working on ourselves together. Like mindfulness itself, it is always vulnerable to resurgent attachments and aversions. Mindful citizenship, like individual mindfulness practice, requires ongoing, patient work.

How might we transform the seven principles of mindfulness into political principles and practices of mindful citizenship? The fit between mindfulness principles and the political ones I am about to propose is imperfect, and a satisfying transposition of the first into the second may depend on theorizing a connection between the psychic, the somatic, and the political in ways that lie beyond the scope of this chapter.[57] Moreover, individual mindfulness practices probably suffer distortion when they become shared ones. Thus, mindful citizenship *departs* from mindfulness principles even as it is inspired by them. As with individual mindfulness, mindful citizenship is not itself a response to the plight of refugees, nor does it dictate any particular response to that plight. Its purpose is to cultivate a more widely shared disposition toward mindfulness in the hopes of encouraging a shared assumption of our political responsibility of hospitality.

Recasting individual practices of mindfulness as political principles and practices makes mindfulness a common project. Accordingly, mindful citizenship demands common referents around which we can nurture such practices in one another and help each other confront and assume our shared responsibility. Appeals to abstract conceptions of suffering and responsibility—even to the awareness that others are suffering—are insufficient because they are too remote from our lived experiences to galvanize our responsive energies. Nor is it enough to agree that we share a political responsibility of hospitality. We must choose referents that evoke concretely the suffering that calls us to responsibility, the privilege that insulates us from it, and the anxieties and resentments to which we must attend in order to assume it. Stories and images can help us do this.[58]

Consider the photograph of Alan Kurdi, a three-year-old Syrian refugee whose body washed ashore on a Turkish beach after the vessel in which his family was fleeing to Greece capsized. He is face-down in the sand, wearing a red T-shirt, blue shorts, and Velcro sneakers. His brother, Galip, and their mother, Rehan, also drowned. Their father, Abdullah, survived. Photos of Abdullah's anguished face also appeared around the world. Emanuel Levinas reminds us of the power of faces when he describes the face-to-face encounter with the Other who calls us to responsibility.[59] The contrast between the bleakness and anguish in those photographs and our own relative comfort may remind us of our privilege. They may also elicit the anxieties and resentments that the acknowledgment of privilege and the call to responsibility can generate. It is easy (and tempting) to recoil from them. But perhaps that is harder to do in the presence of others who may call us back to them. Moreover, while the presence of others can challenge our ability to remain present, their presence may also call us back to ourselves. Being with others may thus enhance our own capacities for mindfulness. We should heed Susan Sontag's warning, however, that

> living with the photographed images of suffering . . . does not necessarily strengthen conscience and the ability to be compassionate. It can also corrupt them. Once one has seen such images, one has started down the road of seeing more—and more. Images transfix. Images anesthetize.[60]

Sontag warns that images can lull rather than provoke engagement, can inure us to suffering rather than draw our attention to it. Mindfulness guards against these possibilities by keeping our attention in the present, oriented toward *this* image until we turn consciously to the next one so that we do not get inundated and anesthetized by others.

Common referents, such as the photographs of Alan and his father, can be sites for the cultivation of mindful citizenship guided by some political principles and shared practices. The political principle that corresponds to non-judging is the suspension of our judgment of others. We cannot suspend our *political* judgment because we have "a right and an obligation to criticize the others with whom we share responsibility."[61] We suspend judgment of those who seek to cultivate mindfulness with us. Mindfulness is difficult because it requires that we let go of habits that shape our lives and shed attachments and aversions to which we are accustomed. It will be harder for some than others because we all face imperatives that challenge our capacities to cultivate mindfulness. A single mother on welfare can devote fewer resources to cultivating mindfulness than can more privileged citizens. If, as Dean Mathiowetz suggests, the leisure associated with mindfulness is a democratic practice,[62] then structural inequality limits its potential for those people who lack leisure. To pass judgment on this mother hinders mindful citizenship just as passing judgment on ourselves hinders mindfulness. We can encourage others (perhaps even our presence will encourage them) in practicing mindfulness, but we should not judge them for their efforts.

The political principle that corresponds to patience with ourselves is patience with each other. We must attend patiently to each other's reactions to the arrivals of newcomers without quick judgment and immediate demands that others change their views, though the assumption of political responsibility ultimately requires that they do. Habits are durable and require time to evolve. Demands for immediate change are bound to produce further anxiety and resentment, which not only harms ourselves and others, but distracts us from our common project. In times of crisis states may need to act before citizens are "ready," and citizens may need to act before states are "ready" (as in the sanctuary movement), but this does not make mindful citizenship less potentially powerful. Indeed, this makes it even more important.

The political principle that corresponds to beginner's mind is openness to others' responses. We often take our own reactions to the world as normal ones. This is how misrecognition turns habits into nature. Being mindful helps us see old habits with new eyes—to see that they are not natural or necessary and may be unhealthy. We can help each other cultivate beginner's mind, pointing out when old habits rear their heads, and so begin to transform them and examine our reactions to the images and stories of Alan's family. This practice might help transform our responses to the arrival of all newcomers.

The political principle that corresponds to trust in ourselves is trust in others, which is crucial for political life.[63] While mindfulness depends on trust in one's own intuition and authority, that trust cannot be blind since our old habits are what hinder us in the first place. Sharing a world means trusting others' intuitions and authority of as well and being willing to consider theirs along with ours. It also depends on trusting others to do the same. This entails sometimes sharing our own sense of how to proceed and sometimes listening quietly to others. Sometimes it means acknowledging that we need help addressing the anxieties and resentments that the arrival of refugees provokes. It also means acknowledging that those in positions of power and privilege may be able to do more to help cultivate mindfulness but must also take care not to use their position to impose on the practices of others or to obscure or to dismiss their anxieties as frivolous. The principle of trust illustrates how distributions of power can shape mindful citizenship.

Nonstriving, acceptance, and letting go correspond to the principle of coexistence, which is related to what Arendt called "the human condition of plurality, the fact that men, not Man, live on the earth and inhabit the world."[64] Like plurality, coexistence is not only a condition of existence. It is also an activity of sharing the world and a necessary condition of political life. The activities that correspond to plurality are living on the earth and inhabiting the world. The activities that correspond to coexistence are implied in the prefix "co-," which means "together" and "in common" but also "mutually," implying reciprocity and care. Just as nonstriving, acceptance, and letting go mean coming to terms with ourselves, coexistence entails the same with respect to others. It means accepting people's anxieties and resentments for what they are, letting go of a desire to change them rather than striving to do so, and letting them unfold as we do our own. That does not mean disengagement from others; rather, it means facilitating their efforts to be mindful. It means drawing and redrawing others' attention to the story of Alan and his family and attending consciously to the reactions it evokes. In all of these ways, the cultivation of mindful citizenship might help us assume our political responsibility of hospitality.

CONCLUSION

The promise of mindful citizenship is that by helping one another let go of our anxieties about and resentments of dislocation that the arrival of refugees evokes, we can better assume the political responsibility of hospitality that arises out of our implication in the structural injustice they suffer. I have said very little about how local, regional, and global operations of power—material, symbolic, discursive, disciplinary, and biopolitical—might shape practices of mindful citizenship or what such practices might mean for the relationship between states, mindful citizens, and civil society. I suspect that there is no single answer to these questions and that only a detailed investigation of the operations of power in a given context can suggest how they might shape practices of mindful citizenship. My purpose here has been a relatively modest one: to suggest that living mindfully, as human beings and citizens, may help us let go of anxieties and resentments about having the vulnerability of our place in the world exposed and assume our political responsibility of hospitality to those who arrive at our borders in desperate need.

NOTES

1. Iris Marion Young, "Responsibility and Global Justice: A Social Connection Model," *Social Philosophy and Policy* 23, no. 1 (2006): 116.
2. Young, "Responsibility and Global Justice," 112.
3. Young, "Responsibility and Global Justice," 112.
4. Young, "Responsibility and Global Justice," 114.
5. Young, "Responsibility and Global Justice," 114.
6. Young, "Responsibility and Global Justice," 114.
7. Hannah Arendt, *The Origins of Totalitarianism* (New York: Harcourt, 1948), 296. See also Serena Parekh, "A Meaningful Place in the World: Hannah Arendt on the Nature of Human Rights," *Journal of Human Rights* 3, no. 1 (2004): 41–52, and Ayten Gündoğdu, *Rightlessness in an Age of Rights: Hannah Arendt and the Contemporary Struggle of Migrants* (Oxford: Oxford University Press, 2015).
8. Gündoğdu, *Rightlessness in an Age of Rights*.
9. See Sohail Hashmi, *State Sovereignty: Change and Persistence in International Relations* (University Park: Pennsylvania State University Press, 2010), and Max Weber, "Politics as a Vocation," in *From Max Weber: Essays in Sociology*, ed. H. H. Gerth and Wright Mills (London: Routledge, 1958).
10. The European Union seems like an obvious exception. However, in the context of the current refugee crisis, many states are aggressively defending their borders.
11. See Philip Pettit, *A Theory of Freedom: From the Psychology to the Politics of Agency* (Oxford: Oxford University Press, 2001).
12. Hedley Bull and Adam Watson, *The Expansion of International Society* (Oxford: Oxford University Press, 1984), 1.
13. Hedley Bull, *The Anarchical Society: A Study of Order in World Politics* (New York: Columbia University Press, 2012), 13.
14. Arendt, *The Origins of Totalitarianism*.
15. Young, "Responsibility and Global Justice," 119.
16. Young, "Responsibility and Global Justice," 119.
17. Young, "Responsibility and Global Justice," 114.
18. See Jacob (Jade) Schiff, "Confronting Political Responsibility: The Problem of Acknowledgment," *Hypatia* 23, no. 3 (2008): 99–117, and Jade Larissa Schiff, *Burdens of Political Responsibility: Narrative and the Cultivation of Responsiveness* (Cambridge: Cambridge University Press, 2014).
19. Pierre Bourdieu, *Outline of a Theory of Practice* (Cambridge: Cambridge University Press, 1977), 78–79.
20. Bourdieu, *Outline of a Theory of Practice*, 78, emphasis added.

21. Bourdieu, *Outline of a Theory of Practice*, 164.
22. See Schiff, *Burdens of Political Responsibility*.
23. See Bourdieu, *Outline of a Theory of Practice*, 168–69.
24. Bourdieu, *Outline of a Theory of Practice*, 169.
25. See Ian Austen, "Syrian Refugees Greeted by Justin Trudeau in Canada," *New York Times*, December 11, 2015, https://www.nytimes.com/2015/12/12/world/americas/syria-refugees-arrive-in-canada.html, and Jodi Kantor and Catrin Einhorn, "Refugees Encounter a Foreign Word: Welcome," *New York Times*, June 30, 2016, https://www.nytimes.com/2016/07/01/world/americas/canada-syrian-refugees.html.
26. See Harriet Agerholm, "Denmark Uses Controversial 'Jewelry Law' to Seize Assets from Refugees for the First Time," *The Independent*, July 1, 2016, http://www.independent.co.uk/news/world/europe/denmark-jewellery-law-migrants-refugees-asylum-seekers-unhcr-united-nations-a7113056.html.
27. See Daniel Dickson, "Swedish Railway Stops Denmark Service over Refugee ID Checks," *Reuters*, December 21, 2015, https://www.reuters.com/article/us-europe-migrants-sweden-denmark/swedish-railway-stops-denmark-service-over-refugee-id-checks-idUSKBN0U41OI20151221.
28. See Barbara Surk and Stephen Castle, "Migrants Diverted to Slovenia after Hungary Closes Border," *New York Times*, October 17, 2015, https://www.nytimes.com/2015/10/18/world/europe/hungary-closes-border-changing-refugees-path.html.
29. James Reynolds, "Slovenia Builds Razor-Wire Fence to Control Migrant Numbers," *BBC News*, November 11, 2015, http://www.bbc.com/news/av/world-europe-34790151/slovenia-builds-razor-wire-fence-to-control-migrant-numbers.
30. See Justin Thomas, "Resentment Is a Reaction That Refugees Don't Deserve," *The National*, August 23, 2015, https://www.thenational.ae/opinion/resentment-is-a-reaction-that-refugees-don-t-deserve-1.62514; Jamie Dettmer, "In Turkey, Resentment Builds over Syrian Refugees," *VOA News*, November 12, 2014, https://www.voanews.com/a/resentment-builds-in-turkey-over-syrian-refugees/2517491.html; and Kareem Fahim, "As Syrians Flee Anew, Neighbors' Altruism Hardens into Resentment," *New York Times*, February 7, 2016, https://www.nytimes.com/2016/02/08/world/middleeast/as-syrians-flee-anew-neighbors-altruism-hardens-into-resentment.html.
31. William E. Connolly, *Political Theory and Modernity* (Ithaca, NY: Cornell University Press, 1989), 138.
32. See Connolly, *Political Theory and Modernity*.
33. Fahim, "As Syrians Flee Anew, Neighbors' Altruism Hardens into Resentment."
34. Friedrich Nietzsche, *The Gay Science: With a Prelude in German Rhymes and an Appendix of Songs*, ed. Bernard Williams, trans. Josefine Nauckhoff (Cambridge: Cambridge University Press, 2001), 125.
35. Connolly, *Political Theory and Modernity*, 141 (quoting Nietzsche).
36. Connolly, *Political Theory and Modernity*, 141. See also William E. Connolly, *Identity/Difference: Democratic Negotiations of Political Paradox*, expanded ed. (Minneapolis: University of Minnesota Press, 2001).
37. Daniel Warner, "We Are All Refugees," *International Journal of Refugee Law* 4, no. 3 (1992): 365–72.

38. Nicholas Xenos, "Refugees: The Modern Political Condition," *Alternatives* 18 (1993): 425; see also Simone Weil, *The Need for Roots: Prelude to a Declaration of Duties toward Mankind*, trans. Arthur Wills (New York: Harper Colophon, 1971).

39. Michael Dillon, "The Scandal of the Refugee: Some Reflections on the 'Inter' of International Relations and Continental Thought," in *Moral Spaces: Rethinking Ethics and World Politics*, ed. David Campbell and Michael Shapiro, 92–125 (Minneapolis: University of Minnesota Press, 1999), 95.

40. See Farah Godrej, "Orthodoxy and Dissent in Hinduism's Meditative Traditions: A Critical Tantric Politics?," *New Political Science* 38, no. 2 (2016): 256–71.

41. Friedrich Nietzsche, *Untimely Meditations*, ed. Daniel Breazeale, trans. R. J. Hollingdale (Cambridge: Cambridge University Press, 1983), 62.

42. Arendt, *The Origins of Totalitarianism*, vii.

43. See Paul Condon, Gaëlle Desbordes, Willa B. Miller, and David DeSteno, "Meditation Increases Compassionate Responses to Suffering," *Psychological Science* 24, no. 10 (2013): 2125–27; see also David DeSteno, "The Kindness Cure," *Atlantic Monthly*, July 21, 2015, https://www.theatlantic.com/health/archive/2015/07/mindfulness-meditation-empathy-compassion/398867.

44. Jon Kabat-Zinn, *Full Catastrophe Living*: *Using the Wisdom of Your Body and Mind to Face Stress, Pain and Illness* (New York: Bantam, 2013), 33.

45. Kabat-Zinn, *Full Catastrophe Living*, 33.

46. Kabat-Zinn, *Full Catastrophe Living*, 35.

47. Kabat-Zinn, *Full Catastrophe Living*, 35.

48. Kabat-Zinn, *Full Catastrophe Living*, 36.

49. Kabat-Zinn, *Full Catastrophe Living*, 26.

50. Kabat-Zinn, *Full Catastrophe Living*, 29.

51. See Anita Chari, "The Political Potential of Mindful Embodiment," *New Political Science* 38, no. 2 (2016): 226–40; Michaele Ferguson, "Symposium: Mindfulness and Politics," *New Political Science* 38, no. 2 (2016): 201–5; Farah Godrej, "Orthodoxy and Dissent in Hinduism's Meditative Traditions: A Critical Tantric Politics?," *New Political Science* 38, no. 2 (2016): 256–71; Dean Mathiowetz, "'Meditation Is Good for Nothing': Leisure as a Democratic Practice," *New Political Science* 38, no. 2 (2016): 241–55; Matthew J. Moore, *Buddhism and Political Theory* (Oxford: Oxford University Press, 2016); Matthew J. Moore, "Buddhism, Mindfulness and Transformative Politics," *New Political Science* 38, no. 2 (2016): 272–82; and James K. Rowe, "Micropolitics and Collective Liberation: Mind/Body Practice and Left Social Movements," *New Political Science* 38, no. 2 (2016): 206–25.

52. Rowe, "Micropolitics and Collective Liberation," 213.

53. Chari, "The Political Potential of Mindful Embodiment."

54. Godrej, "Orthodoxy and Dissent in Hinduism's Meditative Traditions."

55. Iris Marion Young and Martha Nussbaum, *Responsibility for Justice* (Oxford: Oxford University Press, 2010), 118.

56. See, for example, Schiff, *Burdens of Political Responsibility*.

57. William E. Connolly, *Neuropolitics: Thinking, Culture, Speed* (Minneapolis: University of Minnesota Press, 2002) and Romand Coles, *Visionary Pragmatism:*

Radical and Ecological Democracy in Neoliberal Times (Durham, NC: Duke University Press, 2016).

58. See Schiff, *Burdens of Political Responsibility*, and Schiff, "Confronting Political Responsibility."

59. See Emmanuel Levinas, *Totality and Infinity: An Essay on Exteriority*, trans. Alphonso Lingis (Pittsburgh, PA: Duquesne University Press, 1969).

60. Susan Sontag, *On Photography* (New York: Picador, 2001), 20.

61. Young and Nussbaum, *Responsibility for Justice*, 151.

62. See Mathiowetz, "'Meditation Is Good for Nothing.'"

63. See, for example, Mark E. Warren, ed., *Democracy and Trust* (Cambridge: Cambridge University Press, 1999).

64. Hannah Arendt, *The Human Condition* (Chicago: Chicago University Press, 1998), 7.

Chapter Six

On the Limits of Hospitality

Arendt and Balibar on a Universal Right to Politics

Peg Birmingham

> We lost our home, which means the familiarity of daily life. We lost our occupation, which means the confidence that we are of some use in this world. We lost our language, which means the naturalness of reactions, the simplicity of gestures, the unaffected expression of feelings. We left our relatives in the Polish ghettos and our best friends have been killed in concentration camps, and that means the rupture of our private lives.[1]

Hannah Arendt's 1943 essay "We Refugees" begins with an extensive list of losses suffered by refugees, including Arendt, who arrived in New York in 1941, fleeing from the Nazi genocide: loss of home, loss of usefulness, loss of language, loss of freely expressed feelings and gestures, loss of friends, loss of family, loss of private life. An unspeakable silence accompanies these losses, not only the silence of the unspeakable horrors fled but also the silence required by the hospitable, those who welcome yet do not want to hear about the events that forced the flight. The implicit demand of welcome is to fit in, to be agreeable, to be less undesirable:

> Once we could buy our food and ride in the subway without being told we were undesirable. We have become a little hysterical since newspapermen started detecting us and telling us publicly to stop being disagreeable when shopping for milk and bread. We wonder how it can be done; we already are so damnably careful in every moment of our daily lives to avoid anybody guessing who we are, what kind of passport we have, where our birth certificates were filled out—and that Hitler didn't like us. We try the best we can to fit into a world where you have to be sort of politically minded when you buy your food.[2]

Arendt's description of the refugees' precarious existence in carrying out the activities of daily life—buying milk and bread or taking the subway—points to the limits of hospitality. The hospitable invitation is conditional and will be revoked if these conditions are not met.

The expectations of a dinner invitation, for example, is that one is pleasant during the meal, uses the table manners of the host, and engages in conversations that will not be infuriating or depressing, resulting in the table erupting in anger or tears. Certainly, one does not bring along the rest of the family or a bunch of friends who are also hungry. Hospitality is precarious; anything can happen that will upset the meal and lead to the reconsideration of any further invite, hence the carefulness Arendt describes. This is why zones of hospitality such as Derrida describes, while certainly much needed as what we might call ethical places of temporary residence, do not substitute for unconditional or universal political rights. Following Arendt's and Etienne Balibar's differing accounts, I want to explore this claim of a universal right to politics, looking especially at the aporia at the heart of this claim.

The aporetic nature of a universal right to politics emerges when recognizing that while there may be a universal right to politics, politics is never universal. Politics, in other words, is defined by borders and boundaries. Balibar agrees with Arendt when she claims that a "citizen is by definition a citizen among citizens of a country among countries; his rights and duties must be defined and limited not only by those of his fellow citizens, but also by the boundaries of a territory."[3] As Arendt points out, a world without borders or demarcations is a world of one government, and such a globalized unified government is terrifying:

> Philosophy may conceive of the earth as the homeland of human beings and one unwritten law, eternal and valid for all, but politics deals with human beings of many countries and heirs to many pasts. Politically, the task is to think the nature of laws which positively establish demarcations that protect and limit the spaces in which freedom is not a concept, but a living, political reality.[4]

If borders—places of demarcation between inside and outside, included and excluded—are an inescapable condition of politics, necessary for the very institution of the political, then from the outset, the claim of a universal right to politics is aporetic. And this aporia is intensified when we consider another aspect of the modern political space set in motion with the 1789 Declaration of the Rights of Man and the Citizen, a declaration that claims that human rights are universal yet inseparable from the status of citizenship of a particular nation-state.

How, then, do we think a universal right to politics if politics is never universal? How do we think a universal right to politics if this right seems inseparably connected to particular political states? What concept of universality is at work in this "universal right of politics"? These are the questions

I will take up in Arendt's and Balibar's respective understandings of the universality at work in this rights claim. In conclusion, I will return to Arendt's "We Refugees" to think the status of the universal at work in the "We" in the title of her essay.

HANNAH ARENDT AND A UNIVERSAL RIGHT TO POLITICS

In *The Origins of Totalitarianism*, Arendt points out that at the very moment when protection under the auspices of universal human rights was most desperately needed, no such protection was granted. Outside the law and not belonging to any political community, she and her fellow refugees were reduced to "mere naked human beings" in a "condition of complete rightlessness."[5] Her time as a refugee led Arendt to rethink human rights, arguing that human rights cannot be simply the rights of citizen; instead, what is revealed through the stateless refugees is a more fundamental right: the universal right to belong to a political community. She calls this fundamental right the "right to have rights" or the universal right to politics: "We became aware of the existence of a right to have rights . . . the right to belong to some kind of organized community, only when millions of people emerged who had lost and could not regain these rights because of the new global political situation."[6] She describes this new global political situation: "suddenly, there was no place on earth where refugees could go without the severest restriction, no country where they would be assimilated, no territory where they could found a new community of their own. This, moreover, had next to nothing to do with any material problem of overpopulation; it was a problem not of space but of political organization."[7]

For Arendt, the political organization that prevents refugees and the stateless from losing and not regaining rights is the problem of the nation-state that limits human rights to citizens of a nation-state. She argues that in the modern era, despite the claim of the universality of human rights, rights are limited to those who belong to the *unified powerful* will of a sovereign nation-state. The notion of a sovereign, unified, and thereby powerful will is tied to a long tradition that has its origins in Augustine, for whom the problem of being able to act or, more precisely, the inability to act is tied to a divided will. This is his dilemma in the *Confessions*: "I will and I cannot."[8] A powerful will is therefore possible only if the will is one with itself. Arendt points out that this conception of power, located in a unified will, is precisely the conception of power developed in modern political theory, a fact that has serious consequences for the modern formulation of human rights.

Indeed, Arendt argues that the modern understanding of the self as a subject who is the bearer of inalienable rights is inseparable from the notion of the sovereign nation-state that gets it power from the sovereign general will of the people. Human rights, then, are tied up with the question of national emancipation. In this schema, power is always associated with sovereignty and unity—either the unified sovereign will of the individual or the unity of the sovereign general will embodied in the figure of the ruler. Hobbes's frontispiece to *Leviathan* is not only the first but also the best illustration of this figure. To go further, the sovereign will of the nation is unified through a common language, a common history, and a common territory whose borders are the places of inclusion and exclusion. Again, those who are not nationals, those outside the territorial borders of nation-states, belong nowhere and have nowhere to go; they are therefore outside the protection of human rights.

How, then, do we think the universality at work in Arendt's claim of the "right to have rights"? To take up this question, we need to turn to Arendt's anthropology that claims that the human being is a unique and singular beginner. As she writes in the last sentences of *The Origins of Totalitarianism*, quoting Augustine, "That a beginning be made, Man was made, before whom there was nobody."[9] This notion of the human being as a unique beginner who is at the same time thrown into a web or plurality of others is at the center of Arendt's conception of action, freedom, and power. At the same time, Arendt's anthropology of the human being as a beginner is rooted in the ontological event of natality, a contingent and unpredictable event that radically interrupts time. The event of natality interrupts the flow of time as it inserts the new into time. This interruption brings uniqueness and newness into the world. The originary event is unconditioned, even though it is always at the same time through the insertion connected to the conditioned.

In his reading of Arendt's event of natality, Bernard Flynn points out that to whom one owes a debt is revealing.[10] Arendt's debt to Augustine, he argues, is evident in the last lines of *The Origins of Totalitarianism*, wherein she explicitly cites Augustine. Flynn argues that this points to a theological debt at work in Arendt's ontology that has significance for thinking the universality animating the "right to have rights." This fundamental right, he argues, remains rooted in "an ontological framework that moves from rights within an existing political community to a more originary foundation in the event of natality—again, an ahistorical event that interrupts time even as it is an event that inserts each singular and unique being into time"[11] Moreover, according to Flynn's analysis, in the Arendtian schema, we cannot say "universality" in the plural, and therefore it is not connected to the political. The universality of the right to have rights is located in the singular and unique individual, each time, for the first time, prior to whom there was nobody.

While I agree with Flynn that our debts give some insight into who one is and the work that one does, it does not seem to me that a debt necessarily establishes an identity with those to whom one is indebted. After all, Kant recognizes his debt to Hume and Rousseau for waking him from his respective epistemological and moral slumbers, yet Kant's work is certainly not grounded in either thinker's epistemological or ethical assumptions. So too Arendt vis-à-vis Augustine. She takes his notion of the event of beginning but then unmoors it from its theological underpinnings. In her thought, the event of beginning is the *ungrounded* and *unconditioned* appearance of the singular in time. The event of natality, the event of the newcomer, comes from nowhere. This is why when referring to the newcomer, she claims, "Before you, there was nobody." Again, singularity and uniqueness is introduced into the world through the insertion and, thereby, interruption of time that radically disrupts genealogy, lineage, and generation. Again, the event of natality is an unconditioned and therefore groundless event, hence its status as a "miracle."

Here I want to pause to consider the relation between the unconditional event of natality and its worldly insertion. Recently, Adriana Cavarero has indicted Arendt for forgetting that the newcomer does not arrive from nowhere; instead, it is an arrival through the mother and the event of birth. Birth, she argues, is not an unconditioned event; the fundamental event is the mother.[12] Certainly, Arendt is not so naive as to be claiming that one arrives in a world without others, without a mother, without material conditions inseparable from the event of one's actual birth. She devotes several pages in *The Human Condition* to an exploration of the "web of human relations" into which one is thrown on entrance into the world. This would include the newcomer's relation to the mother. In these pages, Arendt speaks of two births in the chapter on political action, arguing that the second birth, the birth into the political space of speech and action, is predicated on a first birth, and she goes further, arguing that the second birth is not added like a superstructure onto the first birth but that the two are infused, suggesting that first physical birth and all that is connected with it—embodiment, the mother, the material conditions into which one is born—remain with and infuse the second birth and are therefore of political concern. Of course, Arendt does not develop this first birth in any detail, and that is a lack in her work, but she does not deny it.

That said, Arendt does deny reducing the ontological event of natality to the event of birth (associated with the *vita activa* encompassing labor, work, and action). In other words, she insists that the ontological and the political be kept apart, speaking to each other from "distant hilltops." If natality is reduced to birth, then the unique, unprecedented, unconditioned being is reduced to her genealogy, generation, and lineage. Still further, to reduce natality to birth is to break with the ontological promise of radical new beginnings that saves the world and the earth from ruin. Hence, the two events—natality and birth—must be viewed as equiprimordial but not identical: Miracle-of-birth.

While Arendt's ontology does not allow for a simple reading of the relation between natality and birth, her insistence on the difference between ontological singularity and political plurality deepens the aporia between the universal and the political, making it difficult to think the universality at work *in* the right to have rights. On Arendt's ontological account, the refugee and the stateless have a universal right to politics, yet there does not seem to be a way to move from the transcendent universal right to its political inscription into plurality. Again, on Arendt's own account, these two dimensions speak to one another from distant hilltops. While each newcomer carries with her the principle of beginning, this principle remains unique and singular, not plural.[13] At this point, I turn to Balibar's thought on the universality at work in the political.

ETIENNE BALIBAR AND THE UNIVERSAL RIGHT IN POLITICS

While Balibar's thought on this universal right is in many ways very close to Arendt's, nevertheless, he is also at a distance from her insofar as he opens up the aporia between the political and the universal by shifting ever so slightly the question. Rather than asking how we can account for a universal right *to* politics, Balibar asks if we can find a universal right *in* politics.

For Balibar, the 1789 Declaration of the Rights of Man and the Citizen announces a new conception of the citizen, one no longer rooted in differences of status and hierarchy, such as the free person versus the slave or the king and his subjects. Instead, the declaration declares that the concepts of man and the citizen are identified, declaring thereby the right of politics for all human beings:

> What is distinctly characteristic of modern citizenship, at least by right or in principle, is the universalization of the status of the citizen. In other words, this status ceases to be a privilege and instead comes to be conceived in terms of universal access, or a universal right to politics: a right not only to political rights (a "right to have rights," as Arendt said), but also to effective political participation.[14]

In other words, it is not the democratic principle as such that marks the revolutionary nature of the declaration of rights—after all, this principle was at work in ancient Greece. Instead, Balibar argues, the declaration is revolutionary insofar as it "*universalizes* the principle of equality, extending the right to political participation to our common humanity or what Marx calls our 'species-being.'[15] Significantly, Balibar refers explicitly to Arendt's "right to have rights" but alters her reading slightly, arguing that the declaration does not separate the universal human being from the citizen but instead declares their identity. The universal is the particular citizen, or, to say it differently, the citizen is the site of universality

Going further, Balibar argues that the declaration announces that freedom emerges only out of equality. Calling this "equaliberty," Balibar claims that the declaration declares its opposition to absolutism and privilege, setting into motion the claim that universal equality and freedom are based on the revolutionary struggle itself: "the universal equality and freedom of human beings is a 'historical universal,' not based in human nature but in political struggle and praxis."[16] This universality, he argues, "excludes exclusion, forbids the denial of citizenship in the name of determinations of condition, status, or nature."[17] This means that the citizens themselves are the site of the constituting power of the political; the citizen-subject becomes sovereign in the sense that citizens, constituted by political participation, are "the subjects of their own incorporation in a system of guarantees and constitutional controls."[18] Citizens as political agents now decide on the distribution of rights, which retain an inherent indeterminacy. Citizen-subjects, therefore, are not simply "the bearers of a demand to be governed by authorities of their choices and under their control."[19] To summarize, for Balibar, the modern declaration of human rights declares the subject a universal *political* subject bearing "a universal right to politics and this right to political subjectivity exists *in practice* to those who are 'unorganized.'[20] Significantly for thinking the status of the refugee, Balibar points out that the difference between man and citizen is *only* the recognition that those who are not organized into the people remain political subjects, part of the "community of belonging."[21]

Contrary to Arendt, Balibar argues that the universality of human rights does not announce itself in an ahistorical event of natality but instead announces "the irreducible human project of being 'through one another' and 'in common.' This differs from Arendt's claim that the unique being is always in a plurality with others but is not constituted by these others. According to Arendt, the unique being reveals through acting who she already is. Contrary to this, Balibar argues that we are from the start "trans-individual," constituted through and by others in our being-in-common. We always already find ourselves in social communities whose relations constitute who we are in our common being. Following Roberto Esposito, he argues that the etymology of community reveals it to be the opposite of immunity: self-protection and propriety. Balibar goes on to argue that the being-in-common finds "its truth in limit situations (which are also situations of political urgency), where the most exterior, the most foreign must be admitted to the sharing of the public space as such, which amounts to saying that the community experiences its greatest capacity to represent the common in the inclusion of the widest difference."[22]

If Balibar is critical of a notion of community in which self-protection and propriety are central, that is, a community in which the "we" is established through proper identifications, he also recognizes that human beings cannot live in a state of pure openness or exposure, or what he also calls "pure disidentifications." Rather than being either "proper (total)" or "pure (free-floating)," Balibar argues that all identity is fundamentally "transindividual," neither purely individual nor purely collective. Thus, he argues that "rather than identities, we must speak of identifications—neither given nor fixed once and for all."[23] Very close to Spinoza, Balibar's anthropological principle claims that the individual is "a construction which is the result of a given regime of communication (affective, economic, and intellectual) with other individuals,"[24] hence his insistence on the transindividuality of identifications as well as his claim that this movement of identification and disidentifications takes place at the level of collective political identities themselves.

Balibar's "universal right to politics" is, then, though from out of a different anthropology and ontology than Arendt's, one indebted in large part (although certainly not entirely) to Spinoza. Unlike Arendt's debt to Augustine, one that is apparent in her notion of a transcendent (although nontheological) universality, Balibar's debt to Spinoza is such that he eliminates every form of transcendence and ideality from his ontology. His materialist ontology rejects not only the dualisms of unity and diversity, of the temporal and the eternal, but also and even more significantly for thinking universalities, the duality of the universal and the singular. As we have seen, the singular citizen-subject is the site of the universal. Thus, Balibar's account of Spinoza could also be an account of his own work:

> His work is not divided into a metaphysics (or an ontology) on the one hand and a politics or an ethics, which are seen as "secondary applications" of "first philosophy" on the other. From the very beginning, his metaphysics is a philosophy of praxis, of activity; and his politics is a philosophy. For it constitutes the field of experience in which human nature acts and strives to achieve liberation.[25]

Unlike Arendt, for whom ontology and politics speak from distant hilltops, Balibar refuses the distinction between ontology and politics. Perhaps more accurately, his ontology is a materialist ontology in which we find ourselves always already in a field of experience in which striving or acting to achieve liberation is the fundamental and pervasive activity. His understanding of the universality of human rights is placed *within* the field of experience even as it retains an aspect of the imprescriptible in this field.

Balibar, therefore, offers a conception of citizenship that emphasizes "a concrete articulation of the rights of man and the rights of the citizen, of responsibility and militant commitment."[26] Citizenship and political communities are always "practical sites of universality" wherein political actors find themselves in a "practical confrontation with the different modalities of exclusion (social, and thus political, for the two notions have never truly been separate) that constitutes the founding moment of citizenship."[27] Here I note his emphasis on the inseparability of social citizenship and social rights from political citizenship and political rights. Following Marx, he argues that social rights must be made universal, not merely reserved for the poor or needy: "they are to be considered as universal, entering into the definition of a new historical figure of human individuality and giving 'labor' the dignity of a title to public recognition."[28] While Arendt does not develop this point, she too includes the right to work along with the right to residence as essential to her notion of the "right to have rights."[29]

Further, Balibar envisions that these work sites of democracy are formed through a "community of alliances" that establishes a new conception of the political, a conception no longer based on the friend–enemy distinction or on idea of a "pre-existing community based on traditional membership and 'roots.'"[30] Political actors do not aspire to be friends, nor are these sites free from hostilities and conflicts. Instead, these historical sites of democracy point to the opposite axiom: "it does not say there are no 'fault lines,' no 'vested hostilities' around them, but it does say that political institutions (the 'polity,' 'civility') precisely arise when hostility becomes a focal point of the elaboration of common interests and historic compromises." He argues that these common interests "express the 'complementarity of the enemies' . . . and this is what makes them politically significant."[31]

Finally, this practical struggle is not the simple demand of inclusion on the part of those who have been excluded. Rather, Balibar argues that political struggle is the "*common operation* or, if you prefer, the '*shared*' *act* of both—for example, those 'with' and those 'without' (papers, citizenship qualifications)—in such a way as to democratize citizenship beginning from its borders, thus 'making right' and civilizing the state and politics."[32] Those who have been excluded are not weak or passive victims; their human rights must not be viewed as humanitarian rights granted to the excluded and marginalized who retain the status of victims; instead, those who have been excluded from the political universal are themselves sites of political agency.

At the same time, while recognizing that the 1789 Declaration of the Rights of Man and the Citizen declares universal citizenship, nonetheless, this universality is inseparable from the status of citizenship of a sovereign state. This is the aporetic gap between universal citizenship and the recognition of this universality by the state. For Balibar, this aporia is at the center of his thinking on sovereignty, governance, and resistance. He argues that nothing violates more the universal right to politics than sovereign borders that act as instruments of control, segregation, and the demarcation of inclusion/exclusion: "The border is the preeminent site where the controls and guarantees of the 'normal' juridical order are suspended (it is truly in the modern constitutional state, the antidemocratic condition of democracy), the site where the 'monopoly of legitimate violence' takes the form of a preventive counterviolence."[33] In such a world, Balibar argues, borders are places of crises, hostilities, and emergencies. Borders are the "limit-situations" in which the concrete instantiation of universal political citizenship must take place. As such, they are sites of political contestation and negotiation. As sites of political contestation, borders are no longer viewed as ahistorical, juridical sites governed by state sovereignty but instead are recognized as constituted through citizen-actors who are themselves part of the border crises. As he points out, this would be the "democratization of the borders," which he rightly claims is something quite different from the abolition of borders.[34] The democratization of the borders occurs when borders become "work sites of democracy," the places of political work by those who cross back and forth between them.

That said, Balibar is not suggesting that a democratic politics could give form to a nonexclusive belonging. Again, he agrees with Arendt: there is a universal right in politics, but politics is never universal. Instead, we must think the *place* of universality as a historical conjuncture (and there is more than one). The site of the universal is a site that must constantly question the origins of universality, how it is constituted, and its internal contradictions. As Balibar points out in his essay "Racism as Universalism," deeply mired in the "great blossoming of universalism—the Enlightenment—were anthropological prejudices regarding race."[35] While the temptation might be to abandon universality altogether, Balibar cautions against such an easy and utopian thought. As he concludes in this essay, the task is to think inside the *place* or *conjunction* of universality—not to abandon it but to transform it from the inside. Such a transformation will not resolve the aporia of a universal right in politics, but it will open up the universality of this right to a different history with a different set of identifications and the transformation of sovereign political borders.[36]

By way of conclusion, I want to return to Arendt's essay "We Refugees," taking up the status of the "We" in its title. As noted at the outset of my remarks, Arendt begins this essay noting the losses and the silences that characterize the refugee's existence, an existence without political or social identity and at the whims of hospitality. She ends the essay by noting that refugees "driven from country to country represent the vanguard of their peoples—if they keep their identity. For the first time Jewish history is not separate but tied up with that of all other nations. The comity of European peoples went to pieces when, and because, it allowed its weakest member to be excluded and persecuted."[37] Arendt notes that refugees not only are the "vanguard of their peoples" but also give figure to a new notion of "peoples" more generally. The refugee is the new figure of the "We." She goes on to qualify this, paradoxically claiming, "but only if refugees are allowed their identities."[38]

With this claim, Arendt is arguing against the demand that refugees assimilate, thereby losing their language, their gestures, their occupations. Assimilation is closely aligned with the status of a guest, dependent on hospitality, careful to conform to the manners of the host. Similar to Balibar's claim that the task of inscribing the universality of political rights is one of the identification and disidentification of collective life, she nonetheless gives some pause to Balibar's claim, pointing out that the retaining of identity is essential to the task of inscribing universality into the political in ways that open up and transform it. Here Arendt is again pointing to the aporetic status of the "we" of "We refugees," a "we" that has the status of both displacement and place, of both identities and nonidentities. The refugee "we" points to political spaces no longer able to bind themselves together through unified homogeneous national wills. Instead, this "we"—the vanguard of a new conception of the people—demands inscribing universal political rights through the new political figure of the refugee.

In *Aesthetic Politics*, F. R. Ankersmit points out that the form of the political in a particular historical epoch is an answer to the problem of violence and destruction.[39] Feudalism, he reminds us, is a response to the collapse of the Carolingian Empire and the raids of the Norse: "By delegating political and military power to the individual baron, count, or bishop, a more or less adequate solution was found for the problems of the public safety facing Europe in that period."[40] The gate into the city is the political form of this new political world. The sovereign state, first as absolute monarchy and then rooted in the sovereign will of the nation-state, was a solution to the religious wars of modern Europe. The territorial sovereign border is the political form of this world.[41]

In our present historical conjunction of globalization and the violence of profound economic inequality, of continual war and the destruction of the environment, sovereign national borders no longer provide a political solution. The contemporary global violence flows back and forth, inside and outside political borders. What, then, is the political form that could provide some solution to the contemporary problem of global destruction and violence? I submit that the figure of the refugee—the UN High Commissioner for Refugees puts the 2016 figure of forcibly displaced persons at 65.3 million—is the contemporary figure of the political. And yet, while the figure of the refugee points to the inability of sovereign borders to contain the violence, it would be incorrect to argue that this figure serves as a political form that might provide a possible answer to the global problem. The figure of refugee is the figure of the inadequacy of the modern political solution of national borders, which, following Arendt, requires a new form of the "We." Following Balibar, this new political form, this "We" that includes the 65.3 million forcibly displaced, will emerge only at the sites where refugees appear as political agents and where the political task of instituting politically a universal right to politics carries out its work.

NOTES

1. Hannah Arendt, "We Refugees," in *The Jewish Writings*, ed. Jerome Kohn and Ron H. Feldman (New York: Schocken Books, 2007), 264–65.
2. Arendt, "We Refugees," 265.
3. Hannah Arendt, *Men in Dark Times* (New York: Harcourt, 1968), 81.
4. Arendt, *Men in Dark Times*, 81.
5. Hannah Arendt, *The Origins of Totalitarianism* (New York: Harcourt, 1948), 96.
6. Arendt, *The Origins of Totalitarianism*, 296–97.
7. Arendt, *The Origins of Totalitarianism*, 295–96.
8. Augustine, *The Confessions*, trans. John Ryan (New York: Image Books, 1960), 196.
9. Arendt, *The Origins of Totalitarianism*, 479.
10. Bernard Flynn, "On the 'Right to Have Rights,'" response to Peg Birmingham, *Hannah Arendt and Human Rights*, American Philosophical Association Book Session, December 30, 2007, unpublished.
11. Flynn, "On the 'Right to Have Rights.'"
12. Adriana Cavarero, *Inclinations*, trans. Amanda Minervini and Adam Sitze (Stanford, CA: Stanford University Press, 2016), 107–20.
13. Arendt claims as well that the ontological principle of beginning makes each human being a beginner who carries this principle throughout his or her existence. The principle of beginning, therefore, makes possible judgments regarding the unprecedented, such as the unprecedented event of totalitarianism; see her essay "Understanding and Politics," in *Essays in Understanding 1930–1954*, ed. Jerome Kohn (New York: Harcourt Brace, 1993), 321.
14. Étienne Balibar, "Is a Philosophy of Human Civic Rights Possible? New Reflections on Equaliberty," *South Atlantic Quarterly* 103, no. 203 (2004): 312.
15. Balibar, "Is a Philosophy of Human Civic Rights Possible?," 312.
16. Étienne Balibar, *Masses, Classes, Ideas: Studies on Politics and Philosophy before and after Marx* (New York: Routledge, 1994), 49.
17. Balibar, "Is a Philosophy of Human Civic Rights Possible?," 312.
18. Balibar, "Is a Philosophy of Human Civic Rights Possible?," 317.

19. Balibar, "Is a Philosophy of Human Civic Rights Possible?," 318.
20. Balibar, "Is a Philosophy of Human Civic Rights Possible?," 318.
21. Balibar, "Is a Philosophy of Human Civic Rights Possible?," 318.
22. Étienne Balibar, *We, the People of Europe? Reflections on Transnational Citizenship*, trans. James Swenson (Princeton, NJ: Princeton University Press, 2004), 71.
23. Étienne Balibar, *Politics and the Other Scene* (New York: Verso, 2002), 29.
24. Étienne Balibar, *Spinoza and Politics*, trans. Peter Snowdon (New York: Verso, 1998), 124.
25. Balibar, *Spinoza and Politics*, 103.
26. Balibar, *We, the People of Europe?*, 49.
27. Balibar, *We, the People of Europe?*, 76–77.
28. Balibar, *We, the People of Europe?*, 220.
29. See Arendt, *The Origins of Totalitarianism*, 286.
30. Balibar, *We, the People of Europe?*, 230.
31. Balibar, *We, the People of Europe?*, 231.
32. Balibar, *We, the People of Europe?*, 77.
33. Balibar, *We, the People of Europe?*, 140.
34. Balibar, *We, the People of Europe?*, 117.
35. Balibar, *Masses, Classes, Ideas*, 196.
36. Balibar, *Masses, Classes, Ideas*, 199.
37. Arendt, "We Refugees," 274.
38. Arendt, "We Refugees," 274.
39. See F. R. Ankersmit, *Aesthetic Politics* (Stanford, CA: Stanford University Press, 1996).
40. Ankersmit, *Aesthetic Politics*, 124.
41. Ankersmit, *Aesthetic Politics*, 124.

Part III

REFUGEE DETENTION AND EXCLUSION TODAY

Chapter Seven

Abolish Refugee Detention

Rethinking International Law and Carceral Humanitarianism

Kelly Oliver

Refugees are considered criminal threats, charity cases, or both. Discussing refugees from Nazi Germany, Hannah Arendt says, "Apparently nobody wants to know that contemporary history has created a new kind of human beings—the kind that are put in concentration camps by their foes and in internments camps by their friends."[1] Today, there may not be concentration camps murdering refugees, but thousands of refugees end up in detention centers, and hundreds of thousands are fenced into camps every year. Incarcerated or interned, they have their basic human rights, as defined by the United Nations in terms of security, freedom of movement, travel documents, and dignity, further breached by their "host" countries. Detention centers and refugee camps are often places of abuse and always places of further trauma.[2] The irony is that people who have the courage to stand up to totalitarian governments and fight for freedom may flee persecution yet in the name of freedom and security find themselves locked up again. Asylum seekers fleeing violence in their own countries meet another kind of violence in their host countries. Those escaping repressive and violent governments at home face repression and violence from their hosts. The freedom and security of refugees is sacrificed in the name of the freedom and security of citizens. The democratic value of an open society quickly closes itself off in the face of mass migration as refugees and asylum seekers are managed, controlled, interrogated, detained, incarcerated, and interned.

Here, I argue for the abolition of refugee camps and detention centers based not only on the deplorable conditions of these places and the fact that innocent people are locked up like criminals but also on the problematic and paradoxical category "refugee." The UN definition of refugee status creates an impossible aporetic subject, required both to be law abiding and, in most cases, to break the law by entering the host country illegally without proper documentation. In addition, refugees are put in a double bind in terms of their ability to effectively testify to their own abuse and persecution. The very violence and trauma they flee to seek asylum can undermine their ability to persuade officials not only of their veracity but also of their position as upstanding citizens escaping persecution; testimony is especially problematic for refugee children. In the end, I suggest an alternative politics of refugees that is not based on the distinction between citizens and noncitizens or between citizens and refugees but rather on earth ethics as an obligation to respond to those with whom we share the planet.

BEYOND HUMAN RIGHTS VIOLATIONS

In 2015, more than a million people fled to Europe seeking asylum, primarily from Syria, Afghanistan, and Iraq. The vast majority of them arrived by sea, making a perilous journey that has cost thousands their lives. Thousands died crossing the Mediterranean Sea, and given that thousands more go missing or are unaccounted for, it is impossible to determine how many people have actually died.[3] Given that many migrants are forced to attempt illegal border crossings and therefore avoid detection by authorities until their dead bodies wash ashore, many more are not counted in statistics of missing or dead.[4] And statistics for early 2016 were significantly higher.[5] In just the first six weeks of 2016, crossings increased tenfold, and so did deaths.[6] Although overall crossings for 2016 were fewer than for the prior year (362,753), deaths outnumbered those for the prior year, totaling more than 5,000 recorded deaths. By late 2017, 160,847 refugees had arrived in Europe via the Mediterranean, and 2,992 refugees died or went missing during the crossing.[7] As of 2017, there are more than 22 million refugees worldwide, global displacement (including internal displacement) has reached more than 65 million people, and 10 million people are considered stateless according to the UN High Commissioner for Refugees (UNHCR).[8] These statistics are mind-boggling.

What is more astounding is that most refugees end up living in camps for decades before resettlement. Unlike refugees from World War II, who were resettled by 1952, many of today's refugees spend substantial portions of their lives in a permanent state of temporary living. For example, the largest refugee camp in the world, Kenya's Dadaab, is now twenty-seven years old. It was built for 90,000 refugees but now "holds more than 420,000. . . . Currently, the number of years a refugee lives in a refugee camp is, on average, 12."[9] Furthermore, conditions in most refugee camps are dangerous and unhealthy, where people are forced to live in overcrowded makeshift tent compounds without adequate basic necessities, such as bathrooms, clothes, and food. For example, in Dunkirk camp in France, more than 3,000 refugees live in rat-infested tents pitched in ankle-deep mud and human waste with only two water faucets; one resident says, "This place is for animals, not for human beings."[10]

Unfortunately, Dunkirk is not an isolated example. Calais, another camp in France near the Channel Tunnel, known as the "Jungle," housed more than 6,000 at its peak in the summer of 2018, most living in squalor. Doctors described it as worse than a war zone with people sleeping in tents surrounded by raw sewage, stagnant water, and mud. One resident told a reporter, "We are humans, not animals."[11] Violent protests and clashes with police throwing tear gas have resulted from the French government bulldozing a large section of the camp in March 2018, further displacing already displaced people.[12] At least 129 children have gone missing since the camp was razed.[13]

The Greek interior minister Panagiotis Kouroublis called the Idomeni camp on Greece's border with Macedonia "a modern-day Dachau, a result of the logic of closed borders."[14] "Despite being planned for just 2,500 people, the camp hosts around 12,000 refugees—many from Syria and Iraq—in wet, cold and muddy conditions," which Red Cross officials warn are rife for the spread of disease.[15] These refugees "feel like we are dying slowly."[16] And, since the route to Greece from Syria has been effectively closed now, refugees flee through Libya, making an even more dangerous crossing of the Mediterranean Sea into Italy—one that led to more than 1,000 people dying and another 4,000 being rescued, in a matter of days, in what a spokesperson for Save the Children called "a massacre."[17]

Thousands of miles away in the United States, refugees live in detention centers that look and are run like prisons, with locked cells, jumpsuits, and all. And processing refugees takes months.[18] The United States operates the world's largest immigration detention system, and most centers provide substandard health care.[19] As in other prisons, conditions in detention centers are often poor, with inadequate health care, lack of facilities and personnel, and preventable deaths, including suicide.[20] A recent investigation into subpar health care in detention centers confirmed that the lack of health care contributed to several deaths: "system-wide problems remain, including a failure to prevent or fix substandard medical care that literally kills people," and that isolation is improperly used to confine people suffering from mental health issues.[21]

In addition, immigrants and asylum seekers have been denied due process and locked up without legal recourse. According to Human Rights Watch, "Most of the hundreds of thousands of people held in this system each year are subject to harsh mandatory detention laws, which do not allow for an individualized review of the decision to detain them during their immigration proceedings."[22] Many asylum seekers suffer in detention centers for months before their cases are resolved.

If we take asylum seekers and refugees as a group, the circumstances of most refugees, whether in U.S. detention centers or in international refugee camps, meet the criteria for genocide set out by the United Nations, which include debilitating living conditions: "Less obvious methods of destruction, such as the deliberate deprivation of resources needed for the group's physical survival and which are available to the rest of the population, such as clean water, food and medical services; Creation of circumstances that could lead to a slow death, such as lack of proper housing, clothing and hygiene or excessive work or physical exertion." Hundreds of thousands of people are forced to live in situations without adequate clean water, food, shelter, and medical care, and even if they do get those basic needs met, it is often at the expense of their personal security, liberty, mental health, and dignity.[23]

Indeed, no matter how many mind-boggling statistics we accumulate, we can never approach the human element of the equation, which cannot be quantified or reduced to a mere number. Furthermore, statistics piled one on top of the other can lead to "disaster fatigue," even for those most committed to help. Perhaps this is why most news stories begin and end with "human interest" angles that focus on the experiences of particular individuals to make the numbers come to life. Many news reports on the refugee crisis in Europe or Africa refer to a "humanitarian crisis" and the lack of human rights or inhumane living conditions. But the rhetoric of humanity cuts both ways. For example, one aid worker in the Calais camp described the situation: "There's no official structure, no camp leadership, just a group of people surviving, a random collection of humanity camped in a field."[24] And the same report says, "Some of the newer British volunteers are cheerful as they hand out supplies. 'It's touching, isn't it?' they say, brightly. 'The humanity is amazing!'"[25] Simultaneously, as we have seen, many of the refugees call on their hosts to treat them like human beings instead of animals.[26] The list of horrors from camps and detention centers goes on and on. And so do the statistics on numbers of displaced and dead, to the point that it becomes impossible to fully fathom the depths of the current "humanitarian crisis."

CARCERAL HUMANITARIANISM

Contemporary detention centers and refugee camps are part and parcel of carceral humanitarianism that turns refugees into criminals and charity cases simultaneously and that, in turn, becomes the troubling justification for locking them up or locking them in, increasingly in dangerous, disease-ridden, sorely inadequate conditions.[27] Refugees and asylum seekers become targets of the new humanitarian military—in the case of Syrian refugees, navies and coast guards operating in the Mediterranean Sea. Their rescue at sea becomes a way of containing their unauthorized movement. Once rescued, migrants are sorted, contained within fences and checkpoints, and monitored. Their freedom of movement is severely limited, and they are often forced to live in deplorable conditions. As Martina Tazzioli argues, migrants escaping wars and famine become shipwrecked people to be rescued in a problematic rescue politics that is as much about statistics as it is quality of life: "the government of migration is grounded on a politics of numbers that sorts people into 'risk' categories," where very few are eventually granted permanent asylum and allowed to legally enter the host country.[28]

With contemporary rescue politics, the military and security approach that treats refugees like prisoners of war, terrorist threats, or criminals melds with the humanitarian approach that treats refugees as charity cases to be rescued and saved. Military and humanitarian organizations operate in tandem, often in coordinated efforts, to both save and contain refugees. In practice, the international laws governing refugee status require illegal entry on the part of asylum seekers, and, in turn, this illegal entry authorizes the host country to detain and interrogate asylum seekers. Indeed, the rights granted to asylum seekers by international law are very similar to the rights granted to criminals, with the significant exception of lack of due process or access to legal counsel. In the name of homeland security in the United States and security against terrorist threats across the globe, in actuality, regardless of international law, asylum seekers have very few rights. The fact that refugee status requires the applicant to make it to a host country and then prove his or her persecution at home means that those fleeing war and famine must have a means of escape (which costs money), make it out of their home countries, make an illegal border crossing (unless they have proper passports and visas, which are extremely difficult if not impossible to obtain in regions fraught with war and violence), and then prove persecution (which is also difficult for those fleeing war or famine). The UN 1951 Convention on Refugees defines a refugee as a person who

> owing to well-founded fear of being persecuted for reasons of race, religion, nationality, membership of a particular social group or political opinion, is outside the country of his nationality and is unable or, owing to such fear, is unwilling to avail himself of the protection of that country; or who, not having a nationality and being outside the country of his former habitual residence as a result of such events, is unable or, owing to such fear, is unwilling to return to it.[29]

Many refugees today who are fleeing war and violence or drought and famine in their home countries do not meet the letter of this definition insofar as they are not being persecuted for reasons of race, religion, nationality, or membership of a particular social group or political opinion. In fact, the largest group of refugees today, those escaping violence in Syria, are not technically refugees according to this definition. In addition, the thousands of women and children escaping gang violence in Central America are not necessarily considered refugees under this definition. The irony is that if and when they reach a host country and are sorted, managed, detained, and fenced into camps, then they become members of a group, "refugees" or "asylum seekers," who are denied basic human rights as defined by the United Nations, and if they are not also persecuted, then they are allowed to slowly perish. If they do not die from violence or starvation at home or on the perilous escape, they face disease and what some refugees call "slow death" in the camps or a lack of basic resources and abuse in detention centers. The international refugee protocol requires that refugees leave their home country and make their way to a possible host country before they can apply for asylum. In other words, they cannot apply for asylum from within their home country. This means that they must find their own way out of a precarious and dangerous situation and face further trauma and violence, only to arrive (if they are lucky) in a host country that accepts them into a camp or detention center where they are further traumatized and even interrogated like criminals or terrorists.

IMPOSSIBLE TESTIMONY

Even the words "refugee" and "asylum" connote criminality. The *Oxford English Dictionary* defines a refugee as "One who, owing to religious persecution or political troubles, seeks refuge in a foreign country: a) Originally applied to the French Huguenots who came to England in 1685 after the revocation of the Edict of Nantes; b) A *runaway fugitive from justice*" (emphasis added).[30] And, asylum is defined first as "A sanctuary or inviolable place of refuge and *protection for criminals and debtors* from which they cannot be removed without sacrilege" and as "A benevolent institution affording shelter and support to some class of the afflicted, the unfortunate, the destitute, e.g. '*a lunatic asylum*'" (emphasis added).[31] From the beginning, then, refugees have been seen as criminals, debtors, and mentally ill. While the words have evolved, their associations have not. Refugees are still treated like criminals, debtors, and mentally ill. Yet it is their social, political, and legal situation that turns them into criminals, debtors, and mentally ill. War, violence, famine, and climate change, combined with national borders, laws of citizenship, and international laws governing refugees, create the refugee as criminal, debtor, and mentally ill. First, the refugee suffers violence and trauma at home, then she makes the perilous escape, leaving behind home and belongings, to make the dangerous journey to seek asylum elsewhere. She suffers violence and trauma, leaves everything behind, becomes homeless, and then becomes a criminal and suffers further trauma because of her status as refugee.

National borders and international conventions governing asylum seekers create the refugee. Moreover, they create her as destitute, criminal, and mentally ill. Insofar as she must leave her home country, she becomes homeless and dependent on others for basic needs; insofar as national and international law requires that she leave her home country and make her request for asylum on foreign soil (and usually to do so as an illegal alien), she is made criminal; and the trauma she has suffered at home, the trauma that justifies and legitimates her status as refugee and asylum seeker, creates her as mentally ill. For, in order to legitimately gain refugee status and be accepted into her host country, she must convincingly testify to the *trauma* of violence and *fear* of persecution. She must convince authorities that she is afraid for her life, that she has been traumatized—in effect, that she has suffered mentally as well as physically.

Yet, as the UNHCR guidelines for interviewing asylum seekers make clear, cultural differences and translation problems are significant dangers in the determination of refugee status. The guidelines give a striking example of the danger of mistranslation:

> A Turkish asylum-seeker, applying for refugee status in Switzerland, stated that he had escaped arrest by hiding in the mountains near his home town. The application was rejected. Among the reasons given was the fact that the town was situated amid hills. For the Swiss interviewer there were no mountains in the region and thus the applicant was considered to be not credible. However, in Turkish, the term "mountain" also applies to hilly regions.[32]

As the guidelines warn, "Notions of time, of truth and falsehood can also vary from culture to culture and give rise to misunderstandings that put the asylum-seekers' credibility in doubt."[33] Yet, in spite of the monumental risk of misinterpretation and mistranslation, every day, interviews determine the fate of asylum seekers based on this faulty process.

The UNHCR guidelines on interviewing asylum seekers also includes several sections on addressing and navigating trauma in order to determine the truth of the applicant's testimony. The guidelines point out that people suffering from trauma may give inconsistent testimony, be unable to testify, or even become aggressive when questioned as a result of trauma. Yet the document also insists on verification of the truth of the testimony and resolving inconsistencies through confrontation techniques. While the UNHCR convention clearly states that an asylum seeker must fear returning to her country and must fear persecution based on belonging to a certain group in particular, the interview guidelines admit that fear may adversely affect the interview process. So how does one testify to fear in a way that is convincing? The guidelines warn against rehearsed scripted testimony and against retraumatizing applicants. So how does an interviewer determine the veracity of claims to fear? How can fear be quantified and accessed? Assuming that fear is an emotional or mental state, what formula can interviewers use to assess the legitimacy of fear insofar as it corresponds to actual events? Indeed, in trauma theory and psychoanalytic theory, trauma is often considered an experience that cannot be put into words, an experience that falls outside of linear time and rational comprehension.

So what does it mean to testify to the trauma of persecution? What does it mean to *prove* trauma, especially mental trauma or posttraumatic stress disorder (PTSD)? Furthermore, how much trauma is enough to justify asylum? And how does one convince administrators and interviewers that one's trauma is real? Although humanitarian aid organizations, including Doctors Without Borders, now include mental health professionals and psychologists, there are woefully inadequate resources to treat mental health issues in refugee camps and migrant detention centers, even though many refugees and asylum seekers fleeing war and violence suffer from PTSD. One study of refugee camps in Germany "found that half of refugees are experiencing psychological distress and mental illness resulting from trauma" and that "one fifth of refugee children are also suffering from PTSD."[34] As historian Michael Barnett suggests, we have entered an era of trauma wherein the violence of persecution at home is measured not only in terms of physical scars but also in terms of mental scars, and humanitarian aid includes treatment not only for physical wounds but also for mental wounds.

We could go further and claim that current international policy and practices governing the treatment and status of refugees require testimony to trauma that puts the refugee into an impossible subject position with regard to his or her own experience.[35] Refugees are required to both prove suffering and trauma in their home countries while also demonstrating that they did everything in their power to overcome those obstacles before fleeing. This is, they must testify to both their helplessness and their own resilience in escape. They must prove both their radical victimization and their own sovereignty. Being accepted as a legitimate refugee requires documentable and verifiable fear and trauma. Yet this position as "shipwrecked" person to be saved or rescued undermines agency and self-sovereignty and creates an aporetic subject position impossible to maintain. Asylum seekers are expected to take matters into their own hands and actively flee violence, but in doing so, they become helpless, passive victims to be rescued—victims of rescue politics.

THE SPECIAL STATUS OF CHILDREN'S TESTIMONY

At the other end of the spectrum, reactionary polices of some countries, such as the United States and Hungary, treat refugees as criminals rather than as charity cases (to use Arendt's binary). Recently, the "zero tolerance" policy of the United States for illegal immigrants has led to dire consequences for asylum seekers, especially parents and children who have been separated at the border. Refugee and migrant children have a special status insofar as (in addition to the translation and language issues raised above) they are often unable to testify to their own refugee status because of their age and their knowledge and experience of their own situation. Current international refugee law does not make special accommodations for children who cannot testify on their own behalf,[36] yet children play a central role in the public visibility of the refugee crisis.

Most of us remember the horror of seeing pictures of the tiny body of three-year-old Alan Kurdi lying face-down on a Turkish beach or the small, ash-covered face of Omran Daqneesh as he was placed in an ambulance in Aleppo. Alan and Omran became tragic "poster children" for the violence in Syria that led to one of the most publicized (if not the biggest) refugee crises in modern history. Today in the United States, we face a border crisis closer to home. While refugees from violence in the Northern Triangle of Central America—El Salvador, Honduras, and Guatemala—have increased dramatically, the recent policies of the Trump administration, including ending temporary protected status, zero tolerance, and the separation of children from their parents, have intensified trauma and harm to refugees and migrants at our own borders.

The most heinous consequence of the Trump administration's zero-tolerance policy is the separation of children from their parents. In just six weeks, between April 19 and May 31, 2018, nearly 2,000 children were taken from their parents. Some parents were told their children were being taken for a bath but then did not see them again.[37] Hundreds of children are being detained in prison-like facilities and locked in cells with dozens of others and with only food and water and very little care.[38] Guards have been instructed not to touch them or even to comfort or care for them.[39] For example, Associated Press News reported,

> Michelle Brane, director of migrant rights at the Women's Refugee Commission, met with a 16-year-old girl who had been taking care of a young girl for three days. The teen and others in their cage thought the girl was 2 years old. "She had to teach other kids in the cell to change her diaper," Brane said. Brane said that after an attorney started to ask questions, agents found the girl's aunt

> and reunited the two. It turned out that the girl was actually 4 years old. Part of the problem was that she didn't speak Spanish, but K'iche, a language indigenous to Guatemala. "She was so traumatized that she wasn't talking," Brane said. "She was just curled up in a little ball."[40]

This example points to the special status of dependent children who cannot yet take care of themselves and cannot articulate their needs, let alone recount their histories, even when they do speak the same language as their captors or officials. Children as young as three years old are facing court alone and being asked to explain why they fled their home countries.[41] Young children often do not know the circumstances that led their parents to flee. Even if they did, they may not be able to articulate those circumstances or the dangers of returning. Obviously, it is unreasonable to expect children to make credible and convincing arguments for asylum. In the words of Dr. Benard Dreyer, director of pediatrics at the New York University School of Medicine, "Given the trauma the children faced in their home country that spurred their families to flee and the pain of being separated from a parent, the expectation that children can mount a legal defense is unconscionable."[42]

American law provides special protections for children, yet refugee and migrant children have been stripped of all but the most basic protections. Given restricted access to facilities and the secrecy surrounding them, it is likely that in some facilities, even the most basic needs are not being met. If citizen-parents treated their children in the way that our government is treating refugee and migrant children—namely, locking them in cages with instructions not to touch them—they could face investigation by Child Protective Services for child neglect and abuse.

The Trump administration is using refugee and migrant children as political pawns to force Congress to negotiate on the issue of immigration and Trump's border wall and to deter parents from seeking asylum or trying to enter the United States illegally.[43] It is morally wrong to punish innocent children for their parent's illegal entry, yet imprisonment, detention, and the accompanying trauma is the penalty to be paid by refugee and migrant children who reach the U.S. border. The policy of zero tolerance is cruel and unusual punishment for both parents and children, guilty of illegal entry (a misdemeanor) or not.

It is important to point out that many of these families are refugees fleeing violence and seeking asylum in the United States. In other words, they are not migrants entering the country illegally except in the sense that most refugees enter their host country illegally, which is to say without proper documentation. Most people fleeing totalitarian regimes have difficulty obtaining passports or other official documentation. The Immigration and Naturalization

Act allows refugees to seek asylum whether they enter through a port of entry or not and whether they have passports or not.[44]

The current zero-tolerance policy of the United States violates not only national law but also international law. The fundamental principle of the UN Convention on Refugees stipulates that a refugee should not be returned to a country where they face serious threats to their life or freedom, what is called the principle of *non-refoulement*. While poverty and climate change may cause displacement and threaten life and freedom and while in these cases the distinction between refugees and economic migrants becomes more difficult, international law is clear that those fleeing persecution in countries that cannot or will not protect them are considered refugees and not migrants. For better or worse, the distinction between refugee and migrant is central to international law protecting refugees from non-refoulement.

The Trump administration is violating international law insofar as it does not recognize the distinction between refugees and migrants.[45] Even those already in the United States are not safe. In May 2018, the Trump administration ended the policy of temporary protected status for 90,000 Central Americans living in the United States, threatening to deport refugees who will face violence and possible death if returned.[46] And, for the record, the current administration has set the lowest cap on refugees in U.S. history.[47]

Tens of thousands of women and children flee violence in the Northern Triangle region of Central America and seek asylum in the United States and Mexico. Worldwide, El Salvador, Honduras, and Guatemala rank first, third, and seventh, respectively, for rates of homicides of women.[48] Most of the refugees from this region are women escaping repeated rape, assault, extortion, threats from armed criminal gangs, watching their children being recruited into gangs or killed, and watching other family members being murdered or disappearing while authorities do nothing. Often, they reach a breaking point when their lives are in imminent danger unless they flee immediately. But escaping presents its own dangers, as women are forced to pay exorbitant fees to "coyotes" and then suffer more rape, beating, and sometimes murder by these human traffickers. If they reach Mexico or the United States, these women face detention, a lack of adequate health care, and lengthy interrogations, which too often exacerbate their psychological trauma, and then there is no guarantee that they will be given asylum rather than sent back home to face more violence.

Today, in addition to these dangers, if they reach what should be safe asylum, women escaping gang violence at home face the trauma of separation from their children. These women risk their lives to protect their children, only to have them taken away. People escaping violence and abuse should be welcomed as refugees and not be treated as criminals. Even when parents cross the border illegally, their children should not be punished, especially not with the trauma of separation and detention. The Trump administration's policies are immoral (if not also illegal). The policy of separating children from their parents is cruel and unusual punishment, in many cases levied against refugees who are protected by international law.

Speaking for herself and other refugees from World War II, Hannah Arendt says, "If we are saved we feel humiliated, and if we are helped we feel degraded."[49] She points out that because refugees "voluntarily" entered detention centers and camps, their interment is justified. This sentiment is alive and well today, as some callously claim that if refugees do not like conditions in the camps, they can stay home or go back home. Yet in what sense is the perilous journey of most refugees "voluntary"? The status of the refugee calls into question categories of active and passive, sovereign and victim, voluntary and forced.

Arendt argues that refugees are considered both as pariahs sucking up resources that could go to rightful citizens and as parvenus, social climbers not truly fleeing violence or trauma but rather migrating for a better life abroad. Arendt's observations are apt today when reactions to images of refugees fleeing violence in Syria include fear of them taking jobs or resources from host countries already dealing with high unemployment and poverty (such as Greece and Turkey) or refugees fleeing violence in the Northern Triangle of Central America or Mexico being referred to as an "infestation" from "shithole" countries by the president of the United States.[50] Some expressed bewilderment as to why Syrian refugees have cell phones and nice clothes if they are so badly off. And, whether seen as charity case or social climber, Arendt says that "history has forced the status of outlaws upon both, upon pariahs and parvenus alike."[51] Today, rescue politics and carceral humanitarianism produce the helpless, homeless refugees as both charity cases and criminals in order to justify detaining, monitoring, controlling, and containing them.

HOSPITALITY AND EARTH ETHICS

We must move beyond both rescue politics and carceral humanitarianism, which entails moving beyond fenced and walled national borders. To do so, we must reconceive of our relationships to other people who share planet Earth beyond citizenship and national identity. Furthermore, we must think of our obligations to others not only in terms of human rights or humanitarian aid but also in terms of radical hospitality and responsibility. I propose an Earth ethics wherein our obligations are based on our common planetary home rather than on our national or individual homes. Rather than see ourselves as Americans or Europeans, offering aid to others less fortunate, we should see ourselves as earthlings sharing the planet. Rather than a rescue politics that requires perilous escape and lifeboat scenarios, we should consider our ethical obligations beyond national borders and beyond mere physical proximity. Once we consider our position in relation to others from an earthly perspective, we can no longer deny our interdependence and our shared dependence on each other and our planetary home.

Jacques Derrida insists that the hospitality is not simply one obligation among others but rather that "ethics is so thoroughly coextensive with the experience of hospitality.[52] Yet there is a tension at the heart of hospitality between the need for a home with doors and windows, fences, and borders—that is, limits—and the openness required by unconditional hospitality. To be a host, one must have a home. Derrida's hyperbolic account of hospitality points to the assumptions of mastery and sovereignty already operating in our everyday notions of hospitality, especially when it comes to welcoming foreigners and refugees.[53]

Certainly, national sovereignty is part and parcel of the law of hospitality, particularly as it is set out in international law concerning refugees and asylum seekers. Yet as Derrida argues, national sovereignty is always in an "autoimmune" relationship with democracy.[54] That is, in order to avoid the worst violence and maintain democracy, we must allow the possibility of the worst to enter. This is the autoimmune logic of hospitality. It must always remain open to what comes, for better or worse. And while our practices of hospitality can never live up to this ideal, without holding onto the concept of just unconditional, impossible hospitality, our everyday practices of hospitality are hollow illusions of hospitality and self-deception at best or alibis for continued violence at worst.

In fact, Derrida claims that as soon as we identify the guest as foreigner (or refugee), we have already done him violence by reducing him to a category that we think we understand. Furthermore, by questioning him, we continue our violence not only because we may do so in a language unknown to him and because we most likely are interrogating him in an unfamiliar legal process but also because we are calling on him to account for himself and thereby subjecting him to our assumed superior judgment.[55]

In light of Derrida's standard of unconditional or just hospitality, the carceral humanitarian aid of refugee camps and detention centers falls far short. Indeed, camps and lockups hardly meet the basic criteria for limited, conditional hospitality. For, with very few exceptions, it is difficult to use the word "hospitality" to describe the situation of most refugees and asylum seekers when they arrive at the borders of their host countries, countries that have barely begun to provide even for the basic needs of refugees and asylum seekers or to provide the basic human rights supposedly guaranteed by international conventions.

So what would it mean to think beyond rights discourse, beyond borders, beyond detention centers and refugee camps, and toward justice as radical hospitality? First, we would have to move beyond notions of national sovereignty and citizenship. Rather than starting with human rights or citizen's rights as the basis of political (or ethical) obligations, we would have to acknowledge our interdependence on this shared planet, our only home. Rather than claim the sovereign right to welcome others into our own homes, we would have to acknowledge that the foundation for that home is Earth itself, which belongs to us not as property but rather as what we share with every other earthling. In other words, the grounds for our claiming any home at all is the home we all share, planet Earth. Insofar as climate change and climate displacement exacerbate if not cause most forced migration on the planet today, we need to come to terms with the fact that Earth is our only home, and therefore we have an obligation to it and to those with whom we share the planet.

In the past seven years, an estimated one person every second has been displaced by a disaster, and that number is on the rise thanks to climate change and poor design and planning.[56] There is evidence that climate change plays a central role in mass migrations in Africa and has led to hundreds of thousands in refugee camps.[57] The problem of climate refugees is only going to get worse, and international law and UN guidelines do not consider those escaping natural disasters and drought or climate change as refugees. Can we say that people fleeing drought and famine or flooding and receding shores in their homelands are being persecuted? In what sense do climate refugees meet the definition of refugees set out in international law?

These questions make clear the need to rethink refugees beyond identity politics that requires one group at war with another or the persecution of one group by another. Even in the Syrian refugee crisis, it is not clear in what sense refugees and asylum seekers are being singled out as part of a group and then targeted for violence, which is a standard criterion for determining refugee status under the UN guidelines. Rather, as I argued above, we could say that they become a group, "refugees" or "asylum seekers," only by virtue of national and international laws that create them as such. They become a group, even a persecuted group, only after they escape violence and famine in their home countries. Earth ethics requires us to begin to think of ourselves and our relation to each other beyond group or national identities and toward interrelationality determined by the interconnectedness of ecosystems and our biosphere. As I have argued elsewhere, we need to embrace an Earth ethics as a response ethics through which we consider our obligations to others as obligations to ourselves and vice versa, for our very survival depends on it.[58]

We need to respond to others in ways that open up rather than close down the possibility of response.

In terms of refugees and asylum seekers, whether they are escaping the violence of civil war, natural disasters, or climate change, they should not be detained, incarcerated, or locked into camps. It is national and international law that makes these people "criminals" when, in practice, they are forced to enter illegally, which, as we have seen, is then used to justify their internment. In sum, refugees are not criminals to be locked up. The current conditions in refugee camps and detention centers violate the basic human rights supposedly guaranteed by international law and UN conventions on refugees and asylum seekers. More than this, rescue politics and carceral humanitarian create an impossible subject position, "the refugee," that simultaneously requires and undermines both national and individual sovereignty. Incarcerating and interning refugees is not only politically wrong in terms of our own standards set out by the United Nations but also ethically wrong in terms of our obligations to each other as coinhabitants of our shared planetary home.

NOTES

1. Hannah Arendt, "We Refugees," in *Altogether Elsewhere: Writers on Exile*, ed. Marc Robinson (Boston: Faber & Faber, 1994), 111.
2. Eleanor Acer and Jessica Chicco, "U.S. Detention of Asylum Seekers: Seeking Protection, Finding Prison," Human Rights First, 2009, https://www.humanrightsfirst.org/wp-content/uploads/pdf/090429-RP-hrf-asylum-detention-report.pdf. See also Megan Granski, Allen Keller, and Homer Venters, "Death Rates among Detained Immigrants in the United States," *International Journal of Environmental Research and Public Health* 12 (2015): 14414–19.
3. "Migrant Crisis: Migration to Europe Explained in Seven Charts," *BBC*, March 4, 2016, http://www.bbc.com/news/world-europe-34131911.
4. See Martina Tazzioli, "The Politics of Counting and the Scene of Rescue: Border Deaths in the Mediterranean," *Radical Philosophy* 192 (2015): 2–6.
5. The UN High Commissioner for Refugees (UNHCR) reports that in the first eight months of 2015, more than 300,000 refugees and migrants crossed the Mediterranean Sea seeking asylum in Europe. More than 2,500 died in those months, and in 2014, 3,500 died. See Melissa Fleming, "Crossings of Mediterranean Sea Exceeds 300,000, Including 200,000 to Greece," *UNHCR: The UN Refugee Agency*, August 28, 2015, http://www.unhcr.org/en-us/news/latest/2015/8/55e06a5b6/crossings-mediterranean-sea-exceed-300000-including-200000-greece.html. See also Tazzioli, "The Politics of Counting and the Scene of Rescue."
6. "Hundreds of Refugees Died on Way to Europe This Year," *Aljazeera*, February 9, 2016, http://www.aljazeera.com/news/2016/02/400-refugees-die-europe-2016-160209133941502.html.

7. "Mediterranean Situation," United Nations High Commissioner for Refugees, Data Portal, November 27, 2017, http://data2.unhcr.org/en/situations/mediterranean.

8. "Figures at a Glance," United Nations High Commissioner for Refugees, November 27, 2017, http://www.unhcr.org/en-us/figures-at-a-glance.html.

9. Mac McClelland, "How to Build a Perfect Refugee Camp," *New York Times Magazine*, February 13, 2014, https://www.nytimes.com/2014/02/16/magazine/how-to-build-a-perfect-refugee-camp.html.

10. "A Closer Look at 'Europe's Worst' Refugee Camp," Sputnik International, January 24, 2016, https://sptnkne.ws/g6w9.

11. Amelia Gentleman, "The Horror of the Calais Refugee Camp: 'We Feel Like We Are Dying Slowly,'" *The Guardian*, November 3, 2015, https://www.theguardian.com/world/2015/nov/03/refugees-horror-calais-jungle-refugee-camp-feel-like-dying-slowly.

12. David Courbet, "Migrants at Calais Camp Given Dignity in Death," *The Local*, May 23, 2016, https://www.thelocal.fr/20160523/migrants-at-calais-camp-given-dignity-in-death.

13. "Almost 130 Refugee Kids Vanish after the 'Calais Jungle' Demolition—Charity," RT, April 3, 2016, https://www.rt.com/news/338217-129-kids-missing-in-calais.

14. Will Worley and Lizzie Dearden, "Greek Refugee Camp Is 'as Bad as a Nazi Concentration Camp,' Says Minister," *Independent*, March 18, 2016, https://www.independent.co.uk/news/world/europe/idomeni-refugee-dachau-nazi-concentration-camp-greek-minister-a6938826.html.

15. Worley and Dearden, "Greek Refugee Camp Is 'as Bad as a Nazi Concentration Camp,' Says Minister."

16. Gentleman, "The Horror of the Calais Refugee Camp."

17. Jim Yardley and Gaia Pianigiani, "Three Days, 700 Deaths on Mediterranean as Migrant Crisis Flares," *New York Times*, May 29, 2016, https://www.nytimes.com/2016/05/30/world/europe/migrants-deaths-mediterranean-libya-italy.html.

18. Devon Cone, "The Process for Interviewing, Vetting, and Resettling Syrian Refugees in America Is Incredibly Long and Thorough," *Foreign Policy*, November 30, 2015, http://foreignpolicy.com/2015/11/30/the-process-for-interviewing-vetting-and-resettling-syrian-refugees-in-america-is-incredibly-long-and-thorough. Thanks to Jennifer Newman for bringing this to my attention.

19. Janet Golden, "What Will Today's Immigration Detention Centers Look Like to Future Americans?," *The Inquirer*, June 22, 2016, http://www.philly.com/philly/blogs/public_health/What-will-todays-immigration-detention-centers-look-like-to-future-Americans-.html.

20. See Granski et al., "Death Rates among Detained Immigrants in the United States."

21. "US: Deaths in Immigration Detention: Newly Released Records Suggest Dangerous Lapses in Medical Care," Human Rights Watch, July 7, 2016, https://www.hrw.org/news/2016/07/07/us-deaths-immigration-detention. See also "Will the Immigration Detention System Finally Get the Reforms It Desperately Needs?,"

Human Rights First, August 7, 2009, https://www.humanrightsfirst.org/2009/08/07/will-the-immigration-detention-system-finally-get-the-reforms-it-desperately-needs.

22. "US: Deaths in Immigration Detention"; "Will the Immigration Detention System Finally Get the Reforms It Desperately Needs?"

23. By all accounts, the term "genocide" was first used by Raphael Lemkin, a Polish Jewish lawyer who fled Nazi Germany to the United States during World War II. Rather than limit genocide to mass murder, Lemkin's definition includes "the destruction of the personal security, liberty, health, dignity, and even the lives of the individuals belonging to [national] groups." See Office of the UN Special Adviser on the Prevention of Genocide, "Analysis Framework," http://www.un.org/ar/preventgenocide/adviser/pdf/osapg_analysis_framework.pdf. Some theorists make a distinction between genocide and politicide wherein victims are targets for their political status. We could argue that refugees are victims of both. Cf. Barbara Harff and Ted Robert Gurr, "Toward Empirical Theory of Genocides and Politicides: Identification and Measurement of Cases since 1945," *International Studies Quarterly* 32, no. 3 (September 1988): 359–71.

24. Gentleman, "The Horror of the Calais Refugee Camp."

25. Gentleman, "The Horror of the Calais Refugee Camp."

26. Gentleman, "The Horror of the Calais Refugee Camp."

27. Tazzioli, "The Politics of Counting and the Scene of Rescue."

28. Tazzioli, "The Politics of Counting and the Scene of Rescue."

29. "The 1951 Refugee Convention," *UNHCR: The UN Refugee Agency*, http://www.unhcr.org/en-us/1951-refugee-convention.html.

30. "refugee, n.," *OED Online*, January 2018, http://www.oed.com/view/Entry/161121.

31. "asylum, n.," *OED Online*, January 2018, http://www.oed.com/view/Entry/12340.

32. "Interviewing Applicants for Refugee Status (RLD 4)," *UNHCR: The UN Refugee Agency*, 1995, http://www.unhcr.org/4d9485a69.pdf. Thanks to Jennifer Newman for bringing these guidelines to my attention.

33. "Interviewing Applicants for Refugee Status (RLD 4)."

34. Deirdre Finnerty, "Migration Crisis: Trauma Takes a Toll on Mental Health," *BBC*, December 22, 2015, http://www.bbc.com/news/world-europe-35102320.

35. For a sustained discussion of the paradox of testifying to your own trauma and oppressions, see Kelly Oliver, *Witnessing: Beyond Recognition* (Minneapolis: University of Minnesota Press, 2001).

36. For an excellent analysis of the special status of refugee children and the inadequacy of current international law, see Long Adams, "Overlooked and Underserved: The Radical Vulnerability and Victimhood of Refugee Children" (honor's thesis, Vanderbilt University, 2018).

37. Reade Levinson and Mica Rosenberg, "U.S. Government Says Nearly 2000 Child Separations at Mexico Border in Under Two Months," *Reuters*, June 15, 2018, https://ca.reuters.com/article/topNews/idCAKBN1JB2SF-OCATP.

38. Sean Sullivan, "Zero Tolerance Policy Means Zero Humanity," *Washington Post*, June 17, 2018, https://www.washingtonpost.com/politics/zero-tolerance-policy-means-zero-humanity-democrats-decry-trump-immigration-policy-after

-tour-of-detention-center/2018/06/17/bbf68b2c-7248-11e8-9780-b1dd6a09b549_story.html?utm_term=.6bbdea79f34c.

39. Laura Bush, "Separating Children from Their Parents at the Border Breaks My Heart," *Washington Post*, June 16, 2018, https://www.washingtonpost.com/opinions/laura-bush-separating-children-from-their-parents-at-the-border-breaks-my-heart/2018/06/17/f2df517a-7287-11e8-9780-b1dd6a09b549_story.html?utm_term=.e2c03ba2fcd6.

40. Nomaan Merchant, "Hundreds of Children Wait in Border Patrol Facility in Texas," *AP News*, June 18, 2018, https://www.apnews.com/amp/9794de32d39d4c6f89fbefaea3780769.

41. Christina Jewett and Shefali Luthra, "Immigrant Toddlers Ordered to Appear in Court Alone," *Texas Tribune*, June 27, 2018, https://www.texastribune.org/2018/06/27/immigrant-toddlers-ordered-appear-court-alone.

42. Jewett and Luthra, "Immigrant Toddlers Ordered to Appear in Court Alone."

43. James Homann, "Trump Team Cannot Get Its Story Straight," *Washington Post*, June 18, 2018, https://www.washingtonpost.com/news/powerpost/paloma/daily-202/2018/06/18/daily-202-trump-team-cannot-get-its-story-straight-on-separating-migrant-families/5b2701f030fb046c468e6ef6/?utm_term=.3cabe6bb1f9d.

44. Jasmine Garsd, "What Zero Tolerance Policy Means for People Fleeing Violence," *PRI*, May 18, 2018, https://www.pri.org/stories/2018-05-18/what-zero-tolerance-policy-border-means-people-fleeing-violence.

45. Garsd, "What Zero Tolerance Policy Means for People Fleeing Violence."

46. See Tal Kopan, "DHS Ends Protections for Nearly 90,000 Central Americans," *CNN*, May 6, 2018, https://www.cnn.com/2018/05/04/politics/immigration-tps-honduras/index.html.

47. Julie Davis and Miriam Jordan, "Trump Plans Limit on Refugees," *New York Times*, September 26, 2017, https://www.nytimes.com/2017/09/26/us/politics/trump-plans-45000-limit-on-refugees-admitted-to-us.html.

48. UNHCR, "Women on the Run," 2015, http://www.unhcr.org/publications/operations/5630f24c6/women-run.html.

49. Arendt, "We Refugees," 114.

50. David Graham, "Trump Says Democrats Want Illegal Immigrants to 'Infest' the U.S.," *The Atlantic*, June 19, 2018, https://www.theatlantic.com/politics/archive/2018/06/trump-immigrants-infest/563159.

51. Graham, "Trump Says Democrats Want Illegal Immigrants to 'Infest' the U.S.," 119.

52. Jacques Derrida, *On Cosmopolitanism and Forgiveness*, trans. Mark Dooley and Michael Hughes (New York: Routledge, 2001), 16–17.

53. Jacques Derrida, "Hospitality," *Angelaki: Journal of the Theoretical Humanities* 5, no. 3 (2000), 14.

54. Derrida, "Hospitality," 5.

55. See Derrida, "Hostipitality"; see also Jacques Derrida, "Hospitality."

56. Norwegian Refugee Council, "19.3 Million Displaced by Disasters but 'Mother Nature Not to Blame' Says New Report," *Internal Displacement Monitoring*

Centre, July 20, 2015, http://www.internal-displacement.org/sites/default/files/inline-files/20150706-GE-2015Press-release-FINAL-v1.pdf.

57. Peter Schwartzstein, "The Climate-Change Refugee Crisis Is Only Just Beginning," *Quartz*, January 31, 2016, https://qz.com/605609/the-climate-change-refugee-crisis-is-only-just-beginning. See also Josh Hrala, "Global Warming Could Trigger a 'Climate Exodus' from The Middle East and North Africa," *Science Alert*, May 4, 2016, https://www.sciencealert.com/global-warming-may-trigger-a-climate-exodus-in-parts-of-the-middle-east-and-north-africa.

58. See Kelly Oliver, *Earth and World* (New York: Columbia University Press, 2015).

Chapter Eight

Beyond the Ethics of Admission

Statelessness, Refugee Camps, and Moral Obligations

Serena Parekh

Statelessness, the existence of millions of people who do not belong in a meaningful sense to any political community, is an increasingly important political problem. On the one hand, there are more than 65 million people who have been forcibly displaced from their homes and have no effective citizenship, the majority of whom remain in this situation for on average seventeen years. On the other hand, each state—rightly or wrongly—believes that it is justified in including only those individuals whom they choose to admit. In other words, most states do not acknowledge an obligation to admit people who have nowhere else to live, and when they do accept refugees, it is considered an ex gratia policy, arising out of generosity rather than the fulfillment of a moral or legal norm. The result is a situation in which a population larger than that of the United Kingdom—one in every 100 of the world's citizens—lives more or less permanently outside the nation-state system, and no state acknowledges political or moral responsibility for this group.[1]

Given the political importance of this phenomenon, I argue in this chapter that philosophers ought to be concerned with clarifying our moral obligations to people living in a condition of statelessness. For the sake of simplicity, I will refer to people in this situation as refugees, though most would not qualify in the legal sense of this term. To do this, I argue that we need to reframe both our understanding of the problem of statelessness in the contemporary world and our understanding of the obligations that this situation gives rise to.

This chapter has two sections. In the first section, I critically assess philosophical analyses of the problem of refugees. Philosophical discourse has focused largely on whether we in the West have moral obligations to admit refugees or whether we can morally justify closing our borders. In other words, philosophers have focused largely on an *ethics of admission.* I show that though this is an important question, it is too narrow. By focusing on admission, philosophers have been effectively concerned with only de jure refugees, people who are eligible for admission to a new country, and have failed to consider the obligations we may have to people who remain outside of all political communities for prolonged periods of time. The focus on the ethics of admission renders the vast majority of refugees normatively invisible and does not fully address the situation of statelessness in the global context described above.

In the second section of the chapter, I argue that in order to understand our moral obligations to both de jure and de facto refugees, we ought to reconceptualize the harm of statelessness as entailing both a legal/political harm (the loss of citizenship) and an *ontological* harm, a deprivation of certain fundamental human qualities. To do this, I draw on the work of Hannah Arendt and show that the ontological deprivation has three distinct though interconnected elements: a reduction to the merely human or bare life, a separation from the common realm of humanity and abandonment, and the diminishment of agency or ability to *act* in the Arendtian sense. Yet it is important to note that for Arendt, though the ontological deprivation of statelessness is a fundamental one, it is not absolute. By this, I mean that though refugees have a diminished capacity to *act* in Arendt's distinct sense, they always retain this ability at a fundamental level. This is because for Arendt, action is rooted in the human condition of *natality*, the fact that we are beings who are born and are beginners by our very nature. Refugees always have the possibility for action. However, what is important about the ontological deprivation is that refugees, in virtue of this status, are deprived of two other conditions that are essential for action: a public space to make opportunities for action more than rare exceptions and an ability to be judged *as* speaking and acting agents. Consequently, I argue that Arendt is able to give us a framework for understanding why statelessness is a fundamental harm yet without denying that refugees retain their humanity and capacity for agency in a basic way.

On my reading of Arendt, the problem with statelessness is that it has these two distinct though interrelated harms: a legal/political harm and an ontological one. The main goal of this chapter is to establish that statelessness ought to be understood as entailing both sets of harms. If we pull these two sets of harms apart, we are better able to see that we can address some of the features of the ontological deprivation even though we may not be able to rectify the political harm through resettlement. I conclude by suggesting that our obligations to refugees will consist in changing our policies and practices toward refugees in order to minimize, if not eliminate, the ontological deprivation. Ultimately, the challenge will be to create spaces and conditions where refugees can be seen and heard, where their action and speech can gain meaning, so that we can come to see them as equal members of our common humanity, whether or not we also acknowledge them as citizens.

REFUGEES AND THE ETHICS OF ADMISSION

Michael Walzer was one of the first philosophers to discuss our moral obligations to refugees, and he initiated the debate by stressing that refugees differ from immigrants in general because of the *moral* dimension of their claims. Refugees, he writes, "make the most forceful claim for admission. 'If you don't take me in,' they say, 'I shall be killed, persecuted, brutally oppressed by the rulers of my own country.'"[2] Walzer defined refugees as people whose moral claims "cannot be met by yielding territory or exporting wealth, but *only* by taking people in."[3] Because he understands refugees as suffering a political loss, the loss of political belonging, he argues that our moral obligations to them can be met *only* by admitting them to our country. This definition laid the foundation for the contemporary debate around moral obligations to refugees in philosophy.

Since Walzer put forth this view, a number of other philosophers have entered the debate. For example, Barbieri, Carens, Cole, Gibney, Miller, Nyers, Singer and Singer, and Wellman, among others, have all written about our moral obligations to refugees.[4] Although there is no consensus on the question of what these obligations are exactly, there is one important point that is agreed on by all these authors: the question of whether we are obliged to admit refugees to our country is *the* primary moral question. Indeed, this question remains the dominant one whether or not you agree that we have had much stronger obligations to admit refugees than we currently do (as people like Benhabib, Barbieri, Carens, and Singer and Singer do) or that states are justified in closing their doors to "all potential immigrants, even refugees desperately seeking asylum from incompetent or corrupt political regimes."[5] Regardless of the outcome, justifying including or excluding the displaced from our political communities has been *the* primary task for philosophers.

Although the ethics of admission remains an important area of concern, I argue below that we ought to expand our philosophical analysis beyond it. Concentrating exclusively on an ethics of admission focuses too narrowly to only one subset of displaced people: those deemed refugees according to the 1951 UN Refugee Convention and thus eligible for resettlement. For the vast majority of refugees, admission to a Western state is not even a possibility in the current international framework. Only about one-fifth of the people who are displaced are eligible for resettlement because they meet the UN criteria of a refugee; of those eligible, only a fraction are ever resettled (less than 1 percent).[6] As Loescher puts it, "The majority of the world's refugees are not offered permanent asylum or opportunity to integrate into local communities by most Third World governments. Rather, they are kept separate and dependent on external assistance provided by the international community."[7] As I show below, our ethical norms must be brought to bear on all people who are "kept separate" from the rest of humanity.

Because normative philosophy conceives of statelessness as primarily a legal and political harm—the loss of citizenship—it is unable to incorporate the deeper harm of statelessness in their analysis of our moral obligations to people in this situation. Consequently, I argue that we ought to turn to the work of Arendt to develop an understanding of statelessness that is more fitting for the contemporary global situation.

ARENDT ON STATELESSNESS: THE LEGAL DIMENSION

Arendt begins her analysis of statelessness in *The Origins of Totalitarianism* with the observation that starting shortly after World War I, the nature of forced migration began to change. While there had always been "war refugees" (as we would call them), what was unique about people fleeing after the war is that they "were welcomed nowhere and could be assimilated nowhere. Once they had left their homelands they remained homeless, once they had left their state they became stateless; once they had been deprived of their human rights they were rightless, the scum of the earth."[8] For Arendt, when a person lost her national citizenship and became stateless, she became "rightless" as well.

To clarify her terminology, Arendt distinguished between de jure and de facto refugees. De jure refugees are people who meet the legal definition of a refugee, as someone fleeing individual political persecution. Such people were not the real issue for Arendt. In fact, she claimed that they were not a "genuine political problem" since besides being relatively few in number, the asylum laws that existed at the time did act as a genuine substitute for national laws.[9] By contrast, de facto refugees, people who are effectively without citizenship regardless of their legal status, made up the "core of statelessness" for Arendt and were in her view identical with "the refugee question."[10] For Arendt, de facto refugees included all people who are forcibly displaced and without any form of effective citizenship or political belonging, regardless of how they are categorized legally (i.e., as refugees, asylum seekers, forcibly displaced, *sans papiers*, internally displaced persons, war refugees, and so on). People in this situation are, in her words, fundamentally rightless; they belong "to no internationally recognizable community whatever" and are thus outside "of mankind as a whole."[11]

What did it mean to become rightless for Arendt? For Arendt, the rightlessness that accompanies statelessness has two dimensions: a legal/political dimension and an ontological one. Legally, it meant that once you cease living under the jurisdiction of your domestic law, you were without the protection of any other law.[12] In other words, once you are removed from your own national law, there is no effective way to treat you as a legal subject. This is tied to her critique of human rights, which were understood as natural and inalienable and thus without the need for positive law to protect them. For her, "the loss of national rights was identical with the loss of human rights."[13] Thus, for refugees, as soon as they lost their citizenship and had only their humanity and human rights to protect them, it turned out that there was no institution willing and able to guarantee them. Human rights proved impossible to enforce outside of a political community.

This point has been somewhat mitigated since Arendt wrote this in 1948 with the advent of numerous human rights treaties and declarations, especially the UN Refugee Convention (1951) and its 1967 Protocol and other treaties concerning refugees, all of which were designed precisely to address people who had lost the protection of their home states. Yet despite this legal progress, the consensus among many scholars is that the legal protection of refugees is at best precarious and at worst nonexistent.[14] Although there is a legal framework in existence for the protection of refugees, many states are still reluctant to acknowledge significant *obligations* to refugees. The most widely accepted obligation, non-refoulement, is often respected in principle though not in practice. Further, few states acknowledge positive obligations to help refugees by admitting them to their states or granting them the right to residence. Most nations feel that they *ought* to help refugees and that it would be wrong simply to let them die of starvation or exposure, but few see it as a moral, political, or legal obligation except in the most minimal sense. The United States, for example, firmly asserts that its policies concerning refugees are not rooted in the fulfillment of any international obligation but ought to be understood as "an exceptional *ex gratia* act provided by the United States in furthering foreign and humanitarian policies."[15] Given this, Arendt's fundamental critique of the way refugees are treated when they are outside of their state remains true: "the prolongation of their lives is due to charity and not to right, for no law exists which could force the nations to feed them."[16]

To summarize, Arendt's first critique of statelessness is that it entails the loss of a political community, and it is only within this political community that human rights can be protected. Despite more than fifty years of changes in international law and human rights conventions around refugees, their rights—both legal and human—remain fundamentally precarious outside the nation-state. Although this is a crucial point in understanding statelessness, it is not Arendt's most fundamental critique of statelessness. If this were the only harm of statelessness, we might say that the ethics of admissions is sufficient to deal with it. This is not the case however. As I argue below, Arendt demonstrated that there is a much more fundamental loss that comes with statelessness. I refer to this loss as the ontological deprivation.

THE ONTOLOGICAL DEPRIVATION

In this section, I argue that for Arendt, statelessness constitutes an ontological deprivation that contains three different dimensions: the loss of identity and reduction to bare life, the expulsion from common humanity, and, finally, the loss of agency understood not as a subjective disposition but as an ability to have your words and actions be recognized as meaningful and politically relevant. It might be objected that being a refugee does not change your *ontological* status, your being-in-the-world, but is better understood as an *epistemological* harm, a harm in how refugees are understood by others. As I argue below, there is certainly a dimension of epistemological harm: refugees are seen not as *who* they are as individuals but as *what* they are, bodies to be cared for, lives to be saved. This is the epistemological harm of misrecognition and a denial of their full humanity. But there also is something deeper going on here. Many refugees, in becoming stateless, come to experience themselves in a different way and come to relate to others and the common world differently. As I argue below, what Arendt is suggesting is that being stateless constitutes a fundamental change in their being, one that should be understood as a kind of ontological harm. This harm stands over and above the political deprivation of being a refugee (loss of citizenship and the rights of citizenship), the epistemological harm (of being misrecognized as less than fully human), and the material deprivation of losing your home and livelihood (and the ability to access food and other material resources). This is a harm that is often not fully appreciated and leads us to misunderstand our moral obligations to refugees.

The ontological deprivation begins with a transformation of personal identity. This transformation had two steps: refugees are first deprived of their original identities and then have their identities replaced with new ones. In Arendt's words, statelessness deprived a person "of all clearly established, officially recognized identity."[17] This was the basis of the most common complaint of refugees, from all levels of society, that "nobody here knows who I am."[18] The loss of a unique personal identity came hand in hand with being given a new identity: that of a human being in general, "without a profession, without a citizenship, without an opinion, without a deed by which to identify and specify himself."[19] Refugees appeared to the outside world as "nothing but human beings," entirely innocent and without responsibility.[20]

Importantly, this new identity rooted in our humanness did not give rise to respect, awe, or humanitarian sentiment as Enlightenment thinkers thought it would; quite the opposite: "the world found nothing sacred in the abstract nakedness of being human."[21] According to the traditional understanding of human rights, if a human being loses her political status, she should be able to fall back on her natural, inalienable human rights. "Actually the opposite is the case," writes Arendt. "It seems that a man who is nothing but a man has lost the very qualities which make it possible for other people to treat him as a fellow-man."[22] In other words, to be purely human is actually to be less than human or, at least, to be human in a way that people cannot recognize.

Why is this necessarily the case? Arendt was the first to observe that once a person is stripped of her political persona and citizenship, she appears as an abstract human being who, precisely because of this abstraction, does not appear to be fully human. Taking up this idea, Giorgio Agamben developed the concept of "bare life" to describe precisely what Arendt was referring to.[23] For Agamben, bare life refers to the separation of biological life from political existence. Agamben claims that the original foundation of politics is the exclusion of bare life. This can be traced to Aristotle's distinction between two fundamental kinds of life: *zoë*, the biological life that we share in common with animals, and *bios*, the kind of life that is distinctive to human beings, embodied in our political capacities for speech and action. Aristotle argued that *zoë*, biological life, ought to be excluded from the polis since politics was concerned with what was distinctly human. For Agamben, though the relationship between bare life and political life is complicated in modernity, bare life still cannot be part of political life and must remain separated from the polis. The modern nation-state, premised on the separation of *bios* and *zoë*, is incapable of dealing with refugees who have become "nothing but human" and must keep them in a permanent state of exclusion.[24] This is why he argues that "there is no autonomous space in the political order of the nation-state for something like the pure human itself."[25]

Taking his cue from Agamben and Arendt, the French anthropologist Michel Agier documents the way that bare life manifests itself in the current refugee regime. As he puts it, refugees "are certainly alive, but they no longer 'exist,' that is, they no longer have a social or political existence apart from their biological one."[26] This is in part because of the rationale for the existence of humanitarian agencies: they are supposed to protect people qua human being, not qua particular identity. Refugees must assume the standpoint of bare life in order to receive aid. Indeed, refugees can make claims for humanitarian aid and protection *only* as *bare life*, or, more specifically, bare life in need of protection as victims. With the loss of identity and reduction to victimhood, aid can come from states that may be either friendly or hostile. Humanitarian aid thus requires the "social and political non-existence of the beneficiaries of aid."[27] Rather than being political *subjects*, they become *objects* of humanitarian aid, bodies to be cared for and protected.

In sum, the first aspect of the ontological deprivation is that refugees are turned into human beings in general and bodies to be cared for rather than retaining their status as individuals with unique identities or political subjects whose particular existence matters. This ontological deprivation is solidified in the political structure such that humanitarian aid is available only on the basis of this transformation.

REJECTION AND ABANDONMENT

The second dimension of the ontological deprivation has to do with the exile from the common world that comes with statelessness. For many, refugee camps are a matter of practical necessity: there is nowhere else to put large groups of unwanted people. Yet for Arendt, I argue, it is important to see these camps as morally problematic because they effectively exclude people from what she referred to as "the common world." This expulsion from the common world is a fundamental aspect of the ontological deprivation.

As Agier puts it, refugees are often *physically* outside of the geographically recognized world. Refugee camps, for example, are often not even on maps, though they may have existed for a decade or longer.[28] Refugees are *economically* outside the common world since they are not permitted to engage in the global economy except through being passive recipients of and entirely dependent on the world's charity for their minimal biological existence. Finally, they are *socially and politically* outside the common world since they are denied social integration and political rights or agency in the states where they reside.[29] Since refugees are not permitted to integrate into the communities where they reside and very few are ever resettled, refugees spend the duration of their lives outside of any social or political community and thus are effectively excluded from the common realm.

For Arendt, this physical, economic, social, and political exclusion has an extra dimension: taken together, they represent the exclusion of refugees from the "common world." This exclusion constitutes part of the ontological deprivation because this means that an individual loses her place in a common public space from which action, speech, and hence identity become meaningful. For her, the common world "is not identical with the earth or with nature. . . . It is related, rather, to the human artifact, the fabrication of human hands, as well as to affairs which go on among those who inhabit the man-made world together."[30] The common world is what both relates us to each other as beings who must share the same worldly space and separates us from each other and allows us to maintain our individual identities. In this sense, the common world is the ground of plurality, our uniqueness and difference that is so fundamental to politics.

SPEECH, ACTION, AND THE THORNY QUESTION OF AGENCY

There is one more crucial element in the ontological deprivation that arises directly as a result of the first two transformations: statelessness diminishes a person's ability to speak and act in a meaningful way. In this sense, a stateless person has her political *agency* diminished, her ability to act in the specific Arendtian sense of the term, as the freedom to act *with* others and have actions and speech recognized as meaningful.

Action for Arendt is connected to *plurality*, the fact that as human we are both alike in fundamental ways and different. This urge to assert our difference within equality is the ontological root of action. This is why for Arendt it is only through action (rather than labor or work) that we reveal who we are as individuals and are able to mark our place in the world. In action and speech, "men show who they are, reveal actively their unique personal identities and thus make their appearance in a human world."[31]

Yet action is a basic human capacity that is rooted in *natality*, the fact that we are beings who are by nature beginners. In this sense of the term, action is not an achievement but a fundamental human capacity. To act in the most general sense means to begin, to set something into motion that can be neither predicted nor controlled. Action thus is "unexpected," and the "fact that man is capable of action means that the unexpected can be expected from him, that he is able to perform what is infinitely improbable."[32] This aspect of action is crucial because it demonstrates that Arendt is committed to the idea that even in the worst conditions—whether it be refugee camps today or concentration camps in the past—humans retain this powerful and surprising capacity to act and to begin.

Given Arendt's understanding of action, it is not surprising that the fundamental harm of statelessness is that it diminishes a person's ability to speak and act in a meaningful way. This occurs in several ways. First, because they are outside of the common world, refugees lack a reliable, durable space in which their actions can be seen and words understood. Recall that for Arendt, without "a politically guaranteed public realm, freedom lacks the worldly space to make its appearance."[33] This is not to say that Arendt believes that action can occur only in an institutionalized public setting or that only citizens can act. For Arendt, action requires a "space of appearance,"[34] and this emerges when people come together to act. Within these minimal conditions, refugees do act and speak. But what is lost with statelessness is the reliability and durability of a space of appearance that is "politically guaranteed." Without this, the political action of refugees is possible and does occur in exceptional circumstances but lacks the conditions that make action consistently meaningful.

This is why Arendt insists that refugees are in a fundamental condition of rightlessness even though they have certain rights in principle, such as freedom of expression or opinion. Without a political community, regardless of whether one is able to say what they think and believe, opinions and actions cease to matter. So fundamental is the intersubjective nature of speech and action that Arendt defines the most fundamental right, the right to have rights, as the right "to live in a framework where one is *judged* by one's actions and opinion."[35] Conversely, the deprivation of human rights "is manifested first and above all in the deprivation of a place in the world which makes opinions significant and actions effective."[36] One no longer has a common public realm to give one's actions and identity meaning. To be sure, it is not that refugees are no longer capable of speech and action but rather that, in their condition of rightlessness, it becomes hard if not impossible to recognize their words and actions as meaningful.[37]

I want to stress that for Arendt, the ontological deprivation is such a fundamental loss not because it means that a person *can* no longer speak or act but because they are no longer *judged* by their words and deeds and are judged instead according to what is "merely given" about their existence: the fact that they are human beings in general and bodies in need of protection. Because action is rooted in natality, it remains a fundamental human capacity even in the most extreme conditions, yet because speech and action are *intersubjective*, they require the presence and *recognition* of others. To be without a meaningful public persona and public stage on which to appear, refugees are judged not according to their actions and opinions—according to "who" they are—but according to how they are seen by others—according to "what" they are. This is why refugees can be treated as bare life, as a body without a meaningful identity, a life to be cared for indistinguishable from other suffering bodies.

For Arendt, what the ontological deprivation entails is that speech and action are no longer meaningful, not to ourselves and those close to us but rather to those who are different from us and in front of whom we try to distinguish ourselves. In other words, without a political persona, speech lacks meaning; it is a "fool's freedom" because it gains no recognition from local nongovernmental organizations, the United Nations, host states, or Western states that may resettle them. What they have lost is action in the Arendtian sense as self-disclosive and world-building. On the contrary, because refugees are seen merely as "what" they are—bodies to be cared for or people who threaten the state—they are often considered to be liars who will say anything to get into "our" country or take more resources. Their speech is thus disvalued, dismissed, and certainly not seen as meaningful.

Let me draw on an example discussed by Didier Fassin to make this point clearer. He tells the story of Marie, a Haitian woman who sought asylum in France in 2000 after being gang-raped in Haiti in the context of generalized political violence. She was denied asylum in France because the gang rape was not thought to be politically motivated and too ordinary to amount to persecution to justify asylum (only 3.3 percent of Haitian applicants received asylum during that period in France).[38] Like the 80 percent of asylum seekers whose applications are turned down, she became an illegal immigrant. After two years of living in isolation and becoming increasingly sicker, malnourished, and depressed, she finally saw a doctor. They learned that she was HIV positive and suffering from advanced AIDS, the result of the gang rape experienced in Haiti. She sought and won asylum on medical grounds, granted under the so-called humanitarian rationale. "Her words about the violence she had suffered were doubted," writes Fassin, "but ultimately her body spoke for her."[39] I use this example to show that for Marie, her words and actions were meaningless to the authorities who had the power to define her either as a legitimate person entitled to asylum and citizenship or as illegitimate, a liar, and illegal. It was only when her body, her bare life, made her suffering and trauma clear that she could be believed. This, I think, is what Arendt has in mind when she argues that stateless brings with it the diminishment of meaningful speech and action: there was simply nobody who found her words meaningful.

In sum, though refugees retain the capacity for action because it is rooted in natality, statelessness deprives them of other fundamental requirements of action: a community to judge their action and speech as meaningful and the possibility for a reliable public space in which to act. The problem with refugee camps is that they systematically deny refugees these latter two conditions and thus make agency as difficult as possible. Life in refugee camps and other spaces of containment amounts to systematic obstacles to agency that undermine the political life of refugees. Again, it is not to say that it is impossible to act—something Arendt explicitly denied—but it creates the conditions where such action is unlikely and difficult, and without a reliable political space where you are judged according to your words and deeds, even our ontologically rooted capacity is not sufficient.[40]

CONCLUSION

To summarize, I have argued above that philosophers ought to take more seriously the ontological deprivation of statelessness described by Arendt in considering our moral obligations to refugees. The ontological deprivation contained three separated but interdependent elements that together showed that statelessness deprives people of certain essential features of their humanity in a fundamental though never absolute way. So understood, this view of statelessness gives rise, I argue, to a different understanding of our obligations to refugees. Given that the vast majority of refugees are never resettled and remain displaced for prolonged periods of time, philosophers ought to be concerned with ethical norms that will help refugees mitigate if not entirely overcome the ontological deprivation and be included in the common realm of humanity. I conclude this chapter by discussing some suggestions that follow from a recognition of the reality of the ontological deprivation.

One ethical obligation that follows from my analysis is to rethink the ethics of long-term encampment and reconsider it as a morally acceptable solution since it effectively excludes people from the common realm and contributes to the diminishment of their ability to speak and act. One way to overcome this aspect of the ontological deprivation is to think of ways that the long-term displaced can be reintegrated back into the common world, even though they may remain without citizenship. For example, some nongovernmental organizations, such as the U.S. Committee for Refugees and Immigrants, advocate for the "temporary local integration" of refugees while a permanent durable solution is negotiated. Here, the UN High Commissioner for Refugees (UNHCR) would fund programs that allow refugees to integrate locally, such as through the funding of educational programs, primary schooling for children, and co-op and other work programs. Rather than funding camps that segregate people from the common world, the UNHCR would fund education, employment, and social services within states that host refugees; this would both allow refugees to be integrated into a political community (temporarily until a more permanent solution is found) and be materially beneficial to host states.[41]

Second, given the influence (financially and politically) that Western states exercise at the UNHCR, members of these states ought to advocate for a more ethical aid policy concerning refugees, one that respects them as members of the common realm and as political agents. This may entail, for example, insisting that when refugee camps are necessary as the only way to provide aid, they respect human rights. Currently, though the Refugee Convention lists rights that all refugees have even while displaced—including the right to earn wages, the right to education, the right to public assistance at the same level as nationals, the right to courts and travel documents, and, perhaps most important, the right to freedom of movement—they are routinely denied to refugees, and this is seen as morally unproblematic. An ethical policy ought to take more seriously the ontological deprivation of statelessness and include ways to mitigate this in our policies concerning refugees.

To be sure, I do not mean to claim that the above suggestions would provide a comprehensive solution to the global refugee crisis. Rather, they are meant simply to point in the direction that our ethical thinking might take. I began this chapter by arguing that political philosophers are mistaken in thinking that our *only* ethical obligation to refugees consists in admitting them into a state. My aim in arguing for the ontological deprivation is to show that when the harm of statelessness is reframed in this way, we see that many other obligations become at least conceivable. If the harm is partly that refugees are excluded from the common realm and are not consistently recognized as political agents, then philosophers ought to be concerned with thinking about ways that this harm can be mitigated if not entirely eliminated in the current global political context. We must be concerned with our ethical obligations to the millions of people who will never be resettled and will spend decades living in refugee camps that are supported, at least in part, by the policies of our states. Given the current global reality, overcoming the ontological deprivation must be seen as a moral imperative.

NOTES

1. See Serena Parekh, *Refugees and the Ethics of Forced Displacement* (New York: Routledge, 2017).
2. Michael Walzer, "The Distribution of Membership," in *Global Justice: Seminal Essays*, ed. Thomas Pogge and Darrel Moellendorf, 145–78 (St. Paul, MN: Paragon House, 2008), 163.
3. Walzer, "The Distribution of Membership," 163.
4. See William Barbieri, *Ethics of Citizenship: Immigration and Group Rights in Germany* (Durham, NC: Duke University Press, 1988); Joseph H. Carens, "Refugees and the Limits of Obligation," *Public Affairs Quarterly* 6, no. 1 (1992): 31–44; Phillip Cole, *Philosophies of Exclusion: Liberal Political Theory and Immigration* (Edinburgh: Edinburgh University Press, 2000); Matthew Gibney, *The Ethics and Politics of Asylum: Liberal Democracy and the Response to Refugees* (Cambridge: Cam-

bridge University Press, 2004); David Miller, *Strangers in Our Midst: The Political Philosophy of Immigration* (Cambridge, MA: Harvard University Press, 2016); Peter Nyers, *Rethinking Refugees: Beyond the State of Emergency* (New York: Routledge, 2006); Peter Singer and Renata Singer, "The Ethics of Refugee Policy," in *Open Borders? Closed Societies? The Ethical and Political Issues*, ed. Mark Gibney, 111–30 (New York: Greenwood Press, 1988); and Christopher Heath Wellman, "Immigration and Freedom of Association," *Ethics* 11 (2008): 109–41.

5. Wellman, "Immigration and Freedom of Association," 109.

6. Specifically, less than 1 percent of the 20 million people that the UN High Commissioner for Refugees considers refugees are ever recommended by the agency for resettlement (cited at http://www.unhcr.org/pages/4a16b1676.html).

7. Gil Loescher and James Milner, "Understanding the Challenge," *Forced Migration Review*, no. 33 (2009): 9.

8. Hannah Arendt, *The Origins of Totalitarianism* (New York: Harcourt, 1948), 267.

9. Arendt, *The Origins of Totalitarianism*, 295.

10. Arendt, *The Origins of Totalitarianism*, 279.

11. Hannah Arendt, *Responsibility and Judgment*, ed. Jerome Kohn (New York: Schocken Books, 2003), 150.

12. Arendt, *The Origins of Totalitarianism*, 286.

13. Arendt, *The Origins of Totalitarianism*, 292.

14. The title of a recent book on the subject is telling; see Marie-Benedicte Dembour and Tobias Kelly, *Are Human Rights for Migrants? Critical Reflections on the Status of Irregular Migrants in Europe and the United States* (New York: Routledge, 2011). For a more Arendtian analysis, see Ayten Gündoğdu, *Rightlessness in the Age of Rights: Hannah Arendt and the Contemporary Struggle of Migrants* (Oxford: Oxford University Press, 2015). Jan Klabbers notes that one reason for this continuing precarious situation is that neither "the 1951 Refugee Convention nor the 1967 Protocol thereto provide anything by way of political rights" (Jan Klabbers, "Hannah Arendt and the Language of Global Governance," in *Hannah Arendt and the Law*, ed. Marco Goldini and Christopher McCorkindale [Portland, OR: Hart Publishing, 2012], 244).

15. From the 1980 U.S. Refugee Act (quoted in Singer and Singer, "The Ethics of Refugee Policy," 116).

16. Arendt, *The Origins of Totalitarianism*, 296.

17. Arendt, *The Origins of Totalitarianism*, 287.

18. Arendt, *The Origins of Totalitarianism*, 287. This is a sentiment that Arendt reported in her own biographical account of life as a refugee in "We Refugees," in *Altogether Elsewhere: Writers on Exile*, ed. Marc Robinson, 110–19 (Boston: Faber & Faber, 1994).

19. Arendt, *The Origins of Totalitarianism*, 302.

20. Arendt, *The Origins of Totalitarianism*, 295.

21. Arendt, *The Origins of Totalitarianism*, 299.

22. Arendt, *The Origins of Totalitarianism*, 300.

23. That Agamben's concept of bare life is the necessary consequence of Arendt's view of statelessness is a position also held by Jacques Rancière. For him, "the radi-

cal suspension of politics in the exception of bare life is the ultimate consequence of Arendt's archipolitical position" (Jacques Rancière, "Who Is the Subject of the Rights of Man?," *South Atlantic Quarterly* 103, no. 2/3 [2004]: 301).

24. That refugees are exemplars of bare life has been much discussed in recent years. For examples of scholars using Agamben to discuss the problem of refugees and statelessness, see Tugba Basaran, "Security, Law, Borders: Spaces of Exclusion," *International Political Sociology* 2 (2008): 339–54; Matthew Coleman and Kevin Grove, "Biopolitics, Biopower, and the Return of Sovereignty," *Environment and Planning D: Society and Space* 27 (2009): 489–507; Roxanne Lynn Doty, "States of Exception on the Mexico-U.S. Border: Security, 'Decisions,' and Civilian Border Patrols," *International Political Sociology* 1 (2007): 113–37; Tobias Hogmann and Benedikt Korf, "Agamben in the Ogaden: Violence and Sovereignty in the Ethiopian-Somali Frontier," *Political Geography* 31 (2012): 205–14; Ronald C. Jennings, "Sovereignty and Political Modernity: A Genealogy of Agamben's Critique of Sovereignty," *Anthropological Theory* 11, no. 1 (2011): 23–61; Fiona Jenkins, "Bare Life: Asylum-Seekers, Australian Politics and Agamben's Critique of Violence," *Australian Journal of Human Rights* 10, no. 1 (2004): 79–95; and Patricia Owens, "Reclaiming 'Bare Life'?: Against Agamben on Refugees," *International Relations* 23, no. 4 (2009): 567–82.

25. Giorgio Agamben, *Homo Sacer: Sovereign Power and Bare Life*, trans. Daniel Heller-Roazen (Stanford, CA: Stanford University Press, 1998), 20. To be clear, I do not mean to suggest that we follow Agamben's analysis concerning refugees to its conclusion. For one, as this statement indicates, Agamben leaves no room for the limited but still present agency of people rendered bare life. Owens ("Reclaiming 'Bare Life'?") argues persuasively that he takes the idea of a refugee as bare life too far. I do, however, want to argue that his development of the concept of bare life and the relation of abandonment remain important concepts in helping us develop a fuller understanding of statelessness in the modern world.

26. Michel Agier, *On the Margins of the World: The Refugee Experience Today* (Malden, MA: Polity Press, 2008), 49.

27. Agier, *On the Margins of the World*, 133.

28. For example, see Zygmunt Bauman, *Liquid Times: Living in an Age of Uncertainty* (Malden, MA: Polity Press, 2007), 38.

29. See Agier, *On the Margins of the World*.

30. Hannah Arendt, *The Human Condition* (Chicago: University of Chicago Press, 1998), 52.

31. Arendt, *The Human Condition*, 179.

32. Arendt, *The Human Condition*, 178.

33. Hannah Arendt, *Essays in Understanding 1930–1954*, ed. Jerome Kohn (New York: Harcourt, 1993), 149.

34. Arendt, *The Human Condition*, 199.

35. Arendt, *The Origins of Totalitarianism*, 296, emphasis added.

36. Arendt, *The Origins of Totalitarianism*, 296.

37. Rancière takes up this point and argues that politics is precisely about deciding what counts as genuine political speech and what is mere noise. See Rancière, "Who Is the Subject of the Rights of Man?"

38. Didier Fassin, *Humanitarian Reason: A Moral History of the Present* (Berkeley: University of California Press, 2012), 142.

39. Fassin, *Humanitarian Reason*,142.

40. How to understand the place of action in the lives of rightless people is a current debate among Arendt scholars. Andrew Schaap ("Enacting the Right to Have Rights: Jacques Rancière's Critique of Hannah Arendt," *European Journal of Political Theory* 10, no. 1 [2011]: 22–45) and Rancière ("Who Is the Subject of the Rights of Man?") stress that for Arendt, refugees are unable to act and claim their right to have rights because they are politically impotent without a political community. By contrast, Barbour argues that for Arendt, refugees retain the capacity to act since nothing more is required for action than a space of appearance and that this space takes shape "anywhere humans come together in word and deed" (Charles Barbour, "Between Politics and Law: Hannah Arendt and the Subject of Rights," in Goldini and McCorkindale, *Hannah Arendt and the Law*, 315). I situate my reading of Arendt between the two. I agree with Barbour against Schaap and Rancière that because action is rooted in natality, it remains a capacity for even rightless people. Yet against Barbour, I want to stress that action requires more than just a space of appearance—it requires a public who will *judge* the action and speech as meaningful. Intersubjective recognition as well as a durable, reliable public space are missing for stateless and rightless individuals.

41. See Merril Smith, "Warehousing Refugees: A Denial of Rights, a Waste of Humanity," in special edition of the *World Refugee Survey*, 38–56 (Washington, DC: U.S. Committee on Refugees and Immigration, 2004).

Chapter Nine

Critiquing Agamben's Refugee

The Ontological Decolonization of Homo Sacer*

Sabeen Ahmed

> If we want to be equal to the absolutely new tasks ahead, we will have to abandon decidedly, without reservation, the fundamental concepts through which we have so far represented the subjects of the political (Man, the Citizen and its rights, but also the sovereign people, the worker, and so forth) and build our political philosophy anew starting from the one and only figure of the refugee.[1]

Giorgio Agamben's essay, a reflection on Hannah Arendt's powerful manifesto "We Refugees," falls neatly in line with his Foucauldian theory of contemporary sovereignty and changing modalities of state violence developed in *Homo Sacer*, but it is the first comprehensive extension of his conceptualization of *homo sacer*—the "limit figure" par excellence—to the figure of the refugee. Much has been written on *homo sacer* in the two decades since the book's publication, from critiques to applications of Agamben's theory beyond the contours of his own project, but few have applied this framework to the formerly colonized subject situated in a (theoretical or material) Western sociopolitical space.[2] In truth, this pursuit is frustrated by Agamben's own ontologization of the modern political subject, particularly when we recall that *homo sacer* is meant to both challenge universalizing Western political concepts and illuminate the threshold of human rights' universal jurisdiction.

In this chapter, I show how *homo sacer* is incapable of typifying the modern refugee—a subject who urgently demands attention but is often overlooked in political theories that take World War II as the exemplary

*I thank the commentators and participants at the many conferences where versions of this chapter were presented for their insight and constructive feedback. I am also profoundly grateful to Lisa Guenther, without whose mentorship and sustained support this chapter would not have reached its final stage.

context of refugee analysis—and instead leaves unresolved her unique space of vulnerability in contemporary political and ethical discourses. To this end, I examine Agamben's *homo sacer* as a figure *ontologically* indexed to a particular political and historical moment—that of the Shoah[3]—and illustrate that the universality Agamben's theory intends is unable to account for a figure who has, historically and politically, been viewed as ontologically *distinct* from the European "standard." As Tawia Ansah suggests, "Agamben's schema installs a dilatory camp as a sovereign, extralegal, and imperialistic decision as the center of thought,"[4] and this schema is often taken for granted in writings, both critical and laudatory, that appropriate and expand on Agamben's theory. Much of the problem in these texts, I suggest here, is the juridical notion of human rights taken for granted as constitutive of the modern political subject. Accordingly, I focus my attention on *homo sacer* as a means of exposing the unacknowledged Eurocentricism undergirding much of contemporary political philosophy that aims to, like Agamben's, "build our political philosophy anew" in an ever-more complex, opaque, and fundamentally pluralist geopolitical landscape.

HOMO SACER, SOVEREIGN POWER, *MUSELMANN*

Agamben's *Homo Sacer* is centered principally around two figures: *homo sacer*, the figure excluded from political life but included in the juridical calculus of the state, and the *sovereign*, the primary author of political ontology with the power to "decide" who is to be *homo sacer*. Historically, *homo sacer* designated the subject singled out by the political ruler of ancient Rome as "sacred": one who was ontologically separate from the body of the polis to which she formerly belonged, who had lost her political right not to be killed, but who could nevertheless not be sacrificed. In Agamben's contemporary reformulation, the liminal space occupied by *homo sacer* is characterized by the subject's loss of political rights—she is no longer the citizen but rather life bare of civic affiliation with her fellow men—and simultaneous vulnerability to state violence, a mirror image of the sovereign's inclusive-exclusion from the law. Sitting at the threshold between political man and animal—*bios* and *zoë*—*homo sacer* exemplifies the subject reduced, socially and politically, to the living dead.

In the contemporary nation-state, which for Agamben increasingly assumes the form of Michel Foucault's *dispositif* of biopolitical governmentality, *homo sacer* is positioned against the "familiar understanding" of man as "the very natural life that . . . is placed at the foundation of the order" and who "vanishes into the figure of the *citizen*, in whom rights inaugurating the biopolitics of modernity are 'preserved.'"[5] The emphasis on the "citizen" finds its juridical origin in the 1789 French Declaration of the Rights of Man and of the Citizen, under which the birth of the nation-state itself necessitates the birth of man qua citizen. As Agamben notes, the "Declaration of Rights represent the originary figure of the inscription of the natural life into the juridico-political order of the nation-state."[6] Today's *homo sacer*, as such, is precisely the *homo sacer* of old insofar as state and sovereign (or, perhaps more accurately, state *as* sovereign) hold jurisdiction—through both creation and protection, the power to make live and let die—over her as subject.

Although the influence of Foucault's work on his understanding of biopower is apparent, Agamben's idea of the paradigmatic realization of biopolitics comes from Carl Schmitt's theory of the "exception": it is the establishment of the "state of exception" wherein all men are *homines sacri* whose bare life is subject to state power, thereby transforming the oppressed population(s) into the generalized category of bare life. In this normalized state of exception—which "allows for the physical elimination not only of political adversaries but of entire categories of citizens who for some reason cannot be integrated into the political system"[7]—it is the status of the citizen stripped of her *bios*, her status as mere *zoë*, that is elevated and becomes the central concern of the state. "In the system of the nation-state," Agamben writes, "the so-called sacred and inalienable rights of man show themselves to lack every protection and reality at the moment in which they can no longer take the form of rights belonging to citizens of a state."[8]

It is for the special attention paid to the citizen in today's nation-state order that the exemplary intersection of sovereign power and biopower is embodied by the Jew of Nazi Germany. It was the Third Reich's calling into question—and ultimately removing—the citizenship status of the Jew that allowed her to be transported to the extermination camp as *homo sacer*. Just as the Roman Senate could declare a citizen *hostis*, a "public enemy," the Nazi regime "radically deprived [*homo sacer*] of any legal status" such that he "could therefore be stripped of his belongings and put to death at any moment."[9] The state's ability to "denationalize" certain members of civil society is precisely what awarded those citizens their new status of "bare life" and simultaneously transformed biopolitics into thanatopolitics. As Agamben observes, the annihilation of the Jews was carried out "not in a mad and giant holocaust but exactly as Hitler had announced . . . as bare life."[10]

In the camps, the exemplary manifestation of biopower for Agamben, the "state of exception," becomes the rule, and the figure of the *Muselmann* emerges. Drawing from Primo Levi, Agamben defines the *Muselmann* as a derogatory term used for camp prisoners who suffered extreme starvation and seeming emotional passivity and apathy. Their appearance—emaciated, weak, bent, and prone from muscular atrophy—"gave the impression of seeing Arabs praying,"[11] which thus earned them the title of "Muslim." Already stripped of juridical personhood through denationalization, the *Muselmann* is beyond even the threshold of the exiled citizen; her state is a source of revulsion for the other prisoners, who themselves see her not as a fellow prisoner but rather as a being no longer fully human: "Auschwitz is the site of an experiment," Agamben tells us, "beyond life and death in which the Jew is transformed into a *Muselmann* and the human being into a non-human."[12]

Significantly, Agamben's discussion of the *Muselmann* incorporates the first proper, albeit brief, mention of race in his theory. What is notable, however, is that race is brought up only to demonstrate how the *Muselmann* is the figure who has transcended race entirely: "the non-Aryan passes into the Jew, the Jew into the deportee, the deportee into the prisoner, until biopolitical caesuras reach their final limit in the camp. That limit is the *Muselmann*. At the point in which the [prisoner] becomes a *Muselmann*, the biopolitics of racism so to speak transcend race."[13] For Agamben, this sort of "color-blind" racism allows only for generalized, equiqualitated exclusions from social and political society, accordingly allowing for (1) ignoring the very real concerns of political subjugation and exclusion qua ethnicity, gender, ability, or sexual orientation; (2) equating citizenship with a nominally universal notion of juridical human rights that does not exist in practice; and consequently (3) an inability to account for the political status of contemporary stateless peoples. Just as Leti Volpp has written of the modern citizen, we might say that *not all* homo sacer *are equal*.[14]

THE SILENCED MINORITY AND ERASURE OF THE SHOAH

Once employed, the removal of ethnic race from biopolitical racism allows Agamben to emphasize *homo sacer*'s generalizability while distancing himself from any critical investigation of racially motivated, state-sponsored violence occurring prior to, during, or after World War II. Even more fundamentally, the danger of this deracialization is the subsequent deflation of oppression as a phenomenon that comes to affect the singular collectivity of *homo sacer* to the same degree: "*homo sacer*" becomes a blanket referent for *all* politically oppressed populations. An immediate implication is the suggestion that all peoples born under the nation-state are those who hold, prima facie, full citizenship or juridical personhood;[15] after all, Agamben qualifies *biopower* as that which reduces all citizens to the status of *homines sacri* such that *homo sacer*, as the antithesis to the citizen proper, emerges only after her citizenship status is actively *removed*.

Given that Hannah Arendt herself emphasizes "race and racism as key ideological elements in the implementation, administration, and justification" of the imperialist underpinnings of Nazi Germany,[16] it is worrying that Agamben's binary reading of state racism overrides nuanced histories of power struggle and the ongoing domination and subjugation of less-than-whole citizens through cultural, political, or socioeconomic mechanisms. Nonetheless, it is one that falls in line with Foucault's conceptualization of biopolitics, in which "racism is bound up with the workings of a State that is obliged to use race, the elimination of race and the purification of race, to exercise its sovereign power."[17] Here, too, racism is "not a truly ethnic racism"[18] but rather a tool used to demarcate segments of the population along lines of political vulnerability and, ultimately, exposure to death.

Neither Foucault's nor Agamben's biopolitical iterations of race consider power apparatuses employed by the state that hierarchize subpopulations therein, to the detriment of any substantial historico-material critique. Recognizing this lacuna, Alexander Weheliye suggests that

> we should remain vigilant about not acquiescing to these monumentalizing protocols . . . because, more often than not, they achieve their aggrandizing effect by not taking into account the historical relationality and conceptual contiguity between Nazi racism and other forms of biopolitics . . . those perfected in colonialism, indigenous genocide, racialized indentured servitude, and racial slavery, for instance.[19]

Contra Weheliye, the power to declare *homo sacer* does for Agamben the same work that racism does for Foucault: both are instruments of biopower that function to define the ontological status of the human being in terms of citizenship, centered entirely on the rights that she possesses.[20]

Crucially, Agamben's erasure of race not only precludes us from constructively utilizing the figure of *homo sacer* in diverse historical contexts but also paints a distorted picture of the *Shoah*—and in particular Auschwitz—itself. Criticizing Agamben for "[effacing] the very historical constitution of this aporia [of Auschwitz], which he structurally appropriates for assimilation into his philosophical discourse,"[21] Esther Marion has problematized Agamben's methodological tendency to subsume historical and theoretical work under a reductivist conceptualization of *homo sacer*. The death camp itself becomes elevated to a status of ontological and metaphysical singularity, situated outside of its own historico-material context and thereby dangerously depoliticized. For Agamben, Auschwitz loses the contingencies of its emergence and becomes a device rather than an event, an idiosyncratic, transcendent moment rather than a manifestation of complex historical developments. Further, the geopolitical territory marking Auschwitz's spatiality is characterized as the totalization of biopolitics—the "suspension of the juridical order itself"[22]—marking the complete dissolution of the juridical in the face of thanatopolitical exceptionalism. The consequence is the construction of an absolutely totalizing biopolitical situation that precludes Auschwitz's ability to serve as a "conduit to an alternative politics" that is able to constructively challenge the very facets of authoritarianism that allowed for its emergence.[23] As Ansah puts it, "Agamben simply fails to show how law actually works, or how the traditional relationship between rule and exception is never a univocal obliteration of one by the other."[24]

Agamben's characterization of *homo sacer* as a product of this exceptional political space leads not only to uncritical abstraction, but also to a mystification of the figure of *homo sacer* herself. Agamben's conceptualization of *homo sacer* as the "newly" denationalized German citizen abandons any critical discussion of the secondhand status of European Jews that had proliferated for centuries leading up to the Shoah, nor does it offer any analysis of deeply problematic international responses to the Shoah itself. Hannah Arendt, for example, makes note of the Dreyfus Affair explicitly in her own writings, highlighting the hypocrisy of the European nation-states' selective adherence to the human rights model. This she uses to emphasize the reluctance with which stateless persons were accepted by European nation-states (and this after being consistently barred from asylum) as indicative of the unique phenomenon of the enemy-from-within that permeates much of European political and historical memory still today.[25] Perhaps most damningly, Arendt charges public discourse of the "refugee crisis" with distracting from the material atrocities that allowed for the influx of statelessness in the first place:

> The new refugees were persecuted not because of what they had done or thought, but because of what they unchangeably were—born into the wrong kind of race or the wrong kind of class or drafted by the wrong kind of government. . . . The more the number of rightless people increased, the greater became the temptation to pay less attention to the deeds of the persecuting governments than to the status of persecuted.[26]

Agamben's failure to address any of these contingencies not only prevents us from utilizing *homo sacer* as a diagnostic tool for concrete spaces of political and humanitarian crises but also fails to adequately portray the *Muselmann* as a figure of historical, social, theological, and political alterity. For this reason, Agamben's "Europeanization" of the Jew for the purposes of his own philosophical thesis should be troubling to any scholar of contemporary political precarity. Marion herself suggests that Agamben ahistorically adopts the figure of the "Holocaust survivor" to serve as a "generic model of subjectivity,"[27] a phenomenon not unique to Agamben and one that overlooks the constellation of sociohistorical events that established the conditions for the possibility of the Shoah emerging in its particular historical moment.

Finally, and as yet little discussed in the critical literature, Agamben makes no clear distinction between the *Muselmann* and actual (Jewish) *refugees*: both groups of stateless persons are, at turns, identified as *homo sacer* despite the profoundly distinct material contexts in which each emerged. That this materiality makes no appearance in Agamben's theory prompts us to ask how, exactly, he believes that the *refugee* has become the *homo sacer* of today. In "Beyond Human Rights," Agamben identifies the contemporary space of exception, in which "the figure that should have embodied human rights more than any other—namely, the refugee—mark[s] instead the radical crisis of the concept,"[28] as the nation-state rather than the camp. The theoretical link between the *Muselmann*–camp crisis and the refugee–nation-state crisis, however, is absent. Agamben simply fails to either philosophically or politically distinguish between or associate the *Muselmann* and the refugee; instead, *both* figures, once ontologically elevated above their historico-material contexts, come to characterize *homo sacer*. As argued by Matthew Sharpe, we might say that Agamben's political theory is "deeply nonpolitical" due to his abstracting from precisely these historico-political contexts, which would have robustly enriched the otherwise generalized ontology of bare life he instead provides.[29]

In line with his ahistoric rendering of the Shoah, it is unsurprising that Agamben fails to mention that the Jewish Holocaust was not the first thanatopolitical manifestation of its kind. Two decades prior, the imperial government of the Ottoman Empire directed the massacre of 1.5 million Armenian citizens—an event that is itself often cited as the first modern genocide. In his infamous Obersalzberg speech revealing his intention to invade Poland, Adolf Hitler himself chillingly declares that

> as to what the weak Western European civilization asserts about me, that is of no account. I have given the command and I shall shoot everyone who utters one word of criticism, for the goal to be obtained in the war is not that of reaching certain lines but of physically demolishing the opponent. Only thus can we gain the living space that we need. Who after all is today speaking about the destruction of the Armenians?[30]

I do not here mean to undermine the severity and gravity of the actions carried out by SS personnel and the Nazi Party more generally. My aim is rather to illustrate that the ideology advanced under Nazism—that of purifying the "master race" through eliminating the "enemy" or "subhuman" race—was not the first instance of its appearance. Rather, as argued by Charles Mills and David Scott, it is crucial that we recognize that the Shoah was the first systematized and widespread use of such an ideology on peoples of *European* descent, or those who were (wrongly) assumed to have constituted, prima facie, the status of full juridical personhood. "The Jewish Holocaust," Mills writes," is by no means a bolt from the blue, an unfathomable anomaly in the development of the West, but unique only in that it represents the use of the Racial Contract against *Europeans*."[31] Indeed, even while Hitler himself acknowledged the Armenian genocide, it is telling that we scarcely read about, for example, the 10 million Congolese natives murdered under King Leopold II's Reign of Terror.[32] It was the very belief in and perpetuation of the notion of subhumanity and justifiable exploitation that drove European colonialism, and Agamben's insistence on the "transcendence of race" experienced by the camp prisoner—never mind the problematics of his appropriation of the *Muselmann* as a generalized subject of oppression—allows him to avoid addressing the racially motivated power dynamics of subjugation imposed on those outside the framework of and prior to Nazi Germany altogether.

THE RIGHT TO BE RIGHTLESS

The phenomenon of denationalization was originally posited by Hannah Arendt as the theft of juridical rights from the Jewish citizen of Nazi Germany. In order to exercise "total domination," the state had to effectively murder juridical man in order to transform the citizen into bare life that could be exploited and exterminated. In *The Origins of Totalitarianism*, Arendt recalls that "the first essential step on the road to total domination is to kill the juridical person in man. This was done, on the one hand, by putting certain categories of people outside the protection of the law and forcing at the same time, through the instrument of denationalization, the nontotalitarian world into recognition of lawlessness."[33] It was due to the loss of these rights—those "which had been thought of and even defined as inalienable, namely the Rights of Man"—that minorities and refugees no longer had "governments to represent and to protect them and therefore were forced to live either under the law of exception of the Minority Treaties . . . or under conditions of absolute lawlessness."[34] Writing as a resident alien in America several years after the end of World War II, Arendt acutely recognized that

> only nationals could be citizens, *only people of the same national origin could enjoy the full protection of legal institutions*, that persons of different nationality needed some law of exception until or unless they were completely assimilated and divorced from their origin . . . [but the European powers] were neither willing nor able to overthrow the laws by which nation-states exist.[35]

While Agamben's understanding of juridical personhood marks a prima facie ontological constitution of man in the nation-state, Arendt's conceptualization of juridical personhood marks a legal designation contingent on Western sociopolitical histories. Both Arendt and Agamben, nevertheless, illuminate the originary source of the refugee as a figure of legal and ethical precarity: the contemporary, Western nation-state system, which holds the ultimate power to categorize and identify persons who *belong* in the nation-state. The removal of juridical personhood is, as such, at the mercy of the sovereign's will: "one is almost tempted to measure the degree of totalitarian infection by the extent to which the concerned governments use their sovereign right of denationalization."[36] Simply put, the noncitizen is the subject who has suffered a social and political death contingent on her selection as *homo sacer*, whose removal from civil society is intended to purify the pure, dominant social body.

Seyla Benhabib, drawing from Arendt's notion of the "right to have rights," offers a contemporary rearticulation of the self-contradictory paradox of juridical and natural rights rooted in the geopolitics of the nation-state system. For Arendt, the Declaration of Rights allowed for "historical rights [to be] replaced by natural rights"[37] and subsequently redefined human dignity as something that had to be granted or guaranteed by the sovereign through acceptance of the subject as a citizen. Loss of citizenship status—which Arendt at turns appears to equate with "statelessness"—accordingly marks the point at which the former citizen has lost all claims to her natural rights *as well as* her political rights. In her contemporary reformulation, Benhabib observes that "in a territorially bound nation-state system, that is, in a 'state-centric' institutional order, one's legal status is dependent on protection by the highest authority that controls the territory upon which one resides and issues the papers to which one is entitled."[38] The extension of human rights is reliant on and sustained by what Benhabib calls "a special sort of social recognition and acceptance—that is, of one's *juridical status* within some *particular concrete political community*."[39] External to this formulation stands the stateless, the noncitizen, whose claim to human rights vanishes alongside her lack of citizenship.

Benhabib's conceptualization is quite in line with that of other contemporary political philosophers, including Jürgen Habermas, Zygmunt Bauman, and Giorgio Agamben himself, who characterizes the refugee similarly:

> The concept of the refugee (and the figure of life that this concept represents) must be resolutely separated from the concept of the rights of man, and we must seriously consider Arendt's claim that *the fates of human rights and the nation-state are bound together such that the decline and crisis of the one necessarily implies the end of the other*. The refugee must be considered for what he is:

> *nothing less than a limit concept that radically calls into question the fundamental categories of the nation-state*, from the birth-nation to the man-citizen link, and that thereby makes it possible to clear the way for a long-overdue renewal of categories in the service of politics in which bare life is no longer separated and excepted, either in the state order or in the figure of human rights.[40]

In "Beyond Human Rights," Agamben expands on his conceptualization of the refugee, again highlighting the denaturalization and denationalization of citizens by European countries after World War I and calling the resulting "citizens without political rights" the "mass [of] statelessness."[41] The emergence of this collectivity as well as the state's inability to regulate it marks, for Agamben, the moment at which sovereignty's impotence makes itself apparent. As such, the denationalized European citizen, the refugee, and the stateless all bring the "originary fiction of sovereignty into crisis" and are, fundamentally, *homines sacri*.[42]

THE COLONIAL UNDERPINNINGS OF NAZI BIOPOLITICS

Having laid out his thesis as such, I suggest that critiques such as Agamben's, which are centered on today's (Western) nation-state model, are unequipped to account for the modern, non-European refugee, principally because we are not apt to recognize the non-European *citizen* as falling within the framework of the historically heterosexist, white, European manifestation of the modern nation-state. If the existence of *homo sacer* is so intimately tied to the prima facie existence of the juridical person, I question how one might interpret the non-European who has been consistently excluded from discourses on juridical rights, whose claim to juridical personhood is itself historically and ontologically absent.[43] Indeed, aside from the term *Muselmann*, Agamben notes that the camps outside of Auschwitz utilized different terms for the same emaciated, walking corpse: donkeys, camels, tired sheiks, and trinkets, among others.[44] Notable here is the racialized underpinnings of these terms—all reminiscent of glittering sands and hot sun, inspiring visions of *keffiyeh*-clad nomads and Romanies wearily wandering across desert dunes—and the literal translation of *Muselmann* as "Muslim." What is especially telling, however, is that the invocation of the figure of the *Muselmann* indicated, "with a kind of ferocious irony," that "the Jews knew that they would not die at Auschwitz as Jews"[45]; they died instead as *Muselmänner*.

Ayten Gündoğdu, much like Seyla Benhabib, examines the contemporary struggle of refugees through an Arendtian rather than an Agambian lens. Following Arendt's theorization of the juridical–natural rights paradox—which "brings to view the inextricable connections between human rights and citizenship"[46]—the noncitizen lacks not only political rights but also her sovereign-granted, "natural" rights. Accordingly, Gündoğdu states, "it becomes very difficult for those deprived of membership in a political community to be recognized as human beings entitled to rights."[47] In her analysis of the biopolitics of human rights, however, Gündoğdu observes that the juridical–natural rights paradox is the product of historically *contingent* conditions, influenced in large part by *imperialist and colonialist ambitions*:

> Rights struggles do not take place in a historical vacuum; certain historical conditions can set obstacles to the political practices of claiming, enacting, and reinventing human rights . . . *[Imperialism] solidifies racial categorizations that hollow out the notion of "humanity" that is central to human rights and international law*, undermines the precarious balance between "nation" and "state," and paves the way for the decline of the constitutional state. . . . This new [state] structure . . . aims to achieve total control by *stratifying people on the basis of naturalized categories of race, ethnicity, and class*, [deploy] mass denaturalizations in the management of its populations, and [give] rise to the massive scales of rightlessness.[48]

To ignore the profoundly sexist and racial elements that have been embedded in human rights discourses is, for Gündoğdu, to disregard the historical and material contexts in which philosophico-juridical discussions of human rights have taken place.

Recognizing the reductivist tendencies in Agamben's writings on *homo sacer*, Gündoğdu states that "it is not surprising that he [Agamben] concludes with a call for a politics that renounces all concepts tied to sovereignty, including human rights and citizenship, since he offers a critique that ends up erasing the complex, ambivalent, and contingent histories of these concepts."[49] That Arendt is attractive to both Benhabib and Gündoğdu is unsurprising given Arendt's strong, situated critique of nation-statehood and European imperialism more generally. As noted by Christopher J. Lee, Arendt illuminated how "imperial expansion, like anti-Semitism, contributed to the deterioration of the nation-state ideal, essentially representing an overextension and compromise of its primary role as a guarantor of individual rights."[50]

The issue of human rights extension within the context of the colonial *territory* is taken up more explicitly by Samera Esmeir, who identifies the "special status" of citizenship in terms of what she calls "juridical humanity." Esmeir's analysis, which looks at the colonial history of Egypt in particular, examines the development of the juridical Egyptian citizen as a means of incorporating the colonized Egyptian into the political framework of colonial law, illustrating the liminization or transformation of these very bodies into *homines sacri* within an ascribed spatial territory. Accordingly, the colonization of Egypt "emerges in a new light—not as dehumanizing Egyptians, but as working to include them in the realm of universal humanity, which colonial law simultaneously facilitated. . . . The French Declaration of the Rights of Man and of the Citizen found a career in colonial reform; European ideas and practices of emancipation became forces of colonization."[51] As a means of realizing the colonial project, the British colonists elevated the Egyptians to the status of, essentially, the human: "to juridically humanize the colonized," Esmeir writes, "[the colonial state] revealed how humanity came to be thought of as something that could be confiscated or allocated."[52]

The commodification of "humanity" in Esmeir's analysis is striking; given that citizenship is widely considered among philosophers as a designation that one can embody or lack, Esmeir is suggesting, much like Arendt, that the very notion of *humanity* is similarly contingent on conferral and dispossession. For Esmeir, it is the *human herself* that is produced through law—once again demonstrating the unintelligible distinction between human and juridical rights—insofar as "human" identifies a status bestowed on a subject who is, otherwise, subhuman, prehuman, or prelegal. As is the case with denationalization, the conferral of juridical humanity serves as a biopolitical tool—albeit inclusionary rather than exclusionary—that aims to extend the boundaries of subjects exposed to sovereign power, working "to include them in the realm of universal humanity."[53]

Discourses on human rights must be cognizant of their theoretical limitations and narrow scope of applicability. Labor activist Erik Forman, for example, offers a strong critique of the liberalist emphasis on the guarantees of the rights of man, noting that "the majority of the planet's inhabitants have *already been living under a permanent state of exception*:

> The test run for the Nazi Holocaust were *the late-Victorian holocausts of mass murder in Africa, the genocidal colonization of the Americas and uncounted colonial massacres*. In the capitalist core, millions have long lived their lives as what Giorgio Agamben termed *homo sacer*—a term from ancient Rome signifying those who are deprived of rights by the state, and subject to extra-judicial violence by the George Zimmermans of the world. Across the capitalist core, immigrants and refugees live without the promise of any kind of liberal human rights, facing possible deportation in any interaction with the authorities.[54]

In response to David Scott's query about Western anxiety—that which "makes the Holocaust the primal scene of the original crime, and the extermination camp the fundamental paradigm of modern Western power"[55]—I suggest that the humanization and subsequent dehumanization of colonized bodies, which frames persons of African or Arab descent in "subhuman" or "depoliticizing" terms, allows for the persistence of a human rights model that takes World War II as paradigmatic of a proper, sociopolitical and ethical *human* suffering. When we take into account the "prehuman" status held by colonized bodies in the eyes of their European colonizers, it is crucial that we examine whether the association of non-European bodies with subhuman status contributes to the erasure thereof from critical analyses of Western-centered political theory. In so doing, we might observe that the phenomenon discussed by Arendt and Agamben—that of "denationalization," or the reduction of one to the status of *homo sacer*—emerges as a footprint of the biopolitical tools of inclusive-exclusion employed under colonialism. *Denationalization*, in other words, *is biopolitical in praxis but colonialist in theory.*

TOWARD A POST–WORLD WAR II REFUGEE

What is especially striking about the modern global refugee crisis—and what I have aimed to shed light on here—is the lack of analysis it has merited in philosophical writings on human rights and statelessness that have historically taken Nazi Germany as the paradigmatic refugee-producing entity. Prior even to the European migrant crisis, the volume of Afghan refugees that began after the 1979 Soviet-Afghan War transformed Afghanistan into the largest refugee-producing country for *thirty-two years*, a massive proportion of whom have taken up refuge in Pakistan.[56] That Afghan refugees or the "Pakistani refugee crisis" have rarely—if ever—featured in philosophical discourses on the refugee is only a testament to the primacy of ethico-political significance placed on *European* bodies, whether as refugees themselves or as economic and cultural "victims" of refugee crises (and, indeed, that Western public discourse on the "refugee crisis" began only after the influx of stateless attempting to migrate to *Europe* is profoundly telling).

Much could be said about the malleability of affect utilized by political powers, and it would be irresponsible to deny the role played by right-wing populist movements in trumpeting the inherent existence of an ideological incompatibility between East and West (and, indeed, the ethico-ideological superiority of the West over the East). Coupled with the Donald Trump's anti-Muslim retweets, blatant disregard of "white nationalist terrorism," and the colloquially termed executive "Muslim ban"—which included Syria, the world's largest source country of refugees at present—the pervasiveness of Islamophobia clouding foreign policy and public opinion cannot be overlooked. And indeed, xenophobic attitudes toward Muslim migrants is especially striking when we recall that the derogatory term for the living corpses of the Nazi camps—those who had transcended religion—was *Muselmann*.

I have not aimed in this chapter to argue for the dissolution of the *homo sacer* as a figure of potential utilization for analyzing current trends in refugee studies. Indeed, there are valuable dimensions of Agamben's theory that have and continue to deserve further exploration in expanded writings on the subject. However, if political philosophers such as Agamben disregard the colonialist echoes still permeating contemporary refugee discourses and instead continue invoking Nazi Germany as the paradigmatic manifestation of contemporary biopolitics, then the burden is on them to respond, for example, to the Greek interior minister Panagiotis Kouroublis's claim in the spring of 2016 that Greece's Idomeni camp was "a modern-day Dachau."[57] In a political era that has grown only more hostile to the non-European refugee since Kouroublis's statements, it is imperative that we recognize the trends and biases underlying our analyses of the most vulnerable and overlooked bodies today. Leti Volpp presciently observed in the early years of the "War on Terror" that "while some might believe in the power of universality—that one can infinitely expand the ambit of who is entitled to rights and freedoms—race and other markers appear and reappear to patrol the borders of belonging to political communities."[58] If we are to problematize the universalizing concepts of politics as Agamben urges we do, we must begin by interrogating a fundamentally Eurocentric intellectual inheritance that is increasingly inadequate to address the social and political crises of a progressively global world.

NOTES

1. Giorgio Agamben, "Beyond Human Rights," *Social Engineering*, no. 15 (2008): 90.
2. This is not to overlook Marcelo Svirsky and Simone Bignall's excellent anthology, *Agamben and Colonialism* (Edinburgh: Edinburgh University Press, 2012), which problematizes Agamben's utilization of the "camp" as the paradigmatic space of exception and instead presents the "colony" as the modern embodiment of sovereign exceptionality. On their account, the anthology examines the "connection between Agamben, colonialism, and post-colonialism—with the post-colonial understood as the 'critical attention to the continuing legacy of colonization in national life'" (Svirsky and Bignall, *Agamben and Colonialism*, 6). Although it is a crucial addition to Agamben scholarship, I part ways with Svirsky and Bignall's project in that I am concerned with the antagonism that characterizes the confrontation between the non-European refugee and the Western "state," in which the non-European is characterized, prima facie, as a hostile Other to the supposed "spirit" of Europeanism. More fundamentally, I regard the premature *ontologization* of the non-European refugee as *Other* as a microcosm of the deeply xenophobic geopolitical Zeitgeist of our era.
3. I use "Shoah" throughout this chapter as a means of differentiating the Jewish Holocaust from other historical uses of the term "holocaust."

4. Tawia Ansah, "Auschwitz as the *Nomos* of Modern Legal Thought," *Law and Literature* 22, no. 1 (2010): 148.

5. Giorgio Agamben, *Homo Sacer: Sovereign Power and Bare Life*, trans. Daniel Heller-Roazen (Stanford, CA: Stanford University Press, 1998), 127.

6. Agamben, *Homo Sacer*, 127.

7. Giorgio Agamben, *State of Exception*, trans. Kevin Attell (Chicago: University of Chicago Press, 2005), 2.

8. Agamben, *Homo Sacer*, 126.

9. Agamben, *State of Exception*, 80.

10. Agamben, *Homo Sacer*, 114.

11. Giorgio Agamben, *Remnants of Auschwitz: The Witness and the Archive*, trans. Daniel Heller-Roazen (New York: Zone Books, 2002), 43.

12. Agamben, *Remnants of Auschwitz*, 52.

13. Agamben, *Remnants of Auschwitz*, 85.

14. I allude here to Leti Volpp's 2002 article "The Citizen and the Terrorist," wherein he argues that "despite the universalizing discourse of citizenship, not all citizens are equal" (Leti Volpp, "The Citizen and the Terrorist," *UCLA Law Review* 49 [2002]: 1596).

15. Were this not the case, Agamben would have to consider nominal "citizens" (sometimes called "fragmented citizens") who hold less juridical standing—normative or legal—than others. We might think of the Dalits in India or third-generation Aboriginal peoples in Canada as examples of such "citizenship."

16. Christopher J. Lee, "Locating Hannah Arendt within Postcolonial Thought: A Prospectus," *College Literature* 38, no. 1 (2011): 101.

17. Michel Foucault, *Society Must Be Defended: Lectures at the Collège de France, 1975–1976*, trans. David Macey (New York: Picador, 2003), 260. Foucault, it should be noted, has been the subject of many important critiques from critical race theorists for what is interpreted as a radically insufficient account of race. See for example Ann Laura Stoler, *Race and the Education of Desire: Foucault's History of Sexuality and the Colonial Order of Things* (Durham, NC: Duke University Press, 1995) and Ann Laura Stoler, *Carnal Knowledge and Imperial Power: Race and the Intimate in Colonial Rule* (Berkeley: University of California Press, 2010).

18. Foucault, *Society Must Be Defended*, 261.

19. Alexander G. Weheliye, *Habeas Viscus: Racializing Assemblages, Biopolitics, and Black Feminist Theories of the Human* (Durham, NC: Duke University Press, 2014), 59.

20. Importantly, I do not suggest that Foucault's and Agamben's theories are irreconcilable with any analysis of the political subject. Leti Volpp, for example, utilizes Foucault's concepts of biopower to advance a more constructive definition of citizenship as "a process of interpellation start[ing] from the perspective that power both subordinates and constitutes one as subject" (Volpp, "The Citizen and the Terrorist," 1592). In the context of the post-9/11 United States, Volpp keenly observes that citizenship as a legal status "does not guarantee that [someone] will be constitutive of the American body politic" (1594).

21. Esther Marion, "The Nazi Genocide and the Writing of the Holocaust Aporia: Ethics and Remnants of Auschwitz," *MLN* 121, no. 4 (2006): 1009.

22. Agamben, *State of Exception*, 4.

23. Ansah, "Auschwitz as the *Nomos* of Modern Legal Thought," 152.

24. Ansah, "Auschwitz as the *Nomos* of Modern Legal Thought," 154.

25. Although it goes beyond the scope of this chapter, it is worth mentioning Manfred Gerstenfeld's analysis of anti-Semitism as a phenomenon emerging from theological discord that has historically driven political and cultural factionalism between the Abrahamic faiths. As Gerstenfeld states, "The core motif of anti-Semitism over more than two millennia was that the Jews embody the most extreme evil. The perception of absolute malevolence has varied over the centuries. For a long time it focused on the alleged eternal responsibility of all Jews—unless they converted—for the death of the founder of Christianity" (Manfred Gerstenfeld, "The Multiple Distortions of Holocaust Memory," *Jewish Political Studies Review* 19, no. 3/4 [2007]: 44). That Agamben draws on the ancient Greek characterization of *homo sacer* as the "sacred"—highlighting the complex theologico-political significance of this figure's invocation—it is troubling that any discussion of the theological underpinnings of contemporary *homo sacer* is absent in his principal work, especially given the religiously motivated foundations of anti-Semitism in Christian European history.

26. Hannah Arendt, *The Origins of Totalitarianism* (New York: Harcourt, 1948), 294. Not surprisingly, we see the same in today's treatment of the "European migrant crisis" and the Syrian Civil War.

27. Marion, "The Nazi Genocide and the Writing of the Holocaust Aporia," 1013.

28. Agamben, *Remnants of Auschwitz*, 92.

29. Matthew Sharpe, "Only Agamben Can *Save* Us? Against the Messianic Turn Recently Adopted in Critical Theory," *The Bible and Critical Theory* 5, no. 3 (2009): 40.2.

30. Adolf Hitler, *Documents on British Foreign Policy, 1919–1939*, 2nd ed., vol. 7, ed. E. L. Woodward and Rohan Butler (London: Her Majesty's Stationery Office, 1954), 258–60.

31. Charles Mills, *The Racial Contract* (Ithaca, NY: Cornell University Press, 1997), 103.

32. In a short article on the Congolese genocide, Liam O'Ceallaigh remarks that "when you kill ten million Africans, you aren't called 'Hitler.' . . . The victims of imperialism are made, like they usually are, invisible" (Liam O'Ceallaigh, "When You Kill Ten Million Africans You Aren't Called 'Hitler,'" *Diary of a Walking Butterfly*, December 22, 2010, http://www.walkingbutterfly.com/2010/12/22/when-you-kill-ten-million-africans-you-arent-called-hitler).

33. Arendt, *The Origins of Totalitarianism*, 447.

34. Arendt, *The Origins of Totalitarianism*, 268–69.

35. Arendt, *The Origins of Totalitarianism*, 275, 273, emphasis added.

36. Arendt, *The Origins of Totalitarianism*, 278.

37. Arendt, *The Origins of Totalitarianism*, 298.

38. Seyla Benhabib, *The Rights of Others: Aliens, Residents, and Citizens* (Cambridge: Cambridge University Press, 2004), 54–55.

39. Benhabib, *The Rights of Others*, 56, emphasis added.

40. Agamben, *Homo Sacer*, 134, emphasis added.

41. Agamben, "Beyond Human Rights," 91.

42. Agamben, "Beyond Human Rights," 93.

43. Refugees aside, this Eurocentric perspective has influenced the philosophical disregard of oppressed bodies—such as poor, LGBTQ, black, Latin, and Jewish members of Western society—the consequences of which have been taken up in recent decades by critical legal theorists, critical theorists of race, queer theorists, and feminist theorists. The formerly colonized body, too, has suffered a similar, philosophical erasure that has only recently been recognized in social and political philosophy, thanks principally to the works of Edward Said, Homi Bhaba, and Gayatri Spivak.

44. See Agamben, *Remnants of Auschwitz*, 42–44.

45. Agamben, *Remnants of Auschwitz*, 45.

46. Ayten Gündoğdu, *Rightlessness in an Age of Rights: Hannah Arendt and the Contemporary Struggle of Migrants* (Oxford: Oxford University Press, 2015), 26.

47. Gündoğdu, *Rightlessness in an Age of Rights*, 26.

48. Gündoğdu, *Rightlessness in an Age of Rights*, 50, emphasis added.

49. Gündoğdu, *Rightlessness in an Age of Rights*, 51. Quite ironically, Agamben himself makes the same observation: "the reasons for such impotence [of politics] lie not only in the selfishness and blindness of bureaucratic apparatuses, but also in the *very ambiguity of the fundamental notions regulating the inscription of the* native *(that is, of life) in the juridical order of the nation-state*" (Agamben, "Beyond Human Rights," 92).

50. Lee, "Locating Hannah Arendt within Postcolonial Thought," 100.

51. Samera Esmeir, *Juridical Humanity: A Colonial History* (Stanford, CA: Stanford University Press, 2012), 8.

52. Esmeir, *Juridical Humanity*, 8.

53. Esmeir, *Juridical Humanity*, 68.

54. Erik Forman, "Fight to Win!," *ROAR: Reflections on a Revolution* 16 (2017): 16, emphasis added.

55. David Scott, "Preface: Soul Captives are Free," *Small Axe* 11, no. 2 (2007): ix.

56. Until the mass exodus of refugees fleeing Syria beginning in 2015, Pakistan was also the largest refugee-hosting country in the world (a position now held by Turkey).

57. Will Worley and Lizzie Dearden, "Greek Refugee Camp Is 'as Bad as a Nazi Concentration Camp,' Says Minister," *Independent*, March 18, 2016, https://www.independent.co.uk/news/world/europe/idomeni-refugee-dachau-nazi-concentration-camp-greek-minister-a6938826.html.

58. Volpp, "The Citizen and the Terrorist," 1595.

Part IV

EXPERIENCES OF IMMIGRATION

Chapter Ten

Political Refugees and Economic Migrants

A Distinction without a Difference?

Chong Un Choe-Smith

Political refugees have a kind of privileged status among other migrants seeking admission to a safe country. Refugees are entitled to special protection under international and domestic law and have access to certain benefits, including admission to a safe country, assistance with resettlement, and a pathway to citizenship. So-called economic migrants, on the other hand, may feel compelled to enter a safe country without inspection and live in the shadows throughout their lives. This chapter takes a closer look at the distinction between political refugees and economic migrants and challenges the practice of prioritizing political refugees. The chapter specifically asks and answers the questions whether the distinction makes a morally significant difference and, alternatively, whether the definition of refugee has been applied in a way that is morally justified.

SPECIAL PROTECTION FOR POLITICAL REFUGEES

Under the UN Refugee Convention and Protocol, a refugee is defined as follows:

> Any person who, . . . owing to well-founded fear of being persecuted for reasons of race, religion, nationality, membership of a particular social group or political opinion, is outside the country of his nationality and is unable or, owing to such fear, is unwilling to avail himself of the protection of that country.[1]

The UN definition of a refugee, which addressed the historical circumstances at the time of its adoption, and its interpretation in different domestic jurisdictions continue to be the subject of controversy and appeals for reform.[2] Some have sought clarification or a broader interpretation of certain terms, such as "a fear of being persecuted" or "political opinion," while others have called for an extension of the grounds for refugee status based on the violation of social and economic rights alone or a better awareness of certain forms of injustice, such as violence against women.[3] Currently, nevertheless, the definition is often narrowly construed by many governments and covers only those who flee their countries of origin for fear of persecution on one of the specified grounds.

For those who are deemed to qualify under the definition, states must afford certain protections, including the protection provided under the principle of non-refoulement. Article 33 of the Convention and Protocol specifically provides, "No Contracting State shall expel or return ('refouler') a refugee in any manner whatsoever to the frontiers of territories where his life or freedom would be threatened on account of his race, religion, nationality, membership of a particular social group or political opinion."[4] States, therefore, under international law, are prohibited from returning an applicant seeking asylum without first adjudicating his or her application.

In the United States, the Refugee Act of 1980, which amended the Immigration and Nationality Act of 1952, also specifies the number of refugees to be admitted per year and authorizes the attorney general to establish a procedure for granting asylum. The Refugee Act provides,

> The Congress declares that it is the historic policy of the United States to respond to the urgent needs of persons subject to persecution in their homelands, including, where appropriate, humanitarian assistance for their care and maintenance in asylum areas, efforts to promote opportunities for resettlement or voluntary repatriation, aid for necessary transportation and processing, admission to this country of refugees of special humanitarian concern to the United States, and transitional assistance to refugees in the United States.[5]

Consistent with international law, the Refugee Act also codifies a version of the principle of non-refoulement:

> The Attorney General shall not deport or return any alien Deportation (other than an alien described in section 241[a][19]) to a country if Attorney General determines that such alien's life or freedom would be threatened in such country on account of race, religion, nationality, membership in a particular social group, or political opinion.[6]

The United States, under these provisions, has a legal duty not to return refugees if their lives are in danger for one of the stated reasons and to adjudicate their applications for asylum. As with the United States, other states are obligated under similar international and domestic laws and policies.

In addition to the legal duty of states, some would argue that states have a moral duty to political refugees. Michael Walzer, for example, argues that political refugees deserve special consideration: "There is, however, one group of needy outsiders whose claims cannot be met by yielding territory or exporting wealth; they can be met only by taking people in."[7] Under Walzer's communitarian and statist perspective, political communities such as states are the closest thing that we have to a world of common meanings in which we share a certain conception of justice, including a conception of distributive justice. Within a political community, we have a shared understanding of what are the social goods, including security and welfare, and the right distribution of these goods. The political community, which is likened to families and clubs, is comprised of morally connected but often unchosen members who collectively have a right to determine even the rules of membership. According to Walzer, membership is itself a social good. With membership comes a share of the social goods. Without membership, a person is in "a condition of infinite danger" without the protection and resources afforded within a state.[8] A refugee who is under the threat of being killed, persecuted, or brutally oppressed in his or her state of origin presents the "most forceful claim for admission."[9] The refugee's admission is still a matter to be determined by collective political will, but among other applicants for admission, the refugee's claim is the most urgent. Under Walzer's view, if a political community can and will accept any group of applicants, they ought to accept political refugees first.

Similar claims also are defended from cosmopolitan perspectives, such as that of Stefan Heuser. Heuser, appealing to the values of liberal democratic states, argues that liberal democratic states ought to extend basic civil rights to those who are stateless and, therefore, whose rights are unprotected. Liberal democracies believe that there should be no human being who is not the subject of civil rights. Political refugees are refugees who have lost civil rights in their country of origin. Political refugees belong to a group whose rights often have been violated by their own governments. Liberal democracies, therefore, should open their borders to political refugees and ensure the protection of their civil rights, even eventually admitting them to full citizenship.[10] Many theorists writing on political asylum, including Heuser and Anna Gotlib in this volume, are concerned primarily with addressing the plight of political refugees and the various ways that they are harmed. When they distinguish political refugees from economic migrants, they usually are not presented with an occasion to delve more deeply into the status of economic migrants. Gotlib focuses on political refugees and the loss of their ability to tell their own stories (i.e., a kind of narrative silencing), which may have wider applications. Heuser focuses on the loss of civil and political rights. Whether for legal or moral reasons, such as the one presented by Heuser, many states extend to refugees special consideration and prioritize them over other migrants seeking admission. The rest of this chapter looks more closely at economic migrants and challenges this practice of prioritizing political refugees over other migrants.

THE (UNCLEAR) DISTINCTION BETWEEN POLITICAL REFUGEES AND ECONOMIC MIGRANTS

One way to challenge the practice of prioritizing refugees over other migrants is to delve more deeply into the distinction between political refugees and economic migrants. To do this, this section extends Henry Shue's argument on the related distinction between security and subsistence rights to argue that the distinction between leaving one's country because of a threat to one's security rights and leaving one's country because of a threat to one's subsistence rights is not as sharp and significant as commonly presumed and, consequently, is inadequate to justify the practice of prioritizing political refugees over so-called economic migrants.

In *Basic Rights*, Shue argues that subsistence rights should be included as among our most basic rights, sometimes referred to by others as "human rights." For Shue, moral rights, generally, are justified demands for social guarantees or arrangements to guard against standard threats.[11] Basic rights specifically are "everyone's *minimum* demands upon the rest of humanity."[12] Basic rights are necessary for the enjoyment of every other right.[13] Shue explains,

> When a right is genuinely basic, any attempt to enjoy any other right by sacrificing the basic right would be quite literally self-defeating, cutting the ground from beneath itself. Therefore, if a right is basic, other, non-basic rights may be sacrificed, if necessary, in order to secure the basic right. But the protection of a basic right may not be sacrificed in order to secure the enjoyment of a non-basic right.[14]

If civil and political rights are considered basic and social and economic rights are considered nonbasic, we can see how one may be prioritized over the other. But Shue argues that certain political rights and economic rights are equally basic.

In particular, Shue claims that the right to subsistence is basic in the same way that the seemingly most urgent political right, namely, the right to physical security, is basic. Physical security includes the right not to be subjected to murder, mayhem, rape, or assault.[15] Economic security or subsistence includes the right to "unpolluted air, unpolluted water, adequate food, adequate clothing, adequate shelter, and minimum preventive public health care."[16] What is physical security if one is dying of starvation? Because a right to subsistence is necessary for the enjoyment of even physical security, the right to subsistence is also a basic right.

Shue specifically challenges a common view that there is a sharp and significant distinction between security and subsistence by casting doubt on the assumption that security rights are negative and subsistence rights are positive. The common view is that security rights are negative in that they require that others refrain from murdering, raping, and the like and that subsistence rights are positive in that they require that others provide clean air, water, food, clothing, and shelter. What Shue carefully shows, however, is that every basic right entails three correlative duties: (1) a duty to avoid depriving, (2) a duty to protect from deprivation, and (3) a duty to aid the deprived. The common assumption is to associate security rights with a duty to avoid depriving and subsistence rights with a duty to aid the deprived. The duty to avoid depriving is generally believed to be the most urgent and also requires the least resources; a person can simply refrain from harming another person. Security rights, however, entail all three correlative duties. "The very most 'negative'-seeming right to liberty, for example, requires positive action by society to protect it and positive action by society to restore it when avoidance and protection both fail."[17] Deprivations are not uncommon, and society must protect from deprivations by establishing domestic and international security measures, including a police force and a standing army. Society also must aid the deprived by establishing a criminal justice system to compensate victims and punish offenders with prosecutors, impartial tribunals, and prisons. Security rights entail all three correlative duties, including positive duties, and, if anything, require the most resources to carry out these duties.

What is even more compelling is that subsistence rights also entail all three correlative duties, including a duty to avoid deprivations. Shue offers a hypothetical but realistic example of intervention in a local economy involving a peasant village where the peasant farmers originally grew black beans that were a staple of the regional diet.[18] The peasant farmers were offered a lease to grow flowers, an employment contract, and equipment to grow a different crop with fewer laborers. This led to a sharp reduction in black bean supply, higher prices, and malnutrition of the children of the laborers who were no longer needed to grow black beans. Shue also offers the actual example of foreign development "aid" in Latin America that imposed austerity measures that harmed the working class and contributed to the spiraling debt and civil unrest.[19] Sometimes all that is necessary to respect the rights of those whose subsistence is threatened is not to interfere with their ability to be self-supporting. Both examples show that subsistence rights also involve the duty to avoid deprivations and that the failure to discharge this duty may result in life-threatening consequences. Both subsistence and security rights are equally basic and equally urgent with respect to living a minimally decent life.

Shue's closer look at security and subsistence rights reveals that the distinction between security and subsistence rights is not as sharp and significant as commonly thought and that the distinction does not justify prioritizing security over subsistence. Similarly, in extending Shue's analysis to migrants, my claim is that the distinction between political refugees and economic migrants is not as sharp and significant and also lacks the justificatory power for prioritizing one over the other.

Although the definition is potentially broader, typically, political refugees are those who have fled their countries of origin to escape threats to their political or civil rights. The basic idea is that their lives are in danger at home and that they are in dire need of a safe country. The term "economic migrant" covers many different individuals and situations, including the following: (1) a worker seeking a job across a border, (2) an individual or family seeking better economic opportunities in a foreign country, (3) an individual or family seeking refuge from a natural disaster, and (4) an individual or family escaping famine and poverty caused by a combination of factors including poor governance, depleted natural resources, and/or possibly historical injustices. By "poverty" I mean living below the level of subsistence, which is the minimum standard of what is necessary for a minimally decent life. The above categories are not mutually exclusive. A person qualifying under category (4) also may fall under categories (1) and (2). Typically, people do not uproot their families to confront the dangers and uncertainties of crossing deserts, seas, or other lands and borders to reach an unwelcoming country unless compelled to by their circumstances. The focus here will be category (4), a group that can also be referred to as "subsistence migrants," or those fleeing their countries of origin to escape famine or poverty. Remaining in their countries of origin would mean living below the level of subsistence with a desperate lack of employment, inadequate food, inadequate shelter, or a lack of clean air or water. I think that a vast majority of economic migrants—more than we are willing to admit—are subsistence migrants.

A common view that underwrites the current policies of prioritizing political refugees over other migrants is that the rights of political refugees are more urgent because they are motivated by fear of persecution.[20] Political refugees are provided a pathway to admission and citizenship, while economic migrants, who enter without inspection, or illegally, are treated as criminals. Unless they already have close relatives in the country, there often is no legal pathway for them. Granted, some states would be reluctant to admit even political refugees without being compelled to by international or domestic law. But, morally speaking, there seems to be little or no justification for prioritizing one over the other.

Regardless of the source of the deprivation, both political refugees and subsistence migrants have been deprived of their basic rights and are in dire need of assistance from a safe country. Both political and subsistence rights are rightfully included as basic rights or minimum demands for social guarantees. Subsistence rights are necessary for the enjoyment of any other right and, therefore, are rightfully included as basic rights. Both security and subsistence are absolutely critical for a minimally decent life. If the violation of security rights justifies asylum in a safe country, then the violation of subsistence rights also justifies the same social guarantee. As Shue explains, "Because the actual deprivation of either can be so very serious—potentially incapacitating, crippling, or fatal—even the threatened deprivation of either can be a powerful weapon against anyone whose security or subsistence is not in fact socially guaranteed."[21] Deprivations or threats of deprivations of either are equally urgent in calling for a response, first from an individual's or group's home country and then from the international moral community. When an individual's or group's home country fails to provide for the enjoyment of these rights, the international moral community has an equal responsibility to protect or provide assistance in response to a violation of one just as much as the other.

Both the security rights of political refugees and the subsistence rights of other migrants are basic rights that are minimum demands for social guarantees against common threats. Both entail the three correlative duties mentioned above, including a duty to avoid deprivations, the duty to protect, and the duty to aid, the last two of which are usually involved in granting asylum. Both involve a violation of the first in their countries of origin. Political refugees may be the victims of an outlaw state, using John Rawls's terms,[22] while economic migrants may be the victims of a burdened society without an effective state to secure their basic rights. In both cases, the duty to avoid deprivations has been grossly neglected or intentionally breached. The only difference may be that, in the case of the political refugee, we can point our fingers more easily at the government of an outlaw state. Identifying who the persecutor is in a burdened society is far more complicated given the joint and several causes of the conditions leading to the migrant's flight.

If the subsistence migrant remains in his own county, he and his family may face starvation from a lack of food, disease from the lack of sanitation and access to health care, and imminent death. In the same way that political refugees walk a kind of tightrope between leaving early enough to get out and not leaving so early that they cannot establish that they were targets of persecution, as James Nickel observes,[23] economic migrants also walk a kind of tightrope between leaving early enough to avoid death and not leaving so early that they cannot receive special humanitarian consideration (e.g., the Special Humanitarian Parole Program for Haitian Orphans).

Interestingly, Nickel also observes that the convenient distinction between political and economic migrants does not track the distinction between those who are under life-threatening conditions and those who are escaping harsh but not life-threatening conditions:

> It is true that those whose claim is based on the danger of death, imprisonment or torture have a stronger claim than those who merely wish to escape harsh conditions. Thus we can imagine that it will sometimes be legitimate for refugee policy to distinguish between applicants on these grounds, to limit the guarantee of safe haven to the former. But this is not the same distinction as the one between political and economic refugees. Under famine the conditions threatening one's life may be economic, and under authoritarian rule the conditions that make one's life harsh (without threatening one's survival or liberty) may be political.[24]

Some economic migrants may be seeking prosperity or better economic opportunities in a foreign country, some are fleeing harsh but maybe not life-threatening conditions, and others (subsistence migrants) are fleeing life-threatening conditions, such as poverty and famine. Similarly, some political migrants are seeking a better or preferred political environment, some are fleeing harsh but not life-threatening political conditions (e.g., minority groups without the same political freedoms as enjoyed by majority groups), and others are fleeing life-threatening conditions, such as threats by government forces of imprisonment or death. The morally relevant distinction is not between so-called political refugees and economic migrants but between those who have at least the chance of a minimally decent life in their own country and those who are being forced out because of life-threatening conditions and are in dire need of a safe country. There is no reason to presume that those who suffer deprivations of economic or social rights are less deserving when considering applications for asylum.

While it may be politically expedient to prioritize political refugees over other migrants, a state's moral duties with regard to the rights of political refugees and the rights of certain economic migrants are the same. There is no clear and morally significant distinction between these two categories of desperate migrants seeking admission, and, therefore, there is no basis for prioritizing one over the other.

WHO QUALIFIES AS A "POLITICAL REFUGEE"?

Another way to challenge the practice of prioritizing refugees over other migrants is to examine more closely the application of the criteria for granting asylum. Even if we accept the current definition of a refugee under domestic and international law, proper administration of refugee law depends crucially on fair decisions as to who qualifies under the definition. But decisions as to who qualifies or does not qualify are far from fair. First, we can look at a historical example of Salvadoran and Guatemalan migrants in the 1980s and James Nickel's critique of the Reagan administration's policies. Next, we can look at the more current example of Central American and Mexican migrants today. While these individuals are often not granted refugee status, these determinations, while possibly politically motivated, are morally arbitrary.

SALVADORAN AND GUATEMALAN MIGRANTS IN THE 1980S

In the 1980s, El Salvador and Guatemala were embroiled in a civil war between oligarchies supported by corrupt military leaders and the rest of the rural population. In El Salvador, government-supported assassins shot and killed Archbishop Oscar Arnulfo Romero while he was performing mass shortly after he had publicly demanded the end of civilian deaths at the hands of Salvadoran soldiers. When Ronald Reagan became president of the United States in 1981, he viewed these civil wars as part of a broader Cold War and sided with the governments against the Marxist-led popular movements. During this time, international human rights organizations regularly reported high levels of repression and violence in El Salvador and Guatemala. In El Salvador, the government-sponsored death squads were responsible for thousands of murders and disappearances of union leaders, community leaders, and suspected guerilla sympathizers. In Guatemala, the government-sponsored paramilitary forces targeted indigenous communities, resulting in thousands of murders, disappearances, and displacements.[25]

As Salvadorans and Guatemalans attempted to flee repression and threats of violence, seeking refuge in other states, the Reagan administration's position was that these migrants did not qualify as political refugees. According to Nickel, the Reagan administration's position specifically included that many migrants from Central America were not motivated primarily by fear of persecution in their homelands, as required for refugee status, but rather by poverty and the hope of better lives and that asylum is required under international and domestic law for those who are specific targets of persecution rather than those who are simply endangered by a civil war.[26]

Nickel criticized the Reagan administration's narrow construction of the right to asylum. State departments are given great discretion in specifying the qualifications for refugee status. There are many possible ways to define these qualifications, and the Reagan administration chose not only a narrow construction but also a politically motivated approach in applying this standard. According to Nickel, the degree of danger required may include the following:

a. Being a personalized target of violence (e.g., one's name is on a death list).
b. Being a member of a group that has been subject to much persecution (for example, being a trade unionist or university student in El Salvador).
c. Being subject to generalized violence (for example, a civil war is being fought in one's immediate area of residence).
d. Having well-founded fears that political developments will occur that will put one in position a, b, or c.[27]

The Reagan administration's policies construed the right to asylum to include only (a), that the applicant for asylum must prove that he or she was a personalized target of violence.

As noted by Nickel, the Reagan administration's conception of the right to asylum placed those seeking asylum in a precarious position:

> Successful flight often requires foresight and advance planning, and thus those who wisely choose to flee in advance of persecution walk a tightrope: they must leave early enough to get out, but not so early that it is impossible for them to prove that they were likely targets of persecution. . . . If we require the threat to be personalized, we will often require people to stay until it is too late.[28]

Nickel criticized the Reagan administration's near wholesale denial of refugee status to those fleeing conflicts in Central America.[29] At the time, only 3 percent of the applications from El Salvador were granted as compared to 30 percent from Poland.[30] These migrants claimed that their lives were in danger as a result of civil war and government-sponsored death squads. The Reagan administration's policy, however, required showing that the migrants were personalized targets of violence. The Reagan administration also sponsored military efforts in support of the governments in El Salvador and Guatemala and were unlikely to acknowledge that these governments were responsible for death squads and other threats of violence. They could not, on the one hand, support these governments and then, on the other, admit refugees claiming to be fleeing violence at the hands of the same governments. The administration arguably circumvented international and domestic law on the protection of refugees to advance its political agenda.

The Reagan administration conveniently placed an extremely difficult burden of proof on Salvadoran and Guatemalan migrants. The administration's convenient position also was to presume that Salvadoran and Guatemalan migrants were merely fleeing poverty or seeking better lives for themselves or their families. The Reagan administration's application of refugee law seemed far from fair and, consequently, left those who were fleeing life-threatening conditions with the options of staying to face their fates at home or entering the United States illegally.

CENTRAL AMERICAN AND MEXICAN MIGRANTS TODAY

Thirty years later, and some of our decisions on applications for protection as political refugees continue to be made for political reasons rather than a state's moral obligation to protect and aid those who have been forcefully displaced. Less than 1 percent of formally recognized refugees are designated as political refugees by state departments and admitted for resettlement.[31] When a refugee flees a repressive regime, one that is also considered illegitimate by the country in which the refugee is seeking admission, state departments seem more responsive to these applications. The U.S. State Department, for example, issues special immigration visas to refugees fleeing war-torn countries who have served alongside the U.S. military or the U.S. Army Corps of Engineers, as with refugees from Iraq and Afghanistan. The Obama administration resettled 84,994 refugees in 2016 and sought to increase this number to 110,000 refugees in 2017, a number that was cut by the Trump administration to 50,000.[32] In 2017, the top ten countries of origin were the Democratic Republic of Congo, Iraq, Syria, Somalia, Myanmar, Ukraine, Bhutan, Iran, Eritrea, and Afghanistan.[33] These are the "winners" in the refugee lottery.

There are, however, many more "losers." When a refugee flees a repressive regime that is not considered illegitimate by the country in which the refugee is seeking admission or when the refugee flees other forms of violence or life-threatening conditions, state departments seem less inclined to grant these applications. For example, today, there are many Central American and Mexican migrants fleeing widespread gang violence and poverty.[34]

After the end of the political conflicts of the 1980s, Central American migrants entered the United States to reunify with family members and to escape natural disasters and continued political and economic instability. While some Central Americans who fled as a result of natural disasters, including those from El Salvador and Honduras, were eligible for temporary protected status, many Central Americans entered illegally across the U.S.–Mexico border.[35] In 2016, U.S. Customs and Border Protection intercepted 46,900 unaccompanied children and more than 70,400 family units arriving from El Salvador, Guatemala, and Honduras.[36] According to Migration Policy Institute estimates, in the period between 2010 and 2014, approximately 1.7 million unauthorized immigrants from Central America resided in the United

States, with Guatemala, El Salvador, and Honduras among the top five represented countries of origin.[37]

The single largest group of illegal immigrants came from Mexico. According to Migration Policy Institute estimates, as of 2013, 6.2 million (56 percent) of the estimated 11 million unauthorized immigrants were from Mexico. In the last part of the twentieth century, Mexican immigrants came to the United States to work as migrant farmworkers. Their pattern of seasonal farm work continued as U.S. law and policy changed. After World War II, private labor contractors used Mexican migrant workers through the 1930s. From 1942 to 1964, under the Bracero Program, a series of agreements between the United States and Mexico authorized the use of Mexican migrant farmworkers. After the Bracero Program ended in 1965 and the United States passed the Immigration and Naturalization Act, which placed numerical quotas on Mexican and other Latin American immigrants, Mexican migrant farmworkers continued their seasonal work in the United States illegally. As tighter border security measures were implemented with the passage of the Immigration Reform and Control Act of 1986, Mexican migrants began to settle in the United States permanently.[38] Some Mexican migrants may qualify as subsistence migrants, as discussed in the previous section, but they are almost categorically labeled "economic migrants," in particular, those perceived as entering a foreign country to seek employment or better lives for their families. In the twenty-first century, Mexican migrants present a unique challenge for the United States because, while their patterns of behavior were set by former laws and practices, the United States became less welcoming of Mexican migrants, preferring instead higher-skilled laborers from other parts of the world.

More importantly for our purposes here, some Mexican migrants today, like migrants from El Salvador and Guatemala, also fled their countries of origin because of threats of violence, albeit not from the government but from widespread gang activity. According to Human Rights Watch, under President Felipe Calderón, criminal gangs contributed to a climate of violence, lawlessness, and fear. Human Rights Watch reported about 250 disappearances, including 149 enforced disappearances, in which state agents directly or indirectly participated in these crimes. Members of the army, navy, federal police, and state and municipal police forces were implicated in these crimes.[39] This number may be a fraction of the total number of disappearances during Calderón's term; information leaked from the Ministry of the Interior and the Federal Prosecutor's Office contained the names of more than 25,000 individuals.[40]

Even if we accept the current definition of a refugee under domestic and international laws, there is a strong case to be made for finding that more

Mexican and Central American migrants should qualify as refugees. Under domestic and international law, a refugee is a person who is outside of his or her country of origin because of a well-founded fear of being persecuted for reasons of race, religion, nationality, membership of a particular social group, or political opinion.[41] First, the migrants described above are fleeing because of a well-founded fear of persecution. They believe that their lives and the lives of their family members are in danger. The evidence of disappearances and other acts of violence, the rampant activity of death squads and criminal gangs, and the broader climate of violence and lawlessness provide support for a claim that the flight is the result of a fear of persecution. Second, the migrants may not be subject to violence because of their race or religion, but they arguably are being persecuted for their political opinion, namely, their position against a corrupt regime or against the present lawless condition, for which the regime has been complicit in bringing about.

The courts have interpreted the category of a person fleeing persecution as a result of one's political opinion narrowly, but there is good reason to believe that the category remains an open possibility. In *Immigration and Naturalization Services v. Elias-Zacarias*,[42] a Guatemalan native's application for asylum was rejected by an immigration judge, and the judge's decision was affirmed by the Board of Immigration Appeals (BIA). The question there was whether the guerrilla's coerced conscription necessarily constitutes persecution as a result of the applicant's political opinion. The U.S. Supreme Court ruled that it did not and that the applicant must show that he refused to be conscripted as a result of his political opinion rather than refusing to be conscripted for other reasons. While the *Elias-Zacarias* decision seemed to support a narrow construction of this particular ground for asylum, there is a strong presumption in favor of the fact finder's judgment on appeal that does not apply in cases in which the fact finder finds the applicant's testimony credible or in cases in which the fact finder's decision was defective in some way.[43]

For example, in *Castro v. Holder*,[44] the U.S. Court of Appeals for the Second Circuit reversed the BIA's judgment in a case involving a Guatemalan native and former police officer who had sought asylum on the grounds of persecution based on his political opinion. The circuit court held that the BIA failed to consider the surrounding circumstances in evaluating the application for asylum. Castro blew the whistle on corrupt law enforcement officers who repeatedly tried to retaliate against him and his wife. After the signing of the Peace Accords in 1996, President Álvaro Arzú abolished the Guatemalan National Police, which had been run by the military, and formed the Guatemalan National Civil Police Force. President Arzú removed many corrupt officers from power. But in 2000, President Alfonso Portillo, who was closely aligned with the former military dictator, succeeded Arzú and reinstated many of the officers who had been previously discharged. Castro reported that there was rampant corruption at all levels of law enforcement, including in the military, judiciary, and government agencies. After observing two supervisors, including his own, engaged in a cocaine transaction in 2001, Castro reported the incident to the regional police commissioner and, when that proved ineffective, reported the incident to the UN Human Rights Verification Mission in Guatemala, an organization set up to monitor the peace process and human rights violations. After a few attempts on his life by the Guatemalan police force, Castro fled to the United States in 2004.

The circuit court explained that opposition to government corruption may constitute a political opinion and that retaliation for someone expressing that opinion may constitute persecution. The relevant questions are whether the applicant's actions were directed toward a governing institution or whether they were directed at isolated, aberrational acts of greed or malfeasance. The court also explained that the surrounding circumstances may be relevant in answering these questions. The shift in power in 2000 and the evidence of widespread corruption in law enforcement supported Castro's application that he was being persecuted for his political position against this corruption. Finding that the immigration judge failed to consider Castro's application within this context, the court overturned the immigration judge's ruling. Such cases suggest that it is possible to qualify as a refugee on grounds that one is fleeing persecution on the basis of one's political opinion despite the court's narrow construction of this basis for asylum.[45]

Since Nickel's critique of the Reagan administration's policies, nevertheless, not much has changed with regard to the current administration's policies concerning Central American and Mexican migrants. There continues to be a near blanket assumption that these migrants do not qualify as refugees and are merely economic migrants fleeing harsh conditions. According to an American Immigration Council report,

> The common thread in [the Department of Homeland Security's] response to the thousands of women and children arriving at the United States' southwest border in 2014 was to employ a multi-prong deterrence strategy consisting of (a) launching a multimedia public awareness campaign [of the dangers of migration]; (b) increasing U.S. assistance to help Mexico secure its southern border region; (c) decreasing the chances of gaining asylum by expediting the removal process; and (d) carrying out raids in January 2016 in search of individuals deemed to have exhausted their asylum claims.[46]

The American Immigration Council report noted that knowledge of the dangers of migration had little effect on migrants' decisions to leave their country of origin.[47] The report rather noted that large percentages of migrants (e.g., 44 percent of Salvadorans) fled because of direct encounters with violent crime:

> We may infer from this analysis of migration intentions that those individuals who do decide to migrate and successfully arrive at the U.S. border are far more likely to fit the profile of refugees than that of economic migrants. Upon arrival, however, they are still subject to the "send a message" policies and practices that are designed to deter others rather than identify and ensure the protection of those fleeing war-like levels of violence.[48]

Rather than receiving special humanitarian consideration and having their applications for asylum fairly evaluated, Central American migrants are faced with "aggressive deterrence strategies" under the Obama and Trump administrations.[49] The Obama administration implemented an in-country refugee/parole program in El Salvador, Guatemala, and Honduras, but the program provides relief only for children with parents who already are lawfully present in the United States. The vast majority of migrants from these countries are denied a legal pathway for admission or citizenship.

It is not entirely clear why Central American and Mexican migrants have been "losers" in the refugee lottery. The long history of interaction between the United States and these Central American countries and Mexico may help to explain the current closed-door policy. The sheer numbers of those flooding the United States border from these countries also may present a migration crisis for the United States, devastating its ability to cope or at least its political will to help. The majority's political will also may be shaped by its cultural biases against nonwhite immigrants.[50] When there is no will, it is convenient to rely on the presumption that these migrants are merely "economic migrants" and so less deserving of our help.

If, however, there was a fairer administration of refugee law, these migrants may be granted asylum and the right to enter the country legally. Rather than the migrants bearing the burden of proving that they survived near death experiences, as the case above suggests, a different policy may recognize that their flight was from a repressive regime or a regime incapable of protecting its own citizens. As argued in the previous section, refugee law largely continues to rely on the distinction between security and subsistence, and so, under the current law, not all circumstances, although equally dire, are equally sufficient for asylum. But, as argued here, even under the current definition, a fairer administration of refugee law could lead to a more proportionate result on applications for asylum by Central American and Mexican nationals as well as minimizing the current crisis today with illegal immigration. A country like the United States may not be able to accommodate every person seeking asylum, but each country should be impartial in evaluating applications rather than playing favorites based on political agendas.

CONCLUSION

When a state's resources are limited, deciding which desperate migrants to admit may present a dilemma. On the one hand, a state can choose political refugees only and slam the door on thousands, even hundreds of thousands, of people who have fled their countries because they cannot provide for themselves and their children the very basic necessities of life. On the other hand, a state can choose both political refugees and subsistence migrants and possibly deprive some of its own citizens the resources they need to live a good life. This chapter has defended the rights of subsistence migrants as equally deserving of admission and safe passage but does not mean to make light of the hard choices before lawmakers and policymakers.

In this chapter, I have argued for an extension of Shue's analysis concerning the distinction between security and subsistence rights to the distinction between political refugees and economic migrants. The distinction is not as clear and significant as many have presumed, and it fails to justify prioritizing one over the other. I have also argued that, as Nickel did in the 1980s, the different treatment of political refugees and economic migrants may be the result of politics as usual rather than any clear distinction between the two and any morally justified basis for different treatment. If the arguments presented here are persuasive, then we ought to reconsider the status of economic migrants and recognize their claims of oppression on the basis of some deprivation of their subsistence rights as equally urgent. We can accomplish this by expanding the definition of a refugee by replacing "fear of being persecuted" with "fear of persecution or oppression" and adding "deprivation of basic necessities" to the short list of qualifying grounds. We can also accomplish this by interpreting "political opinion" more broadly to recognize as adequate the claims of those who flee their countries of origin on the grounds of economic persecution or the deprivation of their subsistence rights, whether by an organized government or some other entity. In either case, refugee law should be applied without politically motivated bias and presumptions concerning the legitimacy of certain governments.

While such proposals may face political opposition, this chapter's focus was on the ethical question of whether the distinction between political refugees and economic migrants was morally justified. The solutions suggested above would require rethinking the priority given to political refugees and treating subsistence migrants with equal consideration. A policy that is concerned with the welfare of current citizens may limit the total number of refugees, but it should not deny admission to certain migrants as merely "economic migrants." The purpose of this chapter was to bring attention to the ways that we harm these so-called economic migrants, most of whom are from the already disadvantaged Global South, by minimizing their claims with this label and once again treating them as inferior because they fall under certain stereotypes or categories defined for them and not others, in this instance, of a refugee who is singled out for persecution by an organized and powerful government. Subsistence migrants sometimes do not have the "luxury" of living under an organized and powerful government. They instead may live in environments overrun by criminal elements and the pervasive consequences of global poverty and foreign intervention. In writing this chapter, my hope is for a fairer system of rules to adjudicate the claims of migrants who are forced to flee their own countries and, maybe equally importantly, for a greater respect and understanding toward subsistence migrants and the millions of illegal immigrants who once may have been subsistence migrants.

NOTES

1. UN General Assembly, "Convention Relating to the Status of Refugees," July 28, 1951, *United Nations Treaty Series*, no. 189; UN General Assembly, "Protocol Relating to the Status of Refugees," January 31, 1967, *United Nations Treaty Series*, no. 606.

2. See, e.g., James C. Hathaway, "The Evolution of Refugee Status in International Law: 1920–1950," *International and Comparative Law Quarterly* 33, no. 2 (1984): 348–80; Carl Bon Tempo, "Reform and Retrenchment: The Refugee Act of 1980 and the Reagan Administration's Refugee Policies," in *Americans at the Gate: The United States and Refugees during the Cold War*, 167–96 (Princeton, NJ: Princeton University Press, 2008); Bassina Farbenblum, "Executive Deference in U.S. Refugee Law: Internationalist Paths through and beyond '*Chevron*,'" *Duke Law Journal* 60, no. 5 (2011): 1059–122; and Daniel Steinbock, "Interpreting the Refugee Definition," *UCLA Law Review* 45 (1998): 733–816.

3. See, e.g., Mark Gibney, "A 'Well-Founded Fear' of Persecution," *Human Rights Quarterly* 10, no. 1 (1988): 109–21; Mark Von Sternberg, "The Developing Law of 'Private' Persecution and Its Implication for the Convention Refugee Definition," *In Defense of the Alien* 21 (1998): 129–50; Kate Jastram, "Economic Harm as a Basis for Refugee Status and the Application of Human Rights Law to the Interpretation of Economic Persecution," in *Critical Issues in International Law: Strategies toward Interpretive Harmony*, ed. James Simeon, 143–73 (Cambridge: Cambridge University Press, 2010); Deborah Anker, "Refugee Protection, Gender-Based Violence and Trafficking in Persons," *In Defense of the Alien* 23 (2000): 129–37; and Todd Stewart Schenk, "A Proposal to Improve the Treatment of Women in Asylum Law: Adding a

'Gender' Category to the International Definition of 'Refugee,'" *Indiana Journal of Global Legal Studies* 2, no. 1 (1994): 301–44.

4. UN General Assembly, "Convention Relating to the Status of Refugees," July 28, 1951, *United Nations Treaty Series*, no. 189; UN General Assembly, "Protocol Relating to the Status of Refugees," January 31, 1967, *United Nations Treaty Series*, no. 606.

5. *Refugee Act of 1980*, Public Law 96-212, *U.S. Statutes at Large* 94 (1980): 102, title 1, sec. 101(a).

6. *Refugee Act of 1980*, Public Law 96-212, *U.S. Statutes at Large* 94 (1980): 102, title 2, sec. 202(e); codified at *U.S. Code* 8 (1980), sec. 1231, subd. (b)(3)(A).

7. Michael Walzer, *Spheres of Justice* (New York: Basic Books, 1983), 48.

8. Walzer, *Spheres of Justice*, 32.

9. Walzer, *Spheres of Justice*, 49.

10. Stefan Hueser, "Is There a Right to Have Rights? The Case of the Right to Asylum," *Ethical Theory and Moral Practice* 11, no. 1 (2008): 7.

11. Henry Shue, *Basic Rights*, 2nd ed. (Princeton, NJ: Princeton University Press, 1996), 34.

12. Shue, *Basic Rights*, 19, emphasis added.

13. Shue, *Basic Rights*, 31.

14. Shue, *Basic Rights*, 19.

15. Shue, *Basic Rights*, 20.

16. Shue, *Basic Rights*, 23.

17. Shue, *Basic Rights*, 53.

18. Shue, *Basic Rights*, 40–42.

19. Shue, *Basic Rights*, 48–50. See also Joseph Stiglitz, *Globalization and Its Discontents* (New York: Norton, 2002).

20. Animesh Ghoshal and Thomas Crowley, "Political versus Economic Refugees," *Review of Social Economy* 41, no. 2 (1983): 131.

21. Shue, *Basic Rights*, 29.

22. John Rawls, *The Law of Peoples* (Cambridge, MA: Harvard University Press, 1999), 4.

23. James Nickel, "Sanctuary, Asylum and Civil Disobedience," *In Defense of the Alien* 8 (1985): 181.

24. Nickel, "Sanctuary, Asylum and Civil Disobedience," 181.

25. See Susan Gzesh, "Central Americans and Asylum Policy in the Reagan Era," *Migration Information Source*, April 1, 2006, http://www.migrationpolicy.org/article/central-americans-and-asylum-policy-reagan-era; Human Rights Watch, "Guatemala Rights Abuses Escalate as Elections Near," November 8, 1990, https://www.hrw.org/report/1990/11/08/guatemala-rights-abuses-escalate-elections-near; and Human Rights Watch, "El Salvador's Decade of Terror: Human Rights since the Assassination of Archbishop Romero," October 1, 1991, https://www.hrw.org/report/1991/10/01/el-salvadors-decade-terror-human-rights-assassination-archbishop-romero.

26. Nickel, "Sanctuary, Asylum and Civil Disobedience," 177–78.

27. Nickel, "Sanctuary, Asylum and Civil Disobedience," 180.

28. Nickel, "Sanctuary, Asylum and Civil Disobedience," 181.

29. Nickel, "Sanctuary, Asylum and Civil Disobedience," 183.

30. Nickel, "Sanctuary, Asylum and Civil Disobedience," 178 n. 4.

31. See Jie Zong and Jeanne Batalova, "Refugees and Asylees in the United States," *Migration Policy*, June 7, 2017, http://www.migrationpolicy.org/article/refugees-and-asylees-united-states.

32. Zong and Batalova, "Refugees and Asylees in the United States."

33. Zong and Batalova, "Refugees and Asylees in the United States."

34. See Jie Zong and Jeanne Batalova, "Mexican Immigrants in the United States," *Migration Policy*, March 17, 2016, http://www.migrationpolicy.org/article/mexican-immigrants-united-states, and Gabriel Lesser and Jeanne Batalova, "Central American Immigrants in the United States," *Migration Policy*, April 5, 2017, http://www.migrationpolicy.org/article/central-american-immigrants-united-states.

35. Lesser and Batalova, "Central American Immigrants in the United States."

36. Lesser and Batalova, "Central American Immigrants in the United States."

37. Lesser and Batalova, "Central American Immigrants in the United States." The statistics suggest that many Salvadoran and Guatemalan nationals were compelled to enter without inspection and then subsequently applied for asylum. Salvadorans and Guatemalans represent a significant percentage of the applicants who successfully apply for asylum affirmatively or defensively in response to removal proceedings, but the percentages are not high: 8.3 and 8 percent, respectively (see Nadwa Mossaad, "Annual Flow Report," *DHS Office of Immigration Statistics*, November 2016, https://www.dhs.gov/sites/default/files/publications/Refugees_Asylees_2015.pdf, and Eyder Peralta, "Why a Single Question Decides the Fate of Central American Migrants," *National Public Radio*, February 25, 2016, http://www.npr.org/2016/02/25/467020627/why-a-single-question-decides-the-fates-of-central-american-migrants).

38. Jie Zong and Jeanne Batalova, "Mexican Immigrants in the United States," *Migration Policy*, October 9, 2014, https://www.migrationpolicy.org/article/mexican-immigrants-united-states-0.

39. Human Rights Watch, "Mexico's Disappeared: The Enduring Costs of a Crisis Ignored," February 20, 2013, https://www.hrw.org/report/2013/02/20/mexicos-disappeared/enduring-cost-crisis-ignored.

40. Human Rights Watch, "Mexico's Disappeared."

41. *Protocol Relating to the Status of Refugees*, January 31, 1967, *United Nations Treaty Series*, no. 606; *Refugee Act of 1980*, Public Law 96-212, *U.S. Statutes at Large* 94 (1980): 102, title 2, sec. 201(a), codified at *U.S. Code* 8 (1980), sec. 1101(a)(42)(A).

42. *Immigration and Naturalization Services v. Elias-Zacarias*, 502 U.S. 478 (1992).

43. We also should note the procedural posture of the case and the standard of review on appeal. Both the immigration judge and the BIA found that, based on his testimony, Elias-Zacarias's flight was motivated by fear of retaliation and the well-being of his family rather than a fear of persecution for his political opinion. Such findings of fact on appeal are upheld unless the appellant proves that no reasonable fact finder could find that he lacked the requisite fear of persecution (*Immigration and Naturalization Services v. Elias-Zacarias*, 502 U.S. at 483–84). There is a strong

presumption in favor of the fact finder's judgment and assessment of the applicant's credibility. This same presumption does not apply when an applicant offers testimony that his flight was motivated by his political opinion and the fact finder finds the testimony credible.

44. *Castro v. Holder*, 597 F.3d 93 (2nd Cir. 2010).

45. The burden of proof is on the alien to establish eligibility for asylum and, specifically, a fear of persecution on the basis of race, religion, political opinion, or one of the other protected bases *and* that the persecution was specifically motivated by that protected basis. *The Real ID Act of 2005*, Public Law 109-13, *U.S. Statutes at Large* 119 (2005): 231, 303, codified as *U.S. Code* 8 (2005), sec. 1158 (b)(1)(B)(i); *INS v. Elias-Zacarias*, 502 U.S. at 483; see also *Rivas-Martinez v. Immigration and Naturalization Service*, 997 F.2d 1143 (5th Cir. 1993).

46. Jonathan Hiskey et al., "Understanding the Central American Refugee Crisis: Why They Are Fleeing and How U.S. Policies Are Failing to Deter Them," *American Immigration Council*, February 2016, https://www.americanimmigrationcouncil.org/sites/default/files/research/understanding_the_central_american_refugee_crisis.pdf, 4.

47. Hiskey et al., "Understanding the Central American Refugee Crisis," 8.

48. Hiskey et al., "Understanding the Central American Refugee Crisis," 2.

49. Hiskey et al., "Understanding the Central American Refugee Crisis," 1.

50. The history of immigration law in the Unites States provides evidence of discriminatory animus with the Chinese Exclusion Act of 1882 and the Immigration Act of 1924, which created a permanent quota system based on citizens who counted as citizens at the time and effectively excluded applicants from nonwhite nations (see, e.g., Mae Ngai, "The Architecture of Race in American Immigration Law: A Reexamination of the Immigration Act of 1924," *Journal of American History* 86 [1999]: 67–92). Ngai explains, "The Immigration Act of 1924 law defined 'nationality' according to country of birth. But that definition did not apply to the American nationality. The statute excluded non-European peoples residing in the United States from the population universe governing the quotas. The law stipulated that 'inhabitants in continental United States in 1920' does not include (1) immigrants from the [Western Hemisphere] or their descendants, (2) aliens ineligible to citizenship or their descendants, (3) the descendants of slave immigrants, or (4) the descendants of the American aborigines [footnote omitted]'" (72).

Chapter Eleven

The Rights of Immigrants and the Duties of Nations

*On Cesar Chavez, Transnational Justice, and the Temporality of Rights**

Eduardo Mendieta

Barack Hussein Obama rose to the White House with the campaign slogan "Yes we can." At the end of his acceptance speech at the 2008 Democratic National Convention in Denver, Colorado, he closed by evoking Martin Luther King Jr.'s "I Have a Dream" speech by quoting the specific lines: "We cannot walk alone. And as we walk, we must make the pledge that we shall always march ahead. We cannot turn back."[1] Few may know that the slogan "Yes we can" was popularized by Cesar Chavez during his decades-long activism and union organizing on behalf of migrant and nonmigrant farmworkers. His slogan was "Si se puede." At the core of Chavez's work on the *causa*, the struggle for the rights of farmworkers, was also the theme of marching and the change that these poor and dignified but exploited and stigmatized workers and members of U.S. society represented. Their marching was a way to make themselves present in the U.S. public sphere and assert their justice claims. Like King, Cesar Chavez was a champion of nonviolent action and the transformative power of *peregrinaje*, pilgrimage, and *penitence*, penance. Above all, Chavez brought to the attention of

*I would like to thank Professor Stanko for the invitation to deliver the 2014 Cesar Chavez Intercultural Lecture at Elmhurst College in Elmhurst, Illinois; to President Alan Ray for his hospitality; and to all the students with whom I shared a wonderful two days there. I also want to thank Professor Mayra Rivera Rivera at the Harvard Divinity School for the invitation to present a different version of this chapter at the Divinity School and to participate in her graduate seminar. I also want to thank Len Lawlor at Pennsylvania State University for the invitation to the university and to all the faculty and graduate students there who also gave me feedback on this work in progress. Finally, I want to thank Kelly Oliver for her unfailing support and mentorship.

the U.S. public the plight of both documented and undocumented Mexican American farmworkers and, eventually, all the undocumented workers who are exploited, marginalized, and treated as outcasts. More than ever, in the contemporary United States, when we are seeing the revival and mainstreaming of white nativism, anti-Latino racism, and blatantly cruel and immoral anti-immigrant policies, such as the so-called repatriation of immigrants who came to the United States as children, we need to hear the voice and be informed by the example of a public intellectual and moral exemplar who championed the rights of immigrants, both irregular and regular, in general and Mexican Americans in particular.

In this chapter, I foreground Cesar Chavez as a unique Latino and U.S. leader who transformed the political culture of the United States, contributed to a unique social justice agenda, and in the process led to a deepening understanding of the vitality and promise of democracy in the United States. Building on one of Chavez's main agendas, the struggle against the injustice of U.S. immigration policies, I want to briefly discuss the nature, sources, and challenges of contemporary immigration. I aim to correlate some of the factors that catalyze emigrations with some of the political and ethical challenges we face as a nation. The thrust of the argument is that when we look at migration as a global challenge, our solutions have to address economic and political causes that require different forms of legal, moral, and ethical responses. In other words, the challenge of migration requires a variety of perspectives, and the solutions have to be multipronged and multilayered. I develop a philosophical approach that correlates the rights of immigrants with the duties of nations. A right entails a corresponding duty, and the question with respect to migration is this: what is the nature of the rights of immigrants, that is, what is their source, and what are the limits or conditions for fulfilling correlative duties? In the final section, I focus on rights as relations but most specifically as temporal relations. All discourse on rights hitherto has suffered from what I would call the "presentist" fallacy, that is, that such discourse thinks of rights as relations among temporally coeval legal subjects. I argue instead that rights are fundamentally about establishing relations across time, both backward and forward. A right is not only a power, a duty, a privilege, and a liability—to use Wesley Newcomb Hohfeld's fourfold description of rights—that is among legal equals but also a way to enter in analogous relationships with "temporal strangers," whether they be past or future generations. A rights claim may have immediacy and most pressing urgency with respect to legal coevals, but it always puts us in distinct legal and moral responsibilities with past and future generations.

CESAR CHAVEZ: WITNESS OF PEACE AND PENITENT OF JUSTICE

Cesar Chavez's activism and labor organizing, spanning as it did four decades, also became the historical register, the social archive, of the transformation that activism underwent in the United States. Chavez, like Martin Luther King Jr. and Malcom X, appealed to an anticolonial language that gave urgency to his struggle that made it command the attention of the American public. Undoubtedly, Chavez's success and the efficacy of La Causa were due to the fact that King, inspired by Gandhi, had made the language of nonviolence the vernacular of U.S. social and political movements during this decisive period in American history. At the same time, Chavez's appeal and success also had to do with the stark way in which he articulated an agenda of social transformation that rejected the language of violence and polarization that we saw in the Black Panthers, the Brown Berets, and the Weather Underground. Along with King's language of civil disobedience, nonviolence, and Christian agape, Chavez also brought in the Black Pride movement's language of autonomy, self-determination, self-reliance, and cultural pride. La Causa was as much about transforming conditions of exploitation and injustice as it was about affirming the cultural pride, political autonomy, and will to self-sufficiency of farmworkers.

Like Martin Luther King Jr., Chavez also drew on the symbolic and moral reservoir of his religion to fashion a distinctive message that resonated with the U.S. moral and religious identity. Chavez drew on his deep popular Catholicism but also on the Mexican American and Latino communities' Catholic sensibilities. Chavez's invocation of La Virgen de Guadalupe, Jesus the Farmer, Jesus the Poor and Friend, the God who is on the side of the poor, and the cross as the sign of the suffering Christ who is in solidarity with the suffering masses of the world appealed to the religiosity of U.S. culture in an authentic way. Thus, Chavez capitalized on the religious sensibilities of the American people while also nourishing his discourse at the well of his own Catholic faith.

At the core of Chavez's distinct politico-religious identity, we find three motifs that give his activism a distinctive character: *pilgrimage*, *penitence*, and *revolution* as the empowerment of the poor.[2] As many may recall, a lot of Chavez's success as an organizer and activist was achieved through the organization of marches across California and the Southwest. These Marchas, or walks, were forms of pilgrimage. A pilgrimage is a religious ritual that is meant to exhibit some form of devotion as well as a form of witnessing.[3] For Chavez, these marches were forms of exhibiting a devotion to the Causa and the witnessing to a quest for justice while living in accordance with the principle of nonviolence.

The second motif, penitence, had to do with Chavez's conviction that witnessing the suffering of the exploited required a suffering on the side of those advocating on their behalf. Penitence for Chavez meant to take on suffering in solidarity and empathy so that by undergoing that suffering, we would do penance but also get transformed to the cause of those who are struggling for justice.[4] Doing penance, submitting oneself to a voluntary form of suffering and privation, was a way to be humanized: "When any person suffers for someone in greater need, that person is human."[5]

The third motif in Chavez's lexicon of justice is that of a revolution. For him, however, this revolution is by the poor, for the poor, with the poor.[6] A true revolution had to establish conditions of equality and participation. If you are excluded and not treated equally in a movement for social justice, then this movement is not for a transformative revolution but rather a movement that aims to perpetuate and create more privileges for some and privations for others. Chavez's reference to revolution was a way for him to talk about deepening democracy. In fact, Chavez linked the language of revolution to what he often referred to as "creative nonviolence."[7] Nonviolence requires more ingenuity and courage than the uses of violence, which is always homogenizing and deindividualizing. Nonviolence was a pedagogy for democracy and, as José-Antonio Orosco notes, a way to begin to "decolonize" the mind.[8] At the center of Chavez's struggle for economic, political, and social justice for farmworkers in general and migrant workers in particular was putting on the democratic political agenda the question of the development of just immigration policies.

THE AGE OF GLOBAL MIGRATIONS

We could say in very general terms that the natural history of humanity is one of migration. We would not have become human without our ancestors' exodus from Africa to populate the world. Every major transition in the history of humanity is also punctuated by massive migrations. Let me just mention the ones that are most notable, at least from our perspective in the United States. First, there is the collapse of the Roman Empire, which is generally described as a collapse but was also determined by the so-called Barbarian Invasion. This invasion, or invasions, however, was but a process that began in the East, Mongolia, China, and what is today Russia, pushing waves of people into central Europe. The Barbarian Invasions that led to the collapse of the Roman Empire were nothing else than massive migrations catalyzed by wars of conquest that rippled across the Eurasian continent. What we know as Europe was literally born out of a massive migration.

The second example is perhaps the second-greatest global migration movement that our species has seen and one that was catalyzed by the so-called discovery of the New World. The peopling of the New World required a massive relocation of people from the Old World. The New World became an escape valve that allowed Europe to deal with its own internal challenges. What world historian Alfred Crosby called the great "Columbian Exchange" was also an exchange and extermination of populations.[9] The key point that I am trying to make is that migration, immigration, and emigration are not new challenges. They are part of the history of our species. We have become who we are today because we have wandered through the world in search of those opportunities that allow us to humanize ourselves.[10]

It can be said safely that contemporary global migration is fueled by poverty, wars, repression, and especially, over the past two decades, global climate change. A more disaggregated analysis, however, reveals that migration is a complex phenomenon. In his 2013 book *Exodus: How Migration Is Changing Our World*, Paul Collier identifies three "big" factors that drive international migration: first, the global income gap; second, the local impediments that offset investment and rewards; and, third, the size of the diaspora population in the target country.[11]

Let me discuss each one of these factors, which I would instead call processes. The global income gap is one way to talk about global inequality. There are many extremely poor people, in fact, the majority of the world population, and very wealthy people, a small minority. But even when we do not focus on the extremes, we can see that there are many humans living on very little and some living on a lot. That we live in the age of mass media has only made it more evident that there are incredible gaps between the have-nots and the haves. Somewhere else, there is a better life; somewhere else, there is a lot more that ought to be shared.

Nonetheless, just because there is putatively a better life somewhere else does not mean that you will pack up and embark on a long, perilous, and often suicidal journey. A migration or an emigration is an investment but also an exodus. Thus, a key factor in migration is the correlation between global blocks to migration and local possibilities for resources that can facilitate the journey. A migration voyage is both a personal and a communal investment that will meet certain constraints and barriers. The harder and higher are the legal and physical barriers, the more substantive and expensive is the individual and collective investment. Thus, when we look at migration, we have to consider the wide spectrum of controls on immigration and the different ways in which nations and cultures deal with migrants who circumvent their respective policies, regulations, and controls.

The third factor has to do with the size of the diaspora in the receiving country: the larger the diasporic community, the larger the corresponding immigration population. In other words, the larger a diasporic community is in a given country, the greater the chances are that there are family members, friends, and contacts who can facilitate immigration. Each country has incurred certain kinds of historical debts or imperial relationships with certain populations that then became permanent immigrant communities within its borders. Immigration in many cases is what Juan Gonzalez has called "the harvest of empire."[12] We can illustrate this by making reference to Indians and Caribbeans in England; Puerto Ricans, Cubans, and Mexicans in the United States; Turks in Germany; North Africans in France; and so on.

In contrast to Collier, then, I would say that immigration is due to both push and pull vectors. Global poverty constitutes the push force. Immigration policies counter this force with different degrees of efficacy across the globe. But local diasporic communities act as a pull force as well. Let me underscore that diasporic communities may be within a nation for reasons other than migration. Here, I like to use Gloria Anzaldúa's expression that for Chicanos and Mexican Americans, it was the border that crossed them and not the other way around, meaning that sometimes immigration to certain countries is the consequence of policies initiated by those countries. Immigration in this sense is always grounded in local histories that are embedded within geopolitical projects and imperial designs.

A look at migration today requires also that we be attentive to the variety of immigrations. In its "2013 World Migration Report," the International Organization for Migration notes that while most migration is from the South to the North in absolute numbers (because the global population of the South is larger than that of the North), this number is almost matched by migration from the South to the South. In other words, migration is a challenge not only for the developed North but also for the developing South. Nonetheless, I want to go back to the corridors and highlight some interesting facts. Migration from the North to the North follows established historical lines. Thus, we have a long historical relationship between Germany and the United States going back already at least two centuries. Note that the same is true for the corridors for South-to-North migration (and for North-to-South migration). In other words, migration does not happen just because the poor want to make it to a rich country. Migration happens because there are push and pull forces within different historically established relationships. Migration is always the evidence of historical debts, liabilities, and responsibilities. It could be said that migration is the weight of history on a nation.

Collier notes that the migration population grew from 92 million in 1960 to 165 million in 2000.[13] This is almost a doubling of people on exodus. This growth is anticipated to increase and accelerate precisely because the income gap between the North and the South has actually become more extreme since the early 2000s. Global inequality has grown only more acute in the past two decades. Add to this the increase in poverty and vulnerability due to the severe weather that we have seen over the past decades due to global warming, and we are indeed living in the age of the Anthropocene, which means also the age of mass human migrations.

HUMAN RIGHTS AND THE RIGHTS OF IMMIGRANTS

The challenge of immigration is Janus faced. On the one side, we have the rights claims and duties of immigrants; on the other, we have the right to self-determination of nations as well as their duties to their citizens and other nationals. In other words, immigration has to do with balancing two sets of rights claims and duties. In this section, I want to address first the rights of immigrants in terms of human rights. I will develop an argument that the right of migration is a fundamental human right. This right to migrate has two pillars. Joseph Carens, in his brilliant 2013 book *The Ethics of Immigration*, makes a useful distinction between two types of human rights. The first type is of general human rights that are inalienable and endowed in the personhood of each and every human being by virtue of their humanity.[14] These human rights are rights against the state and are independent of the state; that is, they are rights that preserve the integrity of the human being against the violence, control, or malignant neglect of any state. These rights are not secured, granted, or guaranteed by any state. In this sense, these rights are prior to the sovereign state. We could say that these rights are prepolitical. The second type of rights are membership-specific human rights; that is, they are rights that place the human being in specific relationships to their politico-legal community. These rights generally take the form of citizenship rights. They are rights that preserve the integrity of persons within political communities.

In the literature on human rights, a different terminology is used. Generally, human rights lawyers talk about first-generation, second-generation, third-generation, and, more recently, fourth-generation rights.[15] First-generation rights refer to what we could call subjective rights, or civil rights. These are rights that have to do with the bodily and symbolic integrity of being human, before and beyond any legitimate political authority. One could say that they are what I called earlier prepolitical rights. Second-generation rights refer to what Carens calls membership-specific rights. They are political rights, or the "right to have rights"—to use Hannah Arendt's terminology—within a polity. Third-generation rights are social rights. They are rights that ensure a basic standard of living, which is why they are debated and there is less consensus on them. Fourth-generation rights, still being debated, are cultural and linguistic rights, that is, the right to one's culture and thus to the language in which that culture lives and is passed on.

The question now is, what kind of right is the right to migrate? It can be argued that it is a right that is supported on two types of rights, or, to use Carens's language, it is a right that is both a general human right (a prepolitical right) and a membership-specific right. The right to migrate is grounded in the most fundamental, the most sacred, of all rights, namely, the right to life. If I have the right to live, then I have a right to secure and procure those things that would enable me to live. If I have a right to my life, then I also have the right to escape, evade, circumvent, and prevent those conditions that would hinder my ability to secure my life and survival.

Thomas Hobbes argued famously in *Leviathan* that by the right of nature, I have a right to enter into a compact that allows me to secure and preserve my life. By the same token, I preserve my right to exit that compact if my life is no longer secured by the sovereign. Of course, Hobbes had no use for human rights or natural rights, but when he talks about the right of nature, what he means is that by the logic of the natural will for self-preservation, we are entitled to create those institutions that would allow us to secure our lives. This intuition is retained in the human right to one's life. Now, the right to emigrate is grounded in this right to secure one's life and to prevent and/or circumvent those conditions that would put it in harm's way. The right to life is meaningless if I do not at the same time have the right to move in order to procure the means for my self-preservation. The right to emigrate is a human right because it is an indispensable condition of possibility for the bodily and symbolic integrity of human beings. In short, the right to life entails the right to motility, or mobility, the right of free movement.

We can then clearly see why no nation-state has the right to prevent citizens from exiting their borders and why, within its borders, citizens can and should be able to move unimpeded. At least this is the basic norm. No nation has a legitimate right not to allow its citizen to exit. The right to emigrate is the right of exit. Only totalitarian and despotic societies prevent their subjects from exiting. When they do so, they are violating the rights of their citizens as well as their human rights. Here, then, we see how the right of migration has two pillars: it is a general human right that all humans claim qua humans, one that is grounded in their right to life, but it is also a membership-specific right, that is, a right that I can claim against my specific nation-state.

Do nations thus have a correlative duty to accept or not turn away immigrants? In other words, if there is a human right to exit, to emigrate, is there a corresponding duty to be allowed to enter into another community? Is the basic right to mobility, which is the right to go anywhere, also the right to expect unimpeded entry? While we have an inalienable right of mobility, we do not have a corresponding right of entry or of arrival. To leave entails also to arrive. Do we have a corresponding right of arrival, a right to place, so to say? Here, human rights come up against the claims of nations that also make rights claims, of which the most important is the right to self-determination and sovereignty.

Interestingly, Immanuel Kant had already taken up this question in his 1795 essay *Toward Perpetual Peace*, where he stipulates that "cosmopolitan right" should be limited to the "conditions of universal hospitality."[16] The most basic of cosmopolitan rights is the right of "hospitality," which means that we all have the right not to be treated with hostility and that he or she may not be turned away if his or her life is in danger.[17] Kant's justification for this right is enlightening. We all have this right of hospitality because the earth is spherical, it belongs to no one, and we all can go anywhere on this sphere. No one has a greater or lesser right to any place on the planet. The earth is owned in common, or, rather, the earth is the commons to which all have access.

While the earth may not be owned by anyone in particular, we find that the earth is divided into territorial nation-states. Kant was aware of this fact. It is for this reason that *Toward Perpetual Peace* is an attempt to come up with the kind of legislation that would lead nations to collaborate toward peace. In this text, Kant called for a federation of nation-states with their respective national boundaries binding and bounding their specific territories. Thus, the right of hospitality reveals the fact of national borders. Kant, however, recognized that no nation has the right to turn away someone if by doing so his or her life would be put in danger. The right of hospitality turns out to be a right of asylum. If I have a right to migrate, I have a correspondingly weak right of entry—but as a right of asylum, not an immediate right of entry as a right to claim membership in the receiving nation. Thus, the right to emigrate does not directly translate into a right to immigrate. Why? Because the right to immigrate is a claim to another political community that has its own corresponding claimants and duties. Thus, so far, we have established that the right to migrate, which is the right to emigrate, derives from the right to motility or mobility, which is indispensable to the right to live, the right to one's life. The right to emigrate, however, does not entail a symmetrical right to immigrate because this is a right claimed of another political community.

We are now in the position of having to ask about the rights that nations may have that may trump the rights of nonnationals.[18] If we use the language of Ronald Dworkin, we can ask more pointedly, if we think of rights as trumps, to what extent do the rights of nations trump the rights of individual human beings? Or, using Carens's language, can membership-specific rights trump general human rights? It is clear that human rights are inalienable rights of humans and that they are prepolitical in the sense that existentially or ontologically, they precede the sovereignty of nation-states. The sovereignty of nations is circumscribed and limited by these rights. We can therefore say that membership-specific rights can never trump general human rights. The former presuppose the latter, or the former are meant to serve the latter. In other words, no nation-state can violate the right to emigrate of any human being, and, by the same token, no nation may categorically turn away anyone if by doing so the life of the requester of hospitality may be put in mortal danger. At most, nations can place limits and controls on those who claim the cosmopolitan right of hospitality, but these are conditional and not categorical.[19]

But if membership-specific rights do not trump general human rights, then what rights do nations have vis-à-vis noncitizens? In other words, do nations have any rights that can act as a type of privilege that would neutralize someone else's claims. Here, I would like to briefly introduce some legal language that American jurist Wesley Newcomb Hohfeld, who lived at the end of the nineteenth century and early part of the twentieth, coined that is extremely useful in helping us understand the syntax of rights discourse. Following Hohfeld, we can understand rights as having a quadratic, or fourfold, structure. Thus, a right is a claim that entails a corresponding duty, a privilege that neutralizes a claim or for which there is a nonclaim, a power that has a corresponding liability, and an immunity that entails a disability.[20]

To translate the right of mobility into Hohfeldian language, we could say that someone has a right to emigrate, for which there is the corresponding duty not to hinder someone's departure. We have the privilege to choose to depart an unsustainable situation, but there is no corresponding duty to so enable us to depart. We have the power to emigrate, which makes some liable to our departure, and we have the right to emigrate, meaning that we have the immunity from prosecution and punishment for wanting to do so. We could perhaps see how this unfolds if we were to talk about the right of hospitality. We have a right to claim hospitality, that is, the right of asylum, but no one specifically has the duty to so grant us such asylum (or perhaps it is a duty of nations that take as their basic point of departure the sacredness and inviolability of human rights). However, our claim to the right of cosmopolitan hospitality does make nations that subscribe to the inalienable rights of humans liable to the claim, which at the same time can never claim an absolute immunity from such a claim.

For the moment, let me turn to what rights that nations have vis-à-vis the rights of nonnationals who claim their human rights from this very nation. Here, I want to begin not with the historical givenness of nation-states but rather with the normative status of nation-states. Nation-states are not simply historical contingencies; they are part and parcel of the unfolding of the normative logic of moral, political, and legal life of societies. A nation is a community of memory, an imagined and imaginary community, with its specific history. But a nation is also a moral claim, or, rather, it exists because it is the performance of normative claims. Nations as normative claims have two groundings: the claim to self-determination and the claim to justice (if we think of nations and countries as instances of some sort of imagined or real social compact or social contract). We could say that nation-states are the embodiment of at the very least two forms of justice: procedural justice and distributive justice. In a nation-state's constitution, the two claims are distributed throughout its citizenship rights, or bill of rights, and division of powers. Now, from this normative standpoint, that nations are actual normative claims, we can see that one of the most important roles nation-states have is precisely the distribution of membership in their political communities. In fact, to use Hobbes's language, nation-states are based on the inalienable right to a compact, to a social contract, that grants me membership within a community of rights bearers.

Michael Walzer has argued in an important essay titled "The Distribution of Membership" that distributive justice presupposes a territorially and legally bounded world.[21] In other words, for a political community to enact distributive justice, it has to be something like a nation-state, that is, a form of political organization that distributes citizenship rights that enable justice claims. I agree with Walzer that nation-states are not simple accidents of history but that they are grounded in normative claims. In Walzer's case, the normative claim is that for us to be able to have distribute justice, we need bounded nations that can take on the task of distributing goods, rights, and so on. But Walzer notes that the primary and most precious of goods a nation can distribute is precisely that of membership. I would translate Walzer's language and say that distribute justice requires that there be political communities that secure the "right to have rights" of its citizens as long as this right does not impinge on the rights of others. Let us hold that thought for the moment and focus on the central idea that Walzer wants us to focus on, namely, that the primary good the nation-state can give is that of membership. In this sense, distributive justice requires that we be able to discriminate among those that have a greater and lesser claim to a fair distribution of social goods via the claim of citizenship rights. This makes it clear that this is one normative pillar for the right of nations to secure their borders and have things like passports and social security numbers. The other pillar for the normativity of nation-states is that they enact self-determination, and this is about the autonomy of peoples or nation-states. Another way of elucidating this other normative pillar is that the right to self-determination is the right to democratic authorship.

THE TIME OF RIGHTS

Thus far, I have been discussing the rights of immigrants, the duties of nations, and the limits of the rights of nations to exclude migrants. This discussion thus far has not included any reference to what I will call the "temporality of rights." By this term, I mean that rights are ways not only to secure a future but also to preserve a past. Rights produce temporality.[22] They allow us to fashion a future that draws on some past. At the very least, they secure our expectations about what is to come. A right is also a temporal claim. From the standpoint of nations, citizenship rights impose on citizens duties to past and future generations. It is in this sense that a nation's claim to its own historical identity is neither simply a claim to a contingent history nor a contingent claim. A nation's claim to its identity is a normative historical claim: it is a claim to its history. Democratic authorship, that is, the claim to self-determination, is thus also a claim to a certain history. At the same time, and to follow Walzer, if one of the most important duties of nations is the duty of distribution of membership, then this duty is a duty to its past and future generation. Indeed, if one of the most important duties of nations is to secure and preserve the membership of its citizens, then one of its duties is to establish bonds across generations and how newcomers can and are enabled to claim membership. For the same reason that nations cannot make their actual physical and political borders impermeable, to exclude "strangers," it also cannot close its temporal borders to "temporal strangers."[23]

The right to emigrate, which is based on the inalienable right of mobility or the right to leave, also has a temporal dimension. As we saw, the right of mobility entails the right of hospitality, or the right of asylum. This is the right to arrive. However, this right of arrival is conditional and temporary. The right of arrival grants refuge or sojourn but not a permanent home or permanent residence. I can stay but only for so long or as long as the welcoming nation allows or is able to grant sojourn without abrogating its duties to its citizens. I thus want to claim that just as the right of nations to self-determination and thus to establish and monitor borders is not absolute and cannot trump the right of migrants, nations also do not have the right to permanently exclude immigrants from membership in their polity. A strong version of this right would be that migrants have a right to claim political membership and that nations have the duty to make sure that migrants in their midst have viable ways of securing membership in such a way that they do not become second-class members or outcasts and an ostracized underclass.

In the case of the United States with its approximately 12.1 million irregular immigrants, a large majority of them of Mexican origin in particular and of Latin American origin in general, the country has a special duty to enact a moral and just immigration policy that, first and most important, does not criminalize irregular migration (which has very specific historical dimensions that are beyond the scope of this chapter) and that, second, creates a pathway to legal residence and eventually naturalization.[24] Furthermore, if we attend to the statistics maintained by the Department of Homeland Security—namely, that 50 percent of the irregular immigrant population in the United States has been in the United States for eleven to twenty years and 28 percent for more than twenty years compared to 34 and 11 percent in 2007, respectively, that is, the equivalent of a generation who thus have neither residency papers nor legal status—then the United States has *a special duty not to deport them and to grant them asylum and secure their right to membership*.[25] Here, I would like to quote Carens from his important essay "The Case for Amnesty": "The moral right of states to apprehend and deport irregular migrants erodes with the passage of time. As irregular migrants become more and more settled, their membership in society grows in moral importance, and the fact that they settled without authorization become correspondingly less relevant."[26] Another way to hold this insight would be to formulate the following principle: the right of motility entails the right of arrival, which has the legal correlate of the duty to grant asylum and permit refugee. The right of arrival entails the right to membership, whether temporary or permanent, which has the legal correlate of the duty to grant the means for either legal residency or permanent citizenship. At the very least, no nation has the right to permanently exclude from its political membership members of that society who may have arrived in its midst by nontraditional means. Temporal strangers are not only the past and future generations of a nation but also those who arrive at different times for different reasons within the borders of that nation.

To conclude, borders are the expression of the normative claim of nations, and specifically, they are exemplars of the political morality of nations that pay reverence to the rights of citizens and human beings in general. Borders, however, cannot be killing zones or mass graves. Borders, as the expression of the normative claim to distributive justice, are claims made in the name of the "right to have rights" that humans have, and, consequently, borders also cannot be impenetrable if only because they are always pierced by the cosmopolitan right to hospitality and the "right to have right" of all humans.

This is in part why I began with Cesar Chavez, whose life was dedicated to the claims of migrant workers and who translated into our political vernacular their justice claims. From Chavez, we learned that borders ought to be the human face of nations and not the mask of tyrants, the helmets of SS soldiers, the sword of terrifying Leviathans, or the killing machines of terrorist nations.[27] This means that immigration policies and thus border control policies have to be developed in accordance with the moral (i.e., normative) claims that nations themselves represent. In this chapter, moreover, I have brought to the forefront the temporal dimensions of the rights of migrants in general and irregular immigrants who have grown up within nations, in the United States especially, in order to make the additional claim that *no nation has the right to permanently exclude immigrants from claiming membership in its community*. A stronger version of this claim would be that nations have a special duty to facilitate the integration of immigrants into their political community. I think that recognition of these stronger and weaker versions of the claims of migrants is particularly important if we begin to realize that the challenges of immigration are going to grow more acute over the coming decades and more and more humans are going to be displaced and become "temporal strangers" in our midst.

EPILOGUE

George Orwell's *1984* presents a prophetic analysis of what I would call "mass-induced hysteria." Orwell writes, "The horrible thing about the Two Minutes of Hate was not that one was obliged to act a part, but that it was impossible to avoid joining in. A hideous ecstasy of fear and vindictiveness, a desire to kill, to torture, to smash faces in with a sledgehammer, seemed to flow through the whole group of people like an electric current, turning one even against one's will into a grimacing, screaming lunatic. And yet the rage that one felt was an abstract, undirected emotion which could be switched from one object to another like the flame of a blowlamp."[28]

Under President Trump, it seems that we have been living through "Two Years of Hate." Hate crimes have increased notably since 2014, when the Federal Bureau of Investigation recorded the lowest rate of hate crimes since statistics began being compiled. In 2016, we saw a significant spike in hate crimes, marking an 11.7 percent increase since 2014, while in 2017, a 12 percent increase was calculated over the 2016 percentages.[29] We witnessed the dramatic events at Charlottesville in August 2017 that led to the most inflammatory statements by a president in recent history and that many took to be endorsements of white supremacist violence. Trump rallies can be described as "the national hour of hate." Above all, however, Trump and his administration have unleashed the machinery of the state on so-called illegal immigrants. There is no favorite object of hate, scorn, derision, and vindictiveness for the hate machine of Trump and his White House than Latinos. All Latinos, in fact, have become suspect. Whether illegal or not, all Latinos have become "undeserving citizens."[30]

It is against this background that, more than ever, we need a Cesar Chavez who will turn our attention to the plight of not simply Mexican Americans—who make up the largest majority of so-called illegal immigrants—but all Latinos, who are guilty by skin color, their accents, and their last names. We Latinos now live in the United States not only as second-class citizens but also as undeserving citizens whose citizenship is effectively suspended until further notice. More than ever, we need the moral vision and fortitude of a Chavez, who always put human dignity, nonviolence, and democracy at the core of his Marchas and his Causa.

NOTES

1. Then presidential nominee Barack Obama's speech is available at http://www.nytimes.com/2008/08/28/us/politics/28text-obama.html.

2. Here, I am relying on José-Antonio Orosco, *Cesar Chavez and the Common Sense of Nonviolence* (Albuquerque: University of New Mexico Press, 2008). See also Ilan Stavans's introduction to Cesar Chavez, *An Organizer's Tale: Speeches* (New York: Penguin, 2008), as well as "A Penitential Procession," in *An Organizer's Tale*, 10–11.

3. Chavez, *An Organizer's Tale*, 12.

4. Chavez, *An Organizer's Tale*, 12.

5. Chavez, *An Organizer's Tale*, 235.

6. Chavez, *An Organizer's Tale*, 14.

7. See Chavez, *An Organizer's Tale*, 64.

8. Orosco, *Cesar Chavez and the Common Sense of Nonviolence*, 52.

9. Alfred W. Crosby, *The Columbian Exchange: Biological and Cultural Consequences of 1492* (Westport, CT: Praeger, 2003).

10. For statistics on global migration, see International Organization for Migration, "2015 Global Migration Trends Factsheet," 2015, http://gmdac.iom.int/global-migration-trends-factsheet.

11. Paul Collier, *Exodus: How Migration Is Changing Our World* (Oxford: Oxford University Press, 2014). For the three big factors, see pp. 38–40. Collier's work has received some critical attention, but, as is evident, I find his discussion of the pull and push processes useful for discussing some (but not all) of the factors that both pull and push people to uproot themselves.

12. Juan Gonzalez, *Harvest of Empire: A History of Latinos in America* (New York: Penguin, 2011).

13. Collier, *Exodus*, 50–51.

14. See Joseph Carens, *The Ethics of Immigration* (Oxford: Oxford University Press, 2013), 90–96.

15. See Jack Donnelly, *Universal Human Rights in Theory and Practice* (Ithaca, NY: Cornell University Press, 2013).

16. Immanuel Kant, *Toward Perpetual Peace and Other Writings on Politics, Peace and History*, ed. Pauline Kleingeld, trans. David L. Colclasure (New Haven, CT: Yale University Press, 2006), 82, Ak 8:357–58.

17. Kant, *Toward Perpetual Peace and Other Writings on Politics, Peace and History*, 82, Ak 8:357–58.

18. See the brief, synoptic, but extremely useful and on-point Christopher Bertram, *Do States Have the Right to Exclude Immigrants?* (Cambridge: Polity Press, 2018).

19. See Eduardo Mendieta, "The Right to Political Membership: Democratic Morality and the Rights of Irregular Immigrants," *Radical Philosophy Review* 14, no. 2 (2011): 177–85.

20. See Wesley Newcomb Hohfeld, "Some Fundamental Legal Conceptions as Applied in Judicial Reasoning," *Yale Law Journal* 23, no. 1 (1913): 16–59. See specifically p. 30.

21. Michael Walzer, "The Distribution of Membership," in *Boundaries: National Autonomy and its Limits*, ed. Peter G. Brown and Henry Shue, 1–35 (Totowa, NJ: Rowman & Littlefield, 1981). See also Michael Walzer, *Spheres of Justice: A Defense of Pluralism and Equality* (New York: Basic Books, 1983), specifically chapter 2, "Membership."

22. Niklas Luhmann, in *Law as a Social System* (New York: Oxford University Press, 2004), from a systems theory approach, refers to law as a system for temporal closure, that is, for regularizing our temporal expectations.

23. Here, I am adopting an expression coined by Melissa Yates in a talk titled "Governing as Strangers: Rethinking Cosmopolitan Strategies of De-Alienation," delivered at the meeting of the Critical Theory Roundtable at Pennsylvania State University, November 11–13, 2016. See also David Miller, *Strangers in Our Midst: The Political Philosophy of Immigration* (Cambridge, MA: Harvard University Press, 2016).

24. See U.S. Department of Homeland Security, "Estimates of the Unauthorized Immigrant Population Residing in the United States," 2014, https://www.dhs.gov/immigration-statistics/population-estimates/unauthorized-resident. See also Valeria Luiselli, *Tell Me How It Ends: An Essay in Forty Questions* (Minneapolis: Coffee House Press, 2017).

25. See U.S. Department of Homeland Security, "Estimates of the Unauthorized Immigrant Population Residing in the United States," figure table 1, p. 4.

26. Joseph H. Carens, *Immigrants and the Right to Stay* (Cambridge, MA: MIT Press, 2010), 18.

27. See Eduardo Mendieta, "Assassination Nation: The Drone as Thanatological Dispositif," in *The Life of Reason in an Age of Terrorism*, ed. Charles Padrón and

Krzysztof Piotr Skrowronski, 61–78 (Leiden: Brill, 2018), and Eduardo Mendieta, "The U.S. Border and the Political Ontology of 'Assassination Nation': Thanatological *Dispositifs*," *Journal of Speculative Philosophy* 31, no. 1 (2017): 82–100. See also Reece Jones, *Violent Borders: Refugees and the Right to Move* (New York: Verso, 2016).

28. George Orwell, *1984* (New York: Everyman's Library, 1992), 16.

29. Brian Levin, Jame Nolan, and John David Reitzel, "New Data Shows US Hate Crimes Continue to Rise in 2017," June 26, 2018, http://theconversation.com/new-data-shows-us-hate-crimes-continued-to-rise-in-2017-97989.

30. Leo R. Chavez, *Anchor Babies and the Challenge of Birthright Citizenship* (Stanford, CA: Stanford University Press, 2017), chapter 1.

Chapter Twelve

The Origin That Never Was

The Loss of Heimat *and New Beginnings*

Gertrude Postl

"*Heimat*: a German word that denotes the relationship of a human being toward a certain spatial social unit. The term forms a contrast to social alienation and usually carries positive connotations. It is often expressed with such terms as 'home' or 'homeland,' but it has been alleged that the word has no English equivalent."[1] The term *Heimat* usually refers to a certain territory, a region, to a place of living, a close-knit social group or family, a linguistic and cultural identity, and it is considered the point of one's origin—where one comes from. It derives said "positive connotations" from its reference to an alleged overall familiarity that organizes and gives meaning to the conduct of one's life, to a place of acceptance and belonging. What is considered home or *Heimat* is that which is known and not strange, not alien, not uncanny, that which remains unquestioned. *Heimat* does not take into account any form of difference (be it within itself or from another). *Heimat* is pure identity, unity, homogeneity; it is the guarantee of a single origin that never was. Thus, the very notion of *Heimat* depends on a distancing from it, on an outside view. Only those who leave the unquestioned familiarity of one's origin will call it *Heimat* or home—there is no necessity for the term as long as everything (behavior, gestures, values, relationships, rituals, and language) has meaning within a given, preestablished context.

The loss of *Heimat* or home is at the core of the refugee experience. No matter how refugees are treated in the country of their destination—be it a welcome or confinement to a camp—they will always be marked by, they will always carry with them, the loss of something called origin, the loss of an unquestioned belonging, the loss of a life where everything had meaning, where everybody understood what they said. This would have been a time during which the notion of *Heimat* or home was not yet part of their vocabulary; there was no need for calling it such. Only through the experience of difference, of a distance, does a notion like *Heimat* become meaningful. One's *Heimat*, one's cultural home, that which is familiar and unquestioned, can be recognized as such only from the outside—only the experience of a different culture, of the loss of home, helps to establish the alleged origin that was never recognized as such when one was still part of it.

> We lost our home, which means the familiarity of daily life. We lost our occupation. . . . We lost our language. . . . We were told to forget . . . we were reminded that the new country would become a new home. . . . The more optimistic among us would even add that their whole former life had been passed in a kind of unconscious exile and only their new country now taught them what a home really looks like.[2]

Hannah Arendt's famous account of the Jewish refugee experience, with its focus on her people's seeming optimism and willingness to assimilate, looks at the loss of *Heimat* as something that can be overcome: "as soon as we were saved . . . we started our new lives."[3] But this account also has a subtext: "our proclaimed cheerfulness is based on a dangerous readiness for death."[4] The suicides of Jewish refugees she mentions are the price paid by some for the inability to seamlessly transition from one country to the next, from one language into another. Leaving one's home is never easy, and making a new home in a strange, yet-unknown country is even harder. What Arendt fails to question, though, is whether the *Heimat* they left and lost ever really was their home. She admits that Jews already had substantial experience with assimilation: "It is the history of a hundred and fifty years of assimilated Jewry."[5] According to Arendt, in order to remain Jews, they had to prove their "non-Jewishness."[6] The home they had to leave behind was never the homogeneous safe haven they made it out to be in retrospect. The German *Heimat* in which Jewish people lived was a *Heimat* only because they were willing to submit to a lifestyle and cultural norms they themselves had never created. Their *Heimat* was a fiction of unity, togetherness, and familiarity; the seeming homogeneity was built on a minority's willingness to adapt, on an overall ignorance of that which disrupted, irritated, undermined the proclaimed cultural homogeneity and identity. The Jewish people have been training for a long time to develop the alleged optimism and the ability to assimilate that Arendt attributes to them. Cultures are never homogeneous, and *Heimat* gains its glorified status only from the outside, after having left it behind:

> *What is proper to a culture is to not be identical to itself.* Not to not have an identity, but not to be able to identify itself, to be able to say "me" or "we." . . . There is no culture or cultural identity without this difference *with itself* . . . "with itself" [*avec soi*] also means "at home (with itself)" [*chez soi*]. . . . In this case, self-difference, difference to itself . . . there is no self-relation, no relation to oneself, no identifica-

> tion with oneself, without culture, but a culture of oneself *as* a culture *of* the other, a culture . . . of the *difference to oneself* . . . a culture never has a single origin.[7]

Trying to understand the notions of home, culture, and origin does not require the refugee experience. Jacques Derrida is here talking about the new Europe, about "Today's Europe"—which is by now a Europe of the past. The contemporary Europe cannot be thought of any longer without taking into account the refugee crisis. Nevertheless, Derrida's observations on home, culture, and origin offer valuable contributions to understanding the contemporary Europe, a Europe put to the test because of the refugee crisis.

Heimat, being "at home," always entails this "difference *with itself*," but as long as one is at home, this difference is not admitted, is overlooked, does not become accessible. The very notion of refugee presupposes that there once was a place the refugee belonged to, a place he or she could claim as their own, a place of identity and familiarity, a place without estrangement, without difference, without any other, a place of origin and rootedness that contributes to defining one's entire being: *Heimat*, home, home country. Refugees are forced to leave their home and home country; they are trying to find a new home. During this process, they are without a home country and most likely without a home. They transition through different countries and through temporary substitute homes, such as camps, shelters, temporary housing arrangements, tents, or cardboard boxes. They have lost their *Heimat*, and they are searching for a new one. The more impossible it becomes to find a new *Heimat*, the stronger the urgency to turn the old one into a place of longing, yearning, and desire—"my *Heimat* is my origin and I am where I came from." To be at home is never questioned as long as one is at home. But through the very process of moving away, the lost origin is elevated to an idealized place; it becomes something else in the process of transitioning away from it. Like Hélène Cixous's memories of the Jardin d'Essais in Algiers, "I didn't want to go to Algeria and thus I preserved intact the ideal beauty of the Jardin d'Essais, as it was invented by my father. . . . I hoped not to go to Algeria long enough, and thus to keep the Jardin d'Essais like a reedition of Paradise on earth . . . Algeria. To go there as in a dream, that would be the ideal I said to myself. To go there as *a dream*, I dreamed."[8] She does not want to go back, as reality might taint the idealized image; better to continue dreaming of that which once was. The meaning of that which is left behind changes through the very process of moving away. While the place of one's cultural origin is an unquestioned identity of context and background, a normalcy taken for granted as long as one lives there and attends to the ordinary conduct of life, it becomes *Heimat* only when threatened or lost. Distance creates the very entity one is in the process of being distanced from; only distance allows encountering "this difference with itself." As a refugee in the midst of a foreign culture, one realizes that "a culture never has a single origin."[9]

However, refugees claim their identity on grounds of this fictional but also real identity of lost origin—the respective nation-state that issued their passport. What they are, what they have been, and what they want to become is as much determined by the construct of *Heimat* they left behind as by the nation-state they are a member of, and both will in turn affect the future home they want to build. A respective nation-state gets imbued with the narrative of *Heimat* and origin. A longing for something that never was, something that gets constituted through the very experience of its loss, will inform the entire transition process from one country to the other. National as well as international laws confirm the fiction as well as the reality: being granted asylum (at least in Europe at the moment) depends on which home country one left behind. Some home countries are preferable over others when it comes to getting the chance for a new home. A passport indicating the membership within a particular nation-state increases or decreases the chance of becoming a member in yet a different nation-state. Transactions of people between nation-states rest on the trust in a legitimate origin, a place of cultural and linguistic identity—only those who can prove that they were members of a nation-state and had a *Heimat* are given the chance to find a new *Heimat* in a new nation-state. Fiction and reality merge; the origin that never was now becomes the condition for the chance to find a new place of belonging. But the refugee experience is per se the experience of difference, the encounter with the other. Thus, the new *Heimat*, a dream in response to a fundamental loss, turns out to be no *Heimat* at all since it will never live up to the standards established by the origin myth of the old one—Arendt's account of the suicides of Jewish refugees although they had been saved. The lived experience of difference and separation is not compatible with a fiction of unity and togetherness.

Discussing the paradoxes of hospitality, Jacques Derrida distinguishes between the foreigner (the one protected under the "law of hospitality") and "the absolute, unknown, anonymous other" to whom, under the command of "absolute hospitality," we should open our home "without asking of them either reciprocity . . . or even their names."[10] Could this distinction help to explain the differences in acceptance/rejection of refugees in Western countries? Could the proximity between "my" *Heimat* and "theirs," the closeness of imagined origins, account for a willingness to open one's borders? Hungary in 1956, Poland in 1981, the wars in the Balkans in the 1990s: in all these instances, European countries were quite welcoming and accommodating toward refugees. Are people coming from Syria, Iraq, Afghanistan, Eritrea, or Sudan perceived as "the absolute, unknown, anonymous other," "treated not as a foreigner but as another barbarian"?[11] Be it fiction or reality, one's origin matters. Geographical distance and too-obvious differences in terms of looks, religion, social practices, or lifestyle pose a threat to the construction of *Heimat* of the respective receiving countries. *Heimat* is not as such identical with the nation-state. If feeling threatened in their imagined identity, different nation-states might recur to their alleged similarities, might create a "super-origin" that also never was. Europe as *Heimat*? The shaky grounds of a European identity that triggers the pressure to fight off a "Muslim invasion" from the Middle East and Africa, an identity that has to defend its hard-won fragile unity against "the absolute, unknown, anonymous other," thereby failing to live up to the standards even of the "law of hospitality"—let alone "absolute hospitality"?

According to the "official discourse"—sanctioned by governments, reiterated by mainstream media, and believed by anybody who does not want to look too closely—a refugee leaves one home behind in order to find a new one somewhere else. Getting from one to the other involves the crossing of barriers or borders or waters or walls or fences. The certainty of finding a new home somewhere else is highly questionable; thus, the process involves the risk of getting stuck in an extended limbo or extended state of homelessness even after having managed to overcome various border obstacles. In the search for a new home, people might end up with no home at all. But originating in a particular home country (having a national identity or citizenship) is the prerequisite for getting the opportunity to be considered for a new home. This "official discourse" rests on the assumption of an identifiable origin (the old *Heimat*) and a clear-cut goal to be reached (the new *Heimat*). The period in between, spent in camps, temporary housing, or shelters, is considered a mere transition, a negligible process, that will eventually disappear in oblivion as soon as the new *Heimat* is found. What matters for the "official discourse" is not the "self-difference, difference to itself . . . a difference at once internal and irreducible to the 'at home' (with itself)."[12] Contrary to Derrida's claim that "a culture never has a single origin," the "official discourse" treats any cultural home or *Heimat* as homogeneous, as a single-origin entity that—if the refugee project succeeds—will be replaced with another homogeneous, self-identical place of home. The origin has been lost, but a replacement will be found—the "official discourse" contributes to creating a "myth of *Heimat*" so as to not face "the difference to itself," meaning the differences within a given country that always existed. That this *Heimat* never was the place it is made out to be in retrospect, after having left it (enforced or otherwise), gets overlooked, not admitted, and repressed.

The homogeneity, cultural identity, sameness, purity, and nondifference implied in the notion of *Heimat* does not allow for the realization that the other, the nonsame, or the outsider has always already been inside. Jews have lived in Germany as long as there existed a Germany, French citizens inhabited Algeria from the time it was colonized by France at the end of the 1820s, and people opposed to the Syrian regime lived inside Syria long before the current civil war started. The list goes on. The specific historical circumstances that force people to leave their *Heimat* or home country differ, but the pattern stays the same—the unwillingness or inability to acknowledge that inside and outside can never be clearly distinguished from each other, that the stranger is always already amongst the natives. Countries and cultures are mixed entities; they are not structured along clearly determinable binary oppositions (here vs. there, us vs. them). Rather, they are woven together in terms of a complex permeability that renders any attempt toward clear separation and identification impossible. As Trinh T. Minh-ha put it, "The named 'other" is never to be found merely over there and outside of oneself, for it is always over here, between Us, within Our discourse that the 'other' becomes a nameable reality . . . cultures are far from being unitary, as they have always owed their existence more to differences, hybridities and alien elements than they really care to acknowledge."[13] The notion of *Heimat* does not admit that there is an outside, that the other is always already among us, that difference is a constituting factor for any type of group identity—be this a nation-state or some other configuration.

Homelands have always expelled their unwanted members, have not admitted the "hybridities and alien elements," and have forced them with subtle as well as violent means to disguise, to assimilate, to go into hiding, or—if no other options was left—to go away. Exclusion, border control, and double standards in treatment and in naming and insisting on an illusory purity of cultural heritage are the main building blocks of any country or nation-state. *Heimat* has always been welcoming only for those who already were part of it. Home, culture, and country were never homogeneous with respect to language, values, lived experiences, belief systems, and so on. Exclusion or denying somebody entry is not just the sad privilege of desired new home countries (at the moment Western, especially European, nations) but has always existed within each culture and nation. Part of the fiction of *Heimat*—and thus the home country or the nation-state—is that within its boundaries, everybody is similar, that values and lived experiences are shared, that a common language, history, and culture binds them together—thus creating the myth of an origin that never was. But there always have been those who did not fit in, who could on grounds of arbitrary decisions be expelled, declared as second-class citizens, or even persecuted and killed—ethnic minorities; other races; members of different, unwanted religions; gays and lesbians; the economically unfit; the unruly; the resentful; those who in their very being embodied and thus revealed the fictional character of the entire *Heimat* construct; and those who visibly represented the cracks and fissures of a *Heimat*-based notion of identity. As the story goes, those who have no *Heimat* have no identity—no matter whether they live inside or outside given national boundaries.

But the status of the outsider, of not fitting in, of being expelled, is also a chance for those driven away—previously not realized spaces and courses of action might emerge that help them escape the traps of the origin myth. They know that having no *Heimat* sharpens the gaze for the "difference *with itself*"; it creates an interest in many cultures and a desire to speak more than one tongue. As Gloria Anzaldúa, speaking from her Chicana experience in the United States, has noted, "As a mestiza I have no country, my homeland cast me out; yet all countries are mine because I am every woman's sister or lover."[14] This mestiza develops a new consciousness, "a consciousness of the Borderlands."[15] Living in "the Borderlands"—as do all those who are cast out, driven away, or forced to leave—opens up possibilities no matter how desperate the experience of the loss of one's *Heimat* might be. In Anzaldúa's account, living in "the Borderlands" (taken as a descriptive term as well as a metaphor) is not limited to all those who had to leave their home; it becomes a political, aesthetical, linguistic program for all of us. If the origin myth does not hold any longer, if the meaning of *Heimat* becomes more and more fragile, where else to live in times like ours than in "Borderlands"? "The new mestiza" becomes the guide for "developing a tolerance for contradictions, a tolerance for ambiguity. . . . She learns to juggle cultures. She has a plural personality, she operates in a pluralistic mode . . . she turns the ambivalence into something else," which leads to "(a) massive uprooting of dualistic thinking in the individual and collective consciousness . . . that . . . brings us to the end of rape, of violence, of war."[16] It is this dualistic thinking that keeps a misguided notion of *Heimat* in place, that contributes to the myth of the origin—we/them, inside/outside, native/foreigner, familiar/strange, and firmly rooted/being displaced. Entering "the Borderlands" and claiming all countries as one's home helps to realize the fictional character of one's original home and the misguided desire to find a substitute. And even though we all, in one way or the other, live in Anzaldúa's "Borderlands," refugees and immigrants have to appropriate the term quite practically in its literal sense—for them, it means to stay in "the Borderlands," to claim all countries, to cross all borders, to speak many languages, to live a cultural crossbreeding and multilayered pluralism, and to question one's own origin myth.

But as stated already, in a certain sense, we are all refugees, immigrants, and foreigners. Moving between countries, languages, and cultures; being at home everywhere and nowhere; constantly crossing borders of many different kinds; and being accustomed to strangeness and still missing the familiar—knowing that "a culture never has a single origin" but still yearning for this one origin that never was, knowing that geographical rootedness is a thing of the past and still being sentimentally attached to elements of one's *Heimat*: contradictions, ambiguities, and uncertainties. Perhaps living in "the Borderlands" can serve as an accurate description for life in the twenty-first century.

As Julia Kristeva has pointed out, we all carry the foreigner in us; we are foreign to ourselves. Discovering our own "disturbing otherness" moves us closer to the actual other, the outsider, the one who allegedly does not belong here: "The foreigner is within me, hence we are all foreigners. If I am a foreigner, there are no foreigners."[17] This realization, in turn, leads to new forms of communities characterized by the absence of any community bond—a "paradoxical community," as Kristeva calls it, "made up of foreigners who are reconciled with themselves to the extent that they recognize themselves as foreigner."[18] Granted, the life of the actual refugee or immigrant differs significantly from the lives we ordinary foreigners have the luxury to live, but still, maybe there is some common ground, some proximity between the so-called native and the refugee/immigrant, that can be and should be further explored. Their experiences are not mutually exclusive; the loss of *Heimat* and the subsequent ongoing movement and search for a temporary replacement apply to both groups, although in a very different sense. "Not belonging to any place, any time, any love. A lost origin, the impossibility to take root, a rummaging memory, the present in abeyance. The space of the foreigner is the moving train, a plane in flight, the very transition that precludes stopping."[19] Here again, we find a fitting image for life in the twenty-first century, typical for many, not only for refugees or foreigners—being constantly on the move, not belonging to anything or anywhere, unrooted, and at home in many places and nowhere.

However, even if the loss of a *Heimat* that never was might constitute some common ground between the refugee and the rest of us, one essential difference remains: some of us have—if not a *Heimat* at least—a home, a house, a place to live. Without an habitable home, without a somewhat functioning, not-war-torn nation-state to live in, the prerequisite for any form of hospitality loses its ground. I can welcome somebody into my house only if I have a house. That, as Derrida points out, recent "techno-scientific possibilities threaten the interiority of the home ('we are no longer at home!')" further complicates matters. "Wherever the 'home' is violated . . . the traditional conditions of hospitality" are threatened.[20] If we have a house but do not feel at home in this house, the likelihood of performing acts of hospitality decreases. Insecurities and fears regarding our respective own Western nation-states are running rampant; sovereignty—be it over one's own house or with respect to one's home country—can no longer be taken for granted. Kristeva's claim that "the foreigner is within me" finds a frightful parallel on the level of the state—the "foreigner" is also within my house, my country, not only as refugee or immigrant but also, in Derrida's account, as the paradox of state-sanctioned forms of surveillance in the service of democratization and transparency of information.[21] Accepting and welcoming "the absolute, unknown, anonymous other" becomes more and more difficult if one is no longer sure about one's own house, one's own country, or one' own inner life, if the loss of one's *Heimat* is an always-present possibility, even without being forced to leave.

But still, and without belittling the horror and despair of the contemporary refugee experience, the inhumane treatment of refugees in camps, through border controls, bureaucratic obstacles, and general hostility—living in "Borderlands," discovering one's own "disturbing otherness," and experiencing the loss of *Heimat*—entails possibilities and offers a chance. Leaving one's *Heimat*—be it as refugee or otherwise—changes the perspective and enables insights that are not accessible when living, speaking, and thinking within the secure confinement of one's original home country. The belief in one origin, one culture, one language, and one *Heimat* is limiting; it reinforces an either/or perception of reality, translated into dualistic patterns of thought and a black-and-white mapping of the world.

Above all, it entails a self-referential, affirmative use of language and writing. The trust in the workings of this one language, in its history and cultural foundation, is indispensable to upholding the belief in *Heimat*. If the language is lost, *Heimat* is lost—so the belief goes. In the words of Hannah Arendt, "We lost our language, which means the naturalness of reactions, the simplicity of gestures, the unaffected expression of feelings."[22] But do we ever lose our original language? Is it not rather the case that it never really leaves us, that we carry it with us wherever we go, thus turning it into the ultimate remnant of *Heimat*? "Exiles, the deported, the expelled, the rootless, the stateless, lawless nomads, absolute foreigners, often continue to recognize the language, what is called the mother tongue, as their ultimate homeland"; thus, language becomes "a *remains* of belonging."[23] However, this somewhat idealized view of the mother tongue is only half of the story—according to Derrida, this language of belonging never fully was mine. Furthermore, this view fails to acknowledge that certain reactions, gestures, and expressions could never be conveyed through one's original language. If only one language is spoken, there always looms the danger of its becoming sterile. Without stimulation from outside, the familiarity of the mother tongue might turn repetitive and exclusive, a mere means of self-assurance and comfort. One only says what one already knows. In that the mother tongue is so clearly related to *Heimat*, we tend to overlook its flaws and deficiencies; most important, we overlook the fact that it never was fully "mine" in the first place. "Language is also the experience of expropriation, of an irreducible *exappropriation*. What is called the 'mother' tongue is already 'the other's language.'"[24] Just as the foreigner—this "absolute, unknown, anonymous other"—is always already among and within us, undermining and endangering the comfortable feeling of being at home in one's *Heimat*, so is the foreign language. Our so-called mother tongue is never fully ours. If "a culture never has a single origin," then it also cannot have just one single language.

"To depart from one's own language of origin . . . to fare like a foreigner in this language, and to return to it via its traveling fragments is also to learn how to be silent and to speak again, differently."[25] Being forced into a new language silences the old one, at least temporarily. But in Trinh Minh-ha's account, this silence is not a dead end, a mute submission to the new status of being an outsider in a foreign land. This enforced silence can be used to linguistically regroup; to train one's hearing, which, for Trinh Minh-ha, is also always a form of seeing ("the question is not so much to choose between sight and speech, as to *see what the eye hears, and hear what the ear sees*"[26]); and to revisit one's own language from the perspective of the linguistic outsider. New possibilities of using one's old language emerge, possibilities that are neither on the side of the mother tongue nor within the new language one has been forced to learn. As Derrida puts it within the context of his discussion of absolute hospitality, "Keeping silent is already a modality of possible speaking."[27] A previously unknown linguistic in-between zone opens up, options never realized before become available, and silence turns into a conveyer of meaning, becoming part of the signifying network itself, partaking in an ongoing interplay with the spoken and written signs.

Not to forget the written signs. How would we know about the origin that never was, about the many different "*Heimats*," that we all carry within us, if it were not for the numerous texts that established and reiterated the origin story and the myth of *Heimat*? Each culture is its own textual *Heimat*—from folk songs and fairy tales to philosophical treatise, novels, poems, and, in more recent periods, movies and TV shows.[28] *Heimat* and the origin that never was manifest themselves also through textual entities that articulate, represent, and confirm the alleged belonging to a group and region. Fortunately, though, this close affiliation between *Heimat* and texts also works in the opposite direction. The activity of writing also helps to put into focus the confinements and limitation of the one mother tongue. Many of those who were driven away by their home country were writers who questioned the very concept of *Heimat* and origin. Maybe those writing refugees should be granted a special place within the exile experience in that they help to convey what it means to encounter the "difference with itself," the "disturbing otherness" within ourselves; in short, they put into words what it means to live in "the Borderlands":

> For a number of writers in exile, the true home is to be found, not in houses, but in writing . . . home has proven to be both a place of confinement and an inexhaustible reservoir from which one can expand. And exile, despite its profound sadness, can be worked through as an experience of crossing boundaries and charting new ground in defiance of newly authorized or old canonical enclosures.[29]

Again, it is not the one or the other. There are "Borderlands" also for writing, the "disturbing otherness" found within oneself turned into a text—yes, one's mother tongue will always be an invaluable resource for any writer, but this very same mother tongue also limits, forces the author to return to that which is already known, and imposes itself as structural and semantic standard that is difficult to escape without excursions beyond the *Heimat* origin, be those excursions enforced or voluntary. One's own language is both "confinement and an inexhaustible reservoir," and it is under this premise that the writer has to be viewed as a permanent exile, never having had a home and never finding a home but nevertheless being at home in an ongoing transitioning process in that thing called "text." "Writers who, in writing, open to research the space of language rather than reduce language to a mere instrument in the service of reason or feelings, are bound like the migrant to wander from country to country . . . they disturb the classical economy of language and representation, and can never be content with any stability of presence."[30]

Maybe it is the writer who best epitomizes the experience of exile, of wandering, of not belonging, of the loss of *Heimat*. Many writers have been exiled—for their willingness to accept "the absolute, unknown, anonymous other," for knowing about "this difference with itself," for discovering "the foreigner within." The writer as mestiza, living in Borderlands, having a new consciousness but also a very old one, going back many centuries and exploring diverse cultural histories; the writer, always threatened with being silenced and nevertheless speaking several languages at once; the writer as the one to express, to put into words and signification, the experience of loss, estrangement, alienation, and homelessness; the writer who dismantles (deconstructs?) the myth of *Heimat*, the belief in the one origin, the one culture, the one language; the writer as the ultimate refugee, immigrant, as the homeless, border-crossing cosmopolitan citizen of the twenty-first century who never really had a *Heimat* but still yearns for one. Or shall we ask the question in reverse? Isn't every refugee, immigrant, and foreigner a potential writer in that his or her experience is—at the same time—inside and outside the established codes of representation? On the one hand, the refugee experience cannot be put into words because it exceeds anything imaginable, cannot be related to an ordinary conduct of life; on the other hand, it has to be put into words to make it accessible to those who at least can still live in the illusion of having a *Heimat*. Only then can they, in an act of absolute hospitality—in spite of their own volatile homes and threatened certainty over their mother tongue—offer a new illusion of *Heimat*, at least temporarily, for a brief moment, "without asking of them either reciprocity . . . or even their names."[31]

NOTES

1. Wikipedia contributors, "Heimat," *Wikipedia: The Free Encyclopedia*, October 4, 2017, https://en.wikipedia.org/wiki/Heimat. I would like to make use of the German term *Heimat* for my discussion of the current refugee crisis, not as alternative to the English term "home" but as an addition. The connotation of *Heimat* is at once broader but also more specific than "home." Both terms will be used interchangeably throughout the text.
2. Hannah Arendt, "We Refugees," in *Altogether Elsewhere: Writers on Exile*, ed. Marc Robinson, 110–19 (Boston: Faber & Faber, 1994), 110.
3. Arendt, "We Refugees," 110.
4. Arendt, "We Refugees," 112.
5. Arendt, "We Refugees," 118.
6. Arendt, "We Refugees," 118.
7. Jacques Derrida, *The Other Heading: Reflections on Today's Europe*, trans. Pascale-Anne Brault and Michael B. Naas (Bloomington: Indiana University Press, 1992), 9–10.
8. Hélène Cixous, "Letter-Beings and Time (2007)," in *The Portable Cixous*, ed. Marta Segarra, 85–95 (New York: Columbia University Press, 2010), 86.
9. Derrida, *The Other Heading*, 10.
10. Jacques Derrida, *Of Hospitality: Anne Dufourmantelle Invites Jacques Derrida to Respond*, trans. Rachel Bowlby (Stanford, CA: Stanford University Press, 2000), 25.
11. Derrida, *Of Hospitality*, 25.
12. Derrida, *The Other Heading*, 10.
13. Trinh T. Minh-ha, *Elsewhere, within Here: Immigration, Refugeeism, and the Boundary Event* (New York: Routledge, 2010), 45.
14. Gloria Anzaldúa, *Borderlands/La Frontera: The New Mestiza* (San Francisco: Aunt Lute Books, 1987), 80.
15. Anzaldúa, *Borderlands/La Frontera*, 77.
16. Anzaldúa, *Borderlands/La Frontera*, 79–80.
17. Julia Kristeva, *Strangers to Ourselves*, trans. Leon S. Roudiez (New York: Columbia University Press, 1991), 192.
18. Kristeva, *Strangers to Ourselves*, 195.
19. Kristeva, *Strangers to Ourselves*, 7–8.

20. Derrida, *Of Hospitality*, 53.
21. See Derrida, *Of Hospitality*, 53–57.
22. Arendt, "We Refugees," 110.
23. Derrida, *Of Hospitality*, 88–89.
24. Derrida, *Of Hospitality*, 89.
25. Minh-ha, *Elsewhere, within Here*, 29.
26. Minh-ha, *Elsewhere, within Here*, 2. For the interaction between seeing, hearing, and writing, see also Cixous, "Letter-Beings and Time (2007)."
27. Derrida, *Of Hospitality*, 135.
28. I also make note of the German movie and literature genres *Heimatfilm* (a film about *Heimat*) and *Heimatroman* (a novel about *Heimat*); furthermore, one of the longest film series in German film history, adapted also for TV, is titled *Heimat*. The original series, starting in 1984, was followed by two sequels; taken together, the entire series covers the period from 1919 to 2000 in Germany.
29. Minh-ha, *Elsewhere, within Here*, 34.
30. Minh-ha, *Elsewhere, within Here*, 34.
31. Derrida, *Of Hospitality*, 25.

Chapter Thirteen

Strangers to Ourselves

Contemporary Horizons

Julia Kristeva,
translated by Lisa Walsh

Étrangers à nous-mêmes

I am addressing you as a foreigner. In fact, "The Foreigner" is the title of an article Roland Barthes wrote about me in the 1970 *Quinzaine Littéraire* when, following my arrival in Paris in December 1965, my first book in French was published. What is a foreigner? A tragedy, an election, a banal status in the inexorable process of globalization? How can one be a foreigner?

TOCCATA AND FUGUE FOR THE FOREIGNER

Foreigner: a strangled rage deep down in my throat, a black angel troubling transparency, an opaque, unfathomable trace. The image of hatred and of the other, a foreigner is neither the romantic victim of our clannish indolence nor the intruder responsible for all the ills of the polis. Neither the apocalypse on the move nor the instant adversary to be eliminated for the sake of appeasing the group. Strangely, the foreigner lives within us: he is the hidden face of our identity, the space that wrecks our abode, the time in which understanding and affinity founder. By recognizing the foreigner within ourselves, we spare ourselves from detesting the foreigner as such. A symptom that precisely turns "we" into a problem, perhaps an impossibility. The foreigner begins when the consciousness of my difference arises and ends when we all acknowledge ourselves as foreigners, unamenable to bonds and communities.[1]

Can the "foreigner," who was the "enemy" in primitive societies, disappear from modern societies?[2]

A secret wound, often unknown to himself, drives him to wander. Unloved, however, he does not acknowledge this wandering: with him, the *challenge* silences the *complaint*. "You have caused me no harm," he disclaims, fiercely.

"It is I who chose to leave"; always absent, always inaccessible to all. Rejection on the one hand, inaccessibility on the other: if one has the strength not to give in, there remains a path to be discovered. Riveted to an elsewhere as certain as it is inaccessible, the foreigner is ready to flee. No obstacle stops him, and all suffering, all insults, all rejections are indifferent to him as he seeks that invisible and promised territory, that country *that does not exist* but that he bears in his dreams, and that must indeed be called a *beyond*.[3]

WHO IS THE FOREIGNER? THE PARADOX

I will come back to this movement toward the *beyond* that inhabits the foreigner, who is, definitively in fact, a being with no fixed identity, whose only homeland is the voyage. "*In via patria*," as Saint Augustine says, thereby reminding everyone of the fact that identity is a question mark: painful or ecstatic. This dimension—where to start if not with the Bernadine monks?—is grounded in metaphysics and philosophy; I will approach it from a psychoanalytic angle to conclude. But first, I will pause to explain a *paradox* at the heart of our *politico-judicial conception of the foreigner*.

The foreigner is the one who is not part of the group, who *does not belong*, the *other*. What kind of alterity is this? All alterity is steeped in fascination and abjection. But not every difference endows one with the attributes of "foreignness." The *group* to which the foreigner does not belong must be a social group structured around a given kind of *political* power. And herein lies the paradox.[4]

If political regulations or legislation generally define the manner in which we posit, modify, and eventually improve the status of foreigners, they also make up a vicious circle, for it is precisely with respect to these laws that foreigners *exist*. Indeed, without a social group structured around a power base and endowed with legislation, this exteriority represented by the foreigner—most often experienced as unfavorable, or at least problematic—would simply not exist. Also, one remarks that it has been philosophical (Greek and Latin Stoicisms with their cosmopolitanism) and religious (Proto-Christianism) movements that, transcending the political dimension of man, granted the foreigner rights equal to those of citizens; these rights, however, may be enjoyed only within the bosom of the *polis of the beyond*, within the bosom of a *spiritual polis*. As we know all too well, this absolute solution to the maladies of foreignness, as espoused by certain religions, clashes with their own religious limits and dogmatism; then the fanatics designate new foreigners, ones who do not share their faith, for new exclusions and persecutions. Political jurisdiction then appears as a safeguard, until its own machinery jams, at a given moment, under the pressure of such and such a social group or political power. One will then call on moral or religious cosmopolitanism, and the rights of man will attempt to preserve the few rights that citizens have deemed appropriate to grant noncitizens. Such checks and balances are the best that democracies have found in order to face foreigners, who have the fearsome privilege of causing a state to confront its other (other state, but also outside the state, nonstate . . .), and, even more so, of causing political reason to confront moral reason."[5]

MAN OR CITIZEN

The rights of man *or* the rights of the citizen?

This discord, the genealogy but also the deterioration of which Hannah Arendt has traced—the one that gave rise to totalitarianism—clearly appears in approaches to the "problem of foreigners" by modern societies. The difficulty engendered by the matter of foreigners is entirely contained within the impasse of the distinction between *citizen* and *man*. Is it not true that in order to found rights that are specific to men of a civilization or a nation—even the most reasonable and most consciously democratic—one is obliged to withdraw such rights from those that are non*citizens*, that is, other *men*. This process means—and this is its extreme consequence—that one can be more or less a man to the extent that one is more or less a citizen, that he who is not a citizen is not fully a man. *Between man and citizen, a scar: the foreigner.* Is he fully a man if he is not a citizen? Not enjoying the rights of citizenship, does he possess his rights of man? If, consciously, one grants foreigners all the rights of man, what is actually left of such rights when one takes away the rights of the citizen?[6]

Such a willfully paroxystic formulation of the modern problem of foreigners does not necessarily presuppose anarchistic, libertarian, or "leftist" demands. It simply points out that, from a legal standpoint, the problem of foreigners follows from a classical logic, the logic of the political group and its pinnacle, the nation-state, a logic that, amenable to improvement (democracies) or degeneration (totalitarianism), acknowledges that it rests on certain exclusions, and, consequently, surrounds itself with other formations—moral and religious, whose absolutist aspirations it nonetheless tempers—in order precisely to confront what it has set aside, in this case the problem of foreigners and a more egalitarian solution.[7]

In today's circumstances of unprecedented global intermixing of foreigners, two extreme solutions are taking shape. Either we are heading toward global United States of all former nation-states: a process that can be contemplated in the long term and that the economic, scientific, and media developments allow one to presuppose. Or else, humanistic cosmopolitanism reveals itself as a utopia, and particularistic aspirations impose the conviction that small political groups are the optimal structures to ensure the survival of humanity.[8]

In the first hypothesis, citizenship is called on to integrate the rights of man to the fullest extent and to dissolve itself in these rights, for if they assimilated the ex-foreigners, nationals would necessarily lose many features and privileges that defined them as such. Other differences would undoubtedly take shape, giving rise to the multinational kaleidoscope of the global United States: sexual, professional, religious, and other differences.[9]

On the contrary, if the nation-states were to survive even longer still, as the fierce preservation of their own interests seems to indicate at present, the unbalance between the rights of man and the rights of the citizen would produce varying degrees of subtle or brutal equilibrium, similarly to what can be observed in France in light of political situations. It would then become necessary to institute a status for foreigners, to prevent abuses on both sides and specify the rights and obligations of both parties. Such a status would have to be temporary and progressive and adapt itself to changes in social needs and attitudes.[10]

Whatever the differences between one country and another, it is possible to generalize that in modern democracies, foreigners are excluded from a *certain number of rights*. Thus, barring a few exceptions, foreigners are excluded from public service. Here, there will be a detailed discussion of this difference between, on the one hand, the rights of man and, on the other, the *civic rights* or *political rights* of foreigners in France. Let us briefly mention the thorny problem of *denying foreigners the right to vote*. We all know the arguments made by each party involved in this complex and difficult conflict: "Foreigners remain faithful to their countries of origins in the end, and can pose a threat to our national independence," some say. "Foreigners share in the building of our economic independence and should therefore enjoy political rights endowing them with the power of decision," respond the others.[11]

No matter what opinion one is led to take concerning this difficult question, one can notice that for certain jurists, "the foreigner is thus reduced to being a passive *object*.[12] Foreigners do not vote and participate neither in the state, nor in Parliament, nor in government; they are "alienated with respect to the legal realm—as they are with respect to the political order and the whole of the institutions of the society in which they live."[13] Add to this the fact that the administration is given the power to interpret, indeed modify, current legislation by way of *regulations* and *decrees*, and this may lead to making the rights of foreigners "second-rate rights."[14] In effect, one can understand those who deplore the exclusion of foreigners from the "symbolic effects of the law": the imaginary investment of the judiciary symbolic—resulting in the fact that, for each and every citizen, the law possesses a "sacred" and therefore affective value—does not function with foreigners. They do not participate in the legal process that leads to the adoption of laws.[15]

The political and the judiciary response, of course, intermingles with the modern world's philosophical conceptions of the foreigner, when it is not inspired by these very ideas. I propose, then, to look back at several key moments in the history of modern thought, moments that were nourished by the confrontation between national man and the diversity of men.

HISTORICAL IDEALITY

The French Enlightenment, then the [Declaration of the] Rights of Man and Citizen, attempt to integrate a deconstruction of political identities *into the political contract itself*, to immanentize the universal in the political. From the eighteenth century on, this may be through the notion of a unity of the "human race" and the judicial, social, and political efforts to put this idea into practice through "living together" within the diversity of cultures at the heart of modern globalization.

On my return from the Interreligious Meeting for Justice and Peace in Assisi (October 2013), Pope Benedict XVI pronounced a sentence that struck me: "No one owns truth." I proposed to friends of the Bernadines the creation of a Montesquieu Circle where believers, priests, rabbis, imams, and humanists would think and work together. Why Montesquieu? According to Ernst Cassirer, Montesquieu, the first thinker to conceptualize and express the notion of a historical *ideal type*, contemplates the *totality of the species* and the political fabric of the globe in terms of the *sociability* and *general spirit* that govern the human species, now finally restored to its actual universality. While he does recognize the weightiness of nationhood, Montesquieu transposes this burden and absorbs it into a border-free political philosophy, a maximal integration of humankind into a moderate, attainable reality.[16]

MAN VERSUS CITIZEN

At the very least, we can say that over the centuries following Montesquieu, nationalism has confirmed the need for his safeguards and security networks. Since the French Revolution, however, and already during the period of the Declaration of the Rights of Man and Citizen (August 16, 1789), the extent to which this horizon remains a horizon is evident, but peaceful governance surreptitiously abandons the notion of the universal. "Men" and their presumed political associations must put their natural egalitarian rights into practice in order to reach the nation's historically "essential political association."[17] The *paradox* we encountered at the outset: Article 1 [of the declaration]. "Men are born free and with equal rights." Article 6. "The law is the expression of the general will; all *citizens* have the right to work toward its formation." In fact, then, *natural* man is universal in vain. As soon as we think him as immediately *political*, he is *national*. With the economic development of Western societies, this slippage in reasoning leads to the creation of the United Nations and, through derivation or deviation, the explosion of nationalism in the nineteenth and twentieth centuries.[18] In any case, after the horrific experiences of contemporary history, one can only admire the ethical and political intuition that, over and above the historical necessity of recognizing the *national* political essence of men, maintains an *inalienable horizon*, one that cannot be reduced to the horizon of national political consciousness and its jurisdiction.

It is with Kant that this modern universalism finds its radical formulation. In his "Idea for a Universal History from a Cosmopolitan Point of View" (1784),[19] he interprets the "moral imperative" on a practical and juridical level, envisaging "a legal external relation among states"[20] and extolling a "Great Society of Nations"—"a united power acting according to decisions reached under the laws of their united will."[21] As soon as it is pronounced, universal rights face a major difficulty: without universal and superior transcendence, how to guarantee this "united will," this country beyond countries where *the* people and *the* countries would integrate their "foreigners," who would no longer be foreigners? Kant himself sees his idea as "fantastical," "crazy," he said, thinking of the Abbé de Saint-Pierre and Rousseau, who preceded him in this vision.[22] He sustains his vision, however, "as the necessary outcome of destitution." Where would this hospitality and this voluntary generosity come from? "Quite simply . . . because the Earth is round," he concludes with pragmatism and naïveté.[23]

The Shoah and intercommunity massacres have continued with renewed vigor in the twenty-first century, bearing *witness* to the fact that, despite considerable advances, the "moral imperative," the finitude of Earth's surface, and the politico-juridical adjustments to international law do not suffice in resolving the sociopolitical difficulties of foreigners. They are even more powerless in the face of this push toward the beyond that takes hold of each of us, more dramatically in the case of foreigners exposed to both the failures of integration and the forces of disintegration. Foreigners not only fail to adhere to any form of supplication but also release the reins of the *life drive* and veer into the *death drive*.

In the face of this absence of "connivance" and "conciliation," we are far from the Stoics and the pacifying tendencies of the *religere* as Kant's "unified will." Ratzinger and Habermas called for a *return to faith*.[24] But which faith? The dialogue between religions does not seem capable of putting an end to the massacres between believers, those of the three monotheisms, but perhaps yet less between the believers of the three monotheisms; even Buddhist serenity is not devoid of explosions against foreign adversaries.

I have the weakness of believing that the development of the humanities, most notably psychoanalysis, never cease to deepen their knowledge of psychic life and contribute an innovative reconstruction of modern humanism within the context of its universalist and cosmopolitan ambitions—in particular, in reaction to the identity confusion lived by foreigners but also the native nationals who welcome them within digital globalization.

UNCANNINESS ACCORDING TO FREUD

Two principal moments in Sigmund Freud's discovery are directly related to our discussion.

His notion of "uncanniness" (*Umheimlich*) invites us to confront the passionate reactions incited by the foreigner, who is assimilated as foreign, threatening, anxiety provoking. For Freud, the foreign foreigner—to whom we turn our backs, whom we reject or persecute, who threatens us. Our charity welcomes, infantilizes, or stimulates the foreign foreigner who does not exist in himself, says Freud. He awakens the fears and traumas that inhabit us, the ones we have forgotten-repressed-censored and through which the encounter with the other—even more so with the foreign other—awakens and actualizes.

You cannot eradicate the foreigner, says psychoanalysis, *every singularity consists in* and *arouses love* and *hate; but you can clarify these within yourself to better welcome them in others. By domesticating foreignness, the fears-anxieties-violences-and-rejections inhabiting you, by giving* meaning to the foreignness in yourself, *you make way for the life of this "interior touch"* (oikeiosis), *a* universal conciliation presiding over the universality *of the "human race."*

This intimate *psychization*[25] of the uneasiness roused by the foreigner invites us to personally accompany migrants as agents of welcome. This psychization does not "resolve" the "problem of foreigners," but it is evident that this psychization can only add to economic, juridical, and social measures. But by interiorizing the political stakes, it makes us responsible and confirms that universalist humanism is a delicate experience—reconstructed in the singular, and very very long term.

To convince you, I will give the extreme example of the mortiferous acting out on the part of (often) adolescent foreigners who are exposed to social disintegration, to profound depression and its manic flip side—or to fundamentalist fanaticism and gangster fanaticism.

FOREIGNNESS AND RADICAL EVIL

Foreignness, strangeness. In effect, new foreigners henceforth disturb globalization in general and the republican pact in particular: demands for rights degenerate into vandalism when gangster and fanatic fundamentalisms aren't fomenting death. Are they really "new" if we think about the nihilism of the late nineteenth century and other devastating, suicidal explosions? But "new" because they act within the context of awakening spiritualities, in the name of a push toward the absolute transformed into what we must no longer call an "ideality" (*divine or secularized universalist*) but rather a "malady of ideality." "New" because in accordance with the conflicts in the Middle East, because in defiance of the French model of secularization and laicity.

The delinquency of "at-risk youth," the fanaticism of the young and the not so young who become kamikazes for the Islamic state in Iraq and the Levant, the resurgence of virulent anti-Semitism reveals a more radical phase of nihilism, a phase epitomized by the "clash of religions." For the most part, this phase affects second-generation French youth who have been damaged by a suffering family milieu, by scholastic and professional failure—disintegrated, unsocialized. Like *all adolescents*, these delayed adolescents have rebelled against the "system," in search of recognition, filled with a quest for an ideal, a yearning for paradise. What differentiates them is that their rush toward the *beyond of malaise* belongs to an explosive violence operating within an inconsistent "ego" and thereby shattering. The ideals themselves disappear, swept away by the most instinctive [*pulsionnelle*] drive [*pulsion*], the absorption of the life drive by the death drive. This disorganization maintains an in-depth grasp of civilization's inner workings, demonstrating the destruction of the prereligious "need to believe" *that constitutes psychic life with and for the other*.

Psychoanalysis ventures on the side of this profound disorganization of the person. This is *disconnection* [*déliaison*]: "'I' do not exist," "nothing but a dauntless drive to disconnect," and the disorganization of ties to the other. It is *deobjectification* ("the other has neither meaning nor value"), where only the malignity of evil triumphs, "radical evil."

What is radical evil? It consists in declaring—and realizing—that human beings are superfluous; they can be killed.

In the state of war between foreigners that has fashioned history, humans have always tried to distinguish between *good* and *evil*, and this results in the collision of values. These very values pass on divergent or concurrent libidinal interests. *Religious man* and *moral man* are constituted by them. More or less guilty and rebellious, they live on values, are preoccupied by them and hope to illuminate them so that one day they will understand each other instead of killing each other.

Right next to debatable *evil* exists another evil: *extreme evil*. Extreme evil sweeps away the meaning of the very distinction between *good* and *evil*, thereby destroying the possibility of acceding to the existence of the other, to meaning, and to oneself. These human "borderline states" don't just find refuge in hospitals or the psychoanalyst's couch but unfurl in sociopolitical catastrophes, in abjection and extermination—such as the Shoah, this horror what defies explanation and reason. Today, new forms of *extreme evil* proliferate in the globalized world, in the throng of *ideality illnesses* spreading within gangster fanaticism.

Is it possible to push analytic listening all the way to the borders of *Homo sapiens* and still practice psychoanalysis in these conditions?

Democracies are facing a historic challenge: are they capable of confronting this *crisis in the need to believe, in the desire to know* when religion can no longer contain this crisis that touches on the foundation of the connections between foreign humans? In these overwhelming times of excesses grounded in social and economic crises (the Mérah case, the Nemmouche case, the Boston marathon's Tsarnaev brothers, the aspiring Syrian martyrs), we are stuck in an anguish that expresses our uncertainty in the face of these colossal concerns.

PSYCHOANALYSIS REINVENTS ITSELF

However, modestly and step-by-step, psychoanalysis is reinventing itself to push back. Thus, and, for example, since 2011, Marie-Rose Moro and I have held a seminar at the Maison de Sollenn—the adolescent unit of the Cochin Hospital, where we question the nature and genesis of our beliefs concerning the sacred, parenthood, illness, unhappiness, speech . . . within the context of a transcultural psychoanalytic clinic with individual patients from multiple cultural universes. We seek to demonstrate that this clinic can be conceived without any religious framework, in an intimate and pagan clinic, a contemporary psychoanalytic clinic. It is within this context that I met Souad.

Souad had been hospitalized for serious anorexia, a cold mortal passion, exhausting episodes of vomiting and bulimia: she was unraveling. This slow suicide, addressed to her family and to the world, had abolished time before transforming itself into radicalization. The faded jeans and baggy sweater disappeared under a burka. Souad erected a wall of silence and lived on the Internet where, with unknown accomplices, she exchanged angry e-mails about her family of "apostates, worse than unbelievers," and arranged her trip "over there" to become the sometimes wife of polygamist fighters, a prolific mother of martyrs, or a kamikaze herself.

Cautious and quiet, recalcitrant about psychoanalysis like many teenagers, Souad nonetheless was open to being surprised by a "multicultural analytic psychotherapy" made up of around ten men and women of all origins and diverse capacities who didn't question each other, nor did they diagnose or judge. They honed their group's empathetic diversity: scattered and plural identifications, a restructured family, a restorative community. Maximum proximity to the affects: frustrated, humiliated, and deadly sensations and arousals. And putting words to her breakdown to accompany this person who clings to barbarity so that rather than fall apart, she will die of pleasure [*jouir à mort*]. The young girl who provokes by describing herself as a "scientific mind," strong in math, physics, and chemistry but "crap" in French and philosophy, begins to enjoy talking about herself, playing with the team, laughing with the others and at herself.

Taking up French again, using language to tame her drives and suffering, finding the words to make them exist, to undo and redo them, to share them. Language, literature, poetry, and theater ensnare meaninglessness and thwart nihilism. Roland Barthes wrote that if you can find meaning in the plenitude of language, the divine void no longer poses a threat. Souad isn't there yet. She's wearing jeans again. It will be a long road. But how many girls won't be lucky like Souad, won't be recognized, listened to, supported?

The accompaniment of "radicalizable" adolescents is part of this worldwide viral war, where Islamic terrorist attacks and our aerial bombings are only the military versions. A viral war because it operates, invisible and invasive, in forms that are just as (if not more so) ancient and resistant, just as inherent and destructive to humanity as viruses are to our cells. Viral war functions through the death drive and the radical evil that live alongside our living organisms and our psychic identities, and in certain circumstances, destroys its host and spreads malignity throughout the world.

I have tried to tell you how this crisis affects me. Am I an optimist? Too much of an optimist? And I ask: What are we doing? Not giving up in the face of evil, nor even in the face of *extreme evil*. Rather, we are patiently pursuing out research—certainly not from some utopic equilibrium but from the fragile *point* defined by Pascal as "perpetual motion." He writes, "Anyone who found the secret of rejoicing in the good without being annoyed by its contrary would have found the point. It is perpetual motion."[26]

What if the experience we lack today in accompanying these "new foreigners" were precisely this "point," this "perpetual motion" toward "the secret of rejoicing in the good without being annoyed by its contrary"? A certain internal experience . . . to accompany foreignness, even at its most explosive.

PRACTICALLY . . .

In conclusion, two propositions.

The foreigner, able to appear as luck opening the group to more fraternity, isn't finished carrying this message of more universality for all men and women in the twenty-first century. But the confusion of this foreign migration becomes so heavy that it exacerbates the fragility of the human condition and aggravates our *search for meaning* by transforming it into maladies of ideality: radical evil spreads under the auspices of holy wars. Foreigners cannot be wedded to their communities, be they prophetic or barbarous—a source of enlightened inquiry but also a source of deadly fanaticism. We should welcome them in their singularity; their impasses are our impasses; they concern us and can be shared.

National identity is not any less of an experience; it is rapidly mutating. In France, at this end of the twentieth century, each of us is destined to remain the same *and* other: without forgetting one's culture of origin but by relativizing it to the point where it coexists with, and even alternates with, the cultures of others. A new homogeneity is improbable, perhaps undesirable. Without its comforting façade, the *Front National*'s rhetoric is reactive, regressive, and suicidal. We are called by the economy, the media, and history to cohabit in one country, France, which is in the process of integration into Europe. Are we on the path to a puzzle-nation made of diverse particularities and whose dominant population remains French for the moment, but for how long?

In the absence of new community ties, religion as salvation might integrate the masses of wanderers and the unordinary into a new consensus, a spiritual "*unanimation*,"[27] something other than the rush toward "more money and more stuff for everyone." For the first time in history, we must live with different people while focusing on our own personal moral codes but without a possible transcendence of a whole containing all our particularities. A paradoxical community is emerging, made up of foreigners who accept each other to the extent that they recognize them as fellow foreigners. The multinational society would thereby be the result of extreme singularity but also conscious of its malaises and its limits. This society consists in an irreducible willingness to help each other in their weakness, a weakness whose other name is our radical foreignness: a kind of *sacredness*. In a new sense already evoked by Kant in *The Critique of Pure Reason* when he predicts a new *ethical* space under the name of a *new "corpus mysticum"* for the world of free will and its moral laws. But isn't St. Augustine, who associates the divine itself with the foreigner, already outlining this by writing, "God through whom we discern that certain things we had deemed essential to ourselves are truly foreign to us, while those we had deemed foreign to us are sometimes ours"?[28]

NOTES

1. Julia Kristeva, *Strangers to Ourselves*, trans. Leon S. Roudiez (New York: Columbia University Press, 1991), 1.
2. Kristeva, *Strangers to Ourselves*, 1.
3. Kristeva, *Strangers to Ourselves*, 5.
4. Kristeva, *Strangers to Ourselves*, 95–96.
5. Kristeva, *Strangers to Ourselves*, 96–97.
6. Kristeva, *Strangers to Ourselves*, 97–98.
7. Kristeva, *Strangers to Ourselves*, 98.
8. Kristeva, *Strangers to Ourselves*, 98.
9. Kristeva, *Strangers to Ourselves*, 98.
10. Kristeva, *Strangers to Ourselves*, 98–99.
11. Kristeva, *Strangers to Ourselves*, 100–101.
12. Danièle Loch, Étranger*: De quel droit?* (Paris: Presses Universitaires de France, 1985), 215.
13. Loch, Étranger, 216.
14. Loch, Étranger, 216.
15. Kristeva, *Strangers to Ourselves*, 100–102.
16. Kristeva, *Strangers to Ourselves*, 127–29.
17. Kristeva, *Strangers to Ourselves*, 148.
18. Kristeva, *Strangers to Ourselves*, 150.
19. Immanuel Kant, "Idea for a Universal History from a Cosmopolitan Point of View," in *Kant: On History*, ed. Lewis White Beck (New York: Bobbs-Merrill, 1963).
20. Kant, "Idea for a Universal History from a Cosmopolitan Point of View," 18.
21. Kant, "Idea for a Universal History from a Cosmopolitan Point of View," 19.
22. Kant, "Idea for a Universal History from a Cosmopolitan Point of View," 23.
23. Kant, "Idea for a Universal History from a Cosmopolitan Point of View," 103.
24. Jürgen Habermas, Joseph Ratzinger, and Jean-Louis Schegel, "Les fondements pré-politiques de l'État démocratique," *Esprit*, no. 306 (2004): 5–28.
25. The original French *psychisation* is Kristeva's neologism. I have modified the word only slightly after considering *subjectivization* as an alternative.
26. Blaise Pascal, *Pensées*, trans. Roger Ariew (New York: Hackett, 2005), 18.
27. Kristeva's neologism.
28. Blaise Pascal, *The Soliloquies of Saint Augustine of Hippo*, trans. Rose E. Cleveland (Charleston, SC: Nabu Press, 2014), 18.

Part V

LISTENING TO REFUGEE VOICES

Chapter Fourteen

I Am Not Your Canvas

Narratives, Nostalgia, and the (Re)claiming of Refugee Voices

Anna Gotlib

The stories of who we are, told by ourselves and by others, come to define and identify us, offering to the world a version of a self that occupies or is excluded from shared moral spaces. The consequences of these narratives are thus in many ways outcome determinative: the dominant story of who one is tends to be fundamentally constitutive of one's place not only in one's immediate community but also in the larger world, resonating throughout the various threads of one's life. And if we grant that words have this sort of power, then it would seem that those who are already, for whatever reasons, disempowered have much to gain or lose, depending on which stories are deployed about them and by whom—and whether these stories are granted uptake.

This chapter, however, is not a defense of the narrative turn in philosophical ethics. As I and others have argued,[1] the claim that stories create (and destroy) identities has more than a little merit, and I proceed with the assumption that the reader will grant at least the possibility that this might be the case. Instead, what this chapter is about is refugees, how their narratives and thus voices are often silenced, and some of the ways that they can be reclaimed, recovered—and heard. Indeed, the current generations of refugees from Syria and other parts of the Middle East are too often forced to enact and embody others' versions of who they are and "assimilate" not only externally to their new location but also internally by submitting to identity-constituting narratives about themselves in which their participation is minimal at best. Specifically, therefore, I address the silencing—the narrative erasure—of refugee voices by both hostile and well-intentioned master public narratives (mostly from the Global North host nations) about who they are, what they desire, and their capabilities and intentions, past histories, and possible futures.[2]

I begin by considering how refugee voices are already liminal and how this liminality positions them in regard to control of their narratives and their moral agency. Second, I examine, both historically and in the current era, the ways in which refugees have been and are narratively erased and their stories made to reflect the socioeconomic and political needs of host societies. Here, I place a special emphasis on the power of the public nature of such narrative silencing. Third, I argue that in order for refugees to reclaim their voices, two moves are required: first, the relinquishing by the Global North of its presumed standing to force identity-defining master narratives—whether ostensibly supportive or decidedly otherwise—on already largely disempowered refugees and, second, by encouraging refugees to tell their own stories regardless of whether these stories reflect the expected, the stereotypical, or the desirable model of the refugee. In other words, I suggest that refugee narratives should be free of the kinds of narrative constraints that limit not only how they view themselves in their present circumstances but also whether they choose to look backward to their past in order to construct an identity that is more fully their own. In so doing, refugees can reclaim themselves as bearers of complex, multicultural identities that resist the master narrative's insistence on xenophobic—or even patriotic and heroic—versions of who they are that only serve to exotify and trivialize their difficult, contested lives. I conclude this section by offering several examples of refugee self-reclamation and suggest that making possible such acts of identity re-creation ought to be the direction in which the Global North directs and broadens its refugee policies, narratives, and moral and political spaces.

REFUGEES AND LIMINALITY

Since this chapter is concerned with the voices and narratives of refugees, a few distinctions must be made. First, refugees differ from immigrants in the sense that the immigrants usually choose to leave their home countries in order to improve their lives (economically, politically, for personal reasons, and so on), and, if they wish, they (most of the time) can return. Refugees, on the other hand, are directly or indirectly forced (by war and violence, economic deprivation, oppression, racism, and so on) to flee, usually with no reasonable prospects of returning. As the 1951 Convention Relating to the Status of Refugees (together with its 1967 amendment) states, refugees are persons outside their country of origin because of a "well-founded fear of persecution" at home and to whom the host state is obligated to offer asylum. Refugees cannot be sent back to a place where their lives or freedom would be at risk from persecution.[3] At the end of 2015, there were 21.3 million refugees worldwide[4] and, more specifically, an estimated 11 million people who had fled their homes as a result of the civil war in Syria, with an additional 13.5 million who are displaced and in need of assistance.[5] Lacking safe homes to which they can return, they look to other nations, specifically the nations of the Global North, for asylum.

Yet the fundamental homelessness of refugees as a growing humanitarian disaster has not moved the Global North to take adequate measures—or, at least, has not moved it sufficiently to offer assistance on the scale that is warranted. For example, the Austrian government made plans to build a fence at its border with Italy to shield itself from the rising migrant numbers.[6] David Cameron, at first embracing the language of "moral responsibility," subsequently announced, under substantial political pressure, that the United Kingdom could accept only 20,000 persons over a five-year period.[7] Indeed, bolstered by fears of the European Union as a failing economic entity, by a growing movement toward nationalism and protectionism, and by a populism that tended to mistrust and reject the "elitism" of the ruling classes,[8] the UK Independence Party's Nigel Farage openly campaigned on a xenophobic and racist antirefugee platform that so frightened the British public that a pro-Brexit vote followed.[9]

And the United States, in the grip of its own antirefugee hysteria,[10] elected Donald Trump, who rose to power on narratives fueled by Islamophobia and fear and mistrust of the other. Indeed, every major Republican candidate in the 2016 presidential race came out against admitting Syrian refugees into the United States.[11]

These antirefugee public speech acts led to policies that effectively closed whatever doors still remained open. And so the refugees found themselves in an impossible position: not able to return, they were also precluded from entering. They were, in other words, politically, economically, physically—and, indeed, morally—liminal. By "liminal," I mean in a state of being in between. More than a condition of uncertainty, their liminality is a kind of social invisibility that is characterized by dislocation from the familiar without at the same time an integration into the new. The past is distant, the present uncertain, and the future often unfathomable, alien, and frightening. As I have argued elsewhere, many refugees—especially those from Syria and other Middle Eastern locations currently trapped in cycles of war, oppression, and deprivation—found themselves in this in-between, caught in a seemingly permanent physical and psychological limbo, unable to return, yet rejected from their intended destinations. Uprootedness, homelessness, and otherness thus become their permanent conditions. No longer belonging to their place of origin—or to any other place at all—what remains is an unending state of transition and liminality.[12] As Hannah Arendt notes, "They are deprived of life, liberty, and the pursuit of happiness, or of equality before the law and freedom of opinion . . . but that they no longer belong to any community whatsoever. . . . They are deprived, not of the right to freedom, but of the right to action; not of the right to think whatever they please, but of the right to opinion."[13]

In many ways, therefore, not only are these refugees on the social and political periphery, but they also have no viable ways to raise their voices to object, to contest their liminality—to be heard by those whose voices carry power over their conditions, indeed, over their lives. As Liisa Malkki argues, refugees find themselves in a kind of "structural invisibility" where this silencing just might be a part of what it means to be a refugee in that they are "systematically" rather than accidentally or inadvertently invisible and inaudible.[14] They are no longer citizens or indeed rightful claim makers of the homes they left behind, but neither are they in a position to make rights claims (or, in fact, any claims) against a new location that has not accepted them as asylum seekers.[15] In refugee camps, illegal settlements, and "unofficial," secret living arrangements, refugees remain in the in-between, between two doors that remain, in all the ways that matter, firmly shut.

Yet refugee liminality does not necessarily end if one of those doors happens to open. In fact, refugee liminality continues even in the face of a favorable outcome of appeals for asylum: even when refugees are granted entry, they are effectively silenced as persons, as selves, while, ostensibly in exchange for safe harbor, their identity-constituting stories are forced into the service of the sociopolitical, economic, and normative needs of host societies. In other words, as they enter a host nation, they become silent archetypes of "the refugee" for the making of whatever new kind of master narrative about them that nation requires: they might become the hero, the pitiable homeless, the compliant striver, the dangerous radical, and so on. They are publicly mythologized, demonized, shaped, and storied by those whose voices have both moral authority and sociopolitical heft. And it is these voices and all those in a given society who follow their dictates who structure and police the boundaries of the moral universe into which the refugees are granted conditional, precarious entry. In this universe, the refugees trade one kind of liminality for another: they may no longer be in between countries or societies, but within their new host nations, they become a liminal "other," a silent cultural canvas—a voiceless and blank other onto which the fears, desires, and anxieties of their hosts are projected via numerous, largely uncontested narratives about who they are as refugees, as persons. In the next section, I examine how this narrative erasure takes place—and the consequences for the refugees' sense of self, their identities, and their ability to re-create and to find their own voices.

MASTER NARRATIVES AND SILENCING

Narratives, Master and Otherwise

Narratives by and about us not only shape our ideas about who we are but also serve as guides and sometimes as boundaries of our place in the social and moral universe. They tell us and others how we can be treated, who we are as moral agents—and whether we are to be viewed as persons.[16] These narratives—these stories that determine and shape our identities—can differ teleologically: they can be good and bad, providing the sort of insight into ourselves that might be constructive and action guiding, or else they can encourage fear or suspicion or serve to indulge our worst instincts and inclinations.

But not all narratives are alike in their power and ability to form enduring, difficult-to-alter stories. Some are told by individuals or groups whose social influence is limited and thus whose ability to form powerful identity-shaping versions of themselves and others are subsequently limited. Other narratives can be "master narratives" that tell us with great conviction and overwhelming force where and how we are socially situated with respect to our duties, claims, and expectations. They can story racial and gender minorities as "less than," as requiring some kind of repair.[17] They can tell women that motherhood is their only "natural" option and that its lack is either a tragedy or else a moral disaster.[18] In these ways, these master narratives, whose narrators often hold high-profile, publicly visible, positions, can silence those over whose identities—and, often, over whose lives—they possess control. And as I argue here, they can similarly silence the voices of refugees by publicly and repeatedly painting versions of them that fit the narrator's agenda—an agenda that may describe the refugee as pleasing, disturbing, or frightening but in any case that has very little to do with how refugees might view (or wish to view) themselves. Importantly, these tellers of powerful narratives usually do not care to hear the (potentially reparative) counterstories of the refugees themselves. Indeed, in their roles as identity-constituting shapers of selves, master narratives "are used to build individual, group or national life stories, and can be both a construction, and a claim of identity. Dominant narratives of refugees have tended to portray them as passive victims, who should be grateful for the assistance they have received and for the chance to start over."[19] Even the nonxenophobic, well-meaning master narratives—the ones designed to inspire empathy for the downtrodden refugee, casting a kindly eye on the homeless migrant—can be both morally and epistemically damaging to the refugee and self-complimentary to the narrators. As Catherine Dauvergne notes, this kind of public humanitarianism typical of the Global North not only shapes the (helpless, lost) identities of those it purports to help in ways that can be disempowering but also is rather self-serving on the part of the narrators, casting them in the best, most flattering light as selfless benefactors.[20] This narrative silencing—indeed, narrative erasure—of refugees takes many forms, and I now turn to a few of the more pernicious examples.

Language, Narrative Erasure, and the "Other"

The stories of who refugees are have historically taken on many forms and guises, shaping many an identity, whether that of individuals or of entire populations. The hero narrative, in vogue during the Cold War era, painted somewhat romanticized images of Soviet and other Eastern bloc refugees as stoic and defiant figures, "struggling for freedom and justice both politically and intellectually. They were figures for us to admire in their defiant stance and personal sacrifice. We could vicariously bask in the nobility of their struggles and have our way of life affirmed for us because they had sought refuge in our society."[21]

How these master narratives took hold of course varied. But what remained consistent was the voice of official, trusted sources of information, such as the *Washington Post*, focusing the public's attention on Soviet human rights abuses while making the case for the necessity of asylum for the heroic Soviet citizens trying to flee totalitarian horrors. Similarly, the *Los Angeles Times* ran five such stories, and in 1977, the *New York Times* ran more than fifty stories addressing the politically fraught plight of Soviet dissidents.[22] This lofty rhetoric was further bolstered by official directives: "The most important of these was the Refugee Act of 1980 [reauthorized in 1991]. This legislation was intended to provide transitional assistance to refugees in the United States, and assist them with, among other things, job training and placement, as well as English language training and cash assistance."[23]

But how much these emplotments reflected the actual lives of Eastern bloc refugees (or those who risked their lives to escape) was dubious at best. That is, while the official Western narratives focused on heroics and defiance, the political prisoners who disappeared into gulags and the oppressed and persecuted Jewish citizens of the Soviet Union who desired asylum were moved by the psychological, physical, and moral traumas of totalitarian oppression while at the same time confronting the impending anguish of exile. As such a refugee myself, the memory of fear, uncertainty, and an unyielding sense of danger were what defined the asylum-seeking experience. In our minds, we were neither heroic nor defiant, and our stories, when told by those who experienced even a part of the refugee drama, reflected the brokenness, the nostalgia, the confusion, and often an ongoing sense of liminality, of the in-between.[24] Yet the master narratives—because their teleologies that had very little to do with those of the refugees that they defined—emphasized the political, the Western democratic victory over the Eastern communist disaster, the nobility of those who ostensibly believe in similar ideologies as the tellers of the triumphant stories. Indeed, the Eastern bloc refugees paid a price for their successful asylum seeking and traded in the liminality of being in between states for narrative erasure, setting aside their own stories of struggle and trauma and loss and becoming, officially, placeholders for a Western Cold War victory.[25]

The current generations of refugees from the Middle East, North Africa, and elsewhere face narrative erasure that is similar but, I would suggest, more extreme and more existentially damaging than those who came before. Asylum seekers, before and after being admitted into a host nation, often face one of three versions of who they are: (less often) as heroic strivers, (more often) as dangerous and threatening, and (increasingly) as passive victims.[26] There are blunt and obvious examples of the "threatening" descriptors: when then-candidate Trump made clear his xenophobia-fueled suspicion of Syrian refugee children, a sufficient number of Americans listened, agreed, and elected a man who declared, "I can look at their [Syrian refugee children's] faces and say, Look, you can't come here. . . . Their parents should always stay with them. But we don't know where their parents come from."[27] But the United States is far from the only nation of the Global North to describe refugees in ways designed to frighten the local populations and make those seeking asylum even more liminal:

> Goodman (2007) noted that media coverage of legislation on asylum-seeking families characterized them in terms usually used to describe animals breeding. . . . Philo and Beattie (1999) observed that the coverage . . . in the British media used the terminology of a natural disaster, presenting Britain as the victim of "floods," even "tidal waves" of immigrants. Lynn and Lea's (2003) analysis of readers' letters to newspapers showed that "asylum seeker" now means "bogus asylum seeker," and genuine refugees are a rarity in the media.[28]

At the same time, "these identities are rarely presented as refugees would construct them, or in their own voices. . . . This is partly a consequence of the fact that while refugees/asylum seekers are subjected to hostility, they rarely have the opportunity to assert their identity in public."[29] This storying of refugees as frightening, unwanted others tends to bring about the following consequences. First, as noted above, the refugees themselves are silenced and made more liminal as noncontributors to the creation of their own identities; second, they internalize the master narrative versions of themselves "as the 'other'"[30]; and, finally, these narratives of heroism or threat tend to affect governmental and social responses in ways that have very little to do with the refugees' needs and the very real oppressive conditions that they are fleeing and everything to do with the existing economic and sociopolitical circumstances of the potential host country. As I have argued elsewhere,[31] because so doing benefits a host nation's geopolitical position, some refugees experience the kind of moral luck that opens doors and welcomes them in. And in cases where no such luck is present, they are either treated as the feared other or else not given the opportunity to enter a country altogether. The point is this: an already marginalized, liminal population is not only further othered by the often self-serving narratives and thus policies of potential host nations but also—because they are marginalized—prevented from offering counter-narratives that might redefine who they are, why they are fleeing, and why they require asylum. The narrative, therefore, is solely unidirectional, allowing those with the narrative, political, and social power not only to determine the outcome of the refugees' asylum seeking but also to be the authors of who these liminal "others" are once they are inside the host nation. Narrative equals control, and control equals power.

But what if refugees were to be painted differently? What if, instead of portraying them as heroes or threats, they are described as victims, as objects of pity and perhaps empathy—as powerless and in need of assistance from the Global North? For example, media coverage in Australia identified asylum seekers as victims with a "human face."[32] Moreover, American media presented the Sudanese "Lost Boys" "as . . . clad only in tattered rags create an image of 'helpless' and destitute refugees in need of American protection."[33] After all, we might think that refugees are humanized by the victimhood narratives: if they are not storied as superhuman heroes or devious threats, then they are themselves running from violence, oppression, and other horrors and are thus perhaps a little less liminal, a bit more sympathetic, and merely searching for a better life. And narrated in this way, would not public policy—and the public itself—respond in a way that is less antagonistic and xenophobic and more welcoming?

The answer is a bit more complicated. For example, the distinction between the narratives and policies of the Obama administration, which tended to embrace the empathetic victim refugee narratives, differed from the current xenophobia of the Trump administration: a delay on the part of President Obama's immigration and security agencies in processing Iraqi refugees in 2011 was limited to a single country in response to a specific threat. Yet President Trump relied on largely vilifying, othering rhetoric and instituted a wider ban on Syrian refugees without specifying a threat that caused confusion, fear, and further liminality on the part of desperate refugees fleeing war, oppression, and other existential threats.[34] So does this suggest that, as a matter of morality and policy, we ought to prefer the victim narrative—is it, in the absence of the hero and the villain narratives, really the best we can do for the refugees?

Ratna Kapur suggests otherwise: the "'look of starvation, helplessness, and victimization' Third World subjects often present in public discourse 'is remarkably familiar to our imaginations, irrespective of the reality.'"[35] Indeed, painting refugees as victims results in two distinct harms. First, there is the emphasis on cultural essentialism, which "'reinforces stereotyped and racist representations of their culture and privileges the culture of the West.'"[36] These stereotypes, in turn, rob the refugees of their own voices, characterizing them solely "by the horrors of the national or international conflicts which they fled, not by the strong religious, cultural or national traditions of the lands from which they came."[37] Second, Kapur argues that the victim narrative is largely paternalistic and invites—indeed encourages—"protectionist measures or rights restrictions for the victim's 'benefit' . . . in a way that strips refugees of agency and hinders refugee empowerment."[38] In other words, victim framing strengthens the master narratives of refugee helplessness while silencing—narratively erasing—refugees as epistemic and moral agents.

What this narrative silencing looks like in practice is described quite vividly by Ece Temelkuran, a Turkish journalist, herself forced into lifesaving flight:

> I was supposed to be writing about a refugee in Istanbul. Then she disappeared. . . . Then I had to disappear myself. So I am now the subject of this text. . . . I am now supposed to fill the shoes of this person called "the victim." Like a refugee waiting for a piece of bread with a stupid ticket in her hands, I should be ready to perform my victimhood whenever the act is called to the intellectual stage. I am now obliged to tell a story, but only the one particular story, the stupid story of my suffering that I hold like a ticket for my passage to the civilized world. . . . The victim should be the victim but nothing else. Otherwise it becomes confusing for the audience.[39]

She continues,

> I remember this man from Somalia I met in a refugee camp on the Tunisian-Libyan border. . . . I was asking the same questions over and over again, "Do you have enough water to meet your daily needs?" "Do you have enough food to eat?" etc. . . . And this man, smiling the most sarcastic smile I've ever seen, asked me in perfect English, "I see it doesn't occur to you to ask me do I have a CV." Now I imitate the same smile to audiences when they are confused by my silly jokes, my defying the cliché of the suffering exile.[40]

And so it seems that the victim narrative is yet another way to silence, to erase, to make small. Thus, as Zahabi-Bekdash argues, all of these narratives—whether heroic, xenophobic, or victim centered—"lump all refugees into one homogenous mass of 'people.' . . . We, citizens and governments, become ventriloquists for refugees, and strip them from the only things they still own; their stories, relationships and experiences as human beings. We forget that there are as many refugee stories, experiences, and identities as there are refugees. We forget how complex identities are."[41] As a result, by granting uptake to these master narratives, we, as members of host nations, not only silence but also create spaces of liminality where refugees are unable to engage as moral agents. Instead, they are systematically storied out of those most powerful moral spaces that allow for identity-constituting practices of creating a place of one's own choosing in the moral universe. Indeed, these broken, limited stories that are told about refugees without their participation mark them as blank canvases on which the deepest needs, anxieties, and political expediencies are projected and that help both the powerful and the powerless forget that "before they became refugees, these people were parents, children, teachers, artisans, doctors and artists."[42] In the next section, I consider how it might be possible to remember.

MEMORY, NOSTALGIA, AND (RE)CLAIMING THE REFUGEE SELF

Refugee Nostalgias

Before I begin, I must note that the task of reclaiming refugee voices and narratives is enormous, and my suggestions are brief and modest. My intent, therefore, is just to begin the conversation. I therefore leave a deeper exploration of political, social, and economic specifics of any identity-(re)constituting refugee policies for another time. So how to begin?

As I suggested earlier, two moves are required for the opening of the requisite moral spaces for refugee voices to be heard. First, there must be a process of letting go of narrative control by the nations of the Global North of their identity-defining narrative practices that exclude the subjects of the stories from authorship. Whether this is socially or politically possible is an empirical question that is best left for further research. But the story and the storytellers must change: instead of insisting on particular (often stereotyped) versions of who refugees are, the message from official sources has to be secondary to refugee voices themselves. And when master narratives do make an appearance, the emphasis ought to be on nonessentialism: refugees are not born—they are made, whether by war, oppression, unbearable living conditions, racism, poverty, and so on. The message has to be clear that they are neither natural kinds (thus, there is no "essential refugee") nor mysterious "others" who must be classified and controlled from the outside. And while this claim about the need for nonessentialist conceptions of refugees might, at first glance, seem clearly obvious and perhaps even banal, evidence suggests that currently this is neither practice nor, in many cases, within the realm of preferred sociopolitical discourse. Indeed, the best that some host nations appear to do at present is to trade their xenophobic, racist rhetoric and turn to the ostensibly less toxic narratives of refugee dependence and victimhood.

Second, I suggest that through official and unofficial (i.e., non–state-sponsored) means, refugees should be encouraged to tell their own stories—and by "their own," I mean those stories grounded in whatever the refugee happens to value—whether she most fervently embraces her hopes for the future or else defines herself via her past, her memories, nostalgias, and longings. And because I take memory and nostalgia to be central drivers in coming to know and define oneself—and in plotting one's story into the future—I suggest that turning to them by those who were torn from their pasts in often violent ways may be the beginning of finding new voices. But not all nostalgias are alike. Specifically, I suggest that if it is indeed possible to reify refugee nostalgia into identity–re-creating practices, one ought to avoid the essentialism of restorative nostalgia while turning to the more fluid, more contemplative, less rigid reflective version.

A brief clarification: what is nostalgia anyway? As I have argued elsewhere, nostalgia is a longing not necessarily only for a place but also for a time or for a certain state of being.[43] The nostalgic longs, and it is this personal, powerful, and potentially motivating longing that I think can be most effective in creating the kinds of narratives that redefine lives. Here, I rely on Svetlana Boym's distinction between two exile-centered approaches to nostalgia: the restorative and the reflective.[44] Restorative nostalgia looks to *nostos* (home), focusing on the singular plot of a "transhistorical reconstruction of the lost home."[45] The stories that restorative nostalgia tells demand an active, exacting restoration of the past, commanding to rebuild and to reestablish what is lost. Restorative nostalgia often drives nationalistic, essentialist master narratives of collective identities that focus on a return to storied "origins."[46] Indeed, "restorative nostalgia does not think of itself as nostalgia, but rather as truth and tradition"[47]—it embraces its own mythologies by trying to reify them. Another way of putting it is this: restorative nostalgia is a totalizing process set against the unfamiliar and the new that, given a refugee's fractured sense of self, is an understandably seductive move. When politically, culturally, or epistemically adrift, as so many refugees are, a longing for a familiar past might very well serve as a blueprint for how things "ought to be." Before long, one is in the thrall of trying to re-create the past while willfully choosing to ignore that such a move may be not only unrealizable but indeed not preferable. In refusing to relinquish any part of one's past self, one might be at risk of foreclosing the possibility of any potential future, thus becoming a permanent exile.

Thus, I suggest that a refugee trying to restore her own voice might turn to what Boym calls reflective nostalgia, which focuses on the *algia* (the longing itself).[48] Reflective nostalgia has more to do with "ambivalences of human longing and belonging. . . . Restorative nostalgia protects the absolute truth, while reflective nostalgia calls it into doubt."[49] Just as it rejects totalizing master narratives, it "explores ways of inhabiting many places at once and imagining different time zones. It loves details, not symbols."[50] A nostalgic of this kind longs for her past but does so indirectly and without a desire to re-create. Instead, she embraces her own ambiguities, the ongoing confusion and convergence of her own backward-looking desires and present realities, and weaves them into a new kind of story, a new kind of self that is reflective of its own fragility, strangeness, and contingency.

How this kind of nostalgia is motivating in a refugee community can be clarified by considering Andreea Ritivoi's slight modification of Boym's analysis. Reflective nostalgia, she notes, "signal[s] the breach [between past and present] and inaugurates a search for the remedy."[51] In other words, here is a kind of nostalgia that does not demand allegiances to the past and therefore does not ensure a kind of narrative insularity that would keep one from engaging with the present. And so, reflective nostalgia creates room for counternarrative—a kind of nostalgic dissidence that offers a space of resistance to oppressive master narratives. Conversant with one's past, a reflective nostalgic recognizes the possibilities for flexible meanings, fragments, and stories in creating a new identity and new possibilities for the self that are not necessarily ground in another's narratives (e.g., of who a refugee essentially is) or in strictly a backward-looking paradigm (e.g., how one cannot go on unless things are exactly as they were preexile). This, in turn, can repair a refugee's broken sense of self by, first, rejecting the master narratives of who she is and, second, through creative acts of imagination, remembering, and re-creating a fluid, different kind of self, a different kind of voice that "can replenish and rebuttress [her] sense of identity by consolidating the ties with [all of her] history."[52] Motivated by a desire for creative self-repair rather than for fitting a preconceived social mold, the reflective nostalgic is engaged in counternarrative acts of resistance that shatter silences. These acts can sometimes be epistemically and morally subversive, pushing not only against the established metanarratives of official pro- or antirefugee pieties but also against their internalization by the refugee herself. The refugees who are guided by reflective nostalgia are thus not led back to their homelands—that door is (mostly) closed. But neither are they left, defenseless and liminal, subject to the whims of the master narratives of their host nations. Instead, they find themselves at that precarious but necessary space of self-redefinition, where the canvas of their lives might be once again their own. I conclude this section with several examples of how reflective nostalgia and memory are already being creatively woven into the practices of refugee life.

I Am Not Your Canvas

As I have argued here, we can build, destroy, and recover ourselves through stories. Thus far, I have only theorized ways of conceiving refugee counter-stories as potentially liberatory, freeing exiles from the oppressive master narratives of those who wield narrative, social, and political power by painting them as angels, demons, or helpless victims. I would like to conclude on a somewhat optimistic note by offering several examples of refugees restoring their own voices, telling their own stories, and through these counternarratives dismantling years of liminality, of narrative erasure, of moral, epistemic, and political disenfranchisement.

In 2010, Latif Mukasa, an artist and LBGTQ rights activist from Uganda, on finding out that there was a warrant for his arrest, fled to the Netherlands, where he was offered asylum. He now guides visitors through what is called the Temporary Museum, which displays the work of refugees and migrants from their own perspectives:

> Mr. Mukasa stopped in front of his own painting, "The Gods of Africa" (2017) depicting a large clownesque figure hovering over a small group of stick figures, painted in hues of green. His work is one of a half dozen that are part of the installation "APKAR (Artist Previously Known as Refugee)" from 2017, all made by former refugees. . . . "As time goes on, I hope I will find a voice again, and this is just a beginning," he said.[53]

In this way drawing on the memory of their homelands and seeking to be heard in their present circumstances, these refugee artists employ nostalgic elements of their homeland, such as dried herbal teas from Syria or paintings of their homeland, but not with a desire to re-create or restore: depicting familiar objects in a different and often strikingly "foreign" manner, they are both looking backward and looking forward in creating new, complex, reflective refugee identities.[54]

In a similar effort to find their own voices amid the strangeness of the new, young female Syrian refugees are using video production and digital photography to narrate and

> [transform] the foreign environment of the refugee camp and their urban communities into new terrain for exploration, self-discovery, self-expression, and empowerment. Taking digital imagery and making video has become a way for

> them to articulate the sometimes unspeakable; . . . and a tool with which they are able to investigate and start to ask themselves and the world around them critical questions . . . digital storytelling offers the possibility not just to change the trajectories of their own personal stories and narratives but also to offer this possibility of change (counter-narratives) to other young refugee girls; offering alternative points of view to individuals in their communities and to the world beyond.[55]

Again, it is the intersectionality of memory and nostalgia, the pain of liminality (even at a young age), and the engagement with the new that makes possible a kind of consolidation of refugee lives that not only counters and challenges master narratives of helplessness and lostness but also serves to rebuild otherwise fractured lives into creative, fluid, and dynamic wholes. As one participant noted, "I want to show the rest of the world that even though we live in a refugee camp, and have different lives, we still have dreams and ambitions. We are creative. We strive to rise above our limitations. I feel it's my responsibility not just to tell the world that truth, but to let people see it for themselves."[56] In other words, this is one voice that no longer accepts its own silence—a voice that will offer its own stories to as many as will listen.

The refugee self-reclamation project can begin with very young children as well. Since 2015, Germany has seen more than a million refugees, and volunteers in North Rhine-Westphalia developed a way for refugee children to find their own voices. In a nation where the refugee crisis has created serious political conflict, these children, by using creative writing as a way to share their stories, have been encouraged to contribute to a book that would address their lives before, during, and after their often-frightening journeys.[57] Not hiding from the pull of their past, nor shying away from the present and the future, they are given the space to say who they were, who they are, and who they hope to become—without being forced to conform to the stifling and limited narratives about what it means to be a refugee child. And as a refugee child myself, I vividly recall that struggle: to give in to the romance of one's past, preexile self while rejecting one's current circumstances and, alternatively, to embrace whatever refugee narrative was in vogue in one's host country—whether one is painted as a villain, a hero, or a victim—because too often, only those two options seemed like the path of least resistance. Or one can do something else: create one's own art, write one's own books, contradict stories about one with stories by one—say something that does not conform to the expected narratives, the expected story lines.

Of course, as can be glimpsed from the several examples above, these nonconforming, counternarrative options require assistance from the host nation—if not from its government, then certainly from its people. It took me a long time to understand the necessity of taking this other, riskier path, and for so many reasons, I am both moved and inspired by the courage that the current generations of refugees, young and old, show in refusing to be a mere canvas for powerful others.

CONCLUSION

I began this chapter with the idea that words—narratives—have a particular kind of power to change, shape, and remake lives. While within philosophical ethics this notion is not new, its application in the given case of refugee silencing and narrative erasure merits discussion and analysis, and that is what I hope to have achieved here. Much has been written about refugee rights as citizens, as claims makers, as people; more has been said about the necessity of not only admitting asylum seekers into host nations but also helping them find a place where they can begin again rather than just providing them with the bare minimum for survival. Yet even given these heartening moves in refugee-focused (mostly) social and political theory, I do not take the moral work of confronting the refugee crisis to be anywhere near completion. The reasons for this are many, but the ones I examined here have less to do with the necessity of admitting refugees into host countries (although I take this to be a moral responsibility that the Global North is, tragically, failing to meet) and more to do with what happens once they are there.

As a refugee myself (because one is never really a "former" refugee—this is not an identity that tends to dissipate, even with the passage of time), I distinctly recall being settled in all the ways that count, by having a place to live, a school to attend, and even new, strange Americans with whom to interact. But I also remember the necessity of keeping a polite, respectful silence when nonrefugee others would remark on my "bravery" or on my "untrustworthy, communist" past or even pitied my clearly secondhand "migrant" clothing. This was their country, I was told, and what they say about me must stand. In the absence of any counterstories told either by fellow refugees or by those whose words seem to define who we were, it took me (and others like me) a long time to understand—and an even longer time to counteract—the political, social, and moral damage of this narrative erasure. Some of us found our own voices. Others never did.

And so now I offer this chapter in the hope that current generations of refugees will be granted not only safe harbor but also the moral spaces where their stories, their voices, and their very selves will finally and unambiguously be their own.

NOTES

1. See Hilde Lindemann, *Damaged Identities, Narrative Repair* (Ithaca, NY: Cornell University Press, 2001), and Howard Brody, *Stories of Sickness* (Oxford: Oxford University Press, 2002).

2. Note that I make the distinction between refugees and immigrants here, which is a distinction against which Choe-Smith argues in chapter 10 of this volume.

3. Anna Gotlib, "Refugees, Narratives, or How to Do Bad Things with Words," *Kennedy Institute of Ethics Journal*, June 20, 2017, https://kiej.georgetown.edu/refugees-narratives-bad-things-words, citing "The Situation at the Sangatte Camp in France," *Refugee Council*, September 7, 2001, http://www.refugeecouncil.org.uk/latest/news/754_the_situation_at_the_sangatte_camp_in_france.

4. "With 1 Human in Every 113 Affected, Forced Displacement Hits Record High," UN High Commissioner for Refugees, June 20, 2016, http://www.unhcr.org/en-us/news/press/2016/6/5763ace54/1-human-113-affected-forced-displacement-hits-record-high.html?query=21.3%20million%20refugees%20worldwide.

5. Syrian Refugees, 2016, http://syrianrefugees.eu.

6. "Migrant Crisis: Austria Passes Controversial New Asylum Law," *BBC*, April 27, 2016, http://www.bbc.com/news/world-europe-36152927.

7. Gotlib, "Refugees, Narratives, or How to Do Bad Things with Words," citing Patrick Wintour, "UK to Take Up to 20,000 Syrian Refugees over Five Years, David Cameron Confirms," *The Guardian*, September 7, 2015, https://www.theguardian.com/world/2015/sep/07/uk-will-accept-up-to-20000-syrian-refugees-david-cameron-confirms.

8. John Mauldin, "3 Reasons Brits Voted for Brexit," *Forbes*, July 5, 2016, https://www.forbes.com/sites/johnmauldin/2016/07/05/3-reasons-brits-voted-for-brexit/#4faea3a51f9d.

9. Katie Forster, "Hate Crimes Soared by 41% after Brexit Vote, Official Figures Reveal," *The Independent*, October 13, 2016, http://www.independent.co.uk/news/uk/crime/brexit-hate-crimes-racism-eu-referendum-vote-attacks-increase-police-figures-official-a7358866.html.

10. See Hatewatch Staff, "American and European Radical Right Attacks Refugees Fueled Anti-Muslim Sentiment," *Southern Poverty Law Center*, October 6, 2015, https://www.splcenter.org/hatewatch/2015/10s/06/american-and-european-radical-right%E2%80%99s-attacks-refugees-fueled-anti-muslim-sentiment, and Robert Steinback, "Activists Attacking Muslims and Islam Are Springing Up around the Country," *Southern Poverty Law Center*, June 17, 2011, https://www.splcenter.org/fighting-hate/intelligence-report/2011/anti-muslim-inner-circle.

11. Gotlib, "Refugees, Narratives, or How to Do Bad Things with Words," citing Paul Waldman, "Republicans' Anti-Refugee Rhetoric Is Shameful and Despicable—and Probably Good Politics," *The Week*, November 18, 2015, http://theweek.com/articles/589395/republicans-antirefugee-rhetoric-shameful-despicable--probably-good-politics.

12. Gotlib, "Refugees, Narratives, or How to Do Bad Things with Words."

13. Hannah Arendt, *The Origins of Totalitarianism* (New York: Harcourt, 1948), 295–96.

14. Liisa Malkki, "Refugees and Exile: From 'Refugee Studies' to the National Order of Things," *Annual Review of Anthropology* 24 (1995): 495–523.

15. Gotlib, "Refugees, Narratives, or How to Do Bad Things with Words."

16. Lindemann, *Damaged Identities, Narrative Repair*.

17. Lindemann, *Damaged Identities, Narrative Repair*.

18. Anna Gotlib, "'But You Would Be the Best Mother': Unwomen, Counterstories, and the Motherhood Mandate," *Journal of Bioethical Inquiry* 13, no. 2 (2016): 327–47.

19. Development Co-operation Directorate, "Refugee Realities: Policy-Making and Recreating the Refugee Narrative," *Organization for Economic Cooperation and Development*, May 19, 2017, https://www.oecd.org/dac/Refugee_Realities_Concept_Note_May%2019.pdf.

20. Catherine Dauvergne, *Humanitarianism, Identity, and Nation: Migration Laws in Canada and Australia* (Vancouver: UBC Press, 2005).

21. Vanessa Pupavac, "New Issues in Refugee Research: Refugees in the 'Sick Role': Stereotyping Refugees and Eroding Refugee Rights," UN High Commissioner for Refugees, Research Paper No. 128, August 2006, http://www.refworld.org/docid/4ff159d32.html, 1–2.

22. Gal Beckerman, *When They Come for Us, We'll Be Gone: The Epic Struggle to Save Soviet Jewry*, Kindle ed. (Mariner Books, 2010).

23. Gotlib, "Refugees, Narratives, or How to Do Bad Things with Words," citing Andorra Bruno, "U.S. Refugee Resettlement Assistance," *Congressional Research Service*, January 4, 2011, https://fas.org/sgp/crs/row/R41570.pdf.

24. Svetlana Boym, "Nostalgia," *Atlas of Transformation*, 2011, http://monumenttotransformation.org/atlas-of-transformation/html/n/nostalgia/nostalgia-svetlana-boym.html.

25. Pupavac, "New Issues in Refugee Research."

26. Ivan Leudar, Jacqueline Hayes, Jiří Nekvapil, and Johanna Turner Baker, "Hostility Themes in Media, Community and Refugee Narratives," *Discourse and Society* 19, no. 2 (2008): 187–221.

27. Nick Allen and Ruth Sherlock, "Donald Trump: 'I'll Look Syrian Children in the Face and Say They Can't Come,'" *The Telegraph*, February 9, 2016, http://www.telegraph.co.uk/news/worldnews/donald-trump/12147515/After-tomorrow-Donald-Trump-could-be-unstoppable.html.

28. Leudar et al., "Hostility Themes in Media, Community and Refugee Narratives," 188.

29. Leudar et al., "Hostility Themes in Media, Community and Refugee Narratives," 188.

30. Leudar et al., "Hostility Themes in Media, Community and Refugee Narratives," 190.

31. Gotlib, "Refugees, Narratives, or How to Do Bad Things with Words."

32. Sarah Steimel, "Refugees as People: The Portrayal of Refugees in American Human Interest Stories," *Journal of Refugee Studies* 23, no. 2 (2010): 219–37, citing

Peter Gale, "The Refugee Crisis and Fear: Populist Politics and Media Discourse," *Journal of Sociology* 40 (2004): 321–40.

33. Steimel, "Refugees as People," 222, citing Melinda B. Robins, "'Lost Boys' and the Promised Land: US Newspaper Coverage of Sudanese Refugees," *Journalism* 4 (2003): 35.

34. Eugene Keily, "Fact Check: Trump's Immigration Policy vs. Obama's," *USA Today*, January 30, 2017, https://www.usatoday.com/story/news/politics/2017/01/30/fact-check-trump-refugee-policy-comparison-obama/97247418.

35. Steimel, "Refugees as People," 232, citing Ratna Kapur, "The Tragedy of Victimization Rhetoric: Resurrecting the 'Native' Subject in International/Post-Colonial Feminist Legal Politics," *Harvard Human Rights Journal* 15 (2002): 2.

36. Steimel, "Refugees as People," citing Kapur, "The Tragedy of Victimization Rhetoric," 6.

37. Steimel, "Refugees as People," citing Kapur, "The Tragedy of Victimization Rhetoric," 6.

38. Steimel, "Refugees as People," citing Kapur, "The Tragedy of Victimization Rhetoric," 6.

39. Ece Temelkuran, "We Want Our Refugees and Exiles to Be Victims," *Literary Hub*, July 27, 2017, http://lithub.com/we-want-our-refugees-and-exiles-to-be-victims.

40. Temelkuran, "We Want Our Refugees and Exiles to Be Victims."

41. Lara Zahabi-Bekdash, "Recreating the Refugees Narratives: From Sympathy to Dignity," *Huffington Post*, http://www.huffingtonpost.com/lara-zahabibekdash-md-phd/recreating-the-refugees-n_b_8610422.html.

42. Zahabi-Bekdash, "Recreating the Refugees Narratives."

43. See Svetlana Boym, *The Future of Nostalgia* (New York: Basic Books, 2002), and Anna Gotlib, "Memory, Sadness and Longing: Exile Nostalgias as Attunement to Loss," in *The Moral Psychology of Sadness*, 183–206 (Lanham, MD: Rowman & Littlefield, 2017).

44. See Boym, *The Future of Nostalgia*.

45. Boym, "Nostalgia."

46. Gotlib, "Memory, Sadness and Longing."

47. Boym, "Nostalgia."

48. Boym, *The Future of Nostalgia*.

49. Boym, "Nostalgia."

50. Boym, "Nostalgia."

51. Andreea Deciu Ritivoi, *Yesterday's Self: Nostalgia and the Immigrant Identity* (Lanham, MD: Rowman & Littlefield, 2002), 39.

52. Ritivoi, *Yesterday's Self*.

53. Nina Siegal, "Refugees Confront the Past through Art, at a Pop-Up Museum," *New York Times*, July 16, 2017, https://www.nytimes.com/2017/07/16/arts/design/asylum-refugees-artists-.html?mcubz=3&_r=0.

54. Siegal, "Refugees Confront the Past through Art, at a Pop-Up Museum."

55. "Syrian Refugee Girls Producing Their Own Narratives," United Nations Alliance of Civilizations, December 8, 2016, https://www.unaoc.org/2016/12/syrian-refugee-girls-producing-their-own-narratives.

56. "Syrian Refugee Girls Producing Their Own Narratives."

57. "Changing the Narrative by Helping Raise Refugee Children's Voices," Teach for All, http://teachforall.org/en/news/changing-narrative-helping-raise-refugee-childrens-voices.

Chapter Fifteen

How to Be a Refug(e)e for a Stranger?

Esther Hutfless and Elisabeth Schäfer

In the early days of August 2017, Kelly Oliver, Ellen Armour, and a group of their students—Sabeen Ahmed, Alison Lutz, Lisa Madura, and Hilary Scarsella—arrived in Vienna to meet with a small group of feminist philosophers affiliated with the University of Vienna in some way or another—Eva-Maria Aigner, Esther Hutfless, Gertrude Postl, Elisabeth Schäfer, and Silvia Stoller. We had been in touch for about two years regarding the workshop, carefully planning and organizing, writing applications for funding, and so on. But moreover, this group of women philosophers has been moved—meaning: is still moved—by current movements in the world, movements of people who are persecuted and suppressed and who have no rights and perspectives in their war-torn and destroyed home countries. We have been and we are moved by the so-called refugee crisis, which strongly affects our present in a broad political sense.

More than 65.6 million people worldwide are in need of protection and assistance as a consequence of forced displacement. Forcibly displaced populations include refugees, internally displaced persons, and asylum seekers. Globally in 2017, more than 40.3 million people were internally displaced as a result of conflict,[1] while 22.5 million are refugees and 2.8 million asylum seekers.[2] Fifty-one percent of the global refugee population are children under age eighteen—the highest proportion in a decade.

So much for the numbers. We are moved not only by them for sure but also by the very singular experience of what this means for each of our lives. Politically and ethically, we are moved by the following question: how to live together?

Being moved as philosophers also means being forced to think. This is a movement, too, a movement that does not necessarily tend to separate itself from others. In our case, it did not. Quite the contrary; we wanted to meet, we wanted to share our thoughts—may they be vague or distinct, fragile or solid. Given all that, a diverse group finally met to think together. Some of us might have had doubts beforehand: would *thinking* really be the appropriate thing to do? Shouldn't we instead support volunteers involved in assistance services for refugees in Austria or the United States or wherever? Or shouldn't we participate in political activism fighting for the rights of refugees? Important questions—for us as well as for many others, we suppose. Nevertheless, meeting and thinking together must not necessarily be a counterpart of needed material support and political activism: No! Rather, it is a necessary and radical part of it. For sure, thinking always needs to find appropriate forms and formats. Paying attention to the form of thinking—to the way we grasp things, others, or the world in thinking—cannot be separated from the process of shaping the world in which we live. The question *How to live together?* is strongly affected by the question *How to think together?*

When strangers meet, modes and forms of living, thinking, and being together have to be invented. How to express oneself? In which language, in which words? There is always more than one. And there is always something that resists expression and translation.

How to talk and think with the other? *With* instead of *about*! How to approximate the other?

Thinking on these questions, the idea of making a film came to mind: a film composed of voices, images, and writing—different layers that touch, create multidimensional planes of storytelling, planes that do not merge into one linearity, planes that do not come to *one* final point.

"Let us not seek to solidify, to turn the otherness of the foreigner into a thing. Let us merely touch it, brush by it, without giving it a permanent structure."[3] A film is a foreigner, too. A film is—in a certain way—a foreign language within the traditional framework of academic philosophy. We are not that trained to see, to listen, to digest, and to answer to the language of films within this context. Thus, as traditionally trained philosophers, it was our decision to leave our familiar terrain of expression. It was our decision to experience a foreign milieu ourselves, to expose ourselves to a foreign milieu of creation, of expression. We had never before made a film. And so in offering our film as a contribution to the workshop, we were offering a fragment of a digestion of that experience—which in itself is of course only a fragment of the multiple perspectives the complexity of the question of the refugee will have given rise to. We are not only thinking of the temporal embeddedness, the connection to the context in which all this is happening. But we do. Right now, as philosophers, as academics, we are suffering with acute indigestion the dangerous populist politics of the United States as well as of Europe. And it doesn't seem right to us, as academics, as teachers engaged in education, in discourse, in philosophy, and in the arts, to continue as if this is not affecting us. How can we continue our work without ignoring the wider context in which it takes place? But also, how can we continue our work without letting it be appropriated by those same events that threaten us? It is our suggestion to productively work on the creation of a space of approximation and encounter, a space to expose ourselves—to each other, to foreigners, to strangers, as strangers, as foreigners. It seems to us that new spaces need to be created—the existing ones are national terrains, enclosed territories. The spaces to meet have to be created elsewhere: in fiction, in the imaginary. A film can be such a space. This is our suggestion. And in our particular artistic and philosophical work, this space is also a garden.

We follow Julia Kristeva and others on this particular point: "Meeting balances wandering. A crossroad of two othernesses, it welcomes the foreigner without tying him down, opening the host to his visitor without committing him."[4] Our film begins with pictures of leaves and branches of a tree moved by the wind. Against this backdrop, one can hear a conversation that takes place while people are lunching together. One of them is a young woman from Afghanistan; her name is Zeynab Jamali.

Little by little, one learns that Zeynab is invited by a German family (actually, it is one of our families, and both the authors of this text and the producers of the film are present in this scene). Zeynab Jamali is invited to have lunch, but she is not only the guest. She is in a very special way also a host because she cooked the meal and has invited those who invited her to share this meal with her. "The meeting often begins with a food fest: bread, salt, and wine. A meal, a nutritive communion . . . this table corner, where they gulp with such pleasure, is covered with the paths of memory: one remembers, makes plans, recites, sings."[5]

As Kristeva tells us, during a meal, the paths of memory are present. Zeynab tells the story of her and her family's flight from Afghanistan. We learn that Zeynab Jamali is a seventeen-year-old young woman from Gizab. After her uncle and her grandmother were killed by the Taliban—both of them refused to deliver their garden to the Taliban, who tried to rob their land—Zeynab and her family fled to Germany. From Gizab, they went via Pakistan to Iran, where they stayed for one month. The Jamalis took the so-called Balkan Route and crossed the mountains in Pakistan and Iran on foot at night and crossed the Aegean Sea between Turkey and Greece in a small boat with sixty others. They finally arrived in Germany on October 15, 2015, after having crossed eight countries: Pakistan, Iran, Turkey, Greece, Macedonia, Serbia, Hungary, and Austria.

In Afghanistan, Zeynab went to school for only half a year. When the family decided to flee, Zeynab, luckily, had not been forced to marry a Taliban man, as happens to many girls from the age of twelve on. Zeynab has now lived in Germany for only one and a half years. Nevertheless, she successfully finished modern secondary school and will now start junior high. Given that she could attend school for only half a year in Afghanistan, this is an extraordinary change. After junior high, Zeynab wants to become a nurse. Her personal metaphor is that she wants to continue her education now, step-by-step on a stairway, which will hopefully henceforth be accessible for her. She is very grateful and very enthusiastic to learn.

Zeynab and her family are currently accepted in Germany but do not have refugee status according to the UNHCR Refugee Convention. They hope that they can stay in Germany.

Zeynab and her family live in a small flat in Bad Karlshafen, Germany, where they finally have a garden with vegetables and fruits again.

Our film refuses to show direct pictures of this meeting and eating scene: on the one hand, to respect Zeynab's religious as well as cultural background and, on the other, due to the ethical and aesthetic decision to develop a slow, cautious, and noncapturing approach to others. The film shows different settings in a garden. The approximately ten-minute scene of Zeynab's narration of her flight is followed by a philosophical reflection on the tension of guests and hosts.

Film Script

Figure 15.1. Source: A film by Esther Hutfless and Elisabeth Schäfer.

How to Be a Refug(e)e for a Stranger? Fragments and Brief Chronicles of the Time of Migration
A film by Esther Hutfless and Elisabeth Schäfer
[*Front credits, white lettering on black screen*]

"Let them be well used; for they are abstracts and brief chronicles of the time"
Hamlet, Act II, Scene 2
[*white lettering on black screen*]

[*impression of branches moved by wind; one can hear Zeynab's voice:* "I have always cried . . . I have always cried . . .]

Figure 15.2. Source: A film by Esther Hutfless and Elisabeth Schäfer.

Fragment I: Preface
[*white lettering on black screen—followed by spoken passages*]

Wie nicht . . .

How not to . . .

. . . speak ABOUT . . . conceptualize . . . use . . . misuse . . . stigmatize . . . normalize . . . exploit . . . colonize . . . know better . . .

How not to . . . think, we are no strangers . . . but the others are . . . how not to hierarchize . . .

"How not to . . ."

. . . "how not to" is the beginning of Hélène Cixous's short text for the program *Le Dernier Caravanserail*,[6] a play written and developed together with Ariane Mnouchkine and many refugees who are members of the Théâtre du Soleil in Paris. The play is based on interviews conducted with refugees living in camps all over France, Indonesia, New Zealand, Australia, and Great Britain.

How not to speak *about* the refugee? Here? Today?

They are present in our imaginary and in the imaginary of our societies; in everyday newspapers; in some Viennese districts more than in others; in camps on the outer borders of Europe; they are spread all over the country and are present in small villages where they live; they are present in many different debates on Western values; in racist and right-wing argumentations which adopt and misuse the feminist fight for equality for their own propaganda and against male Muslim refugees; they are present as religious or conservative others in feminist and left-wing discussions on the often conflicting relation between a radical understanding of hospitality and the core values of a liberal society such as children's, women's, and minority rights; they are present in debates on integration and assimilation; they are present as the uncanny other; as the evil or idealized other.

To which extent is the other allowed to be and remain *the other*?
How to live with the other without assimilating or excluding the other?
Which morally demands does the other have to follow? And which do we?

Where are they? Often we are speaking about the absent. The refugee is an empty signifier. For many people refugees remain ghosts. They have no names, or they have names people cannot spell, they have no faces, but faces of phantasms, like dark, black and wild faces, but they have no singular faces, not the face of Zeynab, the face of Martab, the face of Mohammad, etc. They have no story, no voice. No singular story of their flight. They are nothing but a part of the generalized group of "the refugees." So one hesitates to speak about refugees. Wait, let's stop! Don't speak about them! Let them speak first. Let them tell their stories! Let's listen, let's listen to what they want to say, what they want to ask, what they want to express. But . . . where?! If we do not meet, if we do not see each other so easily?! Where shall we listen to one another?! How to create a space, where we can meet?! Which space?! Where might this space be located, created, invented—if not already done so—in our lives?! In each of our lives?!

How to be a refug(e)e for a stranger?

How not to speak about, but nearby,[7] and with? "How not to replace the words from your lips by my words spoken in good will?," as Hélène Cixous asks.[8]

[*Pause*]

Figure 15.3. Source: A film by Esther Hutfless and Elisabeth Schäfer.

We are uncanny others to each other.
[*white lettering remains on screen*]

Fragment II: Exile
[*white lettering on black screen—followed by spoken passages*]

Etel Adnan, the Lebanese American poet, essayist, and visual artist, writes, "Do I feel as if I live in exile? Yes. But this lasts now for a long long time. It has become my very nature. And I must admit, I did not suffer all too often.

Most of the time, I even felt happy in exile. . . . being a poet I am deeply rooted in languages. Not only in 'my' languages, but in all languages."[9] Etel Adnan was born in 1925 in Beirut. Her mother was a Christian Greek from Smyrna, and her father was Muslim Syrian. Though she grew up speaking Greek and Turkish in a primarily Arabic-speaking society, she was educated at French convent schools, and French became the language in which her early work was first written. She also studied English in her youth, and most of her later work has been first written in this language. Adnan traveled to Paris, where she received a degree in philosophy from the Sorbonne. She then traveled to America, where she continued graduate studies at the University of California, Berkley, and at Harvard University. From 1952 to 1978, she taught philosophy of art at the Dominican University of California in San Rafael.

Poets cross the borders of languages, imaginaries, and cultures. That is their very movement. Adnan says, "That is the reason why a poet embodies the heart of human nature. That is why a poet is so human. Such as a cat is a cat and cherry tree is a cherry tree."[10] A writing human being is a human being. Does this mean we are romanticizing all kinds of border crossings, all kinds of movements, all kinds of exiles? No.

Figure 15.4. Source: A film by Esther Hutfless and Elisabeth Schäfer.

Fragment III: Translation
[*white lettering on black screen—followed by spoken passages*]

"How not to translate?" asks Cixous. "We must translate," she answers.[11] There is no way without translation. How to expose yourself, how to expose ourselves to a stranger?! How to expose yourself to someone, who does not speak your language?! How does a stranger expose herself, himself etc. to you?! We must translate. We must translate ourselves! All of us. All of us involved in the encounter with others, all of us involved in situations, where we do not share the same language, imaginary, culture . . . we must translate. Translation is a process of relationality and reciprocity. It is not a one-way movement. It creates something new. There is also always a loss in translation. We lose something. We lose words, sense, meanings, we even lose ourselves in translation. We get lost in translation. Loss. In German one can say: "*Los gehts*!" It is a phrase for initializing a breakup, a departure, a beginning. To start with something most of the time includes to quit something else. Or to realize that something came to an end. And there is the need for something new. New words, actions, ways of living, moving, thinking or speaking. New habits. New styles. It was Hannah Arendt who enriched western philosophy with the concept of natality. The

Figure 15.5. Source: A film by Esther Hutfless and Elisabeth Schäfer.

power of beginnings is that what radically marks our potentiality to act. It is in her perspective that we are born, that we ourselves have a beginning, which radically forms our actions. And it is not death. Not the end. Not a telos. But the power to begin. To start. To break up. Los! "*Los gehts!*" Hélène Cixous writes about this phrase her mother used for her entire life, even as she arrived in another language for decades, she continues to use this German phrase. She used that phrase in very old age, a few days before she died: "—*Was ist los*? says my mother. What's happening? What's not happening? . . . And silently I cover mama, who is freezing—*Was ist los?* mama moans. *los—los—Los*? What's that? We don't know. It is what we don't know. . . . Have you read *The Book of Los*?—No—No. *The Book of Loss*?—No. *The Book of Los*—Ah! No."[12]

Fragment IV: Transformation
[*white lettering on black screen—followed by spoken passages*]

Oh no. We haven't yet read *The Book of Los*. *The Book of Loss*. Let's read *The Book of Los*. *The Book of Loss*. Let's read *The Book of Was ist los?!* Let's read and get in touch with the not yet read. The not yet experienced. The not yet known. With not yet deciphered signs. Let's enter "signs fiction!"[13] Perhaps we have to translate. Maybe we have to translate *first*. Perhaps we have to start with translation. How not to translate?

Translation does not simply mean that one word, one sentence is translated into another language. The trans* in translation refers to the beyond, the not yet existing, to shiftings, to change and the creation of something new—transformation. There we meet. In signs fiction!

Comment ne pas. . . . *Wie nicht*. . . . How not to . . . reminds us on the Derridean hesitation.[14]
How not to speak *about* the other? How not to speak *about* the refugee?
There is no simple solution for what is called the "refugee crises." No answer how to really live hospitality as an individual, as a whole country. We now have an answer too!
Just storytelling!

When are we really addressing the other? We mean: the other. Are we really addressing the other if we analyze the situation of our societies? If we talk about hospitality: the host on the one side and the guest on the other? Shouldn't we ask: Who is who? Who is the guest of whom? *Wie sich annähern*? How to approximate the other? How to speak *with* the other? And if we really speak with the other, doesn't this mean that we have to become guests ourselves? Guests arriving in a new time, in a new space? How to create a new world, which is a new world not only for guests coming but also for the hosts becoming guests leaving their common world to create a new one together with the others? How to live together? "And what if," as Hélène Cixous asks, "we never arrive? That is the question of the refugee on her journey."[15]

Fragment V: Being Guests of a Guest
[*white lettering on black screen—followed by spoken passages*]

Last week we played badminton with Zeynab Jamali. We played in a garden, where we were guests. Zeynab visited Elisabeth's parents while we were also visiting them. Zeynab is learning German and various other things from Elisabeth's parents. Zeynab invited us to enjoy an Afghan lunch with her. She cooked it together with her mother. When Zeynab, the refugee from Afghanistan, arrived at the house of Elisabeth's parents, she brought with her a huge bundle. She carefully wrapped two big bowls in them. In the bigger one there was rice. Above this was a bowl with chicken. She cooked an Afghan meal together with her mother and invited us, while she was invited by Elisabeth's family. She came as a guest and invited all of us to be her guests. We deconstructed slightly our being hosts, our being guests. And played it as well as we played badminton, trying to keep the ball as long in the air as possible.

We are all guests. We are all strangers. We meet. We all became and become strangers and guests for each other. "Being safe is scary," says the welcoming inscription on of one of the main buildings of this year's 14th *Documenta* in Kassel, one of the biggest art exhibitions in the world. Being thus means not to be safe in a scary way. To take care for our being and well-being, which does not scare us, therefore means to take a risk. Life and taking care for our and each other's lives is an "*élogue du risqué*,"[16] one could sum up with the words of the extraordinary French philosopher Anne Dufourmantelle, who died only a few weeks ago while trying to save children from drowning. What will save us? Maybe the moment when we are courageous enough to take risk, to take care, to be and become strangers and guests for each other. But where? In which garden? In which place? We need spaces to invent, spaces to generate new imaginations, new narrations, we need spaces and passages, where we can translate and transform, where we can invent and develop, where we are able to deconstruct, to lose, to mourn our losses, to start, to shout "*los gehts*!" Hélène Cixous said, when she was asked in Vienna this spring what Western societies might need in times of migration, "We need millions of theatres, to give people access to different languages."

We need spaces to meet. To translate. To transform. Where we all became and become strangers and guests for each other.

[*closing credits, white lettering on black screen*]

A Film by
Esther Hutfless and Elisabeth Schäfer
Medusa Productions 2017

Sounds
PRAED Life in Beirut 2008

Film created for
Refugee Workshop:
A collaborative workshop between Vanderbilt University and the University of Vienna

Thanks to Zeynab Jamali

All Film material has been recorded in a garden.

Figure 15.6. Source: A film by Esther Hutfless and Elisabeth Schäfer.

CONCLUSION

Allowing the spectator to witness the moment—the moment of risk—of being and/or becoming a refug(e)e for a stranger has been the main theme of our aesthetic and philosophical encounter. This is perhaps the very "in-between," the imaginary, the space, that we suggested we seek and delve into at the beginning of this text. This articulated exploration of being and/or becoming a refug(e)e for a stranger seems to *expand* our understanding of living together, leading, one might assume, to a kind of increased—and thus more intensively palpable—shared life. But in order to allow these moments of approximation to reveal themselves, a great patience is required, a willingness to give oneself over to the idea of exposure.

NOTES

1. See Alexandra Bilka et al., "GRID 2016: Global Report on Internal Displacement," *Norwegian Refugee Council*, May 2016, http://www.internal-displacement.org/assets/publications/2016/2016-global-report-internal-displacement-IDMC.pdf.
2. See "Global Trends: Forced Displacement in 2016," UN High Commissioner for Refugees, June 2017, http://www.unhcr.org/5943e8a34.pdf.
3. Julia Kristeva, *Strangers to Ourselves* (New York: Columbia University Press, 1991), 3.
4. Kristeva, *Strangers to Ourselves*, 11.
5. Kristeva, *Strangers to Ourselves*, 11.
6. Hélène Cixous, "Notre Spectacle," trans. Alexandra Grant, *X-TRA* 16, no. 1 (2013), http://x-traonline.org/article/notre-spectacle.
7. Cf. Trinh T. Minh-ha, *Reassemblage*, filmed in 1982 in Senegal.
8. Cixous, "Notre Spectacle."
9. Etel Adnan, *Schreiben in einer fremden Sprache* (Berlin: SuKultur, 2016), 22.
10. Adnan, *Schreiben in einer fremden Sprache*, 22.
11. Cixous, "Notre Spectacle."
12. Hélène Cixous, *Abstracts and Brief Chronicles of the Time: I. Los, A Chapter* (Cambridge: Polity Press, 2016), 378.
13. Cf. Ruth Wolf-Rehfeldt, *SIGNS FICTION* (Berlin: Chert Galerie & Motto Books, 2016).
14. Cf. Cixous, "Notre Spectacle," introduction by Alexandra Grant.
15. Cixous, "Notre Spectacle."
16. Anne Dufourmantelle, *Éloge du risqué* (Paris: Rivages, 2014).

Chapter Sixteen

Echotext. Between Here and There. A Meteoric Meditation

In Response to *How to Be a Refuge(e) for a Stranger?*

Eva-Maria Aigner

1. Approaching. A hospitable space.
This is how you fly.

This short sentence keeps echoing in my ears, seemingly detached from any determinate context, when I watch Esther Hutfless and Elisabeth Schäfer's short film *How to Be a Refuge(e) for a Stranger?*

And indeed, there is a rare tenderness and *lightness*, an airiness at play—in the way the many different voices engage with and pass one another, exchange their own or some stranger's stories. Their tales remain fractured, fragmentary. They are "stories to come": they don't claim to make some definite "point" but commit to their status as being "works in progress" and to their own transitory—thus fluent or even "superfluous" nature. This also means that, to a certain degree, they also remain *secretive*—not in the sense that they "seal themselves off" from interpretation and response but, on the contrary, by proclaiming their own vulnerability (as the "secret" etymologically always also indicates a cut, a wound, an openness toward the other): "There is no simple solution for what is called the refugee crisis. No answer, how to really live hospitality, as an individual, as a whole country. We have no answer too. Just storytelling."[1] As striking as this proclamation of vulnerability might be (and it hits us hard, it makes us feel uneasy, uncomfortable, probably because we rarely encounter it within contemporary academic and *systematic* philosophy[2]), it does not discourage philosophical discourse, but, on the contrary, it entails a call for responsibility. The promise of the secret invites numerous responses, translations; it engages us to "fill in the gaps" of the story, only to erase our own inscriptions again, to start anew, to weigh the words carefully, lovingly, to put them to play.

Approaching tenderly, the voices involved in this particular play evoke a series of different places: a dining table, a garden, a mountain path, a dark forest, a border zone. They are all fragile, precarious places, as we come to realize when we follow the author's hypnotizing readings: they continue to unfold and weave their stories slowly, almost whispering, almost falling into silence at times, as if every word and every intonation is crucial to keep this space alive, to keep the suspense aflight "as long as possible."[3]

By letting itself be traversed by a multiplicity of voices, the movie script thus transforms into a *passage*. While it raises the question of how to create a space where it might be possible to welcome the other and to let him or her arrive, the text itself becomes such a hospitable place, where strangers meet and share bits and pieces of their stories. Their lines of flight cross one another, they touch lightly, exchange an encouraging nod or a smile, a *shibboleth*, a secret word. It is a "text-body" (as you can say in German, *Textkörper*) in transgression, ruptured, caught up in and fully committed to the process of becoming. With Derrida, we could describe this relatively short interval (the movie's run time is 40:59) as an "echo-room" ("*la chambre d'échos*") of voices.[4] Within this space, everything seems to be "up in the air," every seemingly constant meaning in suspense: *Who is the guest, who the host?* Who is speaking? Who is addressing whom? Suddenly, we are not so sure anymore: How (not) to address the other? Do we really address him or her, let the stranger arrive, in our texts? What about the imminent violence, the *cut* that the writing process necessarily implies?

Thus, what is immanently at stake here (among many other things) is the question of how to create a hospitable space *in writing* or, more specifically, within our philosophical writing practices. As Hutfless and Schäfer's quiet and tender approach suggests, this might require to write on the very edges, the margins of what is considered "philosophical writing" in the context of the text-producing industry that the discipline of Western academic philosophy is about to become today. What is so challenging about this approach (again, among many other things) is not only its fully exposed vulnerability that evokes our responsibility for the stories we tell and *how* we tell, recite and rewrite them. The challenge also resides in the appeal to endure this state of absolute suspense—the lightness, the seemingly weightless grace and the confusion that constitute this space of hospitality, the indecisiveness of the *border zone*, *the passage*, where the ghosts continuously rush back and forth, eager to tell their stories:

"I hastily collect some change from my wallet, so we can pass the tollgate, not to obstruct the traffic," says a traveler.

"I put my bag, belt, watch, wallet, jacket, shoes into a small plastic container and wait in line, feeling slightly uneasy while I am watching a stranger taking one step forward through the metal detector, then hesitating as the light signal goes off, stepping back again," says a friend.

2. Surviving. The Hour of the Wolf.

Let me linger at this site for a bit, at this nonplace that is the border. To breathe in its specific atmosphere—to get a *taste* of it, *for* it. Not to *steal off* lightly, as swiftly, clandestinely, and guilty as a thief, or a bird (*voler—voleur*). Birds don't seem to care about borders. But what do I know about the secret life of birds?

What are the possible threats the border zone poses and the immanent chances it grants—with regard to a politics of friendship an ethics of hospitality in writing? How to *survive* at the border (in the double meaning of the word, über-leben in German or *sur-vivre* in French)? Where the bodies appear to lose contour and weight. Because what seems at stake here, in any case, is the survival of a body. And the bodies, they sense it, instinctively, a long time before they even cross: "There is the familiar experience of feeling the border before it is there," says Sandra Noeth in her lecture-performance at Tanzquartier Vienna 2015.[5] The bodies, they know it: they pay close attention, become all ear, they lose volume, they feel light-headed, almost taking flight. Listening, they are moving slower, "even slower than slow-motion."[6] Sandra Noeth observes the many changes the body undergoes when entering this treacherous terrain of the "in-between," how living at the border effects different kinds of bodies:

> Mostly, border zones are populated and inhabited by many different bodies. Waiting, everyday bodies, disciplined and trained ones, invisible ones, bodies in fear. . . . They are projected, suspended, absent, suspicious, hesitating, lazy bodies, bodies in repetition, between action and reaction, response and responsibility. And they . . . put us in touch with a more brittle, preliminary, unstable and incomplete idea of the border. . . . It is disquieting, yes, uneasy. And it asks us to leave any safe position, and yet, there is nothing to do and there is nothing to wait for. The ghosts are already in the house for long.[7]

What the bodies seem to sense here is the process of their own becoming-passage, getting to grips with their own fluent, transient nature and the estrangement that (always, already) haunts and constitutes the "self." They try to keep their balance between absolute transparency and dissolution. Thus, the border opens up a vital chance and mortal danger on both sides.

"When the day slips into a cold and silent night, whenever I cross a border, there is a soft and fluid movement, like dust dancing in the sunlight. A narrow sunlit stream of floating particles. I would stretch out my fingers as if to touch it, imagining my flesh dissolving into water, whirling through the air, splashing to the ground, being drunk up by the dry soil. You can feel the border, a long time before you even cross it. But sometimes it just takes you by surprise," says the tightrope walker.

In "Nature's r," Trinh T. Minh-ha approaches the figure of the border from the image of a sunset. It is this hour of the day, she describes as being "*entre chien et loup*" (quoting Jean Genet), the twilight zone between dog and wolf, when it is impossible to tell one from the other.[8] Like Sandra Noeth, she is observant of the vital transformations the bodies experience when approaching the border—when being confronted with the possible total eclipse of the sun: they vibrate in a strange new light; all senses of distance and volume are flattened and fade into gray, "the colour of ash and of fog . . . between form and formless."[9] They find themselves obscured and dislocated at the plane of "semi-darkness . . . passing from one incarnation to another, turning into . . ."[10], entangled in the process of becoming. Thus, what characterizes this "boundary event" is an "'inconstant feeling,'" as Minh-ha writes, "half hope, half fear, becoming-shadow; the peacefulness of sleep and the anxiety of *transformation*."[11] The ambiguity of this experience lies not (only) in the impossibility to tell who is approaching and crossing—of distinguishing between friend and foe, ally and enemy, domestic and feral. Rather, more radically, this border always appears to cut through the body itself, thus contradicting the common superstition that "we are no strangers, but the others are."[12] We do not know beforehand how our bodies will react when entering the twilight zone. We cannot be sure what we will be able to sacrifice. *But what if we never arrive*? Who will arrive? Will I have become the dog? Or the wolf? Or something stranger still? The guest or the host? The ghost or the haunted? Dead or alive?

3. The Secret. Secretion.
We might never know.

For Derrida (who, as it is well known, had a weakness for borders, for "third terms," the neither-here-nor-there, the twilight), the secret is the crucial condition for the possibility of hospitality. Where there are no secrets, no uncertainties, there is no need, no room for hospitality—just like there is no testimony, no bearing witness, without the shadow or the sting of a doubt. Wherever communication becomes completely transparent, fully translatable, the possibility of (a politics of) friendship and the continuation of a dialogue is erased.

But maybe we have simply lost the *taste* for it. As Minh-ha concedes, again quoting Jean Genet, for contemporary westerners and city dwellers, the hour of the wolf might have lost some of its charm. We don't know much about wolves anymore.[13] What do I know about the secret lives of wolves? The full existential weight of the metamorphosis might be lost on me. After having been presented with all the evidence that, most likely, the sun will rise again in the morning, I might not be able to mourn its possible total eclipse.[14] There might simply be no room, no time for it. This does not necessarily mean that we made a bad bargain: like ever so often we successfully delayed the apocalypse (not now!) and gained a fragile state of stability. *Not to obstruct the traffic*. We gain speed.

But sometimes "being safe is scary," as one of the voices in Hutfless and Schäfer's movie proclaims.[15] National border politics establishes the border as a space of maximal transparency. Rather than the agonizing obscurity of the twilight, the bodies approaching and passing the border zones of the national state often appear to suffer an "overexposure": in this context, the border marks the site where the body literally becomes transparent, where one has to speak and commit to his or her "proper name." Every movement, every response, every waiting hour follows a strictly prescribed protocol here, which makes the time-consuming and often tedious process of translation (almost) unnecessary. Each unforeseen pause raises suspicion: *Who has nothing to hide has nothing to fear.*

This call or, rather, this *passion* for transparency has become even more palpable since the beginning of the so-called European refuge crisis in 2015. (And, to be honest, sometimes, ever so often, it even takes hold of writing. My writing. Each time I try to gloss over the uncertainty, the indecisiveness, the risk that comes with *research*—not to know in advance if I will ever arrive and how to get there. I cannot emphasize this enough, there seems to be an incredible power in this vulnerability, in "weak thought," in not-knowing.) I sense that this call for absolute transparency brings about the risk of a generalized disregard for the secret—and thus also for the *art* of hospitality. It creates an image of the border as a space that can be controlled, guarded, supervised, *illuminated* at all times, day and night. And to be sure, this image seems to have a certain appeal to it. In times of crisis and disorientation, we seem to generally prefer our ghosts properly named: "Stay, speak, speak! I charge thee, speak! [*Exit Ghost*]."[16] Because, after all,

> the spirit that I have seen
> May be the devil, and the devil hath power
> T'assume a pleasing shape; yea, and perhaps
> Out of my weakness and my melancholy,
> As he is very potent with such spirits,
> Abuses me to damn me.[17]

How then to write another tale of the border?

"While I was listening, I was touching his back, his ears, his soft fur, the feathers. It is strange how familiar his wounded skin now feels to me. He is pushing his back against my hand, I am sure I can feel the vibration underneath, we are almost too close now, and my thoughts are wandering off again," says *mama*.

Maybe, the place from where to approach the border is not the checkpoint *but the skin*. A living and breathing body.

In "Circumfession," Derrida gives us a haunting description of a venepuncture.[18] The existential weight of this experience resides not so much in the observation of the "inside" suddenly appearing at the "surface" and fading into the "outside"—a situation that, were it not for the body's ability to heal, could very easily lead to the complete dissolution of the body. (And, again, the bodies, they sense it, instinctively: they take care for their wounds to avoid this total "spillage." This is the law of inertia that is valid for all bodies.) Rather, what makes the venepuncture such an uncanny event is the realization that this has *always already happened*. It continues to happen: "The ghosts are already in the house for long."[19] The secret (secretion) is always already spilled and given away. It is not some hidden meaning stored away in the invisible "depth" of the body but the constant movement and vibration of a border, the fluctuation of microscopic particles at the edges of. . . . Thus, the life-threatening process of the body becoming "superfluous" is, paradoxically, also the condition for its survival, its growth and its becoming: for if it weren't for the porous quality of the skin, the body would suffocate. And as Hutfless and Schäfer's work shows, this also seems to apply to the *Textkörper*. In a welcoming gesture, their script leaves spaces, gives time to breathe in the words, to chew, to digest, rehash, echo, and to answer them. And possibly, to leave a trace.

With regard to the questions I'd like to address here, the venepuncture might serve as a venturing point for an ethics of *inscription*, as it encompasses the whole ambivalence of the boundary event. Derrida seems to hold his breath, watching this event unfold as if hypnotized. Maybe its full existential significance dawns on him only later, when he touches the scar. Every punctuation leaves a scar. And despite his declared taste for the abysmal vertigo that is the boundary event, Derrida never simply dismisses the significance of healing. Most often (not always!) vertigo is a passing condition. We can endure it for only a very brief moment. However, the phantasma of a fully "healed" body turns out to be just as deadly as the dread of a total spillage—of the body losing all volume, all weight. The scar then serves as a kind of midway: while proofing the body's incredible power to heal, it also remains as an inerasable trace of the incision, the infestation, that continuously happens to the body.

4. Between here and there. A meteoric meditation.

At night, we often look out for meteor showers ("we" being the participants of the Refugee Workshop that took place from August 8 to August 10, 2017, at Reichenau an der Rax, Austria, where this text started to write itself).

The meteor, says Derrida, is a transient figure, as "clandestine and guilty as a thief."[20] Arriving from who knows where, it becomes visible only for a very brief moment when passing through the atmosphere. Just like the secret, it appears only in its erasure:

> The meteorite's secret is that it becomes luminous upon, as one says, entering the earth's atmosphere, arriving from who knows where, but in any case from another body from which it has become detached. Then, what is meteoric must be brief, rapid, transitory. Furtive in its lightning passage, that is to say perhaps as clandestine and guilty as a thief. As brief as our still suspended phrase.

—this is how you fly—

a question of time. At the outside of an instant.[21]

While remaining one of his most mysterious and "obscure" figures, the meteor represents the key term at the passage between literature, democracy, and the secret to which Derrida repeatedly returns in his writing. It is the riddle he wants us to decipher and to "meditate" on, endlessly.[22]

What constitutes the "meteoric virtue" of literature for Derrida is its eminent power to keep its meaning, its origin, and its course forever in abeyance. This means that the "becoming-literary"[23] of the text depends on an airiness or light-footedness, an abandonment, a drift, on its being "cut loose" from any fully determinable destination, context, or destination. "Every text," says Derrida, "that is consigned to public space, that is relatively legible or intelligible, but whose content, sense, referent, signatory, and addressee are not fully determinable *realties* . . . can become a *literary* object."[24] Therefore, what characterizes literary writing is its continuous effort to create a hospitable space where the other can arrive, leave his or her inscriptions and signatures. In its indecisiveness, it keeps the possibility to retrace, rewrite, and revisit the text open. It engages the reader, the listener, the passerby in the process of weaving the living, breathing texture that is the story, the *Textkörper*. Because of this "meteoric quality" of literary writing that warrants the right to "ask any question," Derrida also proclaims that literature and democracy are necessarily "co-extensive."[25]

For philosophers, to create a more hospitable space *in writing* thus might require to explore the boundaries of what is conventionally considered to be "proper" or "pure" philosophy. Derrida explicitly addresses this in a radio interview with Elisabeth Weber from 1990 that was published under the title *Passages* in the interview collection *Points* (1992 in French, 1995 in English). Here, Derrida first opts for discerning between the philosophical and the literary text "as far as possible"—and, as he underlines, different disciplines have provided us with a great number of criteria to do so. However, again and again, we find ourselves in situations where discerning between the philosophical experience on the one hand and the literary experience on the other becomes "more risky," as Derrida says.[26] The distinction becomes precarious and therefore also more *adventurous*, elastic, fluent. It is at this moment, when philosophy realizes its own being inhibited by and inheriting language, that the separation ("cut-off") seems to be more harmful than the imminent adulteration of the philosophical and the literary or poetic discourse (the German word for adulteration is *Verwässerung*, which indicates a fluent movement, to make something "water-like"). Therefore, it becomes necessary for philosophy to push the possibilities of the philosophical and the poetic experience of the language[27] and thus also to commit to the becoming-literary of the philosophical text.

What happens to the text-body (*Textkörper*) when it approaches this border zone? In the interview quoted above, Derrida gives a concise answer to this, which—for its clarity and its great relevance for the issues at stake here—I would like to quote in its full length:

> J.D.: . . . to push as far as they can go the philosophical experience *and* the poetic experience of the language. . . .
>
> Q.: In a same text? In the text that one is in the process of writing and working on?
>
> J.D.: It is possible, I believe, only in determined historical situations. One can do it, one must do it. . . . Hence the necessity in fact of making cohabit in a same text or of grafting codes, motifs, registers, voices that are heterogeneous; naturally, one must not do it simply in order to do it or in order to force incompatible things into cohabitation or in order to create confusions—but do it while trying to articulate these different registers, to compose in some way the text so that the articulation of the heterogeneous voices among themselves both causes one to think and causes the language to think, or philosophy in the language.[28]

The text transforms into an echo-room of voices. It becomes readable in its becoming, in its fluidity, as an assemblage of voices. We see this writing "technique" (which exactly contradicts any purely mechanical interpretation of the term) of the echo-room at work in many of Derrida's writings, most prominently in *Glas* and *Feu la Cendre*.[29] And we also recognize it in Hutfless and Schäfer's work. We watch it take place, creating space within the movie script. The echotext effectively deconstructs the conception of writing being a genuinely solitary practice: the text is always already inhibited by numerous voices, stories, multiple characters, and conceptual personae—even in the case of philosophical writing. *The ghosts are already in the house.* They are always already there, traversing and haunting our writing as well as our writing practices and habits. Every text a "House of Fama," where multiple voices cross and exchange their stories—some grave with meaning, some light as birds—they listen, mingle, rub on one another, contradict one another, fall in love with each other, touch, appal, affect each other, grow louder, almost fall into silence—and pass on.

Weber then proceeds to question Derrida about the possible risks of such an approach, namely, the danger of the indeterminable drift or dissemination of the text. Once more, allow me to cite the whole passage here, as it can also be read as a commentary on the figure of the border that I tried to explore earlier in this text:

> Q.: So philosophy does not determine in advance its own destination? . . .
>
> J.D.: Yes. . . . Philosophy is always called upon to transgress the border of the regions of research or knowledge and to ask itself about its own limits, but also about its own destination. Philosophy does not know—from *this point of view* philosophy is a non-knowledge—what its destination is.[30]

Derrida prompts us—as philosophers, as writers—to engage in the "ambiguous adventure" that is the boundary event. As he considers this engagement to be "necessary" under certain historical circumstances ("one must do it"), this also implies an ethical demand, a call for responsibility. To resist the temptation of a complete translatability and transparency of the text and to explore the border zones between poetic, literature and philosophy thus cannot simply be trivialized as a mere "aesthetic" decision. Rather, it seems to become crucial for an ethics of hospitality and friendship. As Derrida shows in the passage above, the condition for this necessary becoming-literary of the text appears to be its decided weakness, its not-knowing. It lies exactly in the acknowledgment of the vulnerability, the "indecisiveness," the airiness, and the drift that characterizes philosophical re-search: not to know if, where, and when we will arrive. It is this frank proclamation of vulnerability and the declared openness of its re-searching movement, its tender and slow approach, that makes Hutfless and Schäfer's work truly inspirational, generous, giving, and hospitable. Watching and reading it, we feel the same light-headed and lighthearted joy we experience when we watch the tightrope walker. Contradictory to a popular view, it does not come from the thrilling prospect of his or her possible fall should he or she lose balance—but from witnessing some-body being able to survive on this fluctuating, erratic, and very treacherous thin line that is the border zone. To observe some-body who truly excels at this art of dancing in the in-between—and be it for only a single short moment.

The meteor always remains a transient figure. How long can we keep it aflight—and endure this confusing and disorienting instant, in which pragmatics is suspended, just for a brief interval of time? "[We] played it as good as we played badminton," says one of the voices, keeping the ball "up in the air," *just as long as possible*.[31]

NOTES

1. Esther Hutfless and Elizabeth Schäfer, *How to Be a Refug(e)e for a Stranger?*, film presented at the Refugee Workshop, Reichenau an der Rax, Austria, August 8–10, 2017.

2. I rely here on a definition of the philosophical "system" or systematic philosophical thought that Jacques Derrida offers in a talk with Maurizio Ferraris from 1993. See Jacques Derrida, *A Taste for the Secret*, trans. Giacomo Donis (Cambridge: Polity Press, 2001), 3–4.

3. See Hutfless and Schäfer, *How to Be a Refug(e)e for a Stranger?*

4. Jacques Derrida, *Béliers. Le dialogue ininterrompu: Entre deux infinis, le poème* (Paris: Galilée, 2003), 59. The passage is missing in the abbreviated English translation by Dutoit and Romanski; see Jacques Derrida, "Uninterrupted Dialogue: Between Two Infinities, the Poem," trans. Thomas Dutoit and Philippe Romanski, *Research in Phenomenology* 34 (2004): 3–19.

5. Sandra Noeth, Kamal Aljafari, and Susanne Valerie Granzer, "Disquieting Movements: Über die Unruhe der Körper und der Bilder," lecture performance presented at the Research Festival Philosophy on Stage #4, Vienna, November 26–29, 2015, http://homepage.univie.ac.at/arno.boehler/php/?p=8936.

6. Hutfless and Schäfer, *How to Be a refuge(e) for a Stranger?*

7. Noeth et al., "Disquieting Movements."

8. See Trinh T. Minh-ha, "Nature's r: A Musical Swoon," in *Elsewhere, within Here: Immigration, Refugeeism and the Boundary Event*, 59–75 (New York: Routledge, 2011), 74.

9. Minh-ha, "Nature's r," 73.

10. Minh-ha, "Nature's r," 73. It is the same mood conveyed by the monochromatic imagery of Hutfless and Schäfer's film, a sequence of garden scenes shot in black and white that evoke the sense of the twilight zone, where it is hard to tell the exact time of day.

11. Minh-ha, "Nature's r," 74–75, emphasis added.

12. Hutfless and Schäfer, *How to be a Refuge(e) for a Stranger?*

13. See Minh-ha, "Nature's r," 75.

14. Minh-ha, "Nature's r," 62. Minh-ha refers to Cheikh Amidou Kane's book *Ambiguous Adventure* in this passage.

15. Ibid., 74–75.

16. William Shakespeare, *Hamlet*, edited by G. R. Hibbard (Oxford: Oxford University Press, 1987), I.1.

17. Shakespeare, *Hamlet*, II.2.

18. Jacques Derrida, "Circumfession," in *Jacques Derrida*, trans. Geoffrey Bennington (Chicago: University of Chicago Press, 1993), 10–11.

19. Noeth et al., "Disquieting Movements."

20. Jacques Derrida, "Literature in Secret," in *The Gift of Death (Second Edition) and Literature in Secret*, trans. David Wills (Chicago: University of Chicago Press, 2008), 139.

21. Derrida, "Literature in Secret," 139. For most of his text, Derrida seems to use the terms of the "meteorite" (cf., e.g., Derrida, "Literature in Secret," 139) and the "meteor" (cf., e.g., Derrida, "Literature in Secret," 142) interchangeably. To emphasize its status as being "still up in the air," I will stick to the word "meteor" in the context of this chapter.

22. Derrida, "Literature in Secret," 142.

23. Derrida, "Literature in Secret," 131.

24. Derrida, "Literature in Secret," 131.

25. See, e.g., Jacques Derrida, "Passions: 'An Oblique Offering,'" in *A Critical Reader*, ed. David Wood (Oxford: Blackwell, 1992), 23.

26. Jacques Derrida, "Passages—From Traumatism to Promise," in *Points . . . Interviews, 1974–1994*, trans. Peggy Kamuf et al. (Stanford, CA: Stanford University Press, 1995), 375.

27. Cf. Derrida, "Passages," 375.

28. Derrida, "Passages," 375.

29. As another remarkable example for such an "echotext," we could regard Virginia Woolf's novel *The Waves*. To tell the life story of her protagonists—six voices, at times more or less distinguishable from one another—within a single day, Woolf choses the image of the rising and falling sun as seen from a shore. We recall this motive also from Trinh T. Minh-ha's text. And like Minh-ha, Woolf attentively observes the change of light as the sun rises and sets and the ever-shifting movements of the waves, evoking the fluent, fugitive, becoming nature of all beings entangled in the web of her story—and of the text itself. See Virginia Woolf, "The Waves," in *Collected Novels of Virginia Woolf*, ed. Stella McNichol, 335–508 (Basingstoke: Palgrave Macmillan, 1992).

30. Derrida, "Passages," 376.

31. Hutfless and Schäfer, *How to be a Refuge(e) for a Stranger?*

Bibliography

Acer, Elanor, and Jessica Chicco. "U.S. Detention of Asylum Seekers: Seeking Protection, Finding Prison." Human Rights First. April 2009 (revised June 2009). https://www.humanrightsfirst.org/wp-content/uploads/pdf/090429-RP-hrf-asylum-detention-report.pdf.

Adams, Long. "Overlooked and Underserved: The Radical Vulnerability and Victimhood of Refugee Children." Honor's thesis, Vanderbilt University, 2018.

Adnan, Etel. *Schreiben in einer fremden Sprache*. Berlin: SuKultur, 2016.

Adorno, Theodor. *Can One Live after Auschwitz? Philosophical Reader*. Edited by Rolf Tiedemann. Translated by Rodney Livingstone. Stanford, CA: Stanford University Press, 2001.

———. *Critical Models: Interventions and Catchwords*. Translated by Henry Pickford. New York: Columbia University Press, 2005.

———. *History and Freedom: Lectures, 1964–1965*. Edited by Rolf Tiedemann. Translated by Rodney Livingstone. Cambridge: Polity Press, 2006.

———. *Minima Moralia*. Translated by E. F. N. Jephcott. New York: Verso, 2006.

———. *Negative Dialectics*. Translated by E. B. Ashton. New York: Verso, 2005.

———. *Problems of Moral Philosophy*. Edited by Thomas Schröder. Translated by Rodney Livingstone. Stanford, CA: Stanford University Press, 2001.

Adorno, Theodor, and Max Horkheimer. *Dialectic of Enlightenment: Philosophical Fragments*. Translated by Edmund Jephcott. Stanford, CA: Stanford University Press, 2002.

Agamben, Giorgio. *Homo Sacer: Sovereign Power and Bare Life*. Translated by Daniel Heller-Roazen. Stanford, CA: Stanford University Press, 1998.

———. *Means without Ends: Notes on Politics*. Translated by Vincenzo Binetti and Cesare Casarino. Minneapolis: University of Minnesota Press, 2000.

———. *Remnants of Auschwitz: The Witness and the Archive*. Translated by Daniel Heller-Roazen. New York: Zone Books, 2002.

———. *State of Exception*. Translated by Kevin Attell. Chicago: University of Chicago Press, 2005.

———. "Beyond Human Rights." *Social Engineering* 15 (2008): 90–95.

Agerholm, Harriet. "Denmark Uses Controversial 'Jewelry Law' to Seize Assets from Refugees for the First Time." *The Independent*. July 1, 2016. http://www.independent.co.uk/news/world/europe/denmark-jewellery-law-migrants-refugees-asylum-seekers-unhcr-united-nations-a7113056.html.

Agier, Michel. *Managing the Undesirables: Refugee Camps and Humanitarian Government*. Translated by David Fernbach. Malden, MA: Polity Press, 2011.

———. *On the Margins of the World: The Refugee Experience Today*. Malden, MA: Polity Press, 2008.

Alcoff, Linda. *Visible Identities: Race, Gender, and the Self*. Oxford: Oxford University Press, 2006.

Aljazeera. "Hundreds of Refugees Died on Way to Europe This Year." February 9, 2016. http://www.aljazeera.com/news/2016/02/400-refugees-die-europe-2016-160209133941502.html.

Allen, Amy. *The End of Progress*. New York: Columbia University Press, 2015.

———. *The Politics of Our Selves*. New York: Columbia University Press, 2008.

Allen, Nick and Ruth Sherlock. "Donald Trump: 'I'll Look Syrian Children in the Face and Say They Can't Come.'" *The Telegraph*. February 9, 2016. http://www.telegraph.co.uk/news/worldnews/donald-trump/12147515/After-tomorrow-Donald-Trump-could-be-unstoppable.html.

Althusser, Lois. *On the Reproduction of Capitalism: Ideology and Ideological State Apparatuses*. New York: Verso, 2014.

Anker, Deborah. "Refugee Protection, Gender-Based Violence and Trafficking in Persons." *In Defense of the Alien* 23 (2000): 129–37.

Ankersmit, F. R. *Aesthetic Politics: Political Philosophy beyond Fact and Value*. Stanford, CA: Stanford University Press, 1996.

Ansah, Tawia. "Auschwitz as the *Nomos* of Modern Legal Thought." *Law and Literature* 22, no. 1 (2010): 142–79.

Anzaldúa, Gloria. *Borderlands/La Frontera: The New Mestiza*. San Francisco: Aunt Lute Books, 1987.

Appiah, Kwame Anthony. *Cosmopolitanism: Ethics in a World of Strangers*. New York: Norton, 2006.

Arendt, Hannah. *Essays in Understanding 1930–1954*. Edited by Jerome Kohn. New York: Harcourt Brace, 1993.

———. *The Human Condition*. Chicago: University of Chicago Press, 1998.

———. *The Jewish Writings*. Edited by Jerome Kohn and Ron H. Feldman. New York: Schocken Books, 2007.

———. *Men in Dark Times*. New York: Harcourt, 1968.

———. *The Origins of Totalitarianism*. New York: Harcourt, 1948.

———. *Responsibility and Judgment*. Edited by Jerome Kohn. New York: Schocken Books, 2003.

———. "We Refugees." In *Altogether Elsewhere: Writers on Exile*, edited by Marc Robinson, 110–19. Boston: Faber & Faber, 1994.

Aristotle. *Politics*. Translated with introduction and notes by C. D. C. Reeve. Indianapolis: Hackett, 1998.

Augustine. *The Confessions*. Translated by John Ryan. New York: Image Books, 1960.

Austen, Ian. "Syrian Refugees Greeted by Justin Trudeau in Canada." *New York Times*. December 11, 2015. https://www.nytimes.com/2015/12/12/world/americas/syria-refugees-arrive-in-canada.html.

Azmanova, Albena. "The Right to Politics and Republican Non-Domination." *Philosophy and Social Criticism* 42, no. 4–5 (2015): 1–11.

Balibar, Étienne. *Citizenship*. Translated by Thomas Scott-Railton. Cambridge, UK: Polity Press, 2015.

———. "Is a Philosophy of Human Civic Rights Possible? New Reflections on Equaliberty." *South Atlantic Quarterly* 103, no. 203 (2004): 311–22.

———. *Masses, Classes, Ideas: Studies on Politics and Philosophy before and after Marx*. New York: Routledge, 1994.

———. *Politics and the Other Scene*. New York: Verso, 2002.

———. *Spinoza and Politics*. Translated by Peter Snowdon. New York: Verso, 1998.

———. *We, the People of Europe?: Reflections on Transnational Citizenship*. Translated by James Swenson. Princeton, NJ: Princeton University Press, 2004.

Barber, Benjamin. *Strong Democracy: Participatory Politics for a New Age* (Berkeley: University of California Press, 1984), 120–21.

Barbieri, William. *Ethics of Citizenship: Immigration and Group Rights in Germany*. Durham, NC: Duke University Press, 1998.

Barbour, Charles. "Between Politics and Law: Hannah Arendt and the Subject of Rights." In *Hannah Arendt and the Law*, edited by Marco Goldoni and Christopher McCorkindale, 307–19. Portland, OR: Hart Publishing, 2012.

Basaran, Tugba. "Security, Law, Borders: Spaces of Exclusion." *International Political Sociology* 2 (2008): 339–54.

Bauman, Zygmunt. *Liquid Times: Living in an Age of Uncertainty*. Malden, MA: Polity Press, 2007.

———. *Strangers at our Door*. Cambridge, UK: Polity Press, 2016.

BBC. "Migrant Crisis: Austria Passes Controversial New Asylum Law." April 27, 2016. http://www.bbc.com/news/world-europe-36152927.

———. "Migrant Crisis: Migration to Europe Explained in Seven Charts." March 4, 2016. http://www.bbc.com/news/world-europe-34131911.

Beckerman, Gal. *When They Come for Us, We'll Be Gone: The Epic Struggle to Save Soviet Jewry*. Kindle Edition. Mariner Books, 2010.

Beitz, Charles R. *The Idea of Human Rights*. Oxford: Oxford University Press, 2009.

Beltrán, Cristina. "'Undocumented, Unafraid, and Unapologetic': DREAM Activists, Immigrant Politics, and the Queering of Democracy." In *From Voice to Influence: Understanding Citizenship in a Digital Age*, edited by Danielle Allen and Jennifer S. Light, 80–104. Chicago: University of Chicago Press, 2015.

Benhabib, Selya. *Another Cosmopolitanism*. Oxford: Oxford University Press, 2006.

———. *Dignity in Adversity: Human Rights in Troubled Times*. Malden, MA: Polity Press, 2011.

———. *The Rights of Others: Aliens, Residents, and Citizens*. Cambridge: Cambridge University Press, 2004.

Benjamin, Walter. *Illuminations*. Translated by Harry Zohn. New York: Schocken Books, 2007.
Bertram, Christopher. *Do States Have the Right to Exclude Migrants*? Cambridge: Polity Press, 2018.
Betts, Alexander. *Survival Migration: Failed Governance and the Crisis of Displacement*. Ithaca, NY: Cornell University Press, 2013.
Bilka, Alexandra, et al. "GRID 2016: Global Report on Internal Displacement." *NRC: Norwegian Refugee Council*. May 2016. http://www.internal-displacement.org/assets/publications/2016/2016-global-report-internal-displacement-IDMC.pdf.
Boltanski, Luc. *Distant Suffering: Politics, Morality and the Media*. Cambridge: Cambridge University Press, 1999.
———. "The Legitimacy of Humanitarian Actions and Their Media Representations: The Case of France." *Ethical Perspectives* 7, no. 1 (2003): 3–16.
Bon Tempo, Carl. *Americans at the Gate: The United States and Refugees during the Cold War*. Princeton, NJ: Princeton University Press, 2008.
Bourdieu, Pierre. *Outline of a Theory of Practice*. Cambridge: Cambridge University Press, 1977.
Boym, Svetlana. *The Future of Nostalgia*. New York: Basic Books, 2002.
———. "Nostalgia." *Atlas of Transformation*. 2011. http://monumenttotransformation.org/atlas-of-transformation/html/n/nostalgia/nostalgia-svetlana-boym.html.
Brody, Howard. *Stories of Sickness*. Oxford: Oxford University Press, 2002.
Brown, Wendy. *States of Injury*. Princeton, NJ: Princeton University Press, 1995.
Bruno, Andorra. "U.S. Refugee Resettlement Assistance." *Congressional Research Service*. January 4, 2011. https://fas.org/sgp/crs/row/R41570.pdf.
Bull, Hedley. *The Anarchical Society: A Study of Order in World Politics*. New York: Columbia University Press, 2012.
Bull, Hedley and Adam Watson. *The Expansion of International Society*. Oxford: Oxford University Press, 1984.
Bulley, Dan. *Migration, Ethics & Power: Spaces of Hospitality in International Politics*. London, UK: SAGE Publications Ltd., 2017.
Bush, Laura. "Separating Children from Their Parents at the Border Breaks My Heart." *Washington Post*. June 16, 2018. https://www.washingtonpost.com/opinions/laura-bush-separating-children-from-their-parents-at-the-border-breaks-my-heart/2018/06/17/f2df517a-7287-11e8-9780-b1dd6a09b549_story.html?utm_term=.e2c03ba2fcd6.
Butler, Judith. *Frames of War*. New York: Verso, 2009.
———. *Giving an Account of Oneself*. New York: Fordham University Press, 2005.
———. *Precarious Life*. New York: Verso, 2004.
Butler, Judith and Athena Athanasiou. *Dispossession: The Performative in the Political*. Cambridge: Polity Press, 2013.
Calloriadis, Cornelius, The Imaginary Institutions of Society (Cambridge, MA: MIT Press, 1987), 373.
Cameron, Jeffrey. "Review: *Exodus: How Migration Is Changing Our World*." *Migration Studies* 1, no. 3 (2013): 375–77.

Cantor, Jodi and Catrin Einhorn. "Refugees Encounter a Foreign Word: Welcome." *New York Times*. July 1, 2016. http://www.nytimes.com/2016/07/01/world/americas/canada-syrian-refugees.html.

Carens, Joseph H. "Aliens and Citizens: The Case for Open Borders." *The Review of Politics* 49, no. 2 (1987): 241–73.

———. *The Ethics of Immigration*. Oxford: Oxford University Press, 2013.

———. *Immigrants and the Right to Stay*. Cambridge, MA: MIT Press, 2010.

———. "Refugees and the Limits of Obligation." *Public Affairs Quarterly* 6, no. 1 (1992): 31–44.

Castoriadis, Cornelius. *The Imaginary Institution of Society*. Cambridge, MA: MIT Press, 1987.

Cavarero, Adriana. *Inclinations*. Translated by Amanda Minervini and Adam Sitze. Stanford, CA: Stanford University Press, 2016.

Chari, Anita. "The Political Potential of Mindful Embodiment." *New Political Science* 38, no. 2 (2016): 226–40.

Chatterjee, Deen K., ed. *The Ethics of Assistance: Morality and the Distant Needy*. New York: Cambridge University Press, 2004.

Chavez, Cesar. *An Organizer's Tale: Speeches*. New York: Penguin, 2008.

Chavez, Leo R. *Anchor Babies and the Challenge of Birthright Citizenship*. Stanford, CA: Stanford University Press, 2017.

Chesterman, Simon, Michael Ignatieff, and Ramesh Thakur, eds. *Making States Work: State Failure and the Crisis of Governance*. New York: United Nations University Press, 2005.

Chimni, B. S. "Globalization, Humanitarianism, and the Erosion of Refugee Protection." *Refugee Studies Center*. Working Paper. Oxford: Oxford University Press, 2000.

Chouliaraki, Lilie. *The Ironic Spectator*. Cambridge: Polity Press, 2013.

———. *The Spectatorship of Suffering*. London: Sage, 2006.

Cixous, Hélène. *Abstracts and Brief Chronicles of the Time: I. Los, A Chapter*. Cambridge: Polity Press, 2016.

———. "Letter-Beings and Time (2007)." In *The Portable Cixous*, edited by Marta Segarra, 85–95. New York: Columbia University Press, 2010.

———. "Notre Spectacle." Translated by Alexandra Grant. *X-TRA* 16, no. 1 (2013). http://x-traonline.org/article/notre-spectacle.

———. *Stigmata: Escaping Texts*. New York: Routledge, 1998.

Code, Lorraine. *Ecological Thinking: The Politics of Epistemic Location*. Oxford: Oxford University Press, 2006.

Cohen, Stanley. *States of Denial: Knowing about Atrocities and Suffering*. Cambridge: Polity Press, 2001.

Cole, Phillip. *Philosophies of Exclusion: Liberal Political Theory and Immigration*. Edinburgh: Edinburgh University Press, 2000.

Coleman, Matthew and Kevin Grove. "Biopolitics, Biopower, and the Return of Sovereignty." *Environment and Planning D: Society and Space* 27 (2009): 489–507.

Coles, Romand. *Visionary Pragmatism: Radical and Ecological Democracy in Neoliberal Times*. Durham, NC: Duke University Press, 2016.

Collier, Paul. *Exodus: How Migration Is Changing Our World*. Oxford: Oxford University Press, 2014.

Condon, Paul, Gaëlle Desbordes, Willa B. Miller, and David DeSteno. "Meditation Increases Compassionate Responses to Suffering." *Psychological Science* 24, no. 10 (2013): 2125–27.

Cone, Devon. "The Process for Interviewing, Vetting, and Resettling Syrian Refugees in America Is Incredibly Long and Thorough." *Foreign Policy*. November 30, 2015. http://foreignpolicy.com/2015/11/30/the-process-for-interviewing-vetting-and-resettling-syrian-refugees-in-america-is-incredibly-long-and-thorough.

Connolly, William E. *Identity/Difference: Democratic Negotiations of Political Paradox, Expanded Edition*. Minneapolis: University of Minnesota Press, 2001.

———. *Neuropolitics: Thinking, Culture, Speed*. Minneapolis: University of Minnesota Press, 2002.

———. *Political Theory and Modernity*. Ithaca, NY: Cornell University Press, 1989.

Courbet, David. "Migrants at Calais Camp Given Dignity in Death." *The Local*. May 23, 2016. https://www.thelocal.fr/20160523/migrants-at-calais-camp-given-dignity-in-death.

Crisp, Jeff and Amy Slaughter. "A Surrogate State? The Role of the UNHCR in Protracted Refugee Situations." *New Issues in Refugee Research*. Research Paper No. 168. January 2009.

Crosby, Alfred W. *The Columbian Exchange: Biological and Cultural Consequences of 1492*. Westport, CT: Praeger, 2003.

Dauvergne, Catherine. *Humanitarianism, Identity, and Nation: Migration Laws in Canada and Australia*. Vancouver: UBC Press, 2005.

Davis, Julie and Miriam Jordan. "Trump Plans Limit on Refugees." *New York Times*. September 26, 2017. https://www.nytimes.com/2017/09/26/us/politics/trump-plans-45000-limit-on-refugees-admitted-to-us.html.

Dawes, James. *That the World May Know: Bearing Witness to Atrocities*. Cambridge, MA: Harvard University Press, 2007.

Dembour, Marie-Benedicte and Tobias Kelly. *Are Human Rights for Migrants? Critical Reflections on the Status of Irregular Migrants in Europe and the United States*. New York: Routledge, 2011.

Derrida, Jacques. *Béliers. Le dialogue ininterrompu: Entre deux infinis, le poème*. Paris: Galilée, 2003.

———. "Circumfession." In *Jacques Derrida*. Translated by Goeffrey Bennington, 3–315. Chicago: University of Chicago Press, 1993.

———. *Cosmopolitanism and Forgiveness*. London: Routledge, 2002.

———. "Hospitality." *Angelaki: Journal of the Theoretical Humanities* 5, no. 3 (2000): 3–18.

———. "Hostipitality." In *Acts of Religion*, edited by Gil Anidjar, 356–420. New York: Routledge, 2002.

———. "Literature in Secret." In *The Gift of Death (Second Edition) and Literature in Secret*, translated by David Wills. Chicago: University of Chicago Press, 2008.

———. *Of Hospitality: Anne Dufourmantelle Invites Jacques Derrida to Respond*. Translated by Rachel Bowlby. Stanford, CA: Stanford University Press, 2000.

———. *On Cosmopolitanism and Forgiveness*. Translated by Mark Dooley and Michael Hughes. New York: Routledge, 2001.

———. *The Other Heading: Reflections on Today's Europe*. Translated by Pascale-Anne Brault and Michael B. Naas. Bloomington: Indiana University Press, 1992.

———. "Passages—From Traumatism to Promise." In *Points . . . Interviews, 1974–1994*, translated by Peggy Kamuf et al., 373–95. Stanford, CA: Stanford University Press, 1995.

———. "Passions: 'An Oblique Offering.'" In *A Critical Reader*, edited by David Wood, 5–35. Oxford: Blackwell, 1992.

———. *A Taste for the Secret*. Translated by Giacomo Donis. Cambridge: Polity Press, 2001.

———. "Tout autre est tout autre." In *The Gift of Death*, translated by David Wills, 82–116. Chicago: University of Chicago Press, 2008.

———. "Uninterrupted Dialogue: Between Two Infinities, the Poem." Translated by Thomas Dutoit and Philippe Romanski. *Research in Phenomenology* 34 (2004): 3–19.

———. "Whom to Give to (Knowing not to Know)." In *The Gift of Death*, translated by David Wills, 54–81. Chicago: University of Chicago Press, 2008.

DeSteno, David. "The Kindness Cure." *Atlantic Monthly*. July 21, 2015. https://www.theatlantic.com/health/archive/2015/07/mindfulness-meditation-empathy-compassion/398867.

Dettmer, Jamie. "In Turkey, Resentment Builds over Syrian Refugees." *VOA News*. November 12, 2014. https://www.voanews.com/a/resentment-builds-in-turkey-over-syrian-refugees/2517491.html.

Development Co-operation Directorate (DCD-DAC). "Refugee Realities: Policy-Making and Recreating the Refugee Narrative." *OECD*. May 19, 2017. https://www.oecd.org/dac/Refugee_Realities_Concept_Note_May%2019.pdf.

de Vries, Hent. "Hospitable Thought." In *Religion and Violence: Philosophical Perspectives from Kant to Derrida*, 293–398. Baltimore: Johns Hopkins University Press, 2002.

Dickson, Daniel. "Swedish Railway Stops Denmark Service over Refugee ID Checks." *Reuters*. December 21, 2015. https://www.reuters.com/article/us-europe-migrants-sweden-denmark/swedish-railway-stops-denmark-service-over-refugee-id-checks-idUSKBN0U41OI20151221.

Dillon, Michael. "The Scandal of the Refugee: Some Reflection on the 'Inter' of International Relations and Continental Thought." In *Moral Spaces: Rethinking Ethics and World Politics*, edited by David Campbell and Michael Shapiro, 92–125. Minneapolis: University of Minnesota Press, 1999.

Dobbs, Leo, ed. "World Refugee Day: UNHCR Report Finds 80 Per Cent of World's Refugees in Developing Countries." *UNHCR: The UN Refugee Agency*. June 20, 2011. http://www.unhcr.org/4dfb66ef9.html.

Donnelly, Aileen. "Alan Kurdi's Father Blames Canada for Death of His Family as PM Suggests He Will Expedite Refugee Applications." *National Post*. September 10, 2015. http://news.nationalpost.com/news/canada/alan-kurdis-father-blames-canada-for-death-of-his-family-as-pm-suggests-he-will-expedite-refugee-applications.

Donnelly, Jack. *Universal Human Rights in Theory and Practice*. Ithaca, NY: Cornell University Press, 2013.

Dotson, Kristie. "A Cautionary Tale: On Limiting Epistemic Oppression." *Frontiers* 33, no. 1 (2012): 24–47.

———. "Conceptualizing Epistemic Oppression." *Social Epistemology* 28, no. 2 (2014): 115–38.

———. "Tracking Epistemic Violence, Tracking Practices of Silencing." *Hypatia* 26, no. 2 (2011): 236–57.

Doty, Roxanne Lynn. "States of Exception on the Mexico-U.S. Border: Security, 'Decisions,' and Civilian Border Patrols." *International Political Sociology* 1 (2007): 113–37.

Dufourmantelle, Anne. *Éloge du risque*. Paris: Rivages, 2014.

Esmeir, Samera. *Juridical Humanity: A Colonial History*. Stanford, CA: Stanford University Press, 2012.

Fahim, Kareem. "As Syrians Flee Anew, Neighbors' Altruism Hardens into Resentment." *New York Times*. February 7, 2016. https://www.nytimes.com/2016/02/08/world/middleeast/as-syrians-flee-anew-neighbors-altruism-hardens-into-resent ment.html.

Falk, Richard. "Refugees, Migrants and World Order." In *The Refugee Crisis and Religion: Secularism, Security and Hospitality in Question*, edited by Luca Mavelli and Erin K. Wilson, 23–34. Lanham, MD: Rowman & Littlefield, 2017.

Farbenblum, Bassina. "Executive Deference in U.S. Refugee Law: Internationalist Paths through and beyond '*Chevron*.'" *Duke Law Journal* 60, no. 5 (2011): 1059–122.

Fassin, Didier. "From Right to Favour." *The Nation*. April 5, 2016. https://www.thenation.com/article/from-right-to-favor.

———. "Humanitarianism: A Nongovernment Government." In *Nongovernmental Politics*, edited by Michael Feher, 149–60. New York: Zone Books, 2007.

———. *Humanitarian Reason: A Moral History of the Present*. Berkeley: University of California Press, 2012.

Fassin, Didier and Mariella Pandolfi, eds. *Contemporary States of Emergency: The Politics of Military and Humanitarian Intervention*. New York: Zone Books, 2010.

FBI Counterterrorism Division. "(U//FOUO) The Radicalization Process: From Conversion to Jihad." *U.S. Federal Bureau of Investigation: Intelligence Assessment*. May 10, 2006. https://cryptome.org/fbi-jihad.pdf.

Federation for American Immigration Reform. "Historical Immigrant Admission Data, 1821–2006." January 2008. https://www.uscis.gov/history-and-genealogy/our-history/agency-history/early-american-immigration-policies.

Feller, Erika, Volker Türk, and Frances Nicholson, eds. *Refugee Protection in International Law: UNHCR's Global Consultations on International Protection*. Cambridge: Cambridge University Press, 2003.

Ferguson, Michaele. "Symposium: Mindfulness and Politics." *New Political Science* 38, no. 2 (2016): 201–5.

Fine, Sarah and Lea Ypi, eds. *Migration in Political Theory: The Ethics of Movement and Membership*. Oxford: Oxford University Press, 2016.

Finnerty, Deirdre. "Migration Crisis: Trauma Takes a Toll on Mental Health." *BBC*. December 22, 2015. http://www.bbc.com/news/world-europe-35102320.

Fleming, Melissa. "Crossings of Mediterranean Sea Exceeds 300,000, Including 200,000 to Greece." United Nations High Commissioner for Refugees. August 28, 2015. http://www.unhcr.org/en-us/news/latest/2015/8/55e06a5b6/crossings-mediterranean-sea-exceed-300000-including-200000-greece.html.

Flynn, Bernard. "On the 'Right to Have Rights.'" Response to Peg Birmingham. *Hannah Arendt and Human Rights*. American Philosophical Association Book Session. December 30, 2007. Unpublished.

Forman, Erik. "Fight to Win!" *ROAR: Reflections on a Revolution*, no. 5 (2017): 12–25.

Forster, Katie. "Hate Crimes Soared by 41% after Brexit Vote, Official Figures Reveal." *The Independent*. October 13, 2016. http://www.independent.co.uk/news/uk/crime/brexit-hate-crimes-racism-eu-referendum-vote-attacks-increase-police-figures-official-a7358866.html.

Foucault, Michel. *The History of Sexuality Volume 1: An Introduction*. Translated by Robert Hurley. New York: Random House, 1978.

———. *Society Must Be Defended: Lectures at the Collège de France, 1975–1976*. Translated by David Macey. New York: Picador, 2003.

Franke, Mark F. N. "Political Exclusion of Refugees in the Ethics of International Relations." In *Ashgate Research Companion to Ethics and International Relations*, edited by Patrick Hayden, 309–28. Surrey: Ashgate, 2009.

Fraser, Nancy. "Rethinking the Public Sphere: A Contribution to the Critique of Actually Existing Democracy." In *Habermas and the Public Sphere*, edited by Craig Calhoun, 109–42. Cambridge, MA: MIT Press, 1992.

Freyenhagen, Fabian. *Adorno's Practical Philosophy: Living Less Wrongly*. Cambridge: Cambridge University Press, 2013.

Fricker, Miranda. *Epistemic Injustice*. Oxford: Oxford University Press, 2007.

Gaita, Raymond. *Good and Evil*. Basingstoke: Palgrave McMillan, 1991.

Gale, Peter. "The Refugee Crisis and Fear: Populist Politics and Media Discourse." *Journal of Sociology* 40 (2004): 321–40.

Garsd, Jasmine. "What Zero Tolerance Policy Means for People Fleeing Violence." *PRI*. May 18, 2018. https://www.pri.org/stories/2018-05-18/what-zero-tolerance-policy-border-means-people-fleeing-violence.

Gatrell, Peter. *The Making of the Modern Refugee*. Oxford, UK: Oxford University Press, 2013.

Gayle, Damien. "David Miliband: Close the World's Refugee Camps." *The Guardian*. May 14, 2016. http://www.theguardian.com/politics/2016/may/14/close-worlds-refugee-camps-says-david-miliband.

Gentleman, Amelia. "The Horror of the Calais Refugee Camp: 'We Feel Like We Are Dying Slowly.'" *The Guardian*. November 3, 2015. https://www.theguardian.com/world/2015/nov/03/refugees-horror-calais-jungle-refugee-camp-feel-like-dying-slowly.

Gerstenfeld, Manfred. "The Multiple Distortions of Holocaust Memory." *Jewish Political Studies Review* 19, no. 3/4 (2007): 35–55.

Gewirth, Allen. *The Community of Rights*. Chicago: University of Chicago Press, 1996.

———. *Human Rights: Essays on Justification and Applications*. Chicago: University of Chicago Press, 1982.

———. *Reason and Morality*. Chicago: University of Chicago Press, 1978.

Ghoshal, Animesh and Thomas Crowley. "Political versus Economic Refugees." *Review of Social Economy* 41, no. 2 (1983): 124–36.

Gibney, Mark. "A 'Well-Founded Fear' of Persecution." *Human Rights Quarterly* 10, no. 1 (1988): 109–21.

Gibney, Matthew. *The Ethics and Politics of Asylum: Liberal Democracy and the Response to Refugees*. Cambridge: Cambridge University Press, 2004.

Gilson, Erinn. *The Ethics of Vulnerability*. New York: Routledge, 2014.

Godrej, Farah. "Orthodoxy and Dissent in Hinduism's Meditative Traditions: A Critical Tantric Politics?" *New Political Science* 38, no. 2 (2016): 256–71.

Golden, Janet. "What Will Today's Immigration Detention Centers Look Like to Future Americans?" *The Inquirer*. June 22, 2016. http://www.philly.com/philly/blogs/public_health/What-will-todays-immigration-detention-centers-look-like-to-future-Americans-.html.

Goldfarb, Jeffrey. *The Politics of Small Things: The Power of the Powerless in Dark Times*. Chicago: University of Chicago Press, 2006.

Gonzalez, Juan. *Harvest of Empire: A History of Latinos in America*. New York: Penguin, 2011.

Goodin, Robert E. "What Is So Special about Our Fellow Countrymen?" *Ethics* 98, no. 4 (1988): 663–86.

Goodwin-Gill, Guy S. and Jane McAdam. *The Refugee in International Law*. Oxford: Oxford University Press, 2007.

Gotlib, Anna. "'But You Would Be the Best Mother': Unwomen, Counterstories, and the Motherhood Mandate." *Journal of Bioethical Inquiry* 13, no. 2 (2016): 327–47.

———. "Memory, Sadness and Longing: Exile Nostalgias as Attunement to Loss." In *The Moral Psychology of Sadness*, 183–206. Lanham, MD: Rowman & Littlefield, 2017.

———. "Refugees, Narratives, or How to Do Bad Things with Words." *Kennedy Institute of Ethics Journal*. June 20, 2017. https://kiej.georgetown.edu/refugees-narratives-bad-things-words.

Graham, David. "Trump Says Democrats Want Illegal Immigrants to 'Infest' the U.S." *The Atlantic*. June 19, 2018. https://www.theatlantic.com/politics/archive/2018/06/trump-immigrants-infest/563159.

Granski, Megan, Allen Keller, and Homer Venters. "Death Rates among Detained Immigrants in the United States." *International Journal of Environmental Research and Public Health* 12 (2015): 14414–19.

Griffin, James. *On Human Rights*. Oxford: Oxford University Press, 2008.

Gündoğdu, Ayten. "'Perplexities of the Rights of Man': Arendt on the Aporias of Human Rights." *European Journal of Political Theory* 11, no. 1 (2012): 4–24.

———. *Rightlessness in an Age of Rights: Hannah Arendt and the Contemporary Struggle of Migrants*. Oxford: Oxford University Press, 2015.

Guterres, António. "Forced Displacement and the Promise of Pluralism." 2014 Annual Pluralism Lecture. United Nations High Commissioner for Refugees. Ottawa. May 29, 2014. http://www.unhcr.org/538d801d6.html.

Gzesh, Susan. "Central Americans and Asylum Policy in the Reagan Era." *Migration Information Source*. April 1, 2006. http://www.migrationpolicy.org/article/central-americans-and-asylum-policy-reagan-era.

Habermas, Jürgen, Joseph Ratzinger, and Jean-Louis Schegel. "Les fondements prépolitiques de l'État démocratique." *Esprit*, no. 306 (2004): 5–28.

Haddad, Emma. *The Refugee in International Society: Between Sovereigns*. Cambridge: Cambridge University Press, 2008.

Hagmann, Tobias and Benedikt Korf. "Agamben in the Ogaden: Violence and Sovereignty in the Ethiopian-Somali Frontier." *Political Geography* 31 (2012): 205–14.

Harff, Barbara and Ted Robert Gurr. "Toward Empirical Theory of Genocides and Politicides: Identification and Measurement of Cases since 1945." *International Studies Quarterly* 32, no. 3 (September 1988): 359–71.

Hashmi, Sohail. *State Sovereignty: Change and Persistence in International Relations*. University Park: Pennsylvania State University Press, 2010.

Hatewatch Staff. "American and European Radical Right Attacks Refugees Fueled Anti-Muslim Sentiment." *Southern Poverty Law Center*. October 6, 2015. https://www.splcenter.org/hatewatch/2015/10s/06/american-and-european-radical-right%E2%80%99s-attacks-refugees-fueled-anti-muslim-sentiment.

Hathaway, James C. "The Evolution of Refugee Status in International Law: 1920–1950." *International and Comparative Law Quarterly* 33, no. 2 (1984): 348–80.

Hathaway, James C. and Michelle Foster. *The Law of Refugee Status*. 2nd ed. Cambridge: Cambridge University Press, 2014.

Hiskey, Jonathan, Abby Córdova, Diana Orcés, and Mary Fran Malone. "Understanding the Central American Refugee Crisis: Why They Are Fleeing and How U.S. Polices Are Failing to Deter Them." *American Immigration Council*. February 2016. https://www.americanimmigrationcouncil.org/sites/default/files/research/understanding_the_central_american_refugee_crisis.pdf.

Hitler, Adolf. *Documents on British Foreign Policy, 1919–1939*. Edited by E. L. Woodward and Rohan Butler. 2nd ed. London: Her Majesty's Stationery Office, 1954.

Hohfeld, Wesley Newcomb. "Some Fundamental Legal Conceptions as Applied in Judicial Reasoning." *Yale Law Journal* 23, no. 1 (1913): 16–59.

Homann, James. "Trump Team Cannot Get Its Story Straight." *Washington Post*. June 18, 2018. https://www.washingtonpost.com/news/powerpost/paloma/daily-202/2018/06/18/daily-202-trump-team-cannot-get-its-story-straight-on-separating-migrant-families/5b2701f030fb046c468e6ef6/?utm_term=.3cabe6bb1f9d.

Honig, Bonnie. *Democracy and the Foreigner*. Princeton, NJ: Princeton University Press, 2001.

Honneth, Axel. *Disrespect: The Normative Foundations of Critical Theory*. Cambridge: Polity Press, 2007.

———. *Pathologies of Reason*. New York: Columbia University Press, 2009.

———. *Reification*. Oxford: Oxford University Press, 2008.

Horkheimer, Max. *Critical Theory: Selected Essays*. New York: Continuum, 2002.

———. *Eclipse of Reason*. Eastford, CT: Martino Fine Books, 2013.

Horowitz, David. "Horowitz's Notepad Special: This Is War." *FrontPageMag*. September 11, 2001. http://archive.frontpagemag.com/readArticle.aspx?ARTID=21215.

Howard, Katherine. "The Right to Have Rights 65 Years Later: Justice Beyond Humanitarianism, Politics Beyond Sovereignty." *Global Justice: Theory, Practice, Rhetoric*, no. 1 (2017): 79–98.

Hrala, Josh. "Global Warming Could Trigger a 'Climate Exodus' from the Middle East And North Africa." *Science Alert*. May 4, 2016. https://www.sciencealert.com/global-warming-may-trigger-a-climate-exodus-in-parts-of-the-middle-east-and-north-africa.

Hueser, Stefan. "Is There a Right to Have Rights? The Case of the Right to Asylum." *Ethical Theory and Moral Practice* 11, no. 1 (2008): 3–13.

Human Rights First. "Will the Immigration Detention System Finally Get the Reforms It Desperately Needs?" August 7, 2009. https://www.humanrightsfirst.org/2009/08/07/will-the-immigration-detention-system-finally-get-the-reforms-it-desperately-needs.

Human Rights Watch. "El Salvador's Decade of Terror: Human Rights since the Assassination of Archbishop Romero." October 1, 1991. https://www.hrw.org/report/1991/10/01/el-salvadors-decade-terror-human-rights-assassination-archbishop-romero.

———. "Guatemala Rights Abuses Escalate as Elections Near." November 8, 1990. https://www.hrw.org/report/1990/11/08/guatemala-rights-abuses-escalate-elections-near.

———. "Mexico's Disappeared: The Enduring Cost of a Crisis Ignored." February 20, 2013. https://www.hrw.org/report/2013/02/20/mexicos-disappeared/enduring-cost-crisis-ignored.

———. "US: Deaths in Immigration Detention: Newly Released Records Suggest Dangerous Lapses in Medical Care." July 7, 2016. https://www.hrw.org/news/2016/07/07/us-deaths-immigration-detention.

Hutfless, Esther and Elisabeth Schäfer. *How to Be a Refug(e)e for a Stranger?* Film presented at Refugee Workshop. Reichenau an der Rax, Austria. August 8–10, 2017.

Hyndman, Jennifer. *Managing Displacement: Refugees and the Politics of Humanitarianism*. Minneapolis: University of Minnesota Press, 2000.

International Federation of Red Cross and Red Crescent Societies. "World Disasters Report 2012: Focus on Forced Migration and Displacement." 2012. http://www.ifrc.org/en/publications-and-reports/world-disasters-report/world-disasters-report-2012---focus-on-forced-migration-and-displacement.

International Organization for Migration. "World Migration Report 2013: Migrant Well-Being and Development." 2013. https://publications.iom.int/system/files/pdf/wmr2013_en.pdf.

———. "2015 Global Migration Trends Factsheet." 2015. http://gmdac.iom.int/global-migration-trends-factsheet.

Ivanovic, Mladjo. "Holding Hands with Death: The Dark Side of Our Humanitarian Present." *Radical Philosophy Review* 19, no. 2 (2016): 359–79.

Jaggar, Alison. *Feminist Politics and Human Nature*. Lanham, MD: Rowman and Littlefield, 1983.

Jastram, Kate. "Economic Harm as a Basis for Refugee Status and the Application of Human Rights Law to the Interpretation of Economic Persecution." In *Critical Issues in International Law*, edited by James Simeon, 143–73. Cambridge: Cambridge University Press, 2010.

Jenkins, Fiona. "Bare Life: Asylum-Seekers, Australian Politics and Agamben's Critique of Violence." *Australian Journal of Human Rights* 10, no. 1 (2004): 79–95.

Jennings, Ronald C. "Sovereignty and Political Modernity: A Genealogy of Agamben's Critique of Sovereignty." *Anthropological Theory* 11, no. 1 (2011): 23–61.

Jewett, Christina and Shefali Luthra. "Immigrant Toddlers Ordered to Appear in Court Alone." *Texas Tribune*. June 27, 2018. https://www.texastribune.org/2018/06/27/immigrant-toddlers-ordered-appear-court-alone.

Jones, Martha S. *Birthright Citizens: A History of Race and Rights in Antebellum America*. Cambridge: Cambridge University Press, 2018.

Jones, Reece. *Violent Borders: Refugees and the Right to Move*. London: Verso, 2016.

Kabat-Zinn, Jon. *Full Catastrophe Living: Using the Wisdom of Your Body and Mind to Face Stress, Pain and Illness*. New York: Bantam, 2013.

Kant, Immanuel. "Idea for a Universal History from a Cosmopolitan Point of View." In *Kant: On History*, edited by Lewis White Beck, 11–26. New York: Bobbs-Merrill, 1963.

———. "Perpetual Peace." *Mount Holyoke*. 1795. http://www.mtholyoke.edu/acad/intrel/kant/kant1.htm.

———. *Toward Perpetual Peace and Other Writings on Politics, Peace and History*. Edited by Pauline Kleingeld. Translated by David L. Colclasure. New Haven, CT: Yale University Press, 2006.

Kantor, Jodi and Catrin Einhorn. "Refugees Encounter a Foreign Word: Welcome." *New York Times*. June 30, 2016. https://www.nytimes.com/2016/07/01/world/americas/canada-syrian-refugees.html.

Kapur, Ratna. "The Tragedy of Victimization Rhetoric: Resurrecting the 'Native' Subject in International/Post-Colonial Feminist Legal Politics." *Harvard Human Rights Journal* 15 (2002): 1–37.

Karim, Faheem. "Slap to a Man's Pride Set Off Tumult in Tunisia." *New York Times*. January 21, 2011. http://www.nytimes.com/2011/01/22/world/africa/22sidi.html.

Kelley, Colin P., Shahrzad Mohtadi, Mark A. Cane, Richard Seager, and Yochanan Kushnir. "Climate Change in the Fertile Crescent and Implications of the Recent Syria Drought." *Proceedings of the National Academy of Sciences of the United States of America* 112, no. 11 (2015): 3241–46.

Kiely, Eugene. "Fact Check: Trump's Immigration Policy vs. Obama's." *USA Today*. January 30, 2017. https://www.usatoday.com/story/news/politics/2017/01/30/fact-check-trump-refugee-policy-comparison-obama/97247418.

Kingsley, Patrick. *The New Odyssey: The Story of the Twenty-First-Century Refugee Crisis*. New York: Liveright Publishing Corporation, 2017.

Klabbers, Jan. "Hannah Arendt and the Language of Global Governance." In *Hannah Arendt and the Law*, edited by Marco Goldoni and Christopher McCorkindale, 229–49. Portland, OR: Hart Publishing, 2012.

Kopan, Tal. "DHS Ends Protections for Nearly 90,000 Central Americans." *CNN*. May 4, 2018. https://www.cnn.com/2018/05/04/politics/immigration-tps-honduras/index.html.

Krause, Monika. "Undocumented Migrants: An Arendtian Perspective." *European Journal of Political Theory* 7, no. 3 (2008): 331–48.

Krayem, Hassan, ed. "The Arab Spring: Revolutions for Deliverance from Authoritarianism." *Change Now! The Arab Network for the Study of Democracy*. August 26, 2014. http://ademocracynet.com/index.php?page=docs&id=75&action=Detail.

Kristeva, Julia. *Strangers to Ourselves*. Translated by Leon S. Roudiez. New York: Columbia University Press, 1991.

Kristof, Nicholas. "We're Helping Deport Kids to Die." *New York Times*. July 17, 2016. http://www.nytimes.com/2016/07/17/opinion/sunday/were-helping-deport-kids-to-die.html?rref=collection%2Fcolumn%2Fnicholas-kristof&action=click&contentCollection=opinion&region=stream&module=stream_unit&version=latest&contentPlacement=2&pgtype=collection&_r=0.

Kurzman, Charles. "Muslim-American Involvement with Violent Extremism." *Triangle Center on Terrorism and Homeland Security*. January 18, 2018. http://sites.duke.edu/tcths/files/2018/01/Kurzman_Muslim-American_Involvement_with_Violent_Extremism_2017.pdf.

Law, Christopher. "'The Ends of *Homo Sacer*': A Review of a Roundtable Discussion on the Work of Giorgio Agamben." *Postmodern Culture* 25, no. 3 (2015). https://search-proquest-com.proxy.library.vanderbilt.edu/docview/1801638751?accountid=14816.

Lee, Christopher J. "Locating Hannah Arendt within Postcolonial Thought: A Prospectus." *College Literature* 38, no. 1 (2011): 95–114.

Lesser, Gabriel and Jeanne Batalova. "Central American Immigrants in the United States." *Migration Policy*. April 5, 2017. http://www.migrationpolicy.org/article/central-american-immigrants-united-states.

Leudar, Ivan, Jacqueline Hayes, Jiří Nekvapil, and Johanna Turner Baker. "Hostility Themes in Media, Community and Refugee Narratives." *Discourse and Society* 19, no. 2 (2008): 187–221.

Levinas, Emmanuel. *Totality and Infinity: An Essay on Exteriority*. Translated by Alphonso Lingis. Pittsburgh, PA: Duquesne University Press, 1969.

Levinson, Reade and Mica Rosenberg. "U.S. Government Says Nearly 2000 Child Separations at Mexico Border in Under Two Months." *Reuters*. June 15, 2018. https://ca.reuters.com/article/topNews/idCAKBN1JB2SF-OCATP.

Lindemann, Hilde. *Damaged Identities, Narrative Repair*. Ithaca, NY: Cornell University Press, 2001.

———. *Holding and Letting Go: The Social Practice of Personal Identities*. Oxford: Oxford University Press, 2014.

Lister, Matthew. "Who Are Refugees?" *Law and Philosophy* 32 (2013): 645–71.

Loch, Daniel. *Étranger: De quel droit?* Paris: Presses Universitaires de France, 1985.

Loescher, Gil. *Beyond Charity: International Cooperation and the Global Refugee Crisis*. Oxford: Oxford University Press, 1993.

Loescher, Gil and James Milner. "Understanding the Challenge." *Forced Migration Review*, no. 33 (2009): 9–11.

Lugones, Maria. *Pilgramages/Peregrinajes: Theorizing Coalition against Multiple Oppressions*. Lanham, MD: Rowman & Littlefield, 2003.

Luhmann, Niklas. *Law as a Social System*. Oxford: Oxford University Press, 2004.

Luiselli, Valeria. *Tell Me How It Ends: An Essay in Forty Questions*. Minneapolis: Coffee House Press, 2017.

Madura, Lisa M. "Global Migration and the Ethics of Hospitality." Master's thesis, University of Nevada, Reno, 2016. ProQuest Dissertations & Theses (AAT 10126137).

Mail Foreign Service. "Death of the Jungle: Incredible Aerial Images Reveal How the Calais Slum Is Now Just Bare Earth after Makeshift Homes Were Flattened by Bulldozers during the Eviction of Thousands of Refugees." *Daily Mail*. March 27, 2016. http://www.dailymail.co.uk/news/article-3511855/Death-Jungle-Incredible-aerial-images-reveal-Calais-slum-just-bare-earth-makeshift-homes-flattened-bulldozers-eviction-thousands-refugees.html#ixzz49ytihWY7.

Malkki, Liisa H. "Refugees and Exile: From 'Refugee Studies' to the National Order of Things." *Annual Review of Anthropology* 24 (1995): 495–523.

Marcuse, Herbert. *An Essay on Liberation*. Boston: Beacon Press, 1969.

———. *One-Dimensional Man*. Boston: Beacon Press, 1968.

Marion, Esther. "The Nazi Genocide and the Writing of the Holocaust Aporia: Ethics and Remnants of Auschwitz." *MLN* 121, no. 4 (2006): 1009–22.

Mathiowetz, Dean. "'Meditation Is Good for Nothing:' Leisure as a Democratic Practice." *New Political Science* 38, no. 2 (2016): 241–55.

Maudlin, John. "3 Reasons Brits Voted for Brexit." *Forbes*. July 5, 2016. https://www.forbes.com/sites/johnmauldin/2016/07/05/3-reasons-brits-voted-for-brexit/#5ffade961f9d.

Mavelli, Luca and Erin K. Wilson, eds. *The Refugee Crisis and Religion: Secularism, Security and Hospitality in Question*. Lanham, MD: Rowman & Littlefield, 2017.

McAfee, Noelle. "Freedom, Psychoanalysis, and the Radical Political Imaginary." In *Literature, Ethics, Morality: American Studies Perspective*, edited by Philipp Schweighauser and Ridvan Askin, 87–99. Tübingen: Gunter Narr Publishing House, 2015.

McClelland, Mac. "How to Build a Perfect Refugee Camp." *New York Times Magazine*. February 13, 2014. https://www.nytimes.com/2014/02/16/magazine/how-to-build-a-perfect-refugee-camp.html.

McIvor, David W. "Bringing Ourselves to Grief: Judith Butler and the Politics of Mourning." *Political Theory* 40, no. 4 (2012): 409–36.

McLuhan, Marshall. *Understanding Media: The Extensions of Man*. New York: McGraw-Hill, 1965.

McLuhan, Marshall and Quentin Fiore. *The Medium Is the Massage: An Inventory of Effects*. New York: Bantam Books, 1967.

Medina, José. *The Epistemology of Resistance*. Oxford: Oxford University Press, 2013.

———. “Toward a Foucaultian Epistemology of Resistance: Counter-Memory, Epistemic Friction, and Guerrilla Pluralism.” *Foucault Studies* 12 (2011): 9–35.

Mendieta, Eduardo. “Assassination Nation: The Drone as Thanatological Dispositif.” In *The Life of Reason in an Age of Terrorism*, edited by Charles Padrón and Kryzsztof Piotr Skrowronski, 61–78. Leiden: Brill, 2018.

———. “The Right to Political Membership: Democratic Morality and the Rights of Irregular Immigrants.” *Radical Philosophy Review* 14, no. 2 (2011): 177–85.

———. “The U.S. Border and the Political Ontology of ‘Assassination Nation’: Thanatological *Dispositifs*.” *Journal of Speculative Philosophy* 31, no. 1 (2017): 82–100.

Merchant, Nomaan. “Hundreds of Children Wait in Border Patrol Facility in Texas.” *AP News*. June 18, 2018. https://www.apnews.com/amp/9794de32d39d4c6f89fbefaea3780769.

Meyers, Diana Tietjens. *Victims Stories and the Advancement of Human Rights*. New York: Oxford University Press, 2016.

Mignolo, Walter D. *The Darker Side of Western Modernity: Global Frames, Decolonial Options*. Durham, DC: Duke University Press, 1997.

———. “The Geopolitics of Knowledge and the Colonial Difference. In *Coloniality at Large*, edited by Mabel Moraña, Enriqué Dussel, and Carlos A. Jáuregui, 181–225. Durham, NC: Duke University Press, 2008.

———. *Local Histories/Global Designs: Coloniality, Subaltern Knowledges, and Border Thinking*. Princeton, NJ: Princeton University Press, 2012.

Miller, David. *Strangers in Our Midst: The Political Philosophy of Immigration*. Cambridge, MA: Harvard University Press, 2016.

Mills, Charles W. *The Racial Contract*. Ithaca, NY: Cornell University Press, 1997.

Minh-ha, Trinh T. *Elsewhere, within Here: Immigration, Refugeeism, and the Boundary Event*. New York: Routledge, 2010.

———. *Reassemblage*. Filmed in 1982 in Senegal.

Minh-ha, Trinh, T. “Nature’s r: A Musical Swoon.” In *Elsewhere, within Here: Immigration, Refugeeism and the Boundary Event*, 59–75. New York: Routledge, 2011.

Momodu, Sulaiman. “Refugees Turn to Ethiopia for Safety and Asylum.” *Africa Renewal*. April 2015. http://www.un.org/africarenewal/magazine/april-2015/refugees-turn-ethiopia-safety-and-asylum.

Moore, Matthew J. *Buddhism and Political Theory*. Oxford: Oxford University Press, 2016.

———. “Buddhism, Mindfulness and Transformative Politics.” *New Political Science* 38, no. 2 (2016): 272–82.

Mossaad, Nadwa. “Annual Flow Report: Refugees and Asylees: 2015.” *DHS Office of Immigration Statistics*. November 2016. https://www.dhs.gov/sites/default/files/publications/Refugees_Asylees_2015.pdf.

Nail, Thomas. *The Figure of the Migrant*. Stanford, CA: Stanford University Press, 2015.

Ngai, Mae M. “The Architecture of Race in American Immigration Law: A Reexamination of the Immigration Act of 1924.” *Journal of American History* 86 (1999): 67–92.

———. *Impossible Subjects: Illegal Aliens and the Making of Modern America*. Princeton, NJ: Princeton University Press, 2004.

Nickel, James. "Sanctuary, Asylum and Civil Disobedience." *In Defense of the Alien* 8 (1985): 176–87.

Nietzsche, Friedrich. *The Gay Science: With a Prelude in German Rhymes and an Appendix of Songs*. Edited by Bernard Williams. Translated by Josefine Nauckhoff. Cambridge: Cambridge University Press, 2001.

———. *Untimely Meditations*. Edited by Daniel Breazeale. Translated by R. J. Hollingdale. Cambridge: Cambridge University Press, 1983.

Noeth, Sandra, Kamal Aljafari, and Susanne Valerie Granzer. "Disquieting Movements: Über die Unruhe der Körper und der Bilder." Lecture performance presented at the Research Festival Philosophy on Stage #4, Vienna. November 26–29, 2015. http://homepage.univie.ac.at/arno.boehler/php/?p=8936.

Norwegian Refugee Council. "19.3 Million Displaced by Disasters but 'Mother Nature Not to Blame' Says New Report." *Internal Displacement Monitoring Centre*. July 20, 2015. http://www.internal-displacement.org/sites/default/files/inline-files/20150706-GE-2015Press-release-FINAL-v1.pdf.

Nowrasteh, Alex. "Terrorism and Immigration: A Risk Analysis." *Cato Institute*. September 13, 2016. https://www.cato.org/publications/policy-analysis/terrorism-immigration-risk-analysis.

Nyers, Peter. *Rethinking Refugees: Beyond the State of Emergency*. New York: Routledge, 2006.

Obama, Barack Hussein. "Democratic Convention Acceptance Speech." Transcript. *New York Times*. August 28, 2008. http://www.nytimes.com/2008/08/28/us/politics/28text-obama.html.

O'Ceallaigh, Liam. "When You Kill Ten Million Africans You Aren't Called 'Hitler.'" *Diary of a Walking Butterfly*. December 22, 2010. http://www.walkingbutterfly.com/2010/12/22/when-you-kill-ten-million-africans-you-arent-called-hitler.

OED Online. "asylum, n." N.d. http://www.oed.com/view/Entry/12340.

———. "refugee, n." N.d. http://www.oed.com/view/Entry/161121.

Oliver, Kelly. *Carceral Humanitarianism: Logics of Refugee Detention*. Minneapolis: University of Minnesota Press, 2017.

———. *Earth and World*. New York: Columbia University Press, 2015.

———. *Witnessing: Beyond Recognition*. Minneapolis: University of Minnesota Press, 2001.

Opondo, Sam Okoth and Michael J. Shapiro. *The New Violent Cartography: Geo-Analysis after the Aesthetic Turn*. Abingdon, OX: Routledge, 2012.

Orosco, José-Antonio. *Cesar Chavez and the Common Sense of Nonviolence*. Albuquerque: University of New Mexico Press, 2008.

Owen, David. "In Loco Civitatis: On the Normative Structure of the International Refugee Regime." In *Migration in Political Theory*, edited by Sarah Fine and Lea Ypi, 269–90. Oxford: Oxford University Press, 2016.

Owens, Patricia. "Reclaiming 'Bare Life'? Against Agamben on Refugees." *International Relations* 23, no. 4 (2009): 567–82.

Parekh, Serena. "A Meaningful Place in the World: Hannah Arendt on the Nature of Human Rights." *Journal of Human Rights* 3, no. 1 (2004): 41–52.

———. *Refugees and the Ethics of Forced Displacement*. New York: Routledge, 2017.

Pascal, Blaise. *Pensées*. Translated by Roger Ariew. New York: Hackett, 2005.

———. *The Soliloquies of Saint Augustine of Hippo*. Translated by Rose E. Cleveland. Charleston, SC: Nabu Press, 2014.

Pawel, Miriam. *The Crusades of Cesar Chavez: A Biography*. New York: Bloomsbury Press, 2014.

Penn Wharton. "The Effects of Immigration on the United States Economy." *Budget Model*. June 27, 2016. http://www.budgetmodel.wharton.upenn.edu/issues/2016/1/27/the-effects-of-immigration-on-the-united-states-economy.

Peralta, Eyder. "Why a Single Question Decides the Fate of Central American Migrants." *National Public Radio*. February 25, 2016. http://www.npr.org/2016/02/25/467020627/why-a-single-question-decides-the-fates-of-central-american-migrants.

Pettit, Philip. *A Theory of Freedom: From the Psychology to the Politics of Agency*. Oxford: Oxford University Press, 2001.

Piggott, Stephen. "Meet the Anti-Muslim Leaders Advising Donald Drumpf and Ted Cruz." *Southern Poverty Law Center*. March 28, 2016. https://www.splcenter.org/hatewatch/2016/03/28/meet-anti-muslim-leaders-advising-donald-trump-and-ted-cruz.

Price, Matthew E. *Rethinking Asylum: History, Purpose, Limits*. Cambridge: Cambridge University Press, 2009.

Pupavac, Vanessa. "New Issues in Refugee Research: Refugees in the 'Sick Role': Stereotyping Refugees and Eroding Refugee Rights." UN High Commissioner for Refugees. Research Paper No. 128. August 2006. http://www.refworld.org/docid/4ff159d32.html.

Rancière, Jacques. "Who Is the Subject of the Rights of Man?" *South Atlantic Quarterly* 103, no. 2/3 (2004): 297–310.

Rawlence, Ben. *City of Thorns: Nine Lives in the World's Largest Refugee Camp*. New York: Picador, 2016.

Rawls, John. *The Law of Peoples*. Cambridge, MA: Harvard University Press, 1999.

———. *A Theory of Justice*. Cambridge, MA: Harvard University Press. 1971.

Redmond, Ron. "Protracted Refugee Situations: Millions Caught in Limbo, with No Solutions in Sight." UN High Commissioner for Refugees. 2006. http://www.un.org/events/tenstories/06/story.asp?storyID=2600#.

Refugee Council. "The Situation at the Sangatte Camp in France." September 7, 2001. https://www.refugeecouncil.org.uk/latest/news/754_the_situation_at_the_sangatte_camp_in_france.

Reynolds, James. "Slovenia Builds Razor-Wire Fence to Control Migrant Numbers." *BBC News*. November 11, 2015. http://www.bbc.com/news/av/world-europe-34790151/slovenia-builds-razor-wire-fence-to-control-migrant-numbers.

Ritivoi, Andreea Deciu. *Yesterday's Self: Nostalgia and the Immigrant Identity*. Lanham, MD: Rowman & Littlefield, 2002.

Robins, Melinda B. "'Lost Boys' and the Promised Land: US Newspaper Coverage of Sudanese Refugees." *Journalism* 4 (2003): 29–49.

Rosen, Michael. *Dignity*. Cambridge, MA: Harvard University Press, 2012.

Rowe, James K. "Micropolitics and Collective Liberation: Mind/Body Practice and Left Social Movements." *New Political Science* 38, no. 2 (2016): 206–25.

RT. "Almost 130 Refugee Kids Vanish after the 'Calais Jungle' Demolition—Charity." April 3, 2016. https://www.rt.com/news/338217-129-kids-missing-in-calais.

Said, Edward. *Orientalism*. New York: Vintage Books, 1999.

Salgado, Sebastião. *Migrations: Humanity in Transition*. New York: Aperture, 2000.

Sari, Yasemin. "Resettlements and a Right to a Place: Resettlement as a Condition for the Sense of Self." Agenda for International Development, (July 7, 2017). http://www.a-id.org/en/news/refugees-and-a-right-to-place-resettlement-as-a-condition for-the-sense-of-self.

Sassen, Saskia. *Expulsions: Brutality and Complexity in the Global Economy*. Cambridge, MA: Belknap Press, 2014.

Scarborough, Rowen. "France Cracks Down on Islamic Radicalism after Paris Attacks, Shutters Mosques." *Washington Times*. January 28, 2016. http://www.washingtontimes.com/news/2016/jan/28/france-cracks-down-on-islamic-radicalism after-par/?page=all.

Schaap, Andrew. "Enacting the Right to Have Rights: Jacques Rancière's Critique of Hannah Arendt." *European Journal of Political Theory* 10, no. 1 (2011): 22–45.

Schenk, Todd Stewart. "A Proposal to Improve the Treatment of Women in Asylum Law: Adding a 'Gender' Category to the International Definition of 'Refugee.'" *Indiana Journal of Global Legal Studies* 2, no. 1 (1994): 301–44.

Schiff, Jacob (Jade). "Confronting Political Responsibility: The Problem of Acknowledgment." *Hypatia: A Journal of Feminist Philosophy* 23, no. 3 (2008): 99–117.

Schiff, Jade Larissa. *Burdens of Political Responsibility: Narrative and the Cultivation of Responsiveness*. Cambridge: Cambridge University Press, 2014.

Schwartzstein, Peter. "The Climate-Change Refugee Crisis Is Only Just Beginning." *Quartz*. January 31, 2016. https://qz.com/605609/the-climate-change-refugee-crisis-is-only-just-beginning.

Scott, David. "Preface: Soul Captives are Free." *Small Axe* 11, no. 2 (2007): v–x.

Shacknove, Andrew E. "Who Is a Refugee?" *Ethics* 95, no. 2 (1985): 274–84.

Shakespeare, William. *Hamlet*. Edited by G. R. Hibbard. New York: Oxford University Press, 1987.

Sharpe, Matthew. "Only Agamben Can *Save* Us? Against the Messianic Turn Recently Adopted in Critical Theory." *The Bible and Critical Theory* 5, no. 3 (2009): 40.1–40.20.

Shue, Henry. *Basic Rights*. 2nd ed. Princeton, NJ: Princeton University Press, 1996.

Siegal, Nina. "Refugees Confront the Past through Art, at a Pop-Up Museum." *New York Times*. July 16, 2017. https://www.nytimes.com/2017/07/16/arts/design/asylum-refugees-artists-.html?mcubz=3&_r=0.

Singer, Peter and Renata Singer. "The Ethics of Refugee Policy." In *Open Borders? Closed Societies? The Ethical and Political Issues*, edited by Mark Gibney, 111–30. New York: Greenwood Press, 1988.

Smith, Merril. "Warehousing Refugees: A Denial of Rights, a Waste of Humanity." In Special Issue of the *World Refugee Survey*, 38–56. Washington, DC: U.S. Committee on Refugees and Immigrants, 2004.

Sontag, Susan. *On Photography*. New York: Picador, 2001.

Sputnik International. "A Closer Look at 'Europe's Worst' Refugee Camp." January 24, 2016. https://sptnkne.ws/g6w9.

Steimel, Sarah. "Refugees as People: The Portrayal of Refugees in American Human Interest Stories." *Journal of Refugee Studies* 23, no. 2 (2010): 219–37.

Steinback, Robert. "Activists Attacking Muslims and Islam Are Springing Up around the Country." *SPLC: Southern Poverty Law Center*. June 17, 2011. https://www.splcenter.org/fighting-hate/intelligence-report/2011/anti-muslim-inner-circle.

Steinbock, Daniel. "Interpreting the Refugee Definition." *UCLA Law Review* 45 (1998): 733–816.

Stevens, Jacob. "Prisons of the Stateless: The Derelictions of the UNHCR." *New Left Review* 42 (2006): 53–67.

Stiglitz, Joseph. *Globalization and Its Discontents*. New York: Norton, 2002.

Sullivan, Sean. "Zero Tolerance Policy Means Zero Humanity." *Washington Post*. June 17, 2018. https://www.washingtonpost.com/politics/zero-tolerance-policy-means-zero-humanity-democrats-decry-trump-immigration-policy-after-tour-of-detention-center/2018/06/17/bbf68b2c-7248-11e8-9780-b1dd6a09b549_story.html?utm_term=.6bbdea79f34c.

Surk, Barbara, and Stephen Castle. "Migrants Diverted to Slovenia after Hungary Closes Border." *New York Times*. October 17, 2015. https://www.nytimes.com/2015/10/18/world/europe/hungary-closes-border-changing-refugees-path.html.

Svirsky, Marcelo and Simone Bignall. *Agamben and Colonialism*. Edinburgh: Edinburgh University Press, 2012.

Syrian Refugees. "Syrian Refugees: A Snapshot of the Crisis—In the Middle East and Europe." September 2016. http://syrianrefugees.eu.

Taylor, Charles. *Modern Social Imaginaries*. Durham, NC: Duke University Press, 2004.

Tazzioli, Martina. "The Politics of Counting and the Scene Of Rescue: Border Deaths on the Mediterranean." *Radical Philosophy* 192 (2015): 2–6.

Teach for All. "Changing the Narrative by Helping Raise Refugee Children's Voices." N.d. http://teachforall.org/en/news/changing-narrative-helping-raise-refugee-childrens-voices.

Temelkuran, Ece. "We Want Our Refugees and Exiles to Be Victims." *Literary Hub*. July 27, 2017. http://lithub.com/we-want-our-refugees-and-exiles-to-be-victims.

Thomas, Justin. "Resentment Is a Reaction That Refugees Don't Deserve." *The National*. August 23, 2015. https://www.thenational.ae/opinion/resentment-is-a-reaction-that-refugees-don-t-deserve-1.62514.

UN Alliance of Civilizations. "Syrian Refugee Girls Producing Their Own Narratives." December 8, 2016. https://www.unaoc.org/2016/12/syrian-refugee-girls-producing-their-own-narratives.

UN General Assembly. "Convention Relating to the Status of Refugees." July 28, 1951. *United Nations Treaty Series* 189. Geneva: UN General Assembly, 1951.

———. "Protocol Relating to the Status of Refugees." January 31, 1967. *United Nations Treaty Series* 606. New York: UN General Assembly, 1967.

UN General Assembly. "Resolution Adopted by the General Assembly on 16 September 2005: 2005 World Summit Outcome." October 24, 2005. http://www.un.org/en/development/desa/population/migration/generalassembly/docs/globalcompact/A_RES_60_1.pdf.

UN High Commissioner for Refugees. "Declaration on Territorial Asylum." A/RES/2312(XXII). December 14, 1967.

———. "Figures at a Glance." N.d. http://www.unhcr.org/en-us/figures-at-a-glance.html.

———. "Global Trends: Forced Displacement in 2014." June 18, 2015. http://www.unhcr.org/556725e69.html.

———. "Global Trends: Forced Displacement in 2016." June 2017. http://www.unhcr.org/5943e8a34.pdf.

———. "Mediterranean Situation." *Data Portal*. N.d. http://data2.unhcr.org/en/situations/mediterranean.

———. "With 1 Human in Every 113 Affected, Forced Displacement Hits Record High." June 20, 2016. http://www.unhcr.org/en-us/news/press/2016/6/5763ace54/1-human-113-affected-forced-displacement-hits-record-high.html?query=21.3%20million%20refugees%20worldwide.

UN Human Rights, Office of the High Commissioner. "Convention against Torture." December 10, 1984. http://www.ohchr.org/EN/ProfessionalInterest/Pages/CAT.aspx.

United We Dream. "About UWD." N.d. http://unitedwedream.org/about/our-missions-goals.

U.S. Citizenship and Immigration Services. "2014 Executive Actions on Immigration." April 15, 2015. http://www.uscis.gov/immigrationaction.

———. "Refugees." October 24, 2017. https://www.uscis.gov/humanitarian/refugees-asylum/refugees.

U.S. Department of Homeland Security. "Estimates of the Unauthorized Immigrant Population Residing in the United States." 2014. https://www.dhs.gov/immigration-statistics/population-estimates/unauthorized-resident.

U.S. Department of State. "Protracted Refugee Situations." N.d. http://www.state gov/j/prm/policyissues/issues/protracted.

Vatican Radio. "Pope: 'Current Migration Crisis Greatest Tragedy after WW2.'" March 22, 2017. http://en.radiovaticana.va/news/2017/03/22/pope_current_migration_crisis_greatest_tragedy_after_ww2_/1300326.

Verdirame, Guglielmo and Barbara Harrell-Bond. *Rights in Exile: Janus-Face Humanitarianism*. New York: Berghahn Books, 2005.

Villamar, María del Carmen Villarreal. "Book Review: *Exodus: How Migration Is Changing Our World.*" *Migraciones Internacionales* 8, no. 1 (2015): 249–53.

Volpp, Leti. "The Citizen and the Terrorist." *UCLA Law Review* 49 (2002): 1575–1600.

Von Sternberg, Mark. "The Developing Law of 'Private' Persecution and Its Implication for the Convention Refugee Definition." *In Defense of the Alien* 21 (1998): 129–50.

Waldman, Paul. "Republicans' Anti-Refugee Rhetoric Is Shameful and Despicable—and Probably Good Politics." *The Week.* November 18, 2015. http://theweek.com/articles/589395/republicans-antirefugee-rhetoric-shameful-despicable--probably-good-politics.

Waldron, Jeremy. *The Harm in Hate Speech.* Cambridge, MA: Harvard University Press, 2012.

Walsh, Bryan. "Alan Kurdi's Story: Behind the Most Heartbreaking Photo of 2015." *Time.* December 29, 2015. http://time.com/4162306/alan-kurdi-syria-drowned-boy-refugee-crisis.

Walzer, Michael. "The Distribution of Membership." In *Boundaries: National Autonomy and Its Limits*, edited by Peter G. Brown and Henry Shue, 1–35. Totowa, NJ: Rowman & Littlefield, 1981.

———. "The Distribution of Membership." In *Global Justice: Seminal Essays*, edited by Thomas Pogge and Darrel Moellendorf, 145–78. St. Paul, MN: Paragon House, 2008.

———. *Spheres of Justice: A Defense of Pluralism and Equality.* New York: Basic Books, 1983.

Warner, Daniel. "We Are All Refugees." *International Journal of Refugee Law* 4, no. 3 (1992): 365–72.

Warren, Mark E., ed. *Democracy and Trust.* Cambridge: Cambridge University Press, 1999.

Weber, Max. *Economy and Society.* Berkeley: University of California Press, 1978.

———. "Politics as a Vocation." In *From Max Weber: Essays in Sociology*, edited by H. H. Gerth and C. Wright Mills, 77–128. London: Routledge, 1958.

Weheliye, Alexander G. *Habeas Viscus: Racializing Assemblages, Biopolitics, and Black Feminist Theories of the Human.* Durham, NC: Duke University Press, 2014.

Weil, Simone. *The Need for Roots: Prelude to a Declaration of Duties toward Mankind.* Translated by Arthur Wills. New York: Harper Colophon, 1971.

Weizman, Eyal. *The Least of All Possible Evils.* New York: Verso, 2011.

Wellman, Christopher Heath. "Immigration and Freedom of Association." *Ethics* 11 (2008): 109–41.

Wendle, John. "The Ominous Story of Syria's Climate Refugees: Farmers Who Have Escaped the Battle-Torn Nation Explain How Drought and Government Abuse Have Driven Social Violence." *Scientific American.* March 2016. https://www.scientificamerican.com/article/ominous-story-of-syria-climate-refugees.

Wessel, Julia Schulze. "On Border Subjects: Rethinking the Figure of the Refugee and the Undocumented Migrant." *Constellations* 23, no. 1 (2016): 46–57.

Wikipedia contributors. "Heimat." *Wikipedia: The Free Encyclopedia.* N.d. https://en.wikipedia.org/wiki/Heimat.

Wintour, Patrick. "UK to Take Up to 20,000 Syrian Refugees over Five Years, David Cameron Confirms." *The Guardian*. September 7, 2015. https://www.theguardian.com/world/2015/sep/07/uk-will-accept-up-to-20000-syrian-refugees-david-cameron-confirms.

Wolf-Rehfeldt, Ruth. *SIGNS FICTION*. Berlin: Chert Galerie & Motto Books, 2016.

Woolf, Virginia. "The Waves." In *Collected Novels of Virginia Woolf*, edited by Stella McNichol, 335–508. Basingstoke: Palgrave Macmillan, 1992.

Worley, Will and Lizzie Dearden. "Greek Refugee Camp Is 'as Bad as a Nazi Concentration Camp,' Says Minister." *Independent*. March 18, 2016. https://www.independent.co.uk/news/world/europe/idomeni-refugee-dachau-nazi-concentration-camp-greek-minister-a6938826.html.

Xenos, Nicholas. "Refugees: The Modern Political Condition." *Alternatives* 18 (1993): 419–30.

Yardley, Jim and Gaia Pianigiani. "Three Days, 700 Deaths on Mediterranean as Migrant Crisis Flares." *New York Times*. May 29, 2016. https://www.nytimes.com/2016/05/30/world/europe/migrants-deaths-mediterranean-libya-italy.html.

Yates, Melissa. "Governing as Strangers: Rethinking Cosmopolitan Strategies of De-Alienation." Presentation at the meeting of the Critical Theory Roundtable, Pennsylvania State University. November 11–13, 2016.

Young, Iris Marion. "Responsibility and Global Justice: A Social Connection Model." *Social Philosophy and Policy* 23, no. 1 (2006): 102–30.

Young, Iris Marion and Martha C. Nussbaum. *Responsibility for Justice*. Oxford: Oxford University Press, 2010.

Zahabi-Bekdash, Lara. "Recreating the Refugees Narratives: From Sympathy to Dignity." *Huffington Post*. http://www.huffingtonpost.com/lara-zahabibekdash-md-phd/recreating-the-refugees-n_b_8610422.html.

Zong, Jie and Jeanne Batalova. "Mexican Immigrants in the United States." *Migration Policy*. October 9, 2014. https://www.migrationpolicy.org/article/mexican-immigrants-united-states-0.

———. "Mexican Immigrants in the United States." *Migration Policy*. March 17, 2016. http://www.migrationpolicy.org/article/mexican-immigrants-united-states.

———. "Refugees and Asylees in the United States." *Migration Policy*. June 7, 2017. http://www.migrationpolicy.org/article/refugees-and-asylees-united-states.

Index

About the Contributors

Sabeen Ahmed is a Provost's Graduate Fellow and PhD candidate in the Department of Philosophy at Vanderbilt University, where she focuses on political ontology, critical refugee studies, contemporary social and political philosophy, and medieval philosophy. Her doctoral dissertation will interrogate the genealogy of international refugee law as a means of exposing the politically motivated, racial underpinnings of the codification of "refugee rights" and its subsequent influence on political ontology. She received her BA in philosophy and BA in Spanish from the University of Virginia and from 2014 to 2015 lived in Antalya, Turkey, as a Fulbright ETA. Her work has been published in *Labyrinth: An International Journal for Philosophy, Value Theory, and Sociocultural Hermeneutics*, *Theory & Event*, and *Philosophy Today*.

Eva-Maria Aigner is a PhD student at the University of Vienna, Austria. She completed her master's degree in philosophy in 2017 with a thesis on Derrida's concept of the "secret." From January to September 2017, she held the position of student assistant in the research project "Artist Philosophers. Philosophy as Arts-Based Research" (AR 275-G21; sponsored by the Austrian Science Fund FWF) at the University of Applied Arts, Vienna (principal investigator: Arno Böhler). Her fields of interest include deconstruction, the ethics of writing, hospitality, arts-based philosophy, negative performance, and the philosophy of silence and the secret.

Peg Birmingham is professor of philosophy at DePaul University. She is the author of *Hannah Arendt and Human Rights: The Predicament of Common*

Responsibility (2006), coeditor (with Philippe van Haute) of *Dissensus Communis: Between Ethics and Politics* (1996), and coeditor (with Anna Yeatman) of *Aporia of Rights: Citizenship in an Era of Human Rights* (2014). She is the editor of *Philosophy Today*.

Chong Un Choe-Smith earned degrees in law from the University of California, Davis, and in philosophy from Georgetown University. She formerly practiced law as a senior appellate court attorney with the California Court of Appeal. She currently serves as an assistant professor of philosophy at California State University, Sacramento. Her areas of expertise are in ethics, political philosophy, and the philosophy of law. Her research and publications address primarily issues in human rights, animal rights, and global justice.

Anna Gotlib was born in Leningrad (now St. Petersburg), USSR, and fled with her family to the United States. She is currently an assistant professor of philosophy at Brooklyn College of the City University of New York. Prior to her academic career, she practiced international law in the United States and abroad, focusing on labor law disputes and related issues. Her areas of research and teaching include bioethics/medical ethics, moral psychology, social and political psychology, philosophy of law, and feminist philosophy. Her work has been published in *Hypatia*, *The International Journal of Feminist Approaches to Bioethics*, *Journal of Bioethical Inquiry*, *Humana Mente*, the *Kennedy Institute of Ethics Journal*, and several edited collections. She has two edited volumes on the emotions of sadness and regret published with Roman & Littlefield and is currently working on a monograph on memory, identity, and nostalgia.

Esther Hutfless is a lecturer at the Department of Philosophy at the University of Vienna and the Psychoanalytic Academy of Vienna and a psychoanalyst with the Vienna Psychoanalytic Association (Wiener Arbeitskreis für Psychoanalyse). Her main teaching and research areas include phenomenology, deconstruction, psychoanalysis, feminist philosophy, ontology, écriture féminine, and queer theory. She is the founder of the Vienna-based research group "Queering Psychoanalysis" and in 2017, with Barbara Zach, edited a volume titled *Queering Psychoanalysis*, which serves as the first German anthology on the topic.

Mladjo Ivanovic is a visiting professor in the Department of Philosophy at Grand Valley State University. His research focuses on moral, political, and environmental challenges tied to the forceful displacement and migration of people, particularly by examining both the sociohistorical and political contexts of human vulnerability and exclusion (contexts such as gender, race, poverty, violence, colonialism, environmental degradation, and climate change). He is also engaged with humanitarian nonprofit and nongovernmental organizations in Serbia, Greece, and Turkey and serves as an adviser for various student organizations that deal with humanitarianism and social justice.

Julia Kristeva is professor emeritus at University Paris Diderot and visiting professor at Columbia University, having worked in the fields of philosophy, linguistics, feminist studies, literary criticism, and psychoanalysis. Her many books and essays span a wide range of subjects, including social and political commentary, psychoanalytic theory, feminist philosophy, linguistics and semiotics, and art and literary theory. Her publications include *Powers of Horror: An Essay on Abjection* (1982), *Strangers to Ourselves* (1991), and *Crisis of the European Subjects* (2000), to name a few, and she most recently published a book with husband Phillipe Sollers titled *Marriage as a Fine Art* (2016). In addition to being a prolific and influential academician and novelist, she is a trained psychoanalyst, founder of the Simone de Beauvoir Prize committee, and the recipient of the Holberg Prize in 2004 and the Hannah Arendt Prize in 2006 and was awarded Commander of the French Legion of Honor in 2014.

Lisa Madura is a graduate fellow in philosophy at Vanderbilt University, where she works in social and political philosophy and critical phenomenology. In 2016, she received an MA from the University of Nevada, Reno, where she studied nineteenth- and twentieth-century continental philosophy. Her thesis, titled "Global Migration and the Ethics of Hospitality," brings the works of Husserl, Levinas, and Derrida to bear on issues concerning immigration and forced migration. Her research is broadly oriented around the phenomenology of habit and perception, social ontology, and group-based oppression and the global politics of inclusion.

Nöelle McAfee is professor of philosophy and director of the Psychoanalytic Studies Program at Emory University; she is also a fourth-year academic candidate at the Emory University Psychoanalytic Institute. She is coeditor of the *Kettering Review* and the author of *Democracy and the Political Unconscious* (2008), *Julia Kristeva* (2003), *Habermas, Kristeva, and Citizenship* (2000), and numerous articles and book chapters. During the past decade, she has worked on projects for the Kettering Foundation, the Ford Foundation, and the MacArthur Foundation. Her coedited volumes include a special issue of the philosophy journal *Hypatia* on feminist engagements in democratic theory and an edited volume titled *Democratizing Deliberation: A Political Theory Anthology* (2012). She is also codirector of the Public Philosophy Network and coeditor of the *Kettering Review*. She is currently completing a book manuscript titled *Fear of Breakdown: Politics and the Work of Mourning* and working on an intellectual biography of the late political theorist Benjamin R. Barber.

Eduardo Mendieta is professor of philosophy, associate director of the Rock Ethics Institute, and affiliated faculty at the School of International Affairs and the Bioethics Program at Penn State University. He is the author of *The Adventures of Transcendental Philosophy* (2002) and *Global Fragments: Globalizations, Latinamericanisms, and Critical Theory* (2007). He is also coeditor with Jonathan VanAntwerpen of *The Power of Religion in the Public Sphere* (2011), with Craig Calhoun and Jonathan VanAntwerpen of *Habermas and Religion* (2013), and with Stuart Elden of *Reading Kant's Geography* (2011). His most recent publication is a book titled *The Philosophical Animal* (2018). He is the 2017 recipient of the Frantz Fanon Outstanding Achievements Award.

Kelly Oliver is W. Alton Jones Professor of Philosophy at Vanderbilt University. She is the author of fifteen scholarly books, including most recently: *Carceral Humanitarianism: The Logic of Refugee Detention* (2017); *Hunting Girls: Sexual Violence from The Hunger Games to Campus Rape*, winner of a 2016 *Choice* Magazine Award (2016); *Earth and World: Philosophy after the Apollo Missions* (2015); *Technologies of Life and Death: From Cloning to Capital Punishment* (2013); and, perhaps her best-known work, *Witnessing: Beyond Recognition* (2001). Her work has been translated into eight languages. Most recently, she has published three novels in *The Jessica James, Cowgirl Philosopher* mystery series (IPPY award for best mystery and finalists for a *Forward* Magazine Award for best mystery, the Silver Falchion Award, and the Claymore Award).

David Owen is professor of social and political philosophy at the University of Southampton. He has published widely across both analytic and continental traditions. His authored and edited books include *Michel Foucault* (2014), *Prospects of Citizenship* (2011), *Nietzsche's Genealogy of Morality* (2007), *Recognition and Power* (2007), and *Multiculturalism and Political Theory* (2007). His recent articles include "Refugees, Fairness and Taking Up Slack," *Moral Philosophy and Politics* (2016), "Soul-Blindness, Police and Black Lives Matter" (coauthored with Jonathan Havercroft), *Political Theory*

(2016), and "Machiavelli's *Il Principe* and the Politics of Glory," *European Journal of Political Theory* (2015). He is currently working on projects on Nietzsche and on the political ethics of migration.

Serena Parekh is an associate professor of philosophy at Northeastern University in Boston, where she is the director of the Politics, Philosophy, and Economics Program and editor of the *American Philosophical Association Newsletter on Feminism and Philosophy*. Her primary philosophical interests are in social and political philosophy, feminist theory, and continental philosophy. Her most recent book is *Refugees and the Ethics of Forced Displacement* (2017). Her first book, *Hannah Arendt and the Challenge of Modernity: A Phenomenology of Human Rights*, was published in 2008 and translated into Chinese. She has also published numerous articles on social and political philosophy in *Hypatia, Philosophy and Social Criticism*, and *Human Rights Quarterly*.

Gertrude Postl is professor of philosophy and women and gender studies at Suffolk County Community College in Selden, New York. Her research focuses on feminist philosophy, especially the intersection between body and language (Luce Irigaray, Julia Kristeva, and Hélène Cixous), and the political implications of the notions of reading/writing, author, and text (Roland Barthes and Jacques Derrida). Her publications include *Weibliches Sprechen: Feministische Entwürfe zu Sprache und Geschlecht* (1991), *Contemporary Feminist Philosophy in German* (special issue editor of *Hypatia: A Journal of Feminist Philosophy*, 2005), *Hélène Cixous: Das Lachen der Medusa zusammen mit aktuellen Beiträgen* (coeditor with Esther Hutfless and Elisabeth Schäfer, 2013), and an entry, "Language, Writing, and Difference," in *The Routledge Companion to Feminist Philosophy* (2017).

Elisabeth Schäfer is affiliated with the Department of Philosophy at the University of Vienna, where she has taught since 2010, and the University of Applied Arts, Vienna. Her main research and teaching areas include deconstruction, queer-feminist philosophy, écriture féminine (Trans*Writing), thinking the body, and performance philosophy. From 2014 to 2017, she held a postdoctoral position with the research project "Artist Philosophers: Philosophy AS Arts-Based Research," sponsored by the Austrian Science Funds FWF (AR 275-G21) at the University of Applied Arts, Vienna, headed by Arno Böhler. Her current research project is titled "Trans*Writing. Immanence and Transformation. Towards a Political, Ethical and Aesthetical Theory of Writing as Artistic Research."

Jade Schiff is assistant professor of politics at Oberlin College. In her work, she explores questions of suffering, vulnerability, and responsibility and approaches them from the perspectives of political theory, psychoanalysis, phenomenology, and literary criticism. She is the author of *Burdens of Political Responsibility: Narrative and the Cultivation of Responsiveness* (2014). Other work has appeared or is forthcoming in *Critical Review of International Social and Political Philosophy*, *European Journal of Political Theory*, *Hypatia*, *Millennium*, *Philosophy and Social Criticism*, *Review of International Studies*, *Signs*, and *Telos*.

www.ingramcontent.com/pod-product-compliance
Ingram Content Group UK Ltd.
Pitfield, Milton Keynes, MK11 3LW, UK
UKHW012035150926
475560UK00001B/26